Working Women, Literary Ladies

Working Women, Literary Ladies

The Industrial Revolution and Female Aspiration

Sylvia Jenkins Cook

OXFORD

UNIVERSITY PRESS

2008

OXFORD
UNIVERSITY PRESS

Oxford University Press, Inc., publishes works that further
Oxford University's objective of excellence
in research, scholarship, and education.

Oxford   New York
Auckland   Cape Town   Dar es Salaam   Hong Kong   Karachi
Kuala Lumpur   Madrid   Melbourne   Mexico City   Nairobi
New Delhi   Shanghai   Taipei   Toronto

With offices in
Argentina   Austria   Brazil   Chile   Czech Republic   France   Greece
Guatemala   Hungary   Italy   Japan   Poland   Portugal   Singapore
South Korea   Switzerland   Thailand   Turkey   Ukraine   Vietnam

Published by Oxford University Press, Inc.
198 Madison Avenue, New York, New York 10016

www.oup.com

Oxford is a registered trademark of Oxford University Press

Library of Congress Cataloging-in-Publication Data
Cook, Sylvia Jenkins, 1943–
Working women, literary ladies : the industrial revolution
and female aspiration / by Sylvia Jenkins Cook.
p. cm.
Includes bibliographical references and index.
ISBN 978-0-19-532780-9; 978-0-19-532781-6 (pbk.)
1. American literature—Women authors—History and criticism. 2. American literature—
19th century—History and criticism. 3. American literature—20th century—History
and criticism. 4. Working class writings, American—History and criticism.
5. Working class women in literature. 6. Working class women—United States—
Intellectual life—19th century. 7. Working class women—United States—
Intellectual life—20th century. 8. Women and literature—United States—
History—19th century. 9. Women and literature—United States—
History—20th century. I. Title. PS217.W64C66 2007
810.9'352623—dc22   2007014908

1 3 5 7 9 8 6 4 2
Printed in the United States of America
on acid-free paper

For Rachel and Rebecca

Acknowledgments

I would like to thank the University of Missouri for a Research Board Award and the University of Missouri–St. Louis for a Research Award. These have provided me with valuable time to work on this book. I would also like to thank the ever-helpful and genial staff of the Thomas Jefferson Library at the University of Missouri–St. Louis for all their efforts on my behalf. I am grateful too to the readers and editors at Oxford University Press for their expert comments and suggestions.

As ever, I owe my greatest debt of gratitude to Richard Cook for his valuable advice and unfailing faith and encouragement, and to my mother, Georgina B. Jenkins, for everything I have learned from her.

Contents

Working Women, Literary Ladies

Introduction

"Mind amongst the Spindles"

All American ladies are more or less literary.
—HARRIET MARTINEAU, 1837

A working girl is a human being, with a heart, with desires, with
aspirations, with ideas and ideals.
—PAULINE NEWMAN, 1915

This book is about a literary phenomenon that raised major social, cultural, and ethical questions during the industrialization of the United States. The phenomenon is the curious Romantic literariness of several successive generations of American working-class women who presumed to pursue a life of the mind while performing labors of the body. The questions raised concern the relationship of literature and intellectual activity to perceptions of women's nature and capacities, to working-class consciousness, and to debates over what constituted a full life for women workers in a rapidly changing world. These questions are part of a literary discourse produced by working women themselves, and by their middle-class female allies, observers, and critics, designated here as literary ladies. The working women and the literary ladies of the title share the common ground of gender and mental ambition but are separated by the barrier of class and by the kind of work considered appropriate to their social status. The terms are suggestive and fluid, however, rather than definitive. Wage-earning factory women were accused of genteel affectations in their amateur literary endeavors and bourgeois women, who attempted to write professionally for money, were stigmatized as unladylike. Thus "working women" and "literary ladies" are necessarily evolving and somewhat elastic categories. The other important contributors to the industrial discourse are Romantic and reformist male writers who, perhaps innocently and unintentionally, stimulated unprecedented aspirations in a newly awakened and literate female audience, thus helping inspire a phenomenon they did not always endorse.

The first anticipation of the phenomenon came remarkably early in the industrializing process, in 1814, when Sarah Savage of Salem, Massachusetts, published her first novel, *The Factory Girl*. It is an account of the endeavors of Mary Burnam, a selfless young woman, to use her experiences in the newly mechanized workplace of the American factory for the good of others. Mary earns vitally needed income for her family, volunteers to teach factory children in her limited spare time, and sets an example to her more self-indulgent workmates of self-control and self-sacrifice. Her reward, after several years of arduous work, is marriage to a widower with two sons, a return to a life of purely domestic service, and, in recognition of her literary proclivities, a gift from her new family of a Bible and a writing desk. Mary thus provides a model for the new working woman of unselfishness and dedication to the service of others—not, perhaps, very different from the old model for the housebound woman, except that she has added wage-earning to her other chores. However, Savage's inclusion of both reading and writing material among Mary's rewards is the first small hint of a revolution in factory women's lives in nineteenth-century America that would alter their own mental awareness and their reputation in the consciousness of others as profoundly as factory labor would change their material world.

Mary is the modest fictional avatar of a phenomenon that would, in an 1844 book title, be designated by the startling metonymy *Mind amongst the Spindles*. An anthology of literature by American factory women, published in England, the inventive title perfectly encapsulates both the book's contents and the implicit incongruity of its existence. If, in midcentury, "heart" was a favored emblem for womanhood, and "hand" the convenient label for industrial worker, the surprising manifestation of "mind" among female operatives was a national and even an international sensation. Initially it was the consequence of a cluster of circumstances peculiar to the establishment of cotton manufacture in New England—of factory villages that were consciously designed to avoid duplicating the degraded conditions of English industrial workers; of an operative population of young women educated in public schools, inured to hard work, and eager for new experiences; and of a context of intellectual and literary ferment that generated lyceums, libraries, lecture tours, periodicals, and improvement circles throughout the region. Although the literariness of these first American factory women was undoubtedly used as a promotional tool by their employers, it was not easily contained or restricted by manufacturers' boosterism.[1] Even as the New England factories became progressively more like the English Manchester they had meant to avoid, the dream of a mindful life of reading, writing, and self-culture did not disappear from the consciousness of workers or from their literary record. Although it abated somewhat in the decades after the Civil War, the heady appeal of books and authorship emerged again with renewed power at the end of the century. Now it appeared in immigrant women who labored in sweatshops but still clung to the vision of a fuller life that would satisfy the needs of the spirit as well as the body.

This fervent pursuit of a life of complete development was marked by a notable literary outpouring from working women themselves as well as from middle-class writers, especially women, who were fascinated with the aspirations and the predicament of the new factory girls. Romantic reformers, feminists, utopians, Christians, socialists, and anarchists scrutinized working women in an extensive array of essays, novels, and documentary reporting. Workers, from New England farmers' daughters who flocked to the cotton mills in Lowell early in the nineteenth century to east European Jewish immigrants who flooded into the New York garment industry early in the twentieth, wrote and edited their own journals and created their own poems, stories, and memoirs. They became for the first time the agents of their own representation as well as famously eager consumers of the printed word. So keen was their literary appetite that, by the middle of the century, New England factories formally banned (and even fired) workers for reading in the work-rooms: "To the praise / Of mill-girls be the need of such a rule" wrote their poet, Lucy Larcom (*Idyl* 128). By the end of the century, when journalists began to descend into the world of the lower classes to report on working-class women's lives, they noted repeatedly the avid reading and discussion of books among them. An 1895 advice book for working women even warned them against joining clubs "for which papers must be prepared and in which discussions are rampant" (qtd. in Eisenstein 89). Nevertheless, women, and especially immigrant Jewish women, flocked to such self-education groups and reported with relish on their "rampant" literary evenings. These working women and their observers jointly participated in a literary discourse that reflected the hopes, the fears, and the bewilderment of a still young republic about the emergence of the formerly silent voices of working-class women, and they pursued vigorous debates about the role of literariness and culture in a newly industrializing democracy.[2]

In his study of working-class self-culture (or what he labels the "autodidact" impulse) in Britain during the same period, Jonathan Rose has found little evidence of working women's participation in such a movement there. Similarly, scholars of British working-class literature have repeatedly noted the relative absence of women's contributions to it in the nineteenth century. In the United States, however, despite many eventual grim similarities in the impact of industrialization on workers' lives, working-class women, particularly factory workers, took a more prominent part as authors and as subjects in the literary and intellectual discourse of industrial life. This book attempts to explore some of the issues raised by their presence. It examines, in a variety of different literary works, the imaginative response to the coincidence of a number of seemingly discrete but historically connected events. These include the beginnings of economic independence for working women; the impact on them of democratic and Romantic ideals of selfhood; the expectations of traditional female roles; the expansion of the literary marketplace and of access to literacy and education; the frequent investigation, celebration, and denigration of working-class women by writers from other classes; their ambiguous presence in the writing of literary ladies; and finally their own literary efforts in the context of their factory experiences.[3]

The first reservation about the benefits of literariness in factory women, ironically, occurred in the later novels of Sarah Savage, who had begun her career by promoting their reading and writing abilities as an accessory to their female virtue. Savage, herself a member of the middle class, had saluted her heroine's literacy in *The Factory Girl* and, through Mary Burnam's Bible study and teaching, made it central to her selfless capacity to serve others. However, no small part of Mary's success as a reader and teacher of the Bible comes from her empathy with biblical characters, her pleasure in her understanding of the text, and her ability to convey the meaning to her pupils. By the time Savage wrote her second novel, *Filial Affection* (1820), she had recognized a curious moral dilemma in the ardent embrace of literature, even for religious purposes. Not only might other aspects of literature prove more absorbing than its religious message but its study might arouse feelings of personal autonomy that undermined dependence on God. Thus, one of her characters in the novel confesses: "the amusements of literature engrossed my thoughts to the exclusion of Him who...made me capable of entering into the feelings of the poet, and of following the historian. I felt too independent, possessing as I vainly thought, the means of happiness within myself" (qtd. in Moore 249). Literature, even when intended for didactic purposes, is ominously capable, in Savage's view, of captivating the mind and of furthering a "vain" sense of innate human ability and worldly agency. By the time she published her last novel, *Trial and Self-Discipline*, in 1835, Savage had come to have precisely the same misgivings about the value of factories that she had about the literariness that was so closely connected with them: she feared that they would nurture "a spirit of self-reliance, an earthly spirit, looking only to this low world for aid, for support" (qtd. in Moore 258). The pattern in Savage's writing of associating working women with factories, of factories with enhanced independence and literary opportunities, and of such opportunities with both virtuous female selflessness and ominous female self-reliance is an early intimation that working women's literacy might present a serious challenge to traditional Christian and gendered notions of selfhood. Factory work, for the purpose of earning a living, and literary work, as a means of self-expression, were each novel ventures for women, beyond their traditional domestic role. These two newly linked activities might be assimilated into codes of selflessness or provoke bold excursions into new kinds of self-awareness that questioned long-held assumptions about woman's modest nature and unselfish ambitions.[4]

The same concerns about self-denial and self-development, sometimes described in terms of "true" and "new" womanhood, were also central to the literature of middle-class women at the time. However, the working

women's debate was compounded by a further challenge to the appropriateness of their literary ambitions, not as an affirmation or a betrayal of
their religion and their sex but as a measure of their allegiance to their own
working-class culture. In becoming literary, did they also become "ladies"
and risk abandoning the interests of workers for the values of a bourgeois culture hostile or indifferent to their own economic class? When the
operatives of Lowell, Massachusetts, first began, in 1840, to publish their
literary magazine, the *Lowell Offering*, one of their keenest motives was to
take up their pens to defend the respectability of factory women against
charges of moral degradation and sexual looseness. However, the feminine decorum and literariness they affirmed through their writing, coupled
with the obvious interests of factory proprietors in promoting a workers'
magazine that avoided industrial controversies, soon brought the charge
from more radical women that they were traitors to their class and tools
of capitalist manipulation and oppression. The literary eloquence of Harriet Farley, the *Offering*'s editor, quickly became the focus of her political
antagonists' scorn. The radical women called on their own rhetorical skills
to satirize and parody her Latinate vocabulary and to mock the linguistic
finesse of "the *honorable, refined, lady-like* Miss F." They italicized her verbal
affectations ("*erroneous impressions*" "*consolatory* assurance," "constitutional
inability") and ridiculed her elegantly deferential style: "I have been *favored*
with a specimen of *refined* literature, from the pen of one of the *geniuses* of
the age, and feel myself highly honored with a passing notice from such a
high source."[5]

Although accusations against Harriet Farley of class treachery and middle-
class collaboration may not have been wholly baseless, the same charges
were made even against working women with impeccably radical credentials when they showed too keen a taste for literature and culture. When
Emma Goldman, perhaps America's most notorious anarchist, founded her
magazine *Mother Earth* in 1906, her interest in writers and artists brought
the remarkable charge that the journal was not "revolutionary enough"
(Morton 47). Fania Cohn, an official in the International Ladies Garment
Workers Union, suffered a similar challenge to her class *bona fides* when she
helped establish a Workers' University in 1918, with a number of classes on
literature and art that proved especially appealing to women members. Her
union leaders warned her that she was "encouraging middle-class fantasies" that might "educate workers out of their class" (Orleck 179–80). The
notion that intellectual interests and literary concerns were innately the
provenance of the middle class could of course justify workers' efforts to
appropriate and adapt them to their own ends just as readily as it could
imply bourgeois cultural authority. Nevertheless, suspicions that the life of
the mind might be class-bound created tensions about working women's
literariness comparable to the anxieties generated by their gender.

It might be easy to conclude that working-class women were thus doubly excluded, by both class and gender expectations, from participating fully

in a culture of literacy and mental aspiration. However, such a conclusion would ignore not only the remarkable concern and empathy for their situation among many middle-class and feminist writers but also the curious malleability of the literary imagination itself. In fact, the protean literary productions of the period belie, as much as they endorse, the simpler politics of class and gender identity. A couple of examples may suggest these complications. In 1853, eight years after Margaret Fuller's *Woman in the Nineteenth Century* was published, the feminist journal, *The Una* published a serialized novel, *Stray Leaves from a Seamstress's Journal,* in which an anonymous seamstress sharply criticizes the bourgeois limitations of Fuller's conceptions of female self-culture, complaining that "a veil is between her and the rude, practical, every-day working world." The seamstress suggests that if Fuller could only come into the "cheerless comfortless homes" of the working class, "where there is nothing beautiful," she might then realize "how difficult, how almost impossible is self development, where there is only the means of keeping soul and body together" (qtd. in L. Reynolds 231–32). The seamstress's remarks seem like the opportune incursion of an adversarial, proletarian voice into a middle-class feminist periodical. However, *The Una* was the project of an elite group of highly educated women whose editor, Pauline Wright Davis, acknowledged her practice of "'writing over various signatures, in order to give variety'" to her journal. She also published many anonymous "letters to the editor," quite possibly written by herself to enhance informed debates (Conrad 162, 170). Thus the fictional worker may well have been the mouthpiece of the actual bourgeoise, trying to speak on behalf of the voiceless subaltern. An interesting variation on a similar theme occurs in Theresa Malkiel's 1910 novel *The Diary of a Shirtwaist Striker.* In this case, the fictional narrator of the diary is apparently a native-born and more privileged woman who observes and comments in amazement on the alien, frizzy-haired, gesticulating immigrants who organize the strike. Malkiel was herself one of those alien, immigrant "others" but chose, as a writer, to imagine her fictional world from an assumed nativist and insider's perspective, in an interesting subversion of speaking on behalf of the "other" class.

This switching and merging of class identity, between middle-class author and working-class diarist and between immigrant author and native persona, is only one manifestation of the literary inventiveness of women writers exploring new conceptions of female self-culture. If such literary efforts to cross the barriers of social circumstance and class prejudice often served to expose the sturdiness of the barriers, they nevertheless showed where breeches might be made and how definitions of working women and literary ladies might evolve and change, even within fairly short historical periods. In her essay "Class, Gender, and a History of Metonymy," Wai Chee Dimock has noted the danger of seeking a unitary or "generalizable identity" in the writings of nineteenth-century women workers and has indicated the ever present literary possibilities for "nonalignment" between individual and class, or individual and gender. Rather than a fixed identity among working women, she finds "a series of momentary postures, at once unevenly developed and imperfectly aligned" (93, 94). The same observation might be made about the literary ladies who participated in the intellectual exchange that emerged in tandem with the industrializing process—the imperfections and inconsistencies of their class alignments and their assumptions of various imaginative postures blurred any fixed identity that might be reduced to metonymic representation. As a matter of historical development, literary ladies could and did become working women, and working women could and did become literary ladies. Margaret Fuller began her career as an elite Boston bluestocking; then she became an employed working woman in New York, then an unmarried mother in Italy, and finally a countess before she died in a shipwreck with her husband, her baby, and her unpublished manuscripts. Lucy Larcom began her working career as a ten-year-old child laborer in the Lowell mills before becoming a successful and esteemed professional poet; Emma Goldman was a sweatshop worker, a prisoner, a nurse, a lecturer, an editor, an associate of many eminent figures and, eventually, a deported alien. Such a variety of identities within individual lives demonstrates not only a degree of class mobility but also the fluidity of these women's self-representation and of their perception by others. They are both the producers and the products of a new literary consciousness emanating from the working woman herself and reflecting back on her, a consciousness first timidly noted in the fictional Mary Burnam and then, a century later, brought to its logical and flamboyant culmination in Emma Goldman, larger in life than any Romantic imagination could have envisioned or any traditional author could have feared.

This book begins with a chapter that explores how two middle-class women writers shaped early and dramatically different versions of the new female factory worker. It juxtaposes Sarah Savage's 1814 novel *The Factory Girl* (about the virtuous Mary Burnam) with Catharine Williams's 1833 account, *Fall River: An Authentic Narrative*, of the miserable life and gruesome death of Sarah Maria Cornell, an actual factory operative. Cornell's tainted sexual reputation, her history of shoplifting, and her camp meeting predilections contrast starkly with the habits of the self-disciplined and rational Mary Burnam. Significantly, the only quality shared by the factual and the fictional factory workers is that both are readers and writers who aspire to a larger life for both body and mind. Both are, however, equally imaginative constructions, based on a mixture of historical fact and literary invention, created by more affluent writers fascinated with the new realm of wage-earning women. Together Savage and Williams establish conflicting reputations for the woman worker that anticipate her imminent (and distinctive) written invention of herself.

Chapter 2 focuses on the factory women's magazine the *Lowell Offering* (1840–45) as one of the primary emanations of the phenomenon of "mind amongst the spindles." It examines the controversial role of its main editor, Harriet Farley—as a champion of factory opportunities, a defender of operatives' morality, and an ardent advocate and model of working women's literacy. The *Offering* has been frequently criticized, in its own day and ever since, for its lack of political militancy in challenging the abuses of the factory system and for its ladylike gentility, as witnessed in its lack of opposition to industrial conditions and its seeming preference for traditional modes of demure literariness. Nonetheless, an investigation of the entire run of the magazine is a valuable guide not only to the impact of new experiences and conflicting obligations on working women but also to their experimentation with the literary forms most appropriate to their self-representation. Although many of the contributions to the *Offering* are conventional in the extreme, some of the authors show a keen awareness of the Romantic literary context of the times, while others begin to develop incipient modes of literary realism that allow them to explore the paradoxes of their situation.[6]

Chapter 3 examines the *Dial* (1840–44), the magazine of the American Romantics, which appeared in New England almost exactly contemporaneously with the *Lowell Offering*. The *Dial*'s contributors, like the *Offering*'s, although in more ethereal mode, explored the possibilities for the full development of mind, soul, and body within the context of the dramatic changes in mid-nineteenth-century American society. Like the *Offering*, for much of its duration the *Dial* was under the editorship of a woman, in this case Margaret Fuller, who tried to expand the Romantic ideals of male transcendentalists and test their applicability to women. Although she did not extend this expansion to women outside her own social and educational class during her *Dial* years, she demonstrated in her writing new possibilities and directions for intellectually ambitious women and in her life the quest for new work and untried experiences. While many transcendentalists, like Emerson, remained distinctly class-bound in their daily lives, they celebrated in their writing a hope for individual intellectual autonomy that recognized no limits. Thus they made a profound impression on a much broader range of people than the brief list of subscribers to their little magazine might suggest, including working women who went unmentioned in their pages but read them avidly for what the former Lowell operative Lucy Larcom described in "R. W. E.," her sonnet to Emerson, as "a sense of widening worlds and ampler air."[7]

Chapter 4 looks at three male novelists who emerged from the Romantic movement in America—Sylvester Judd, Nathaniel Hawthorne, and Herman Melville. In contrast to the majority of the *Dial*'s transcendental contributors, all of them acknowledged in their writing the dynamic changes in the conditions and aspirations of working-class women and the impact of their intrusion into the cultural and literary discourse of the day. In different ways, each reflected in his fiction transformations in literary genre, method, and content in response to this new social consciousness. In doing so, like the working women who contributed to the *Lowell Offering*, these authors emphasized the primacy of fiction as a literary mode adaptable both to new authorial concerns and a new reading audience.

Chapter 5 takes up fiction of a very different kind from the ambitious efforts of Judd, Hawthorne, and Melville to develop a genre suitable to an altered sense of contemporary reality and looks at approximately a dozen "factory" novels that were written in midcentury, in rapid reaction to the experiences of working women in Lowell and similar New England industrial settings. These novels display a range of popular fictional modes, from didactic Sunday school tracts to murder mysteries and sensational seduction stories. They also align themselves with diverse ideological and political responses to the benefits of factory labor for women. Most remarkably, however, and without exception, they *all* focus on the literacy of factory women, on their enthusiasm for reading and lecture-going, and on their dedication to writing. This literariness emerges in these novels as a multivalent symbol for the incongruity of the new working woman's identity, whether as the assertive proclaimer of her own new-found subjectivity or as the dupe of cheap novels and romantic fantasies.

Chapter 6 explores in detail one of the most striking literary products of a nineteenth-century factory woman, Lucy Larcom's 1875 epic poem *An Idyl of Work*. Written in an epic mode that is rare in women's writing, and virtually unique in working-class women's writing, this long poem depicts early American factory women as the emblematic voices and models of a democratic republic of body and mind. Larcom's poetic workers are also thinkers and writers, women whose active literary engagement enables them to form a transcendent link between the physical and spiritual realms of their existence. Although she readily concedes in her preface to the poem that the *actual* conditions in factories have deteriorated seriously since the earlier generation she depicts, Larcom's female operatives nonetheless represent an ideal of work, community, and thought that was to endure far beyond the unique circumstances where it took form.

Chapter 7 turns to the later decades of the nineteenth century, when women's factory labor was no longer a novelty, and industrial and class tensions were increasingly becoming the focus of reforming writers. While working women continued to seek lives that satisfied the needs of body and spirit, middle-class women novelists and male fiction writers for the Knights of Labor offered them literary models of religious sublimation rather than the more secular salvation of intellectual culture.[8] Educated and more affluent women, like Rebecca Harding Davis, Elizabeth Stuart Phelps, and Louisa May Alcott, who sympathized keenly with working women's material deprivation, and who struggled to vindicate their own creative ambitions, nevertheless recommended Christianity and its otherworldly rewards rather than the mental and artistic subjectivity they were themselves trying to assert. One notable exception to the consolations of religion proffered by Knights and ladies alike was Marie Howland's utopian and communitarian novel *The Familistère* (1874). Howland, herself a former Lowell worker, challenged not only religious piety as a female virtue but also conventional attitudes toward sexuality, capitalism, and private property. In doing so, she anticipated some of the more radical working-class attitudes of the generation of immigrant women who followed her.

The concluding chapter considers some dramatic changes in the population of working women by the beginning of the twentieth century, as well as continuities of the same ideals that had animated the earliest female industrial workers. It juxtaposes the hopes for self-culture of a generation of Jewish immigrants from eastern Europe who worked in the sweatshops of New York with those of the earlier Lowell workers, and explores the fiction they wrote and that was written about them. It looks closely at Emma Goldman as an extreme manifestation, both celebrated and notorious, of the consequences of working women's aspirations to literariness and self-reliance. Like Margaret Fuller, Goldman edited a literary periodical, *Mother Earth*, asserted the Romantic primacy of her individual mind, and ignored the sexual restrictions of her time. Like Fuller's working-class contemporaries, she appropriated from the Romantic ideals of transcendentalism principles that had probably not been developed with someone like herself in mind. Like those factory workers, too, she was a passionate reader and writer and, like them, she was the subject, sometimes admired, frequently ridiculed, of other people's fascinated fictions.

Any account of the ways the literary aspirations of several generations of working-class women were entangled with the entrenched class and gender assumptions underlying mental culture must choose a somewhat arbitrary stopping point. In the case of this book, it is the early twentieth century, when working-class women had become firmly established in the industrial workplace, when distinctions between suitable literary content for men and women were being finely drawn, and when discriminations between elite culture and popular entertainment were being made ever more narrowly on the basis of class.[9] One advantage of being members of the second sex and the lower class was that working women were not carefully schooled in the subtle implications of their choices of cheap fiction or classic novels, movies or live theatre, music halls or lectures. In this they had more freedom than the literary ladies who sought to be their friends, models, and guardians. If their reading was more casually promiscuous and their authorial ambitions less inhibited by cultural standards, working women nevertheless continued to demonstrate an intellectual liveliness in the midst of their monotonous daily labor. In doing so, they provided an ongoing response to Lucy Larcom's troubled question in *An Idyl of Work* (142): "how to save/Mind from machinery's clutches."

I

"A Tangled Skein"

Early Factory Women, Self-Reliance, and Self-Sacrifice

"She has worked in a Factory," is almost enough to damn to infamy the
most worthy and virtuous girl.
—ORESTES BROWNSON, 1840

But I believe it would be good for every girl, rich or poor, to spend a
year in a mill. It is a good physical discipline. It may even invigorate the
mind, while it puts every heart in communication with our age, and
in possession of its independent and progressive spirit. It will give you
independence. And how little independence many of our American
women have!
—DAY KELLOGG LEE, 1854

In 1814, Sarah Savage published a novel with the suggestive and prescient
title *The Factory Girl*, a fusion of two key terms in the literary and social
controversies of the century to come. It is an account of the exemplary
career of the chaste, dutiful, and charitable Mary Burnam, who labors
cheerfully in a cotton mill to support her ailing grandmother. Mary is
eventually rewarded by marriage to a prosperous widower and by the
highly emblematic gifts from her stepchildren of a handsome Bible and a
portable writing desk. The novel imagines a factory woman who is a noble
synthesis of industriousness, rational religion, and improving literacy. Less
than twenty years later, in 1833, Catharine Williams published *Fall River:
An Authentic Narrative*, a cautionary true account of Sarah Maria Cornell,
a female factory worker with a distinctly less elevated reputation. From
the early disgrace of shoplifting and expulsion from her local church to
her grisly death, hanged, pregnant and abused, leaving only a small cache
of letters behind, Cornell's history is the moral antithesis of Mary's. Her
story combines similar elements—factory employment, spiritual aspiration,
and a desire to participate in public discourse—into an account of degradation and disaster. Together the two books, both by middle-class women
about working-class women, one an explicit fiction, the other a blend of
fact and fictitiousness, establish crucial elements in the early debate on the
impact of the industrial revolution on American women and of the literary
response to it. The legacy of Mary's writing desk and Sarah Maria's letters,

and the focus in each work on the writing and speaking of the factory workers, suggest from the start that the operatives' own literacy and literariness would form an important strand in this discourse. The role of religion in each woman's story also anticipates later controversies over the impact of Christianity, for good or ill, on factory women's aspirations to be more than mere "hands" in the new industrial world.

In these early nineteenth-century books, the debate about the potential benefits or harmfulness of factories and the wider realm of consciousness to which they introduced their female workers is framed in religious terms, intensely concentrated on working women's moral and sexual conduct. The factory and its milieu could be the road to moral salvation and financial security or sexual perdition and social disgrace. The factory experience could foster such virtues as hard work and self-discipline, and enable republican farmers' daughters to contribute to the mortgaged family home, the support of parents, or the education of a talented brother. It could offer opportunities for education and social exchange, and provide a wider sphere for the operation of mind as well as body. But what if that sphere also proved to be a larger arena of temptation? What if it offered the factory girl frivolous trinkets on which to spend her wages, easy access to seductive pleasures, the absence of a domestic community to support and guide her? Or a dangerous sense of her own autonomy? What if, most ominously, the young woman's religious training did not provide a bulwark against the radical ideas she might encounter when she ventured into the public workplace? What if new sects and movements drew her away from earlier orthodoxies? What if the books she was so eager to read and the lectures she was so ready to attend encouraged a self-culture and application of literacy at odds with traditional religious codes of service and sacrifice? Savage and Williams consider particularly these questions of the relationship of religious belief to the unprecedented experiences of the factory world and to women's enhanced opportunities there for literacy and self-expression. The difference in their conclusions suggests how dynamically and provocatively the circumstances and the consciousness of working women were changing in the first decades of their industrial experience.

Curiously, neither author is especially interested in the new physical conditions of labor in the factories, or in the nature of the mechanized work itself. What intrigues them is the same question that permeates many of the novels of seduction and betrayal of the previous century: how will formerly sheltered woman react to the dramatic transition from the familiar to the unfamiliar and now, specifically, from the fireside to the workplace? Earlier novels had transferred rural beauties to urban sophistication, or women of modest means to surroundings of lavish wealth, where female decorum and purity were challenged and the outcome was appropriately vindicated by marriage or death. These earlier novels had also frequently suggested the consequences of appropriate and inappropriate reading on impressionable womanly minds.[1] The factory settings of Savage and Williams bring novelty to the formula but, more important, begin to hint that the female operatives themselves might shift the terms of the debate to preoccupations beyond a narrow focus on their sexual and moral conduct, even though both accounts do indeed reach conventional conclusions of heroines wed or dead. While they scarcely hint at concerns about the kind of economic and social reforms that would occupy later working women, both books place considerable emphasis on the mental life of their protagonists, on their spiritual beliefs, on their reading and their interest in the understanding and interpretation of texts, and on their role as teachers, speakers, and writers. Together they constitute a suggestive introduction to the literary outpouring throughout the nineteenth century by and about working women—about their new self-awareness, their conflicting reputations, and their capacity to be active agents in their own lives—that would trace their first short steps from farm to factory in New England, and eventually encompass their much larger movement, as immigrants, between continents and cultures.

The earliest stage of the transition from home to the new world of New England mills was, according to the historian Thomas Dublin, a less dramatic transformation in women's working lives than would come later, when women would move entirely away from familiar environments and routines.[2] Early in the nineteenth century, farm women began to perform "outwork" on machine-spun cotton in their homes, receiving credit in the form of store purchases in return for their labor, or they worked in small local factories that, according to Dublin, "did not so much replace household manufacture as complement it" (*Women* 4). By 1814, the year Savage's *Factory Girl* was published, there were about twenty-five cotton mills in New England, and Savage, a native of Salem, might easily observe those nearby in Beverly and Danvers. Her novel suggests that within a very short time some mill workers had acquired a compromised moral reputation. When Mary Burnam, the incipient factory girl, announces her intention of going out to work to her grandmother, the older woman replies "It will, indeed, it will be a sad day to me when you go into the factory; for I shall be thinking all the time, what your poor father would say, were he alive, to have you get your bread in such a manner." The older Mrs. Burnam quickly acknowledges the virtue of being "industrious" and of working, not for fine clothes, but for the comforts of others, but she is troubled that Mary's coworkers will be people who are not "good and serious" (3–4).

The cultural significance of seriousness and levity resonates throughout the first century of American fiction, from Hannah Foster's flighty Eliza Whitman in *The Coquette* (1797) to Nathaniel Hawthorne's allegory of jollity and gloom contending for an empire in "The Maypole of Merry Mount" (1837) to Henry James's satire in *The Europeans* (1878) of playful foreigners and humorless Bostonians. The female factory world presents yet another arena for testing this set of residual Puritan antitheses and for suggesting the particular dangers for working-class women who stray from sobriety into pleasure-seeking, whether in their physical or their mental pursuits. Savage's dutiful Mary resolutely refuses to smile at her workmates' "capital joking" (12) and risks the label of "*Miss Propriety*" (19) by refusing to go to a dance. She is courted by her fickle fellow worker William Raymond, who jilts her for a woman of "thoughtless levity" (71). When William wins $400 in a lottery, he abandons his new wife and child, "believing that there would be no end to his fortune" (85). Mary solemnly rejects personal indulgences in favor of renunciation, and then takes care to disguise the toll her nobility is taking on her health and emotions. When she becomes ill, she appears so "pleasant and cheerful" that she hardly can be believed to be "as sick as she was represented" (57); when William turns to the other woman, she suppresses her envy of her rival and even presents her with a gift; and when her beloved grandmother dies, she restrains her own grief in order to soothe others. It might indeed seem, from the evidence of this earliest American industrial novel, that being a good "factory girl" is simply taking to extremes woman's traditional role of self-sacrifice for the sake of others.

Thomas B. Lovell has, however, fully and very interestingly explored an alternative and more positive reading of this first fictional factory experience that argues for a more empowering understanding of Mary Burnam's career, beyond the context of the "separate spheres" paradigm that has dominated much of the critical discussion of women's roles and their writing in the nineteenth century. Lovell proposes that Savage's version of the factory world represents a growth in opportunity for her heroine and a way for her to enter more fully on to the stage of life by venturing beyond woman's traditional domestic realm. The public workplace offers Mary larger scope for continuing the practice of her female virtue. Thus Lovell sees the novel as an early and significant alternative to the notion that separate spheres, of private life for women and public life for men, were the norm for the culture and literature of the age. His interpretation deliberately counters both the theory developed by Ann Douglas, in which the private world of women is criticized as sentimental and anti-intellectual, because it is detached from commerce and industry; and Jane Tompkins's alternative theory, whereby women are able to create, in their domestic realm, a moral critique of the values of the marketplace. Lovell argues that "our contemporary emphasis on the distinction between spheres prevents us from acknowledging another view, one that imagines a smooth continuity between the concerns of the household and the concerns of the workplace, and a participation in the workplace founded on principles usually associated with the domestic sphere" (4). For Lovell, Savage's novel neither extols the private sphere, at the expense of the public arena for women's action, nor suggests a demeaning lack of connection between the domestic and the public environment.

Not only does Savage's factory world act as a kind of "moral incubator" (11) for female virtue, in Lovell's view, but it also encourages in women a pattern of rational economic calculation that can be imported back from their factory ventures into domestic life. Thus Mary's final decision to marry a widower with children puts marriage and mothering on the same reasoned exchange basis as wage labor in the factory: "Mary sees her decision in market-like terms, trading the costs and benefits of one situation for those of another.... Furthermore, wage labor provides a rational basis for determining one's responsibilities and calculating the effects of one's actions" (17). Contrary to later Marxist notions of workers as the products of their own machine labor, or the pervasive and denigrating metonymic designation of them as "hands," Savage's novel suggests that "women workers create themselves" and become more human by reason of their wage-earning industrial work (18). Lovell notes that such a version of factory fiction allays many contemporary concerns about the entry of women into the workplace. Not only is their womanly virtue uncompromised but it is enhanced and expanded before being drawn back again into the domestic world of marriage and child-raising. However, in acknowledging a rational economic calculation on the part of the woman worker, and a sense of the personal satisfaction it brings, Savage is also the first of many writers, including many women workers themselves, to insist on the pleasure women felt not just at the valuable uses of their labor, but at the prospective power of earning wages. Savage's heroine is elated by the prospect of doing good for others, but such altruism was scarcely the only source of satisfaction for the working woman.

When Mary is first hired at the factory, the "lightness of her heart, was only rivalled by her steps, as she returned home filled with anticipations of future pleasure, from having it in her power to procure for her grandmother the comforts which declining life made peculiarly needful" (9–10). That such an emphasis on the rewards of work, sacrifice, and virtue was a providential combination for proprietors of factories, even more than for workers, has caused many commentators on New England's early industrial experiments to question the sincerity of the convictions of owners who actively promoted Christian piety and Bible study among their workers when the outcome was likely to be so profitable for themselves. Historians of the early labor movement have often noted the double-sidedness of an owners' policy that equated hard work with virtue and salvation, and encouraged the religious education of their workers. Apparently self-serving, it was nevertheless also a direct outgrowth of their stern Protestant tradition. If its intention was the policing of mill operatives, it derived from a theology that emphasized the need for self-discipline. Jonathan Prude comments that "by following the long line of Protestant moralizing that fused righteousness with diligence, mill masters could simultaneously assert concern for their workers' well-being and strive to inculcate values encouraging productivity," an argument that he notes is "not necessarily hypocritical" (94). Hannah Josephson likewise observes that cotton manufacturers managed initially, with a seamless combination of devious and benevolent paternalism, to acquire a reputation for high-mindedness and integrity while, at the same time, becoming enormously rich (63–74). However, if the motives of the owners were double-edged, their encouragement of religion and learning in their workers was also two-sided in its consequences, since spiritual and intellectual pursuits proved notoriously difficult to keep within bounds, especially in the volatile context of the religious awakenings and philosophical and literary movements of the first half of the nineteenth century.

Apart from the specific ideas such developments generated, the sheer emotional enthusiasm of factory workers for the pursuit of both religion and book learning soon came to be such a problem for the owners that they had to make rules to restrain it. By the 1840s, among the causes that could bring a dishonorable discharge from the mills of Lowell, Massachusetts, were "reading in the mill," pretending sickness "to go to meeting," and "religious frenzy" (qtd. in Zonderman 150). Savage's Mary Burnam never oversteps the bounds of religious restraint or scholarly ambition, although her engagement with Bible study and teaching is certainly among the keenest of her interests. Sarah Maria Cornell, on the other hand, is quickly drawn to the extremes of her new-found interests and proves distinctly less amenable to the rational economic and moral calculations of factory logic.

Mary Burnam is the product of an early religious education that has emphasized the close scrutiny of biblical texts and has also made a virtue of the act of reading, with its lessons in empathy and aesthetics. Mr. Danforth, a neighbor, has enlivened family evenings in the Burnam household by reading aloud "some useful or entertaining book" (25); he has recommended the story of the prodigal son because it is "entertaining" (31) and the accounts of Joseph, Moses, and Ruth because they are "beautiful and pathetic" (30). The psychology of reading in order to indulge a taste for delight and pathos, and thereby to imbibe some valuable religious and moral precepts, is central to the novel. Children are to be encouraged to have a lively interest in character, curiosity is to be awakened, compassion aroused, and exciting events to be related until they are so sensitive in the art of reading that they can anticipate the climax and outcome of a story. Mr. Seymore, the village clergyman, recounts with satisfaction the tale of a child "who on reading the history of Job, when she arrived at the highest point of his suffering, clasped her little hands and exclaimed, (while her whole countenance was expressive of fearful apprehension,) 'Oh! I am afraid now he will curse God'" (30). Such faith in the power of narrative and the moral compulsion of literature by means of its fascination is pervasive in the nineteenth-century novel; its corollary is an equal degree of misgiving about the negative effects of misdirected reading in the wrong kinds of books, which are legion. Many later industrial novels focus on the dire consequences of women immersing themselves in books and beliefs that lead them astray. Women, like children, are depicted as much more susceptible to these mental influences, more noble in their triumphs when they do not permit their minds to range too distantly from holy writ, more wretched in their falls when their thoughts are allowed to explore too far afield.

Savage is obviously in something of a quandary in trying to advocate the advantages of reading, education, and broader awareness for women without endorsing their possibly deleterious effects on dangerous feelings of independence and self-sufficiency. She notes the impulse to intellectual enquiry, even in Mary's untutored grandmother: "She did not know the meaning of the word *philosophy*; but yet, no one was more pleased to examine and observe the effects of the machines and instruments. ... The term *natural history* she could not have defined; but was practically acquainted with some of its most useful branches" (14–15). When Mary successfully convinces her friend Nancy to embark on regular study of the Bible, and argues with her fellow workers to change their self-indulgent behavior, she has to face the problem of her own successful self-assertion and agency in accomplishing even such worthy goals. On this occasion, she finds a satisfactory resolution to any unseemly satisfaction in her own power: "Though she was too humble to believe her influence extensive, she thought it right to act as if it were so. For she considered that Providence often employs humble means to effect important purposes" (22). Mary is thus capable of subordinating her skills as a literary interpreter and her success as a teacher to her modest role in a divine plan, but Savage has nevertheless admitted, even in this most humble of heroines, the need for ever-increasing vigilance over the factory woman's intellectual pursuits.

Although Savage is not especially interested in depicting the material conditions of factory life, her novel inevitably reveals some of the social circumstances that will later constitute the central tropes of factory literature. On the first day of Mary's employment, we hear the tolling of the factory bell that will reverberate through generations of workers' lives and their literary record. Savage's acknowledgment of it immediately places her outside the class of writers for whom the metonym of the coming mechanical age was the intrusion of the locomotive's whistle into their pastoral peace, rather than the pervasive presence of clanging bells and the deafening roar of manufacturing machinery. Later, when factory women began to write of their own experiences, this physical presence of sound, ordering the routine of their days and isolating them into their own minds as they worked, is one of the dominant images of their new consciousness of industrial labor.

Mary's job is reeling cotton and, although we are told that she attempts to describe the complicated operation to her interested grandmother, Savage assumes less curiosity on the part of the reader and provides no details. The other girls get angry when their spools are tangled and are "cold, and hungry, and tired" (13) at the end of the day, but Savage does not pursue the subject of working conditions, although later novelists would more than compensate for her omission. An exception to her sparse account of factory life that is likely to trouble a modern reader more than an early nineteenth century one is the employment of children and their consequent inability to go to school. The concern for their education is raised in the novel by Dr. Mandeville, himself one of the proprietors of the mill, who provides an interesting perspective on the causes of child labor: "In these establishments the labours of children are so useful, as to render their wages a temptation to parents to deprive their offspring of the advantages of education; and, for an immediate supply of pressing wants, to rob them of their just rights—the benefit of those publick schools, which were founded peculiarly for the advantage of the poor" (37). The humanitarian doctor solves the difficulty expediently by offering Mary a "small reward" for teaching a Sunday Charity School, a task she gladly takes on in addition to her six-day factory job and the care of her grandmother and another aged relative. Mary shares her educational advantages willingly with the children and is delighted to think that she is thereby "doing service acceptable to heaven" (52). Thus the factory woman's literacy, in Savage's ideal version, serves both God and the proprietor's conscience.

Mary's rigorous moral nature leads her to worry about whether her friend William's admirable behavior is an instance of true virtue or merely an attempt to win her esteem. However, she does not question the equity and justice of a system that makes the labor of children necessary to their parents, and then compensates for the deficiency in their education by exploiting the services of other factory workers. Similarly, Mary's finely tuned conscience causes her to reproach her fellow workers for spending money to hire a sleigh to take them to a dance when they have turned a beggar away from the factory door, but she does not question the causes of the old man's indigence. Savage uses her novel to investigate the private moral concerns of a model female worker rather than to challenge systems and organizations that were changing the whole structure of people's lives. The Christian morality her characters adhere to, or depart from, is a personal one in which individuals bear ultimate responsibility for their conduct. There is as yet no sign of concern in Savage's writing that women workers might use their newly developed literacy to challenge the very system that had enabled it, or to serve themselves as well as others. Nor are there any hints of the development of a group consciousness among workers based on commonalities of class or gender. Nevertheless, the constant yoking, in this early literature of factory experience, of women's physical venture into the public sphere of work and their mental excursions into new realms of reading and thought hints from the start at the possibility of profound consequences arising from these widening horizons.

In Mary Burnam's fictional world, the realms of reading, religion, and factory work blend harmoniously to swell the reach of her virtue, but even in the demure Mary, the symbiosis breeds confidence and authority and, if the implications of the writing desk are pursued, perhaps even future authorship as well. When she came to write her second novel, *Filial Affection* (1820), Savage further developed the incipient paradox barely hinted at in Mary's enthusiastic literacy. In this novel, she is more explicit about the subversive possibilities of reading and writing, even when embraced for religious ends. One of her characters suggests that literature can be so engrossing, and the human capacity for imaginative empathy so empowering, that it leads to delusions of responsibility for one's own spiritual existence and well-being: "I felt too independent, possessing as I vainly thought, the means of happiness within myself" (qtd. in Moore 249). The potent effect of both reading and writing is to create a "vain" illusion of one's personal agency in the process of transcending the everyday world, an agency that should belong by rights only to the divine power who made the human capable, in the words of Savage's character, "of entering into the feelings of the poet" (qtd. in Moore 249). By the end of her long literary career, Sarah Savage was using the term "self-reliance" to describe the change that had come into women's lives with their entry into the world of industrial labor. The effects of that new milieu are seemingly closely allied to the effects of the enhanced literacy that had aroused her apprehensions about the development of feelings of independence and autonomy. In her last novel, appropriately named *Trial and Self-Discipline* (1835), one of her characters avers that while she "is not sorry for the improvement that factories have made in the life of New England," she is concerned "for the spirit which I fear will grow up with them—a spirit of self-reliance, an earthly spirit, looking only to this low world for aid, for support." Mary Burnam is, as yet, far from embracing the Romantic and Emersonian implications that later attached to the term "self-reliance," but even in this, her first novel of a factory woman, Savage seems to sense that Mary is venturing prudently where others may plunge with abandon.[3]

Less than two decades after Savage's novel, Catharine Williams's *Fall River: An Authentic Narrative* demonstrated how rapidly the idealized harmonious synthesis of hard work, dutiful religion, and intellectual activity that constituted the fiction of Mary Burnam could disintegrate into the sordid experiences that formed the true-life crime story of Sarah Maria Cornell. It also suggested how rapidly the circumstances of women's factory labor were changing. Williams's *Fall River* was published in 1833, possibly at the suggestion of the representatives of the local manufacturing community, and the actual events it dealt with were recent and highly sensational. Sarah Maria Cornell was an unmarried factory worker, employed in one of the mills in Fall River, Massachusetts, until her departure from the town early one day in December 1832. The next morning her body was found hanged from a farmer's haystack roof in Tiverton, Rhode Island. The death appeared initially to be a suicide, but when it was discovered that she was pregnant, that her body bore the marks of physical abuse, and that she had left behind in her trunk a letter saying "If I am missing enquire of the Rev. E. K. Avery," the suspicion of murder arose. Ephraim Avery, a

Methodist minister, was charged and tried for the murder in 1833. After his controversial acquittal by the jury, he attempted to rehabilitate himself by preaching to the factory women in Lowell, Massachusetts. However, after being burned in effigy, he turned his career westward and left to take up farming in Ohio. The events and evidence in the case were of such a nature as to provoke widespread and enduring fascination: apart from the ongoing newspaper coverage, there were numerous poems, ballads, and a play written within the year, and Catharine Williams notes that the factory woman's grave had already, in 1833, "been the pilgrimage of thousands from all different sections of the country" (62). Over a century and a half later, scholarly books were still being written investigating the case, and novels based on it have continued to appear.[4]

The ostensible "authentic narrative" that constitutes Williams's *Fall River* belongs without question to that literary genre of true crime accounts that, according to Joyce Carol Oates, have enormous popularity but may also rise to distinction, particularly if the crimes described have "a certain symbolic magnitude" (31). From simple ballad to mystery novel to scholarly monograph, every commentator on the tragedy of Sarah Maria Cornell has found a moral or a suggestive encounter of values, but with the exception of Williams, all have turned to conventional literary genres in the realm of imaginative or nonfiction literature to reveal their insights. Only Williams felt the need to create a wholly new hybrid literary mode for her version of the "symbolic magnitude" of the Tiverton affair. Her mode proved to be an amalgam of historical and legal detective work, grisly forensic and medical details, cool analysis, impassioned rhetoric, fanciful recreation of scenes, scholarly footnotes, personal anecdotes, transcribed letters, and original poetry. Her book anticipates by over a century the kind of extravaganza of invention and documentation that James Agee and Walker Evans found necessary to record their excitement and outrage at the grim lives of Alabama tenant farmers in *Let Us Now Praise Famous Men* (1940). Like the later book, *Fall River* reveals an intriguing collision of middle-class author and working-class subject in an emotionally fraught situation. However, Williams is writing at the beginning, rather than the culmination, of a tradition of documentary literature and has not yet, like Agee, become suspicious of sensationalism or inhibited by any sense of trespassing on her social and economic inferior. She feels no compunction about imagining the factory woman's feelings, transferring her own experiences to her, or putting words into her mouth. Nonetheless, she also includes in her book sixteen transcribed letters written by the worker herself, and in so doing, she enables an alternative and perhaps more truly "authentic narrative" to emerge, in striking contrast to her own flamboyant assemblage of facts and opinion. While noting that Williams's narrative borrows from both the formulas of fiction and the conventions of factual reporting, it is important to acknowledge that many of the authors who described the early industrial experience did so in mixed modes of observation, imagination, memoir, fact, and invention. A single writer might, in her career, respond to the factory world in poetry, journalism, fiction, and autobiography. Novels of industrial life often have the kind of details that are consonant with the historical record, while the historical record itself draws evidence from imaginative sources. The literary traditions of the nineteenth century permitted novelists and poets, like Charles Dickens, Frances Trollope, and John Greenleaf Whittier, to publish "true" accounts of factory life, while actual factory workers, like Lucy Larcom and Marie Howland, produced Romantic epics and utopian fictions. Such latitude in the factual reporting and the stylistic and formal shaping of subject and theme in factory literature challenges both the authority of first-person experience as a guarantee of authenticity and equally subverts the notion that there is no extratextual correspondence for the imaginings of factory fiction. A book like Williams's *Fall River*, which embarks openly on a course outside the guidelines of any traditional genre, tends to raise more questions about the author's veracity and bias than conventional literary forms because it draws so much attention to its innovative techniques and rhetorical excesses, but the result is a vision of a working woman that is more complex and ambiguous than Savage's Sunday-school novel. It is also a reminder of what David Reynolds has noted in *Beneath the American Renaissance*—that much of the sensational literature of the period provides a counterweight to the "village pastoralism and victorious moral exemplars" proffered by conventional and domestic popular writers as "mythic correctives for thorny realities" (182).

The high drama and emotional extremes of *Fall River* are a measure of the great changes that had occurred in industry in the almost twenty years between that book and Savage's conventional novel. In 1814, a woman's move from home to factory meant exposure to some radically new experiences but also a good deal of continuity with a familiar world. The more drastic changes involved strictly regulated work hours and conditions, close supervision, a new social circle of workmates, wages for her work, and a workplace outside the private home. However, the nature of the earliest factory work was not entirely dissimilar to the hand-spinning and weaving of textiles women were already accustomed to in the household. In Thomas Dublin's study *Women at Work*, he notes the close initial association of the two work spaces in the earliest industrial years: "By mechanizing the slowest, most laborious steps in the production process, the carding and fulling mills actually contributed to increasing production of cloth in the home" (4). Not only did the first mills operate in tandem with home industry but the first mill workers lived at home, returning daily to their family life and domestic environment. Mary Burnam, Savage's "factory girl," could continue the care of her grandmother, her former friendships with the Danforths, and her attendance at her regular church while she encountered the novelty of employment. By the 1830s, the function of factories and the living conditions of the workers had changed considerably as "factory textile production began to compete with, and displace, household manufactures" (5). What later became known as the "Waltham system" severed the close connection between worker and home and changed the circumstances of both work and private life. This system integrated all the manufacturing steps at a single location that was often remote from adjoining towns, so that the owners had to recruit labor from much more distant sources and provide company-built boardinghouses in which the new workers could live (17–18). The women workers were now distant from family, friends, and church, free to make new social and religious affiliations, to save or spend their incomes, and to extend the sphere of their virtue or their temptation into a wider arena. Fall River, the setting of Sarah Maria Cornell's story, was one of the communities that underwent a transformation in a single decade from "small-scale craft production and family farming ... to a radical division of labor and mechanization in manufacturing and to commercial agriculture" (Lazerow 74). Whereas in 1812 Fall River was a village with a population of less than one hundred, by 1833 it had more than five thousand inhabitants, thirteen factories, and seven churches—two Congregationalist, two Baptist, one Free-Will Baptist, one Unitarian, and one Methodist (C. Williams 9). It is around the controversial role of the newer churches in the workers' lives that Williams concentrates much of the "symbolic magnitude" of Cornell's experiences.

The success of Baptist and Methodist churches in Fall River in attracting a greater number of mill workers and laborers than the more establishment Congregationalists, and the penchant of these newer churches for conducting fervent religious revivals, was a sign of a larger change in American Protestantism in the early nineteenth century. Jama Lazerow describes it as a movement away from the stern Calvinism of the past to a "more optimistic, and democratic, view of human destiny." She argues that "the rigidity and determinism of a life framed around conditional election, total human depravity, and an inscrutable, arbitrary, and sometimes malevolent Deity gave way to a more malleable and open world, offering the possibility of universal salvation through the free moral agency of children capable of doing good under a benevolent, loving God" (24). However, it is precisely the influence of these more popular and populist sects (and specifically Methodism), with their emphasis on emotional excess and self-absorption, that Catharine Williams, in *Fall River*, berates and blames for the downfall of her factory girl.

In contrast to Sarah Savage's depiction of the fruitful collaboration of religious education and factory opportunity in expanding her heroine's good works, Williams opposes her protagonist's irrational religion and its dangerous appeal to the more rational prospect of independence factory employment offers young women. She argues: "There is no way that grown up girls in the present state of society can get better wages—nor where their payment is so sure. And the privilege of working in the manufactories to such is a great one" (168). This opportunity may unfortunately be sullied, according to Williams, by the false religion of Methodism and the wiles of seductive preachers. Although Cornell, the factory woman, insists in her letters on her autonomous responsibility for her moral obligations and failures, Williams depicts her as a victim of manipulation by a villainous clergyman, by a larger conspiracy of fellow Methodists attempting to cover up his crime, and by a religious sect that encourages emotional excess and self-deception. Williams is, of course, careful to insist that she is not in any way excusing any sexual looseness on the part of the working woman. She suggests that she would judge such misconduct on Cornell's part very harshly, at one point even commenting that if the mill girl was honestly guilty of inviting the minister "to come to her room to pray with her, *she courted destruction*, and might almost be said to deserve the fate it is supposed she met with at his hands" (80). However, Williams projects the mill girl's situation into the context of a much larger controversy over the role of Christian churches (and especially evangelical and revivalist denominations) in the process of industrialization. For Williams, the "symbolic magnitude" of the events of Fall River necessitates an excoriation of Methodism and a defense of the factory system; for later scholars of the events, the circle of significance broadens farther to a consideration of the predicament of working women caught between two male-controlled institutions, the church and the factory; and still farther to expose a bleak vision of Jacksonian America as a society of "hard labor, dislocation, loneliness, violence, and injustice" (Caldwell xxi).

From Williams onward, commentators on the Fall River events (sometimes also known as the Tiverton affair or tragedy, after the location of the corpse) have tended to depict Sarah Maria Cornell as a product of forces largely beyond her limited control, despite her own insistence that she is a free moral agent. This tension between determining circumstances (often controlled by wealthy men) and the individual agency of the factory woman is at the core of almost all the literature in the nineteenth century that explores working-class women's first encounters with industrial labor. Williams, as a more privileged woman, investigates in reportorial detail the external conditions that shape Cornell's world and deprive her of power. However, she simultaneously explores a more personal link between herself and the dead factory worker—a link between two women separated by social class, training, and fortune but brought into almost mysterious sisterhood by the sympathies of their common gender.

She describes in great detail a visit she has made to the grave of the dead woman, an occasion full of portents suggesting her own future role in speaking for Sarah Maria Cornell and clarifying the enigma of her life. Borrowing from the literary conventions of the Romantic and the gothic, she evokes the occasion:

> It was on the evening of the first of July. The moon was then at its full, yet a kind of shadowy darkness hung over the spot, blending the outlines of the surrounding landscape so as to render

them nearly indistinct. For some time I stood wondering, without dreaming of the cause, but upon looking up, discovered the moon was in an eclipse. There was a singular coincidence in it certainly, and it forcibly reminded me of the dark and mysterious fate of her who reposed beneath. I watched it as the shadow slid from the moon's disk, and I felt that confidence which I have ever felt since, that the mystery of darkness which envelopes the story and hides the sad fate of that unfortunate victim will one day be dispersed. (62–63)

Williams's account then shifts dramatically into the present tense as she feels "a spell breathing around that none can withstand: the effect is absolutely irresistible. It is a humble grave, in a solitary spot. It is the grave of a poor factory girl, but from that grave a voice seems to issue, noiseless as that still small one, that speaks to the conscience of the sinner, but whose tones nevertheless sink deep into the heart" (62). She immediately composes a poem addressed to Cornell that is full of womanly empathy and class-based pity:

> Poor victim of man's lawless passion,
> Though e'er so tenderly carest—
> Better to trust the raging ocean,
> Than lean upon his stormy breast....
> On thy poor wearied breast the turf
> Lies quite as soft as on the rich:
> What now to thee the scorn and mirth
> Of sanctimonious hypocrites. (63)

She presents the episode as virtually a divine justification of her efforts to speak on behalf of Cornell, giving words to that "noiseless" voice from the grave. She hints that her own voice is the final link in a chain from the "still, small" voice of God, to the silenced voice of the factory woman, to the inspired voice of her poem and her consequent mediation of the story of the working woman's tragedy.

The eerily spiritual mood of the graveyard scene is not, however, the dominant tone of Williams's narrative. She begins the book with a confession of her state of high embarrassment at the indecent and odious details she will be forced to relate, and begs to be forgiven if she errs "on the side of delicacy" in her recreation of events (6). Thus, with an obligatory bow to feminine sensibilities, and ample notification that there is much prurient detail to be negotiated and many serious morals to be drawn, Williams moves quickly into her account. The first chapter is a history and geography of the town of Fall River that is composed of an eccentric combination of economic statistics; church, crime, and military history;

and lyrical appreciation of the "beautiful cascades," "fairy landscapes," and "enchanting" views that form the picturesque environment of the town (7, 13). There are forty thousand spindles in operation, thirteen manufactories, seven churches, and one "lowly grave on the side of yonder hill," which warns the young and beautiful against "the wiles of man" and "the encroachments of vice" (8–9, 15). Williams's calculated movement between the rhetoric of industrial promotion and that of sensational fiction brings into immediate juxtaposition two of the favorite literary tropes of the time for the discussion of woman's place, but she rapidly proceeds in her next chapter to an even more controversial topic, for which there were not such convenient formulas.

Williams moves immediately from the large historical context to the personal story of Sarah Maria Cornell. She recreates a private interview between the factory woman and a doctor, complete with dialogue and quotation marks, in which he discovers her pregnancy and the efforts of Avery to persuade her to take oil of tansy, a powerful abortifacient, and fatal at the dosage the minister advised. A remarkable literary transition, during this interview, from Williams's third-person narrative voice to Cornell's direct "reported" speech, is made with considerable finesse. The narrator begins by noting the directions to the doctor's house in Fall River and observing that "It was on the evening of the 8th of October 1832, that the Doctor was summoned to the parlor to see a lady who desired to speak with him" (17). Following the two participants into their private exchange, the narrator then reports in indirect speech that "He begged her to be seated: while drawing a chair opposite, he endeavoured to penetrate so deep a grief and ascertain the cause of this visit" (17–18). The lady's reply comes in indirect speech, but with the curious addition of the quotation marks that normally signal a direct report: "'She had come she said to consult him on the subject of her health. She had not been well for some time, and wished to ascertain with certainty the nature of her disease'" (18). This novel conversation, wherein the parties involved speak of themselves in indirect speech but with the punctuation of quoted speech, continues while the symptoms are repeated and clarified, whereupon the doctor asks, "'Are you married, madam?'" and with this dramatic revelation of the conjugal nature of the "illness," the dialogue continues in the conventional "I/you" exchange of direct speech. Cornell tells the doctor that Avery is the father of her child; he delicately asks where the "interview" that caused the pregnancy took place, and is informed: "'Our *interview*, sir, was at the late Camp Meeting in Thompson, Con'" (19). Thus, before the narrative of the death and discovery of the body is presented, Williams has supplied a vivid, first-person—as it were—account of the minister's paternity and his efforts to destroy both mother and child. The doctor's sympathy, his trust in Cornell, and his gentlemanly discretion are the prelude to the chapter's grisly climax, the discovery of the "murdered maid's" abused and mutilated body (29). For this revelation,

Williams decides not to let her feminine fastidiousness obscure the "odious details" of swellings and bruises, of the death cord "nearly half an inch imbedded in the flesh," the tongue that "protruded through her teeth," and an arm that "snapt" when the woman who was laying out the body attempted to adjust it (23, 26). The graphic evidence of the minister's villainy and cruelty is thus juxtaposed to the decorous and kindly concern of the doctor. At the trial of the minister, the doctor's account of his conversation with Cornell was ruled inadmissible as hearsay, but Williams did not assume any such constraints in publishing her version.[5] In her preface, she justifies her invention of this first interview between the doctor and "the unfortunate heroine of the tale" with the authorial defense that "it is said the phraseology is improved without altering the facts" (6).

Williams's willingness to improve on the details of Cornell's story is revealed equally in another episode in her book where she takes her graveyard-assigned role as spokesperson for the voiceless factory woman a step further. Not only does she invent fictitious dialogue for a factual meeting, she projects an account of her own lengthy personal experiences (as a woman in attendance at a camp meeting) into her conclusions about Sarah Maria Cornell. This blurring of identity between the middle-class author and the working-class subject into a more generic assertion of female experience shifts her analysis away from the class-based circumstances that she did not share with the factory woman. Her agenda is an attack on Methodism and a defense of factories, a project best served by emphasizing gender solidarity and downplaying discrepancies of class interest. Thus the final chapter of *Fall River*, labeled "Appendix," although it contains the culmination and the major conclusions of the narrative, is largely a first-person recollection by Williams of a visit *she* made to a camp meeting in Smithfield, Rhode Island, some "ten or twelve years" previously (143). Although Williams admits that, during the time her account has been locked in her desk, the regulations governing camp meetings have become more strict, and the disorders lessened, she nevertheless imposes her prior experiences of the immorality and threats to women at revival meetings onto the latter-day adventures of Cornell, the factory woman, who was a known frequenter of such meetings. By substituting her own camp history, Williams is able to depict the excesses at their worst from the perspective of a modest and vulnerable female, while furthering her didactic condemnation of Methodists, and associating their practices with Cornell's seduction and death: "That her latest misfortune was occasioned by her attendance there, cannot be doubted" (143).

Williams objects first to the indecencies that inevitably attended camp meetings, regardless of their organizers' intentions: "Who can prevent the neighborhood of a Camp Meeting from swarming with drunkards and gamblers, and horse jockies and pickpockets, and offenders of every other description, who go about seeking whom they may devour" (145). She notes extreme intoxication, profanity, and much sexual jostling of young ladies, who said that "whenever they closed their eyes, and tried to engage in prayer, they were aroused by some of the men pressing so near, they could almost feel the pulsation of their hearts, and sometimes press their arms, etc" (152). She berates the lack of sanitation, the offensive smell, the blowing and blinding dust, the constant commotion, and the noise, which "could not have been exceeded by the confusion of Babel" (161). However, all of these degradations and violations of civilized codes of conduct are depicted not merely as the regrettable consequences of camp meeting activity but as endemic to the religious practice itself. Williams labels this practice "spiritual dissipation" (146) and castigates it as superstition, fanaticism, and emotional incontinence. She observes a woman lying on straw in a hysterical fit, another "with her clothes torn and her locks dishevelled, wringing her hands and mourning that the people were not more engaged" (153), some worshipers "throwing themselves in the dirt and calling loudly for mercy" (154), and a man in "strong convulsions" (155). People writhe, shudder, shriek, groan, and call out "'I'm full—I'm running over'" (162). Others stamp, slap hands, and knock fists together in their frenzy, causing Williams to comment sardonically that "this scene of discordant noise and unseemly riot...was what they called 'the power of God'" (162).

Although Williams is particularly insistent in noting the exposed and vulnerable condition of young women (in accordance with her theories on the role of the camp meeting in the sexual fall of Cornell), she also pays a good deal of attention to the general composition of the groups that are most engaged in the rituals. She notes, for example, the "bad English" of one of the preachers and the fact that although some of his hearers smile, another class of people listens with profound attention. She also observes "an African upon a stump at some distance...collecting a great crowd around him, who were listening with open ears and gaping mouths," and she mimics his dialect: "'Deble fader of lies; he be liar from beginnin. Some say poor niger hab no shoule. Vel dat I don't know, but dis I know, I got something in my body make me feel tumfortable.'" These remarks are greeted with laughter and shouts of "glory, hallelujah" from the "profane rabble" (155, 159). By the time Williams and her respectable friends withdraw in a state of shock from the uncouth company in which they have been mingling, there are many hints that the class of people who have been lured by these Methodist excesses are not the educated, intellectually curious middle class who are "modest, practical and retiring christians, who mind their own concerns, and pursue the even tenor of their way" (169) but an underclass of laborers, Africans, and speakers of poor English. Williams then carefully distinguishes between the deleterious effects of camp meetings on this lower class of people and the positive effects of factory labor on the same class of people, and especially on women. She resists forcefully other efforts that were being made at the time to connect the details of Cornell's case to her employment in a factory. She vigorously refutes those who say that "vice was not regarded among that portion of society as it was in any other community; that there was little regard to morals among them, or that persons could not have been tolerated and associated with as we know she was—and finally that it ought to be a warning to parents not to let a daughter go to those places, which was going to certain ruin" (168). Williams concludes that "nothing can be more unjust" than the suggestion that factories might be responsible for loose conduct among the workers when, in fact, all her carefully assembled evidence from Fall River and her own experience suggests that religious dissipation was the primary cause of women's ruin.

David Kasserman, a historian who has conducted the most exhaustive survey of all of the documents connected with the death of Sarah Maria Cornell at Fall River, has concluded that Catharine Williams probably undertook her investigation of the death and subsequent scandal at the direct suggestion of proponents of the factory system. He finds that the writing of the book was most likely proposed to Williams by a member of the Fall River Committee, a group whose vested interest was in defending their manufacturing community. At the beginning of her book, Williams says that "who first proposed it, is of no consequence" (3), but Kasserman makes a strong case for other voices, besides the supernatural one emanating from the grave, being involved in encouraging and facilitating her endeavor. He notes that "she enjoyed remarkable cooperation" in gathering her story in Fall River, and that her account of the mystery clearly resolves any ambiguities in favor of the factories and against the Methodists. Whether such a resolution is in any sense a betrayal of Williams's sense of sisterhood with Cornell on behalf of an ultimate class affiliation with the manufacturers is difficult to determine, since there is little doubt that Williams saw genuine advantages for young women in the factories, as she did equally in more discreet and decorous religious practices. The most traditional of the Protestant churches in Fall River was the Congregational Church, which was associated in a number of ways not only with the Fall River Committee but also with a long New England heritage. The Methodist Church, by contrast, was associated with outsiders and certainly, after the trial, suffered in terms of its membership and reputation. Eventually Methodism would come to be a more accepted and establishment denomination, particularly with the growth of even more apparently subversive sects and schools of thought. Kasserman notes that in time "the Methodists were able to unite with the community against other groups whose ideologies were more threatening to New Englanders' perception of an acceptable social order" (Kasserman 235, 238, 252–53). However, in 1833, for Williams, the Methodists were the carriers of the threateningly alien challenges to a stable society, and thus it was on Avery and his denomination that she focused her animus.

Williams was interested in the hypocrisy of a single clergyman and the particular cultural practice of the camp meeting less in themselves than as symptoms of an entire religious code that undermined rationality and restraint, and seemed to have a particular appeal for people who were already on the outer margins of society—Africans, speakers of poor English, and female factory workers. She admits that she finds a "wonderful mystery" in the allure of Methodism for a woman like Cornell and she decides that, in order to be fair to her, she should permit Cornell's letters to "speak for her" (101). Thus she incorporates into her text sixteen of Cornell's letters, constituting almost the entirety of the seventh chapter of her book. Noting that the letters are "full of Methodism, and relating mostly to her religious feelings" (101), Williams expresses direct disapproval for the self-accusation and public humiliation encouraged by the denomination. Her use of the letters seems intended to expose the unbalanced and excessively emotional nature of Methodism, but the authentic voice of Cornell, suddenly intruded into Williams's narration, produces an effect less consonant with Williams's intentions. Cornell's voice, emerging from her letters, reveals a mysterious glimpse into the mind of a solitary woman who may be a pawn of fate, a dupe of religion, or a victim of all the vicissitudes of the Industrial Revolution but who wants to understand her world, live intensely, acknowledge responsibility, and believe that she has some control over the course of her life. The allegorical power struggle between Methodism and the factory that commentators, from Williams to Kasserman, see as the "symbolic magnitude" of her story tends to recede (although the letters do indeed contain much corroborating evidence for these theories) before the presence of Cornell's own voice. Acutely isolated, despite the elaborate institutions of church, state, and industry that surround her, and constantly uprooted, she despairingly tries to make connections that affirm her presence in the world.

Williams's inclusion of the factory woman's letters as a way of demonstrating the depredations of Methodism is thus both successful and risky for her purposes. There is no question that letter after letter shows Cornell's self-abasing preoccupation with her own sinfulness and with the ecstatically joyful possibilities of forgiveness and salvation. "[A]las my heart is hard," she writes, "and I am as prone to sin as the sparks that fly upward. Oh my sister pray for me, that God in his infinite mercy pour the sweet refreshings of his grace on my soul" (104). A year later, writing to the same sister, she confesses "If I were summoned before his judgment bar could I answer with a clear conscience to having performed my duty? I fear I could not" (106) and later, to her brother and sister, "God in mercy has shown me the depravity of my own wicked heart" (109). There are also frequent admonitions and homilies addressed to these family members, many quotations from the Bible, and habitual recourse to a language full of religious formulas and conventions. The rational Williams condemns such enthusiasm, but Cornell also reveals enough of the circumstances of her life in the letters to suggest that the origins of these seemingly morbid hopes and fears lie not just in the immoderation of a dissolute religion but in a cluster of conditions and hopes for which Methodism seemed, in her situation, the only available remedy.

Cornell lives in a world pervaded by uncertainty, sudden loss, and death, which she records almost obsessively: "The solemn bell has just summoned another fellow-mortal into eternity...a tall stout robust negro" (105). Elsewhere she takes note of "several shocking cases of suicide within a few months here, one of which a man about 30 cut his throat yesterday a few rods from me....About the first of February a young man shot himself before my face and eyes, I was looking out of my window....A girl belonging to this establishment threw herself into the river" (117). Her concern for the death of others is matched and exceeded by her sense of loneliness and even abandonment by family members and old friends. Her first letter to her sister, when she is seventeen, comments "We have been so long separated that we should not know each other by sight" (103), but she urges the pleasure of their correspondence. The next letter again emphasizes the importance of maintaining contact: "Although we are strangers we ought not to be deprived of the privilege of writing to each other" (104). Her letters are a litany of friendlessness and reminders to others of her existence: "I have not been so contented here, being far from any friend or connexion" (107); "I should be pleased could we all meet once more, but I don't expect we ever shall" (108); "I enjoy myself as well as I could expect among strangers" (116); "More than two years have past by since I have seen any of you, or indeed scarce seen one individual that I ever saw before" (120); "I am your affectionate though absent child" (124).

A surprising number of the letters emphasize the act of writing itself as a central means of maintaining connection in this newly fragmented world: "After waiting nearly six months for a letter in vain, I take up my pen to address those of my dear friends who are near and dear to me by the ties of nature" (114); "Once more I take up my pen to write a few lines to my parents, as nearly six months have again elapsed since I have heard from you" (116); "I desire like wise to be remembered to the Rev. David Austin, tell him I wrote to him some months since, but as he has not answered my letter I conclude he has forgotten or wishes to forget me" (118); "My Dear Mother—It seems a long time since I have heard from you, and I almost begin to think you have forgotten me or you would have written before this" (118); "it appears to me if you were in the land of the living and possest a parent's feelings you would have written before this" (122). Although her letters seem to have gone largely unanswered, they are acts of self-assertion and communication, and give persuasive evidence about the cause of her attraction to a church that offered her exactly the kind of opportunities for participation, recognition, and communication that she sought so avidly in her correspondence.

The reasons for Cornell's estrangement undoubtedly arose in part from her own misconduct, which made her painfully sensitive to real and apparent snubs from family and friends. By the time she was in her early twenties, she had acquired a reputation for unpaid bills, shoplifting, and lewd behavior and, as a consequence, she was apparently ostracized by factory and church, as well as her family (Kasserman 30–43). She wrote to her sister, Lucretia, and her brother-in-law, "I want you should forgive me and bury what is past in oblivion and I hope my future good conduct may reward you" (110); to her mother, "Tell cousin Polly and my other friends in Providence, that I hope they will forget and forgive what is past" (114), and "I am your unworthy daughter" (119). In terms of a moral code of honesty and chastity, there seems to have been no real difference between the standards of Cornell's family, her society, and those of the Methodists and other denominations. The letters do not especially indict the Methodists, as Williams intended, because all the authorities in the erring woman's world seem to conspire to remind her of her misbehavior.

In addition to her isolation by a guilty conscience, Cornell's letters demonstrate her extraordinary dependency on the whim of employers and the hazards of factory life, as well as the easy opportunities to succumb to temptation. One of the few periods of stability and reasonable contentment in her short, unhappy life occurred when she lived in Slatersville, working as a weaver, and boarding with a good family. She made positive steps toward reconciliation with her family, she visited her sister and her new baby, she enjoyed the Methodist meetings and the preaching of Elder Tailor, and she wrote repeatedly of her deep attachment to the place: "Sometimes, when I think of leaving Slatersville, it strikes a dread upon me. Can I ever leave this delightful spot, where I have enjoyed so many delightful seasons and privileges, it seems to be a place highly favoured by God" (111). She wrote to her mother a few months later, "I expect the Lord willing to spend my days in Slatersville" (112). After almost three good years there, the factory Cornell worked in was destroyed by fire. She managed to get work at another factory nearby that would still keep her within reach of the meeting that had come to mean so much to her, but that job ended in a summer of low water that made weaving impossible. Responding to her mother's criticism that she was a "moving planet," Cornell makes her frequent moves seem part of her religious code: "I am connected with a people that do not believe in tarrying in one place longer than a year or two years at most at any one time—and I am with them in sentiment believing with the Apostle that we should be as strangers and pilgrims having here no continuing city or abiding place, but seek one to come" (120). Thus she makes fire, drought, and all the arbitrariness of factory employment seem secondary to her personal choice rather than evidence of her lack of it.

By contrast, Williams, despite her desire to defend the factory world, suggests that Cornell's shoplifting is a consequence of "the temptations and allurements of a commercial town." She even implies a direct connection between these minor material temptations and Cornell's ultimate fall: "being often in the shops where these articles for which she had so long sighed presented themselves before her—she at length possessed herself of some of them, trifling indeed in amount, but destined to prove her entire destruction in this world as respected character and every thing else" (69).

Interestingly, in all the evidence of her letters, Cornell herself never suggests any such rationalizations for her misconduct. While Williams's intention in including Cornell's letters is to expose the distorted emotionalism of Methodists, Cornell's correspondence suggests implicitly why she would have turned to the members of a denomination "different in their views and opinions from that which any of my friends have embraced" (121). Bereft of her family and early connections, she found a community in the Methodists who met together almost daily. In a life of hard labor, in which she felt at times "almost beat out" (116), they offered "good times" (112), and their camp meetings were undoubtedly a recreation for body, mind, and spirit, to judge from her recollection of one held at Cape Cod. She writes:

> I went to Camp Meeting in August, as usual was gone ten days, cast anchor three days—went ashore three miles from where we set sail, having in company upwards of two hundred, fourteen of which were Methodist Ministers. Had about twelve sermons preached on board, and one on the shore—dug clams—had plenty of good codfish, crackers and coffee—and on the eleventh day reached Boston wharf in better health and better spirits than when I left. (122–23)

Cornell's account suggests that she found in her church meeting all the vital elements of a good and healthy life, physical, mental, and spiritual. If it was not quite the "bread and roses" to which later working women aspired, it was certainly a release and recreation from being "nearly beat out." Cornell's religion did indeed, as Williams argued, emphasize sin, abasement, and self-accusation, but it also insisted on the ability of the "sinner" to make a choice. Writing to her sister, Cornell says, "Yesterday I heard a discourse from these words, 'Why halt ye between two opinions, choose you this day whom you will serve, if the Lord be God serve him, if Baal then serve him.' I have thought seriously about this text" (106). Methodism offered Cornell not only the option of making a decision but also the chance to think seriously about a text, an activity that Williams did not perhaps see as of great importance to a factory girl, but one that would have an increasing allure for working women, permitting them a very different identity from that of mere "hands," in the industrial age ahead. Later working women would find a broader array of reading material than Biblical texts, a wider arena for speaking their opinions than a Methodist meeting, and a more eager audience for their writing than Cornell's reluctant family. Nevertheless, her letters show the importance of such desires, desires Williams preferred to attribute to the more sinister aspects of Methodism, rather than to a need on the part of the young factory woman for something more than the practical rewards of factory employment and the rational compensations of traditional religious duties.

The dialogue that emerges in *Fall River* from the juxtaposition of the views of the middle-class anti-Methodist woman and the working-class

Methodist is not quite the opposition of common sense and enthusiasm, dignity and abasement, stability and novelty that would have best served Williams's pro-factory argument. The entry of the factory woman's voice shifts the terms of the debate. While the voice Williams relays from the grave speaks the traditional tale of seduction and betrayal, Cornell's voice in her letters ponders choices, meditates on the meaning of words, and speaks subjectively about what most engages her mind. Jama Lazerow, in her exploration of the interaction between religion and the working class in America before the Civil War, speculates on the reasons for Methodism's particular appeal to "society's poor and outcast." She notes a number of areas of likely compatibility between the denomination and the social group—a certain fraternity between the membership of congregations and itinerant and uneducated ministers, the "egalitarian and down-to-earth style" of meetings and revivals, and the "close-knit structure" of the organization that offered "a surrogate community amidst the fragmentation of the capitalist revolution." Besides these democratic and republican aspects, Lazerow also finds "potentially radical social implications" in Methodism in its offer of a psychology of "total and sudden change" in the lives of its adherents (Lazerow 85–86). David Kasserman comments on the unusual degree of participation the denomination offered its women members, encouraging them to speak in public discourse and giving them the opportunity to hold some positions of authority (38). Such theories are well supported by the evidence of Cornell's letters, especially in relation to the value of an intimate community and an ever-present chance of change and redemption. It is not difficult to see why such a working-class group of people, tightly organized, prone to emotional display, believing in dramatic and sudden alterations in human affairs, and open to a new public and authoritative role for women might seem threatening to an industrial enterprise based on the reasoned calculations of factory promoters. Less apparent, in 1833, was the occasion offered to the factory woman for the serious study of texts, as both reader and thinker, and the determination that she should accept responsibility for herself and the vagaries of her own life. Yet these options, too, involved a potentially revolutionary change in women's ways of accommodating and resisting their new life in the factories. Religion and literacy, envisaged by the original factory proprietors as compatible with the industrial endeavor, could combine with the novelty of the new work experience in unanticipated ways. One outcome might be the traditional self-sacrifice of Mary Burnam, another the disturbing self-accusation of Sarah Maria Cornell, but it is apparent that both responses derived from social stereotypes and literary formulas about women that would require drastic revision when the factory women's own experiences and voices entered more fully into the discourse.

Both Sarah Savage and Catharine Williams recognize and endorse the larger opportunities provided for women by factories, but they also anticipate uneasily that they are writing at the beginning of a great change in

women's lives, whose future is unknown. Savage clings to a traditional ideal
of feminine virtue, even as she advocates for the factory and for a largely
nonsectarian Christianity that, for women at least, is premised on self-
sacrificial service to others. However, between *The Factory Girl*, her first
book, and *Trial and Self-Discipline*, her last, she demonstrated her increasing
misgivings about the values that might grow up among the women in
New England factories. Williams projected her fears about the development of socially subversive behavior among a marginalized group of people
onto Methodists, but, like Savage, she also acknowledged that factory workers were already being stigmatized and stereotyped for certain kinds of
immorality, primarily their sexual misconduct. This was an area that the
literary conventions of the novel, with their traditional emphasis on courtship, marriage, seduction, and betrayal, were in some ways well prepared
to address. In the case of *The Factory Girl,* the virtuous Mary Burnam is
initially attracted to the fickle William and his philosophy of pleasure, but
she is released by William's abandonment of her and eventually marries a
respectable widower with a ready-made family of children. She thus passes
instantly from celibacy to motherhood. Sarah Maria Cornell, by contrast,
early acquired a reputation for lewdness, was treated for gonorrhea, and
died pregnant and unwed (Kasserman 56). Her sexual, medical, and men-
strual histories were minutely scrutinized in the courts, with a display of
evidence unlikely ever to occur in any nineteenth-century novel. Catharine Williams's literary pastiche in *Fall River* is an important example of an
effort by a woman writer to negotiate the territory between the conventions of the novel, in terms of morality and sexual content, and those of the
gross realities of the court record.[6] The literary gulf between the fictional
formulas of seduction and betrayal and the graphic naturalism of the legal
transcript, the autopsy, and the account book would gradually be narrowed
in the realist and naturalist novels of the later nineteenth century, although
not without risk to those authors, particularly women, who attempted to
speak of working women's lives with greater candor. The larger debate
over working women's sexuality would grow only more contentious and
complex, especially when working women themselves chose to enter it and
alter its terms.

The other moral criticism that both Savage and Williams make of
factory women is of their increasing worldliness, frivolity, and materialism,
which both authors subordinate and connect to the more serious sin of
unchaste behavior. Mary Burnam resists the exact temptations into which
Sarah Maria Cornell falls, but both authors are generally in agreement as to
what those temptations are. Early in *The Factory Girl,* we are told that Mary's
motive for going out to work is *not* to buy fine clothes for herself, with the
clear implication that it is a common motive for other women. Sarah Maria
Cornell's first fall comes about through "love of dress, and show, and ornament," which induces her to steal some minor items of costume and to fail
to pay her bills for a silk dress, a bonnet, and a shawl (Kasserman 33–34).

The desire for such finery rapidly became, in the imaginative literature by upper-class writers about factory women, the synecdoche for female vanity and selfishness, in opposition to working for the welfare of the family, and the motif came to take on ever-increasing complications related to women's nature, their rights, and their obligations.

The economic system that established factories and their employment of women also encouraged the consumption of commodities and provided stores in factory towns where goods were temptingly displayed. Factory women were encouraged to be respectable, not only in their conduct but also in their appearance, and they logically looked to the dress and ornaments of middle-class women as models of such respectability. A steady stream of visitors, from government officials to foreign dignitaries, toured the early factories and gazed at the women's dress and demeanor, making exacting judgments on them. They were enticed to spend their wages on finery and praised for their refined appearance yet berated for materialism and envy.[7] When a team of archeologists excavated the grounds of the factory boarding houses of the Boott Mills in Lowell, Massachusetts, in the 1990s, they commented that all the jewelry they found was made "from imitation materials that looked valuable, but were not," from black glass buttons, imitating the jet made fashionable by Queen Victoria, to fake tortoise-shell hair combs. These combs imitated expensive originals inaccessible to working-class women but they used them for the very utilitarian purpose of keeping their long hair from becoming entangled in the moving machinery (Mrozowski et al. 78, 80). A minor class war was waged in the papers of Lowell in the 1840s over the rights of working women to wear gold watches and generally confuse their observers about what social class they belonged to. Once again, when working women themselves joined the debate, the question of their selfishness and vanity in spending their wages produced contradictory and paradoxical responses, compounded from their conflicting religious, class, and gender loyalties, and contributed to some of the liveliest and wittiest of their new writing.

Although Savage and Williams present very different examples of factory women who resist or succumb to temptation, their protagonists do have certain interests and abilities in common that would eventually come to play at least as large a role in factory literature as women's vanity and sexual morality. Both Mary Burnam and Sarah Maria Cornell are readers, thinkers, teachers, and writers, limited certainly in their access to education and intellectual material but profoundly affected (whether falsely in Williams's view of Cornell or rightly in Savage's view of Burnam) by their interests in theology. Both women think deeply about the texts they study; both are eager to speak out, Mary in her Sunday school class, Cornell in her meetings, where, she claimed proudly, she "could pray and exhort, as well as any of them" (qtd. in Kasserman 38). Both are communicators, as well as learners and thinkers. The final image of Mary is with a writing desk, and it was Cornell's final letter that ensured the arrest and trial of Avery.

Both women drew their faith and moral codes from the rather narrow range of religious literature and education that was available to them, but they were living on the edge of a period of intellectual ferment when the opportunities of factory women to gain access to books, lectures, schooling, new theories, and intellectual movements were rapidly increasing. Many of the lyceums, libraries, lecture series, and seminaries in New England were given active support by factories, as was the publication of the women's writing in little magazines. The results of working women's engagement both as readers and as writers were certainly not foreseen when Sarah Savage recorded her misgivings about the advent of "self-reliance" for factory women, or even when Catharine Williams felt called on to improve the missives of Maria Cornell with her own constructed version of that worker's personal history. However, only a few years after the sensational Tiverton affair, the Lowell workers who had burned E. K. Avery in effigy would create a very different kind of sensation when they began to write and publish their own versions of their lives, and to consider their intellectual and artistic aspirations, as well as their economic conditions and ethical conduct, as appropriate subjects for public literary discourse.

2

"Ideal Mill Girls"

The *Lowell Offering* and Female Aspiration

Let us look upon our Lyceums, our Common Schools, our Mechanics'
Literary Associations, the Periodical of our Laboring Females; upon all
that is indigenous to our Republic, and say with the spirit of the Roman
Cornelia, "These, *these are our jewels.*"
—HARRIET FARLEY, 1842

They were the ideal mill-girls, full of hopes, desires, aspirations; poets of
the loom, spinners of verse, artists of factory-life.
—HARRIET ROBINSON, 1898

When Sarah Savage warned, in 1838, of the dangers of "self-reliance"
for factory women, she was anticipating the increasing worldliness
and independence derived from their industrial labor more than attitudes
inspired by Emerson's 1840 essay of the same title. Nevertheless, Romantic beliefs in the cultivation of the self and the creative spirit permeated
the minds of the workers of Lowell as surely as those of the philosophers
of Concord and helped to promote, in the following decade, an extraordinary outpouring of literature from those workers. Their fiction, essays,
poetry, and criticism would fill the pages of a host of new publications
in New England—the *Factory Girl's Garland*, the *Ladies' Pearl*, the *New
England Offering*, the *Olive Leaf and Factory Girl's Repository*, the *Operatives'
Magazine*, the *Voice of Industry,* and, most notably, the *Lowell Offering*, the
journal whose fame would quickly cross the Atlantic and give rise to the
significantly named anthology *Mind amongst the Spindles* (1844).[1] The
efforts of newly employed working-class women to articulate their sense
of their changing identity coincided, in the New England of the 1840s,
with the intellectual ferment of the group of Romantic transcendentalists coalescing in Concord who were simultaneously considering by what
literary means they might circulate their ideas. Concord Romantics and
Lowell literary working women had discrete intellectual and social interests,
and even within each of these groups there was no ideological consensus.
Yet, despite the elusiveness and volatility of discourse within these groups,
certain preoccupations recur in their writing that reveal a nexus of concerns central to the contemporary life of the mind, a nexus that has been

obscured by labels such as "Concord" and "Lowell" that have created separate historical mythologies in a realm where there were many mutual interests.[2] These mutual concerns focus particularly on the relationship of work to identity; on whether all work is honorable or whether exploitive work may become debasing and dehumanizing; and on whether it is possible to obtain a desirable balance between mental and manual labor. Writers from both groups also found themselves at the center of controversies about the connection of literary work to social class and gender; the extent to which increasing materialism tainted both individual and social values; and the best ways to improve their world, whether through individual self-culture or by communal and societal reforms. Repeatedly, too, they investigated the role of literature as a means of coming to terms with their rapidly changing world, and began to develop new genres and modes of expression appropriate to their new ideas.

The intensity, inventiveness, and variety of the literary discourse emerging from "Concord" and "Lowell" in the 1840s is a consequence of the dramatic social and industrial developments of the time, and also of widespread literacy and the high value placed on reading and writing at all social levels in the culture of New England. Ronald Zboray, in his study of nineteenth-century American reading habits, notes that the 1840 federal census in the United States "showed basic literacy rates far outpacing those of the rest of the world" and, in the next census, showed the Northeast with the highest literacy in the Union (36, 199–200). Zboray thoroughly explores the roles of family, church, school, and community organizations such as lyceums and mechanics' institutes in enhancing literacy and endorsing the printed word as the tool of democracy. Not only did literacy enable the intellectual discourse of the day but the activities of reading and writing were themselves among the most extensive subjects of debate among Romantics and mill workers alike. As with the controversies on the value of work, they debated whether reading, too, might be ennobling or degrading; whether the demands of marketplace and audience might offer exhilarating opportunities for people hitherto excluded or marginalized from the realms of literature, or, more ominously, whether they might intensify the commodification of the printed media in order to satisfy consumers' appetites and publishers' profits. For factory workers, entering the literary field for the first time as both subjects and authors, the debate generated a remarkable degree of self-consciousness about their own reading and writing and led them to produce both solemn and playful explorations of the moral, aesthetic, and political dimensions of literature. Perhaps because there was not yet a single, conventional genre for them to work in, they wrote poems, essays, sketches, tales, parodies, and allegories and experimented with original approaches to fiction. They transmitted their ideas in books and lectures, journals and newspapers. However, as with many of the most interesting developments in the field of letters, the first agent of their dissemination was, like those of the transcendentalists, a short-lived and highly provocative little magazine.

In 1839, Nathaniel Hawthorne wrote to Henry Wadsworth Longfellow that he found it "intolerable that there should not be a single belles-lettres journal in New England" (qtd. in Myerson 31). Literary historians have noted the subsequent emergence, in July 1840, of the first issue of the *Dial: A Magazine for Literature, Philosophy, and Religion*, the transcendentalist journal that enjoyed both obscurity and notoriety until its demise in 1844. However, the *Dial* was not the only journal of belles-lettres to appear in 1840 in New England, for in the same year following Hawthorne's complaint, the *Lowell Offering* began to publish the literary work of female factory operatives. With a life span almost identical to that of the *Dial*, the *Offering* ran until 1845, winning fame and approval for its modest aspirations and revealing some distinct convergences with the preoccupations and even with the publishing circumstances of its more elevated and ambitious contemporary. Both journals emerged, almost simultaneously, from small discussion groups that had developed in response to the intellectual, philosophical, and political ferment of the late 1830s. The *Dial* was generated by the Hedge Club (later the Transcendental Club), a group consisting mostly of male, mainly Unitarian ministers, while the *Offering* was the product of one of Lowell's several Unitarian- and Congregational-sponsored Mutual Self-Improvement Clubs, whose membership was composed of female textile workers. Both journals had women editors for the larger portion of their lives, with Margaret Fuller at the *Dial* from 1840 to 1842 and Harriot Curtis and Harriet Farley at the *Lowell Offering* from 1842 to 1845.[3] Both magazines were open to writing in many forms and styles. Harriet Robinson, one of the *Offering*'s contributors, summarized its variety thus: "There were allegories, poems, conversations on physiology, astronomy, and other scientific subjects, dissertations on poetry, and on the beauties of nature, didactic pieces on highly moral and religious subjects, translations from French and Latin, stories of factory and other life, sketches of local New England history, and sometimes the chapters of a novel" (69). The *Dial*'s wide range of literary modes was not markedly dissimilar, although it was definitely less interested in fiction; in the field of translation, its predilection was notably for works of German origin. There was apparently mutual interest between the two magazines: Robinson mentions the *Dial* among the subscriptions of a Lowell boardinghouse (56–57), and the editor of the *Dial* sent a congratulatory message to the *Lowell Offering* saluting its success.

While the *Dial* has been of great interest to literary historians and the *Offering* to labor historians, the symbiosis of Romantic, religious, literary, and social concerns in these two regional yet curiously cosmopolitan little magazines has been neglected in scholarly work that has developed two distinctly different provenances for literariness and for working-class history. On the literary side, Lawrence Buell omits from his imposing account of *New England Literary Culture* the "subliterary" efforts of writers who dealt with urbanization and industrialization, noting that "their comparative absence from my book is one of its acts of repression, since to most New

England imaginations during the early nineteenth century the saga of the Lowell textile mills was certainly as enthralling as the saga of Natty Bumppo." Buell's avowedly aesthetic judgment leads him to focus instead on "New England literature of the most sophisticated kind," by "major writers," in which "urban settings and industrial images are conspicuous mainly through their minimization" (301). Philip Foner, the eminent labor historian, makes a more overtly political judgment, in the arrangement of his anthology of the writings of New England factory women, when he divides them into "Genteel" and "Militant" categories. The former are those with literary aspirations, associated with the *Lowell Offering,* the latter those with union and reformist agendas, associated primarily with the *Voice of Industry* (17, 55). Foner's use of the words "genteel" and "militant" for his two groups of factory women suggests more than two politically opposed sets of responses to the factory system. The label "genteel" makes an implicit association of literariness with bourgeois class values and thereby hints at a betrayal of working-class loyalties. Whether such a betrayal is an inevitable consequence of workers aspiring to be authors and artists is a continuous undercurrent in the literary history of a new age that brought widespread literacy for the first time.

Both Buell and Foner imply tacitly that the literary and the class-conscious modes of thought belong to different intellectual spheres, different classes, and perhaps even different gender affiliations. For Buell, the *Offering* isn't elevated enough to be literary, and for Foner it is too literary to be working-class. The editors of the *Offering* themselves conceded both charges—its possible literary shortcomings and their reluctance to turn it into a forum for complaints about working conditions. In a carefully worded preface to the second series of the magazine in April 1841, the editor, Abel Thomas, wrote: "In estimating the talent of the writers for the Offering, the fact should be remembered, that they are actively employed in the Mills for more than twelve hours out of every twenty-four." He added that such lengthy manual employment, "though...not excessive, must in some measure unfit the individual for the full development of mental power" (1: iv).[4] In closing the same volume, Harriet Farley, writing as "Ella," noted that the charge had been made that the *Offering* "does not expose all the evils, and miseries, and mortifications, attendant upon a factory life," to which she responded that "we have never...pledged ourselves to disseminate a knowledge of every petty evil and inconvenience of the manufacturing system" (1: 376). Yet, even allowing for its acknowledged aesthetic limitations and the definite lack of a reformist agenda, this journal of factory belles-lettres was more than a quaint working-class imitation of a middle-class norm, or a tool of the proprietors. If it did not encourage working women to engage in direct challenges to the political and economic authorities that dominated their lives, it did enable them to insert their voices into the intellectual and artistic debates of the day, to demonstrate that the "hands" had minds, and that those minds were vigorously involved in thinking about the identities that others were so ready to impose on them. It also permitted them to explore the efficacy of literature itself as an appropriate medium for members of their class and sex, and even to experiment in the development of new genres of writing and new modes of expression that might help them adapt this formerly "genteel" pursuit to their own interests.

Not surprisingly, a central and persistent preoccupation of the authors of the *Offering* that links them to Savage's *Factory Girl* and to Sarah Maria Cornell of *Fall River*, and concurrently to Romantics and reformers, was with their public reputation as working women and the degree of its accuracy in reflecting their actual experiences. In their own time, as well as in the later historical record, the female factory operatives of Lowell were the objects of an extraordinary amount of observation and analysis. Visits to the Lowell mills, initially orchestrated by owners as an early venture into public relations, became a requisite part of a tour of the United States by foreign visitors such as Charles Dickens and Harriet Martineau. The operatives were repeatedly gazed at and questioned by a host of the curious and the concerned, from President Andrew Jackson to newspaper reporters and a special committee for the Massachusetts legislature (Robinson 67, 50, 135–48). Such minute and reiterated scrutiny can only have heightened for factory women their intense consciousness both of the group impression they were making and of their separate and private identities. From the immediate empirical evidence of their daily lives, they must have been aware that their labor constituted one of the great social controversies of the age. However, even the greatest of controversies needs a succinct and challenging formulation, and for the operatives themselves as well as for both advocates and opponents of the factory system, it came in the most provocative way, in "The Laboring Classes," an 1840 essay in the *Boston Quarterly Review* by Orestes Brownson.

Brownson, born and reared, as he put it, "in the class of proletaries," was in 1840 a transcendentalist, a Unitarian minister, a member of the Hedge Club, and a radical partisan of the working class. He was at once a compelling and incongruous link between the world of Romantic reformers and that of factory women. A largely self-educated man with a powerful intellect, who was "temperamentally extremist in all his ways," he provoked the bitter resentment of his allies and the ridicule of his antagonists for his continual readiness to turn against his current allegiances and endorse new creeds. The *Boston Quarterly Review* was Brownson's own little magazine, begun in 1838 as a forum for his opinions on "the problem of the Destiny of Man and of Society."[5] It lasted for four years, during which he engaged and alienated transcendentalists and factory workers alike with the scathing extravagance of his arguments, and he provoked spirited responses from both the *Lowell Offering* and the *Dial* to his polemical opinions on the degeneracy of the American working class and the inadequacy of philosophies of self-culture to remedy the evils of industrial capitalism.

"The Laboring Classes" first appeared in the July 1840 issue of the *Boston Quarterly Review* in the innocuous disguise of a review of Thomas Carlyle's *Chartism*. A second essay, also called "The Laboring Classes," appeared in the October issue of the same year, responding to some of the numerous objections to the first. Marginally more temperate in tone, it essentially reiterated and developed the ideas that had given such offense in the first, but now with references to eminent precedents for Brownson's positions. At the core of his argument was his assumption that there existed in modern society fundamentally antagonistic class relationships that tended inevitably toward violent and bloody conflict. He defined these "classes" by means of various sets of oppositions—employers and operatives, rich and poor, the middle class and proletarians—but their relationship was fixed as long as it was based on wage labor, which in itself was incapable of raising any operative from poverty to wealth. For Brownson, the consequence of wage labor was a working class that would inevitably deteriorate, in terms of material welfare and oppression, to a status beneath that of chattel slaves, and whose moral condition would decline proportionally with physical circumstances and social status. He argued that "the laborer at wages has all the disadvantages of freedom and none of its blessings, while the slave, if denied the blessings, is freed from the disadvantages" (368). Having denounced wage labor in general, Brownson then turned specifically to the group of women employed in factories and insisted that their debasement by wage labor was not just physical and spiritual, but moral: "the great mass wear out their health, spirits, and morals, without becoming one whit better off than when they commenced labor" (369). His critique of factory women's impaired reputations culminated in his notorious assertion that the phrase "she has worked in a Factory" was "almost enough to damn to infamy the most worthy and virtuous girl" (370).

Brownson then turned to proposals to "emancipate the proletaries" and immediately and caustically dismissed some of the most favored means of Romantic reformers and operatives alike for improving women's lives, namely education, and that particularly American version of it that he referred to, after William Ellery Channing, as "self-culture" (373, 375). He professed to have "little faith in the power of education to elevate a people compelled to labor from twelve to sixteen hours a day," and argued that "A swarm of naked and starving urchins crowded into a schoolroom will make little proficiency in the 'Humanities'" (365). While he certainly did not dismiss the power of education for the laboring classes ("For God's sake beware how you kindle within them the intellectual spark and make them aware that they too are men"), Brownson was wary of improvements that operated only on the private person and not in the public sphere (365). Thus he resisted reformers who "tell us that we want not external changes, but internal; and therefore instead of declaiming against society and seeking to disturb existing social arrangements, we should confine ourselves to the individual reason and conscience; seek merely to lead the individual to repentance, and to reformation of life" (373). Such an idea, he twice pronounced ironically, was "a capital theory" (373, 374) and concluded: "Self-culture is a good thing, but it cannot abolish inequality, nor restore men to their rights" (375). Brownson here set terms for the debate that echoed through many decades, on whether material improvements would precede or follow intellectual awareness, whether the individual must first be reformed before there is hope for society and whether systemic change is a necessary prelude to the betterment of the individual. For the factory women of the *Lowell Offering*, his essay went to the heart of their factory aspirations and their battle to shape a new identity.

The reform proposals Brownson went on to make revealed at once his radical political vision and his eccentricity. His first step toward "emancipating the proletaries" was to abolish the priesthood and "resuscitate the Christianity of Christ" (388). His next proposal, scarcely so revolutionary by 1840, was to "destroy the power of the Banks over the government" (392), followed by the destruction of "all monopolies, of all PRIVILEGE" (393), and finally the abolition of the inheritance of property, which he believed would inevitably bring on bloodshed and war (394–95). He then reiterated and developed his original proposals in much greater detail, aligning himself with the proletariat, as one of its members who was giving "utterance to their views and feelings," and promising to adhere to what he had said about their condition, "at least, until the laboring classes themselves rise up and accuse us of misrepresenting them." Unhappily for Brownson, the *Lowell Offering* was quick to make precisely and repeatedly the accusation of misrepresentation he had challenged them to make, an act that was profoundly disturbing to his faith in radical reform, coming, as it did, directly "from the base of the social organization" (460, 461). However, it is important to note that the entire focus of the *Offering*'s challenge to Brownson was based *not* on his revolutionary proposals for change but on his perceived insults to the moral standing and good reputation of factory women.

The main response was made by Harriet Farley, who would eventually become editor. Later scholars have attributed her defense of the respectability and autonomy of her coworkers in part to her failure to understand the larger issues in Brownson's article, and in part to the compromised editorial position of the magazine, in its refusal to engage directly in criticisms of employers. Scholars have differed on whether the *Offering*'s editorial line, in attacking Brownson, was a consequence of the owners' deliberate manipulation, of the more indirect hegemony of their values among the workers, or even—as Sarah Bagley, a disaffected contributor, put it—because "the very position of the *Offering* as a factory girls' magazine, precludes the possibilities of neutrality."[6] Nevertheless, while most of the editorials and many of the articles in the *Offering* explicitly and vigorously rejected Brownson's portrait of the slavish degradation and implied looseness of factory women and substituted the officially preferred image of respectability and decorum, the magazine, as a whole, reveals a much more complicated view of them and their lives than its outraged rebuttal of "The Laboring Classes" might suggest. The women authors provide a portrait of themselves that qualifies their well-publicized self-culture (of which Brownson was so contemptuous) and their extreme moral sensitivity to any impugning of their virtue, by producing not only genteel sentiments but also a literary mixture of self-deprecating ironies, moral incongruities, vernacular humor, and intermittent feminism toward the new material culture and ethical dilemmas in which they found themselves. While much of their writing is in the vein of religious idealism, and is conventionally decorous and imitative in both form and content, they also begin the more radical process of developing imaginative literary modes that anticipate later realism. Such modes permitted them more complex responses to the societal values that dominated their lives than mere resistance to the terms set by Brownson or acquiescence to those of their employers.

The first issue of the *Lowell Offering* appeared in October 1840, and although it did not mention Brownson directly, the "Editorial Corner" took note of the fact that "An opinion extensively prevails, not merely beyond the limits of Massachusetts, that the Manufacturing city of Lowell is a nucleus of depravity and ignorance." The editor, Abel Thomas, the minister of the city's Second Universalist Church, immediately defended the operatives' "morality and intelligence," in respect of which "they will not suffer in comparison with the inhabitants of any part of moral and enlightened New England" (ser. 1, no. 1: 16). Thomas's contention that the Lowell workers were examples of pervasive regional superiority, rather than class debasement, was furthered by the *Offering*'s chosen epigraph, from Thomas Gray's "Elegy in a Country Churchyard":

Full many a gem of purest ray serene,
The dark, unfathomed caves of ocean bear;
Full many a flower is born to blush unseen,
And waste its sweetness on the desert air. (ser. 1, no. 1, cover)

These lines hint that the obscure voices now destined to be heard in the new magazine are those naturally associated with a distinct gender rather than a social class. The words "purest" "sweetness," and "blush" all carry traditional suggestions of feminine virtue and daintiness. Thus Brownson's class-based tirade was placed, by Thomas's *Offering* editorial and by the carefully chosen epigraph, in the context of a particular geographic and gendered type—the New England girl. The *Offering*'s contributors, however, reveal in their writing a much more fluid and less categorical sense of themselves than the labels of others, whether contemporary reformers and defenders, or later critics and historians who align them with limited class, gender, regional, and religious definitions. Farley herself insisted, in the next issue of the magazine, that "there are among us *all sorts* of girls," and vigorously resisted the suggestion that there was a Lowell "type," either better or worse than the norm (ser. 1, no. 2: 18). Although she defended her fellow workers against Brownson's charges, she was careful to insist on the variety of character and motives among the operatives. Farley seems already to anticipate the metonymic tendency in the treatment of nineteenth-century working women later identified by Wai Chee Dimock, and the distortions that arose from it. Dimock has noted and resisted the imposition of a representative type on newly industrialized women, arguing that "the bodies of the women told one story, their inspirations and aspirations told another, and their organized strikes, it would seen, told yet a third" (93). She questions the likelihood of finding a "generalizable identity," even in the evidence of their writing (94), and suggests therefore that, rather than looking for the "explanatory fullness inductively derivable from the text," we look instead at the evidence of "discrepancy, noncoincidence, off-centeredness" (91). By looking at some of the incongruities and inconsistencies in their world, it may be possible to better understand the dilemmas of the women of Lowell in articulating their new experiences, finding literary terms appropriate to translating them, and avoiding acquiescence to the labels and agendas of others.

The *Lowell Offering* had very rapidly to come to terms with those agendas and with the contradictions in factory women's public image in responding not only to Brownson but also to the many enthusiastic press reviews of the new magazine. Although the reviews were often warmly congratulatory, many of them seemed to agree that Brownson's stereotype of the degraded factory woman was indeed pervasive. The *Pawtucket Gazette* cheered the *Offering*'s rebuttal of that negative image and hoped that the magazine would be "a triumphant refutation of the ungenerous and illiberal doctrines of those who profess to consider female factory operatives as destitute of intelligence and refinement." The *Portland Transcript* acknowledged that "the idea prevails pretty extensively that the operatives of our factories are persons sunk low in the depths of ignorance," and the *Maine Banner* asserted, "let no one hereafter despise the Lowell Factory girls" (all qtd. in *Offering*, ser. 1, no. 2, preface). Thus even the papers that defended factory women's good name acceded to the humiliating terms of the debate, set not by the women themselves but by their partisan detractors and defenders. Throughout the years of its existence, the pages of the *Offering* are filled with repudiations—some bitter, some reasoned, some witty, and some sanctimonious—of the contemptuous labeling of the factory girl that suggest the continuing prevalence of the practice. It apparently already had sufficient currency as early as 1814 for Sarah Savage to try to overturn it, and it was widespread enough in 1833 for Catharine Williams to respond specifically to those who believed of the operatives "that there was little regard to morals among them" (168). By 1840, despite the proprietors' emphasis on the New England origins and sturdy Puritan roots of their workers, despite strict boardinghouse regimens and churchgoing requirements, despite lyceums and improvement societies, the stereotype was still apparently pervasive enough to raise the question of why it had such enduring resonance, and especially why it was so devastating for women workers.

One powerful reason why the reputation of factory workers was such a touchstone for debate was that the British example was ever present in the eyes of owners, reformers, workers, and public alike, and liable to evoke a general consensus of revulsion for their debased condition. The frequently stated purpose of New England manufacturers was to avoid such an outcome; the mission of reformers was to insist on their failure. The gender of the factory workers added extra complications to the debate, for as David Kasserman comments in his study of the Fall River affair and the grisly death of Sarah Maria Cornell, "most Americans in the 1830s believed that women's physical nature dictated a unique psychological balance that, while extremely sensitive to moral issues, limited their rational capacities and made them the inevitable wards of males" (257). This ominous implication, that women might fall from virtue if not placed in the most carefully guarded circumstances, was furthered by the fact that the consequences of such a fall were so disastrous. However, the argument that women were in need of protection and oversight also proved a convenient one: it could readily accommodate a variety of expedient justifications for purporting to defend women against exposure and exploitation, while serving the interests of the defenders of their supposed vulnerability. Caroline Ware, in her history of early New England manufacturing, finds that the men who were most opposed to factory work for women were those who feared that women might come to prefer wage labor in mills to unpaid labor in households; often they were farmers, "whose real grievance was that the factories had drawn off the supply of dairy-maids" (216). Their rationales were more self-serving than their professed concerns: "The ambition of woman should be to beautify and adorn the domestic circle,...yet how often do we see them declining to labor in a family, and preferring the quasi-slavery of a cotton factory" (qtd. in C. Ware 216). Clearly those who attacked the fragile virtue of factory women and used terms like "wage-slavery" ranged from genuinely sympathetic radicals like Brownson to those who feared any change in women's position. They included even southern slaveholders, who relished invidious comparisons between "the hireling and the slave" whereby they might divert criticism from their own brand of exploitation, and challenge the hypocrisy of their New England critics who supposedly cared more about distant than local iniquities.[7]

The dilemma for factory women who chose to respond to attacks on themselves by denying their immorality and ignorance, and affirming their uprightness and independence, was that they appeared to play directly into the hands of the owners. If they claimed to be respectable, their bosses took credit for a system that preserved their virtue. If they admitted to degradation by industrial exploitation, they risked tainting themselves with the devastating associations of "ruin," a term that, for women, had an exclusively sexual connotation. David Zonderman notes that two distinct moral codes emerged among factory women in response to this quandary: "one spoke of preserving virtue through vigilance and critical judgement against any immodest women, for corruption was due to individual weakness; the other called for action in reaching out to troubled women who were victimized, for corruption came from the factory system as a whole" (133). Historians and literary critics have consistently identified the *Lowell Offering* with the first code, and thus with those who affirmed the dignity of labor and the need for women employees to be the guardians of their own moral conduct. The *Factory Girl's Garland*, the *Factory Girls' Album*, and especially the *Voice of Industry*, by contrast, all engaged in vigorous exposés of industrial exploitation and blamed factories for the deteriorating condition of workers. The literary tenor of the times may be gauged by the fact that these journals, too, included many imaginative works of poetry and fiction among their offerings, albeit distinctly subordinated to their radical political interests. Benita Eisler describes the *Garland,* the *Album,* and some of the other "hard-hitting reformist" journals as mixtures of "essentially agitprop" editorials and popular literary "trash" culled from commercial, middle-class women's magazines (41). The *Offering,* true to its emphasis on the individual rather than the generic factory woman, tried to publish only original literary compositions by female operatives, while the more politically militant papers placed less emphasis on the sources and content of their creative contributions. Thus there is not an exact opposition between the literary journal with the conservative politics and the radical journals with their contempt for genteel literariness. The desire to combine imaginative literature with revelations of the lives of factory operatives was an important element on both sides, and both conceded, in their mixed offerings, their mingled concerns for the mental as well as the physical condition of the workers.

One of the essays Philip Foner includes in the "Genteel Factory Girls" section of his anthology *Factory Girls* demonstrates the extent to which even a "militant" factory woman might benefit from a "genteel" literary apprenticeship. "Pleasures of Factory Life," published in the *Lowell Offering* in 1840, makes all the standard defenses of life in Lowell, from churches and lyceums to benevolent mill superintendents and work-rooms that have "more the appearance of a flower garden than a workshop" (36). The piece was written by Sarah Bagley, who later went on to become a radical contributor to the *Voice of Industry* and the public scourge of Harriet Farley and the *Offering.* Undoubtedly, she changed her positive response to factory life during the course of her career at Lowell, but it also seems likely that she, as well as many other young women, did not have many models of a woman's way of writing that were not mainly derived from bourgeois literary paradigms. Bagley's other notable contribution to the *Offering* was her series "Tales of Factory Life," brief fictions that were pious and conventional in the extreme. Yet they also show the young author beginning to explore the ironic and exclamatory modes she would eventually use for very different ends in the *Voice of Industry*. By 1845, when Bagley began her public feud with Farley over the *Offering*'s pro-factory bias, she had honed her rhetorical skills and become a worthy opponent for the eloquent and mellifluous Farley. Ironically, it was the *Offering* that had given her her first public forum and the opportunity to acquire a persuasive style.

The argument between Bagley and Farley did not erupt until 1845, after the *Offering* had ceased publication, when Bagley was reported by the *Lowell Advertiser* to have claimed at an Independence Day workers' rally that "she had written articles in relation to the condition of the operatives, and their insertion had been invariably *refused!*" (qtd. in Foner 58). The debate between the two women, conducted in the columns of the *Lowell Advertiser* and the *Voice of Industry*, quickly moved from civility to insult, as Bagley rejected Farley's professions of political neutrality and polarized their positions as enemy and friend of an exploitive factory system. Farley attempted to claim a common ground for all those whose concern was "to raise the operative": "The Labor Question is the great Reform taper of the day. William Ellery Channing, Lydia Maria Child, and many others, work upon the same side with Geo. Ripley, Michael Walsh, and Sarah Bagley. In each of these I find something in which I can and must sympathize, though they are widely different" (qtd. in Foner 65). Bagley energetically rejected any alliance between the values of the *Offering* and the interests of the operatives, asking rhetorically: "[Had] its columns ever contended against oppression or abuse in any form?" (qtd. in Foner 67). When Farley tried to capture the moral high ground of the debate with good manners and conciliatory gestures, Bagley replied: "I have been *favored* with a specimen of *refined* literature, from the pen of one of the *geniuses* of the age, and feel myself highly honored with a passing notice from such a *high* source" (qtd. in Foner 66). Her parody of Farley's elegant condescension and imposing vocabulary left no doubt that she was constructing a ladylike antagonist with an opposing class affiliation.

Many labor historians followed Bagley in assuming an ultimate betrayal of the economic interests of the operatives by Farley and the *Offering*. Norman Ware summarized Farley's career there by saying that she began "by defending the operatives against the attacks that were leveled at the corporations and finished by defending the corporations at the expense of the operatives" (90). More recently, Thomas Dublin and David Zonderman have found much of interest and value in the *Offering*, focusing less on its absence of polemics and more on its contents as documentary evidence of the dramatic personal changes in the first factory women's lives. In the context of literary rather than social history, debates over the extent of Farley's collaboration with the owners have obscured the important steps she took, as editor and author, to encourage new literary modes that might be appropriate to the experiences of working-class women. Unlike Sarah

Bagley and the writers for the militant *Voice of Industry,* she was more interested in the aesthetic ends of literature than in propaganda. She was also unwilling to concede that the literary manner was, de facto, treacherous to working-class interests. She appeared to recognize much that was effete and dishonest in the realm of traditional literature, and she did her best to define and encourage alternatives. Although it must be admitted that she had only occasional and limited successes in the *Offering,* whose pages were indeed largely dominated by the pious and the conventional, nevertheless she proved to be a thoughtful theorist about fiction and literary realism, and she anticipated the struggles of many later women and working-class writers to find a suitable form for encompassing their untold experiences.

One of the first signs of the incongruous experiences of the Lowell women was instantly manifest in the visual appearance of their new magazine. No reader can have overlooked the startling visual disjuncture between the demure cover with its sedate table of contents and the immediate display of extravagantly worded advertisements within that cover. The stark juxtaposition of the cultural and the commercial indicates the pervasiveness of the marketplace as an environment for these working women and their literary aspirations. Though they professed that they did not wish to be dragged into the arena of political and economic disputes (5: 284), they were forced to acknowledge from the outset that they operated in a material as well as an intellectual and spiritual context, and this materialism was bound to affect the form and content of their writing. The *Offering*'s famously iconic cover, an engraving of a woman with book in hand, framed by greenery and natural objects, with factory buildings, church spire, and schoolhouse in the distance, did not appear until late in the life of the magazine.[8] Its imagery of an idealized landscape midway between rural and urban surroundings, with the institutions of physical, spiritual, and mental endeavor in the background, suggested the desire for a balanced integration of the elements of human life. Notably missing from the symbolic buildings in the Romanticized background of the cover is the store, but in fact this emblem of getting and spending is an insistent presence in the magazine from the beginning, and some of the liveliest contributions are those that address this mercenary reality.

The only art work on the original 1840 cover was a continuous border of alternating fleurs-de-lis and posies around the edge, within which was the title, the *Lowell Offering,* and its modest explanation, "A repository of original articles on various subjects, written by factory operatives." The price, 6¼ cents, is the most prominent feature of the page, which also contains the epigraph from Gray's *Elegy,* and a table of contents listing such pious and demure titles as "The Mother's Love," "Beauty of Leaves," "Woman's Proper Sphere," "Longings of the Spirit," and "Divine Love." The first inside page is consequently distinctly jarring for a reader expecting "gems of purest ray serene" or "longings of the spirit." It displays a tightly packed double-column listing of advertisements for Lowell businesses, intent on arousing quite other than spiritual longings in the operatives. A Miss H. Sanborn offers "Millinery Goods, comprising in part Bonnet and Cap Ribbons, artificial Flowers, Caps and Bonnets of every variety, to suit the prevailing fashions." Philip T. White presents "Cloths, Cassimeres and Vestings ... All Garments cut in the latest style"; A. B. French, "Dealer in Fruit, Cakes, Confectionary and Fancy Goods," promises wedding cakes likewise "trimmed in the latest style," and Mrs. M. Brown declares that her dresses are made "according to the latest fashions." No desert flower in Lowell needs to "blush unseen," for S. P. Howes is eager to provide her portrait or miniature painting, and George W. Ward, dentist, will ensure that "her beautiful Porcelain or incorruptible Teeth" will be made "in a style which, in respect to imitation of nature, firmness, durability and elegance, is not surpassed in any of the American or European cities." The final two pages of the first issue of the *Offering* are again filled with double columns of advertisements for all manner of consumer goods, from books to jewelry and clothing, all described in terms of variety, style, and high fashion. Several of the businesses give their location as "under" Lowell's various churches, suggesting a certain literalness to Orestes Brownson's accusation against the clergy, that "not a few of our churches rest on Mammon for their foundation. The basement is a trader's shop" (369). Before the essays, the stories, the poems, and the editorials of the *Offering* comes the fundamental materialist culture of the new urban marketplace. One of the essays in the first issue, a devout meditation entitled "Beauty and Wealth," concludes by affirming the necessity of seeking spiritual treasures, an admonition that seems more than merely formulaic in the tempting presence of Mr. French's fancy confectionery or George Ward's incorruptible teeth.

The moral duty to work hard, the hope of spiritual rewards, the payment of earthly wages, the pleasure of worldly goods—these were the somewhat incongruous promises of the Lowell factories to women workers. The owners endorsed church attendance and religious practices as a means of encouraging diligence and imposing social control, but as in the case of Sarah Maria Cornell, they risked considerable unpredictability in how the women applied their beliefs. Almost universally, the operatives who came to work in the Lowell mills brought deep attachments to their largely Protestant denominations, and the owners reinforced these loyalties by insisting that workers attend church. In addition, "some manufacturers built churches and supported ministers to instill in the operatives the principles of hard work, thrift, sobriety, and obedience—all characteristic of a dutiful employee" (Zonderman 152). There was always a risk that religious enthusiasm might become excessive, in the lure of camp meetings, and in the extreme responses of workers who displayed "religious frenzy," or were discovered "pretending 'sickness to go to meeting'" (qtd. in Zonderman 150). There was also the possibility that some churches outside the proprietors' oversight might support workers' protests against their employers. However, a deeper complication of the factories' endorsement of Christianity was the religion's emphasis on antimaterialism and its revulsion from the attachment to earthly goods. The consequent misgivings of operatives, drawn to factories by their needs and those of their families, lured by opportunities for indulgence, and warned by the lessons of the Bible against greed and vanity, became the foundation of some of their most original contributions to the *Offering*, and of their development of literary styles that advanced beyond the conventions of the didactic and the celebratory to accommodate some of the novel ironies of their situation.

Thomas Dublin's collection of working women's letters, *Farm to Factory*, reveals how acute their consciousness of this new materialism was. One young woman, Sarah Hogdon writes in her first letter home a request that her mother will pray for her, "that it may not be said of me ... that I have sold my soul for the gay vanitys of this world" (42). However, her friend, Wealthy Page, with whom Sarah went to Lowell, suggests that the gay vanities may already be in the ascendant, for she adds a telling postscript to her letter home the same month: "Sarah has bought her a very handsome Scotch gingham two shillings pr yard" (46). Many of the women's letters itemize in detail their expenditures and anticipated purchases, interspersed with accounts of Bible study classes and their faith in divine providence. Another collection, of Emeline Larcom's letters to her mother, regularly includes mention of enclosures of dollars from her earnings, accompanied by a reminder of a superior economy that must eventually prevail. She writes, "and ma, as you are poor in this world's goods, perhaps it will all be for our good, for as you love your children and cannot express it by bestowing on us the riches of the earth, you will pray for us more earnestly that we may have true riches" (qtd. in Dublin, "Mill," 225). In the *Offering*, the economic implications of such letters become more explicit. One story suggests a certain vengeful satisfaction when a cruelly mistreated servant runs away to Lowell and soon has $400 in her bank account. In another, "Ann and Myself," a schoolteacher is at first scornful of factory girls until she discovers their greater earning power, whereupon she joins them. Some of the *Offering*'s anecdotes show the women's dawning recognition that their incomes alter their perceived value as donors and spenders. One somewhat embittered writer notes, in "The Silver Cup," that workers are constantly being dunned for contributions to religious societies or for gifts for Sunday school teachers, while an editorial complains that the boardinghouses are regularly invaded by peddlers and professors, equally touting their goods. However, there is also a strong countertendency for the women to incorporate their new-found wage earning into traditional tales of sacrifice, justifying its value in paying for a brother's education or the support of a widowed mother, and noting the folly of those workers who spend their wages frivolously or selfishly.

The relationship Emeline Larcom noted in her letter to her mother between "true riches" and "this world's goods," or between God and Mammon, is interestingly reflected from the other side of the pulpit in the writing of William Scoresby, an English clergyman who visited Lowell in 1844. He wrote a book boosting the American industrial enterprise as a model to English capitalists and to the British factory population. Scoresby approved of the physical conditions of the Lowell operatives, from the commodious beds and hearty meals in boardinghouses to the workers' hospital, and especially the "extensive ranges of well-furnished shops, brilliantly lighted up, and continuing so until nine o'clock, or a little later" (31). His celebration of commerce and manufacturing concludes with the pious affirmation that "true, self-denying religion can alone chasten the inordinate love of gain," a statement that sits somewhat anomalously alongside his approval of Lowell's alluring shops, "brilliantly lighted" and open late at night to tempt women who have been at work for twelve hours. Surrounded by opportunities to earn, temptations to spend, obligations to be thrifty, and constant reminders of Christian charity and asceticism, the operatives might well have tried to formulate a convenient rationale comparable to that of their employers, for whom, as Hannah Josephson notes, moneymaking was now a virtue (115). Among the common vindications offered for the women's pursuit of money were their desires to pay off farm mortgages, support aging parents, and send brothers to study at Dartmouth and Harvard. Harriet Farley tried to bring some candor to the debate by cutting through the saintly self-righteousness of such justifications and equally by refuting counter-accusations of greed, vanity, and foolishness in wage-earners' spendthrift habits. In "Defense of Factory Girls," her first such refutation, Farley asserts a middle moral ground and a realistically pragmatic rationale for women who come to work in the factories: she argues that "there are few occupations which can exhibit so many gradations of piety and intelligence," and virtually none in which women can earn comparable wages. Thus factory labor is, "in money-loving New England, one of the most lucrative female employments" (ser. 1, no. 2: 18). However, Farley's worldly mediation between God and Mammon and her wariness of any single moral label for working women did not at first have any imaginative equivalent in the poems, allegories, and fiction of the magazine, although she strove hard to encourage appropriate new modes.

The difficulty of the literary challenge for these aspiring writers is illustrated in one of the essays most often cited from the *Offering*, "Gold Watches," signed by "A Factory Girl." The piece reveals the conflicting attitudes of a working woman who is caught between the self-assertive pleasure of her earned right to a little conspicuous consumption and her self-restraining obligation, as a Christian, to refrain from worldly display. It takes as its "text" a sentence from an article published a year earlier by Sarah Josepha Hale in *Godey's Lady's Book*. In it, Hale chastises "ladies" for imagining that dress can function as a mark of distinction by noting that "many of the factory girls wear gold watches, and an imitation, at least, of all the ornaments which grace the daughters of our most opulent citizens" (2: 377). The *Offering's* author is satirically outraged at the disappearing distinctions between ladies and factory girls: "O the times! O the manners! Alas! How very sadly the world has changed! The time was when the *lady* could be distinguished from the *no-lady* by her dress, as far as the eye could reach; but now, you might stand in the same room, and, judging by their outward appearance, you could not tell 'which was which'" (377). The author's clear intention is to ridicule snobbishness and assert that factory women are "as good as anyone" in their rights to wear the ornaments and clothes that their hard-earned wages have paid for. However, a second intention quickly emerges in her admission that, just like the *Godey's* ladies, the operatives have begun to make their fashionable attire a sign of their superiority, and to "put on an air of haughty contempt, which would do honor (or disgrace) to the proudest lady in the court of Victoria" (378). Thus while the writer argues that factory women have every right to wear the pretty dresses and gold watches that show they are not to be considered inferior, she also insists that they are under a moral and religious obligation not to use their clothing and ornaments as symptoms of their superiority, especially over other women who might be shamed by the contrast (378). The class consciousness of the essay on one hand and its antimaterialism on the other cannot be neatly resolved into a balanced paradox. Although the "Factory Girl" asserts that "we see things more as they really are, and not through the false medium which misleads the aristocracy," what she sees is an unbridgeable conflict between her sense of economic fairness and her sense of Christian, womanly conduct. If she claims a just reward for herself as a working woman, she risks placing a vain emphasis on earthly treasures. Instead of a resolution, what began as ridicule of the bourgeoisie ends in a retreat into a conventional sermon to her fellow workers: "Let us caution each other; let us watch over and endeavor to improve each other . . . and if we succeed, it will finally be acknowledged that Factory Girls shine forth in ornaments far more valuable than *Gold Watches*" (379).

A similar pattern of emergent social realism, finally subordinated to more traditional religious idealism, is apparent in a short story by "Lucinda" (one of Farley's many pseudonyms), called "Evening Before Pay-day." Four factory women, Dorcas, Rosina, Lucy, and Elizabeth, are debating their personal economies, which range from Dorcas's miserliness through Elizabeth's spendthrift ways, Lucy's balanced economy, and Rosina's saintly sacrifices. Each woman's habits provide a way to investigate the social texture of the factory world and how the operatives view their wages, although since it is Farley's story, the adequacy of those wages will not come under consideration. Dorcas's life is dominated by her swelling bankbook and, rather than spend money, she employs her spare time reading free tracts that are delivered to the boardinghouses. Her activity leads to a discussion of the price of religion in Lowell, where a year's seat in one of the more expensive churches costs a week's wages. Elizabeth is much less interested in the cost of religion than in the cost of "beautiful new damask silk shawls which are now so fashionable." She is the most frivolous and worldly of the four friends but also the most vivacious and the wittiest, a sinister combination, as these avid readers of Hannah Foster's account of "Eliza Wharton" in her novel *The Coquette* would quickly have recognized. In fact Lizzy Walters (a virtual echo of the name) almost quotes Eliza when she says, "I shall sow all my wild oats now, and when I am an old maid I will be as steady, though *not quite* so stingy, as Dorcas" (1:242). Lucy, who appears to have established a balanced middle ground for her budget ("a pretty new, though cheap bonnet ... [a] quarter's pew-rent, and a year's subscription to the Lowell Offering"), is as bland as her expenditures (243). Having established in the first part of the story a mode of pragmatism whose central standards appear to be moderation and diversity in the allocation of one's resources, the author shifts the focus to Rosina, the one member of the group who neither spends nor saves. She also moves to an utterly different ethical system that has nothing in common with the values formerly broached. Rosina, it appears, is sending virtually all her wages home to her widowed mother to pay for the care of her mortally ill twin sister. Her budget is fully allocated to the duties of love, an expenditure that has little reference to her friends' worldly account books. By abandoning the debates of Dorcas, Lizzy, and Lucy for the heroic sacrifice of Rosina, Farley subsumes the worldly context of her story to the otherworldly, and abandons the real to the ideal. When she returns to her "payday" theme at the end, the word is now charged with the suggestion of heavenly rather than earthly rewards, but the story contains, without fully confronting, the tension between the two different ways of thinking about ethics and earnings. Melville would later explore the same conflict, between the reasonable demands of self-interest and the unreasonable demands of Christian charity, in the character of his prosperous lawyer in "Bartleby the Scrivener," with a corrosively ironic portrayal of his comfortably bourgeois, male protagonist. The working-class women of Lowell, earning wages for the first time, were not such ripe satirical targets in their struggles to reconcile selfish and unselfish impulses as Melville's expedient lawyer, but in the end, several of the *Offering*'s contributors did discover, in realist comedy, a way of giving voice to some of the ironies of their situation.

The moral incongruity between the materialism of the factory world and the spiritual values of religion is only one of several disparities between proprietors' schemes and workers' experiences that emerge in their literary accounts of their changing consciousness. The boardinghouse system was one of the most promoted advantages of New England factory villages, providing safe and decent facilities for young women far from their families' protection. While it might have been intended for this purpose, or as a more devious scheme to control the nonworking hours of employees' lives, one clear and possibly unanticipated result of it was the intense mutual awareness that developed among the women. Lucy Larcom, one of the youngest *Offering* contributors, who was later to pursue a successful professional career as a poet, wrote about this intimate boardinghouse communion: "One great advantage which came to these many stranger girls through being brought together, away from their own homes, was that it taught them to go out of themselves, and enter into the lives of others. Home-life, when one always stays at home, is necessarily narrowing" (*New* 178). Larcom, who was neither a radical nor a feminist, depicts boardinghouse empathy as both an ethical and an intellectual benefit, and goes on to suggest that it expanded the domestic ideal of family harmony into a larger arena. However, that arena was specifically defined within the boardinghouse system by the social class and single sex of the operatives living there, and thus it constituted a distinct shift from the kind of communal loyalties engendered by a traditional family. If the ultimate community that was being fostered was, in Larcom's ideal, the whole human family, nevertheless, the immediate group within which the factory women came to know and affiliate with one another was that of female wage earners. This class and gender solidarity emerged directly in the women's later industrial activism and, more indirectly, in the consciousness in their writing that they were part of a new generation of working women whose experiences were fraught with unusual significance. Thus they documented repeatedly their farewells to rural families, the loading of trunks and baskets on to carriages, the apprehensive journey to the factory town, the terrors of the arrival, and the gradual assimilation into new communities. Their personal psychological dramas reflected not only the larger historical transition in their society from rural and agricultural to urban and industrial but also a new awareness of class and gender interests that raised dilemmas for both their employers and themselves.

One of the most vexing questions that arose for them was the relationship between their sex and their work: how did traditional gender expectations for women fit with the demands of wage-earning, industrial workers? To some extent it was clearly in the interests of the owners to nourish the traditionally feminine virtues of obedience, loyalty, respectability, and duty in female employees, but distinctly less so to encourage delicacy, dependency, vulnerability, and sensitivity in young women who were laboring seventy hours a week in a confined, noisy, and overheated environment. It was also very much in the owners' interests to put their young female workforce on display to generate publicity for their enterprise. This practice necessitated the relentless exposure of factory women to the gaze of all comers, but most frequently to that of curious male visitors. William Scoresby's account of his observations and comparisons of Lowell operatives to English factory women reveals some of the awkward and unintended ironies that arose when factory proponents imposed ladylike stereotypes on working women, and encouraged watchful men to note the feminine details of their appearance. Scoresby's impressions come as he watches several hundred young women streaming from the mills at dinner time:

> They were neatly dressed, and clean in their persons; many with
> their hair nicely arranged, and not a few with it flowing in carefully

curled ringlets. . . . Many wore veils and some carried silk parasols.
By no means a few were exceedingly well-looking, more pallid
than the factory-girls with us, and generally slight in their figure.
There was not the slightest appearance of boldness or vulgarity;
on the contrary, a very becoming propriety and respectability of
manner, approaching, with some, to genteel. (16)

Scoresby contrasts the levity of English factory girls' behavior with the
demure demeanor of Americans and warns that "a bold, rude, vulgar and
immodest girl is a disgusting creature, and a disgrace to her sex" (17). His
clear preference for the pale, slender, decorously veiled ladies of Lowell
over the brash, loud English girls who go "in the streets without bonnet or
cap or sufficient covering" (18) posits a bourgeois ideal for working-class
women, one to whose paradoxes Lucy Larcom later reacts in her long narrative poem of factory life *An Idyl of Work.* Her pale-faced Eleanor, one of
the factory women in the poem, has "too much / Of the fine-lady look
. . . For any working-girl" and soon is forced, by her declining health, to
withdraw from the mill (19). While the hoydenish Isabel in the poem gets
spots of grease from the factory machinery on the ruffles of her dress, the
genteel Eleanor walks "past the oily wheels immaculate." However, her
scrupulous daintiness is no defense against the rigors of labor, and she is on
her deathbed by the end of the poem (20). The tainted Isabel (both morally
and physically) is, by contrast, about to marry a stalwart young carpenter.
Larcom's satire of the jarring requirements of delicacy and sturdiness in
factory women was the product of her later years of reflection on her mill
experiences, but neither long meditation nor poetic subtlety were required
for workers to perceive the conflicting standards of fragility and endurance
that were being imposed on them. Even Harriet Farley, often seen as col-
laborating with the owners in furthering the genteel reputation of workers,
notes in the *Offering* the impact of factory work on these much-observed
female bodies. In her "Letters from Susan," she warns that after a year or
two in the mill, women have to "procure shoes a size or two larger" as a
result of their long hours of standing at work, and "the right hand, which
is the one used in stopping and starting the loom, becomes larger than the
left" (4: 170). Thus were the bodies of Scoresby's pale, slender, and good-
looking young women distorted by the very industrial enterprise that put
them on display for their femininity.

Among many eminent men who came to Lowell to view the women,
two of the most notable were President Andrew Jackson and Charles Dickens, both of whom expressed suitable appreciation for the parade of female
attractiveness, decorum, and diligence. The women's responses, however,
were not perhaps as grateful as might have been supposed. When Jackson
visited in 1833, twenty-five hundred cotton mill workers marched before
him, clad in white muslin dresses with blue sashes, carrying parasols over
their bare heads. The president's famed response was "Very pretty women,

by the Eternal," a comment he might have wished to rethink when the same workers went on strike in 1836 and marched through the streets, singing "Oh! isn't it a pity, such a pretty girl as I—/Should be sent to the factory to pine away and die?"[9] Dickens's visit to Lowell in 1841 resulted in almost the only wholly laudatory section of his *American Notes*. He found the women well-dressed, healthy, and with appropriate manners and deportment, but what impressed him most was their cultural life and particularly their writing: "Firstly, there is a joint-stock piano in a great many of the boarding-houses. Secondly, nearly all these young ladies subscribe to circulating libraries. Thirdly, they have got up among themselves a periodical called the *Lowell Offering* [which] ... will compare advantageously with a great many English Annuals" (89-90). Although Dickens seemed to endorse the same image of factory women Harriet Farley was accused of promoting, her editorial response to Dickens's praise in the *Offering* is curiously muted: "We trust that we feel grateful for his kindness, and proud of his approval; but we fear that we do not deserve all this commendation, that we are not worthy of such flattering compliments" (3: 95). Farley is perhaps resisting a note of condescension and insisting that, although her journal may not have achieved the highest literary quality, she and the other contributors are well aware of what constitutes excellence. Perhaps any judgment, disinterested or not, was unacceptable to the editor of a magazine so devoted to self-scrutiny as was the *Offering*. Its writers had inherited a rigorous tradition of introspection from their ancestors; they lived in an age when philosophies of self-knowledge, self-reliance, and self-improvement abounded. They were the focus of fascinated observers who wrote paeans and puffery, encomiums and diatribes about them. It is scarcely to be wondered at that they sometimes resisted even the most flattering versions of the selves so many others were eager to define for them.

Modest as the *Offering*'s contributors were about their abilities as authors, they nonetheless were acutely aware of the significance of having their writing published. They engaged in frequent discussions that reveal much about their literary tastes, their reading habits, and their meditations on the advantages and drawbacks of the various modes of writing they might pursue. The Lowell workers have acquired an almost legendary reputation for the avidity and range of their reading, and factories had to make special regulations (frequently violated) governing where and when reading was permissible. Although books and Bibles were confiscated in the workrooms, and workers were even fired for "reading in the mill," the women found many ingenious ways to evade these rules (qtd. in Zonderman 150). Harriet Farley, in one of her editorials, asks why factory women are "more inclined to read than other laboring females." She answers (rather candidly) that it is because "fatigue disposes to a sedentary recreation"; because (unlike other women), "their Sabbaths are more wholly their own"; and because the facilities in a manufacturing town are rich in resources "for the gratification of every literary taste, or preference" (3: 143). She suggests that

factory work is especially congenial to the process of reflection and composition, because its noise "deadens every other sound" and "many of the
best articles in the Offering we know to have been composed in the mill"
(3: 164). Whatever the causes—devotional, escapist, self-indulgent, educational—the factory workers' reading is one of the activities most frequently
documented in their writing. Harriet Robinson gives an account of one
of her mother's boarders who had come from the state of Maine to work
in the factory "for the express purpose of getting books, usually novels, to
read, that she could not find in her native place. She read from two to four
volumes a week" (26). Several operatives wrote accounts of their own and
their companions' reading choices. One compiled a list of the magazines
and periodicals available in her boardinghouse:

> Among us, there are regularly received fifteen papers and peri-
> odicals. These are as follows: Boston Daily Times; Signs of the
> Times; Herald of Freedom; Christian Herald, two copies; Chris-
> tian Register; Vox Populi; Literary Souvenir; Boston Pilot; Young
> Catholic's Friend; Star of Bethlehem; Lowell Offering, three
> copies; Magazine, one copy. We also regularly *borrow* the Non-
> Resistant, the Liberator, the Lady's Book, The Ladies' Pearl . . . ; also
> the Ladies' Companion. Many other papers are occasionally bor-
> rowed. (1: 364)

The ambitious Lucy Larcom also tackled *Blackwood's* and the *Westminster*
and *Edinburgh* reviews, and Harriet Farley added *Grahams* to the list.[10] Religious, devotional, literary, cultural, and abolitionist interests are the main
emphases, together with an added preference for magazines deliberately
directed to women.

The accounts of books read, like those of magazines, naturally tend
to come from the women with the highest literary ambitions, but they
nevertheless provide some sense of the canonical reading within the group,
and of the debates readers engaged in. Harriet Farley, under the pseudonym
"Ella," contributed an early essay to the *Offering* that suggests that the hierarchy of literature in her world is not greatly at variance, especially if one
looks at the pre-nineteenth-century authors, with the standards that still
prevail in literary studies: Homer, Virgil, Shakespeare, Milton, Dryden, and
Spenser. Closer to her contemporary world she mentions Burns, Byron, Sir
Walter Scott, and, among American authors, Irving, Cooper, and Bryant.
More interesting is her choice of three women writers: the English Romantic poet Felicia Hemans, and the Americans Lydia Sigourney and Catharine Sedgwick. Later, her editorials indicate considerable familiarity with
the work of Dickens and the factory novels of Frances Trollope and Charlotte Elizabeth Tonna. Lucy Larcom adds Pope, Wordsworth, Coleridge,
and Tennyson to the list of favored poets, Caroline Kirkland to the women
prose writers and, once again, notes the popularity of Hemans. Harriet
Robinson mentions Emerson, Bryant, Longfellow, Lowell, and Whittier as

writers "whose influence cannot be overestimated in bringing an ideal element into our hitherto prosaic New England life," but her account of her own and other operatives' reading leans heavily toward devotional literature and fiction. She reveals some hesitation, or even embarrassment, on the subject of novel reading, a very contentious one for moralists and guardians of women's mental lives in the period. She affirms first that "novels were not very popular with us" but then admits that "such books as 'Charlotte Temple,' 'Eliza Wharton,' 'Maria Monk,' 'The Arabian Nights,' 'The Mysteries of Udolpho,' 'Abbelino, the Bravo of Venice,' or 'The Castle of Otranto,' were sometimes taken from the circulating library, read with delight, and secretly lent from one young girl to another."[11] By means of such borrowing, Robinson says, she read the novels of Richardson, Madame D'Arblay, Fielding, Smollett, Cooper, Scott, and Captain Marryat.

The suitability both of reading fiction and of writing it, the beneficial and harmful influences of literature, and even the dangers of "cold intellectualism" were all debated in the pages of the *Offering* (5: 47). A lengthy exchange between "Annette" and "Ella" (both pseudonyms used by Farley) entitled "Fiction: A Dialogue" rehearses many of the central arguments over the value and danger of fiction and novels (2: 250–61). Annette, the antagonist of fiction, at first refuses even to use the word to describe her friend's productions, preferring a list of trivializing alternative terms to suggest the insubstantiality of the genre: "Pray what are you writing now? 'One of your dreams, allegories, reveries, metaphors, or some such *jack-o'-lanthorn* thing,' as somebody says of somebody's writings." She proposes that there is "so much of the lofty, beautiful, and inspiring, in the *true*, that I must ever regret your leaving the clear, sunny height, for the dark, mazy vale" (250–51). Arguing that "works of fiction have a most demoralizing and weakening effect upon the mind," she specifically regrets the effects of fiction on women, who are drawn from their duties into a world of trite love stories that encourage them in false sentiments. Borrowing from the rhetoric of the temperance movement, she calls these women consumers of "ardent spirits" and "inebriate novel-readers" (252, 253). Ella responds reasonably and methodically to all of Annette's objections, and even expands on her accusations in order to answer them more fully. She implicitly accedes to some of Annette's analogies to novel reading as a guilty habit when she acknowledges that "the practice of our common readers of fiction, is to *keep silence* when they are attacked, and still go on, amidst the anathemas, and under the proscriptions, of those who are the sworn enemies of this department of literature" (251). The extravagance of the analogies for fiction as a kind of addictive drug suggests how seriously the issue was taken.

Ella responds to the charge of lack of weightiness and truth in fiction by immediately invoking not only its paradoxical capacity to tell the truth but also its appeal to a yearning for the ideal. She sees this aspiration (admittedly by citing the science of phrenology) as a God-given mental faculty, a "propensity to dream, to imagine, to create other and lovelier scenes, and people them with different, and far more beauteous beings" (252–3). Ella shows herself to be poised at an interesting early divergence of Romantic and realist theories of fiction, and she goes on to distinguish between the romancer, "who creates those bewitching palaces, or fairy nooks, or frowning castles, and peoples them … with forms of unnatural beauty, grace, and perfection," and the novelist, "who takes his rule and compass, and marks his chart from the real shore around him, and then creates the mimic vessels with which he is to illustrate the dangers or pleasures of the passage across the real sea" (253). She traces the history of fiction from its beginnings in wild legend and romance to the novels of Scott and Edgeworth, and finally to the contemporary novel, where she notes both a democratization of subject matter and a more tempered and reasonable vision of human existence. Using terms that will later become familiar in the canon of literary realism, she praises those novelists who "portray the feelings, manners, etc., as naturally as possible: as much in accordance, not only with real life, but also common life." They no longer depict a world in which "virtue was too often rewarded … and vice too signally punished, to be in accordance with our observations of real life" (259). Even more pragmatically, Ella admits that she does not know how she could endure the factories and boardinghouses without the escapism fiction provides. She rejects society's cant about the "pernicious effects of novel-reading" by arguing that inveterate devourers of fiction would surely otherwise be doing something worse than reading novels. She suggests that those who do not satisfy their voracious predilection for reading might otherwise be, "if women, tattlers, meddlers, and busy-bodies; or if men, street-loungers and tavern visitors." Thus, novel reading serves to keep them "out of a vast deal of mischief" (255). Ella's playful support for fiction as opiate and distraction does not, however, detract from the remarkable seriousness and energy with which the dialogue considers this genre and endorses it as the literary mode best suited to deal with the realities of commonplace life.

In 1842, when Harriet Farley contributed this defense of novels and the commonplace to the *Offering*, she was not yet editor of the magazine. In October of that year, she and Harriot Curtis took over the editorial chair from Abel Thomas, and Farley was soon involved in controversies about the nature of the fictional realism she chose to publish. In 1843 she began the serial publication of *The Smuggler*, a novel by her coeditor, Harriot Curtis, which employed some of the more controversial aspects of the realist novel and was roundly attacked for them in a very angry letter to the editor. The correspondent objected to *The Smuggler*'s vulgar profanity and to its defamation of the American character, both evils deemed even more repugnant, according to the correspondent, in a woman author writing for an audience of women. Farley defended the profane language vigorously as necessary to a "truthful delineation" of character, arguing that to make smugglers talk like saints would have been "worse than nonsense," and not to have them talk at all "would have materially detracted from the interest of the story" (4: 119). To the letter writer's accusation that the novel slandered the American character by depicting the financial success of a villain, Farley betrayed a flash of class consciousness: "Does not the swindler walk openly our streets, receiving bows and smiles and invitations to places to which no honest laborer can obtain admittance, if he is only suspected—not *detected*?" She suggests that if the hero had been a poor man, "the sins of his youth would be brought in array against him; but we are not of those who would advocate a stricter state of morals for the poor than for the rich. Indeed, it might be very naturally required that those who have less temptation should have more virtue" (119). Farley then dismisses the parallel implication in the letter that there should be a different moral code for the two sexes, and claims herself to be of the school that advocates, in fiction, "a faithful transcript of the evils and vices of real life." She concludes her spirited defense of *The Smuggler* by claiming that it is a preferable fiction "to thousands which are published in those magazines, whose principal recommendation is, that 'nothing will be found in them which any parent need fear to place in the hands of his children;' and which are filled with namby-pamby things, that are incapable of doing either harm or good." Farley certainly appears to align herself here with those who saw in the realist novel a capacity to unmask social hypocrisy and expose the inequities of current attitudes toward class and gender. She mocks as "namby-pamby" literature that fears mimetic candor or shies away from realistic language (4: 120). She is daring in her advocacy of those new aspects of fiction that appeared most subversive in her time and particularly for her sex. Such fiction was, for both Farley and Curtis, a way to expose sophistry and humbug—that there was not more of it in the *Lowell Offering* does not seem to have been for lack of editorial encouragement.

Despite Farley's belief that fiction should be a "faithful transcript of the evils and vices of real life" (4: 120), the *Offering* was not yet ready to challenge the literary taboos against the depiction of sex, disease, violence, and degradation that would become the hallmarks of later literary naturalism. There were, however, significant efforts, some discreet, some playful, to tackle shocking or risky subjects. The magazine published numerous attacks on the evils of drinking, a popular reform movement for women to support, but prostitution, unwed pregnancy, and abortion go unmentioned, except for some essays asking for greater tolerance and less cruelty toward fellow workers who may have erred and fallen. Occasionally a conventionally pious topic provided an opportunity for an author to push beyond the boundaries of a "namby-pamby" style. A sketch, possibly by Farley herself, called "A Sufferer" has a typically didactic purpose—to require the reader to meditate on the afflictions of others—but her literary method is to dwell graphically on the minute physical details of the mortification of the body. She describes a sequence of decay and pain in her subject, who is first required to have an arm amputated, then develops a tumor on his other shoulder that takes "the form of '*rose-cancer*'; evolving itself into a large corrosive, running sore. Next, an abscess formed in the back part of the shoulder, working so violently as to push the blade-bone to the distance of inches from its proper place. The discharges from this abscess, when opened, were astonishingly copious. His whole body, with the exception of the remaining arm, became distended, like one bloated with a universal dropsy" (2: 211). While the story, on one level, emphasizes the traditional virtues of patience and acquiescence to necessity, what is striking is the clinical precision and detachment of the language—it seems to derive, like much of later naturalism, more from a medical textbook than a religious or political tract.[12] Its unflinching observation of the destruction of the body moves far beyond the more traditional female formula of invoking horrors that are then omitted as being too dire to report. Farley's accounts of the distortions of the hands and feet of the factory workers by their labor also suggests her willingness to set an example of candor and directness to other writers who were perhaps too ready to associate literary style with discreet circumspection.

Some very different fictional restrictions are extended in more playful and ebullient ways in the *Offering*'s comic stories, "The White Dress; or Village Aristocracy," and "Kissing," both written by "Kate," one of the pseudonyms of Harriot Curtis. "The White Dress" tackles both racial and social stereotyping. The story juxtaposes an uncommon black girl, Ruth Mingo, who is "the most genteel and elegantly formed female in the country of any color; and withal a good and virtuous girl" against some "common" white girls who nonetheless suffer from the author's invented label of "exclusiveism" and believe themselves to be "*the quality*" (3: 170, 169). However, the story's comeuppance for the arrogant whites is to find themselves embarrassed to be on display in church, wearing the same new dress pattern as the demure black. It is a rather tempered irony, although nonetheless an indication of a willingness to tackle a political issue. "Kissing" is a witty story that meditates on the value to men and women alike of a taxonomy not of species but of kisses: "How much more important to general happiness, is a significant and *understood* meaning of kisses, than a knowledge of the particular class and species of the inanimate curiosities flung from the briny wave" (243). The plea for such a classification is illustrated by an anecdote of misunderstanding between the sexes based on a misinterpreted kiss, but the novelty of the story lies less in the execution of its plot than in a certain saucy vitality that is prepared to discuss the difference "between the kiss snatched *publicly* with a *smack* from the pouting lips of the laughing hoiden, and the silent kiss, imprinted stealthily and noiselessly upon the same lips" (242–43). Curtis and Farley, for all their unwillingness to take on critiques of women's economic oppression, were less timid about challenging attitudes toward female decorum implicit in their society and the consequent diminution of the force of women's writing.[13]

These small movements toward realism are not characteristic of most of the submissions to the *Offering,* but they are frequent enough to suggest a developing trend. Although debates still continue today about the origins and ideology of this amorphous and contested mode, there exists a limited consensus on the appeal of realism to women writers because of its emphasis on a circumscribed and knowable sphere of home, family, community, and workplace. Realism values acuteness of local and temporal observations, precision, a vernacular voice, and a capacity for mimetic representation of detail, the latter talent thought in the nineteenth century to be a particular gift of women. Realism explores the interaction of character and the material world, especially the world of money, capitalism, and the commodification of everyday life. It challenges Romantic and idealist values by testing them in the crucible of the mundane, and finds satire, irony, and parody appropriate modes for exposing conflicts and incongruities.[14] The freshest and most original contributions to the *Offering* are those that come closest to this realist mode. Often their impact is reinforced by their juxtaposition to the kinds of pious, romantic, farfetched, and formulaic literature they satirize, a distinct advantage of the magazine's eclectic format for raising the consciousness of its readers.

The very first issue of the first series of the *Offering* presents just such an incongruous positioning. A distinctly conservative essay on "Woman's Proper Sphere" is followed by the lively and irreverent "Recollections of an Old Maid," two pieces that show enormous divergences in attitude and style among the operatives in treating the role of women. The essay is a tribute to female domesticity, sympathy, and humility, in fact just the kind of piece that earned the magazine its genteel reputation. It insists that woman's true sphere is private and asks, apparently with no sense of irony from its factory author, why a woman should "leave the pleasant duties that await her at her own fireside." The writer warns the woman who would stray abroad: "Let her beware that in the *enlargement* of the circle, the *nature* of its influence be not changed." The language is formal, literary, and metaphorical, characterized by phrases such as "the poisoned arrows of slander," "elevating and ennobling is the duty," "methinks, a holier ambition," and the "gaudy flowers of flattery" (ser. 1, no. 1: 3–4). The "Old Maid's Recollections" are prefaced by a letter to the editor from the author, "Betsey," that suggests a very different voice and vision of womanhood: "That I have never been married, is not my own fault, for I never refused an offer in my life" (4). The writer defends old maids vigorously and humorously: "They form a large proportion of our authoresses; they are the founders and pillars of Anti-Slavery, Moral Reform, and all sorts of religious and charitable societies; and last, (though not least), in country towns where no weekly sheet is published, they are extremely useful in carrying the news." The "recollections" that follow the introductory letter contrast sharply with the pious dispensations of sympathy and moral influence from "woman's proper sphere." First the author introduces her protagonist, Ruthy; she was "pale and slender as the lily of the vale, and her little soft white hands would of themselves have been a sufficient guarantee of her claims to lady-ship" (5). By comparison, the author confesses that she was "about as broad as I was long, with a face as round as a full moon, and cheeks as red as peony, and owned a pair of hands which had been lengthened and wid-ened, thickened and roughened, reddened and toughened, by long and inti-mate acquaintance with the wash-tub, scouring-cloth, and broom-stick" (5). Ruthy quickly becomes a caricature of the nineteenth-century lady, with "delicate nerves, the dyspepsia, and long finger-nails." She "never appeared lively, and seldom in any degree cheerful"; she lacks "that hilarity which is the result of health and vigor"; and she fills her books with poems and morbid quotations that mawkishly anticipate Mark Twain's Emmeline Grangerford:

> I know that soon my time must come
> And I shall be glad to go;
> For the world at best is a weary place,
> And my pulse is getting low. (6)

Ruthy plays the piano and reads a great deal of poetry, and lacks only a "beautiful name" like "Henrietta, or Georgiana, or Seraphina, or Celestina" to be a perfect lady. However, when Ruthy becomes a penniless orphan in need of someone to maintain her, she rather drastically marries a widower with seven children, ten cows, "and all the other appurtenances of a large farm" (6). The stage seems set for a bitter denouement, but the story's witty realism permits Ruthy's salvation from neurasthenia through her immer-sion in meaningful work. She is saved from her effete delicacy by useful labor so that, by the end, she is healthy and hearty, can make butter and cheese, and has "almost wholly given up the piano, but plays admirably upon the cook-stove" (7). The realist story, like the idealist essay, does not remove the heroine from the household—instead that sphere becomes a center of work and productivity: Ruthy makes butter and cheese rather than exuding holy influences.

One other curious way "Recollections of an Old Maid" presages a future central anomaly of realist fiction is in its attitude to art itself. Ruthy's unhealthy effeminacy is signaled by the fact that "she played on the piano" and "read a great deal of poetry" (6); her realist recovery is measured by the extent to which she is able to abandon these indulgences in favor of practical activities. The paradox of a new aesthetic mode premised on anti-aestheticism already hints at the ever more inward turning ironies of realism that reach their climax in the work of William Dean Howells, a writer who would surely have delighted in the early efforts of factory women. In a sec-ond set, "Recollections of Betsey, No. 2," in the next issue of the *Offering*, the pseudonymous "Betsey" pursues once again her literary debunking of behavior and language that is refined and artificial. Her protagonist, Caroline, is "in bondage to a set of laws, the basis of which seemed to be, that nature was always vulgar" (ser. 1, no. 2: 21). Caroline pursues her "*beau ideal*" by marrying a Boston merchant who fails in his business and abandons her, while her pragmatic, plain-Jane antagonist marries a young man who peddles a more modest and unromantic range of merchandise: "he kept an assortment of calico and molasses, thread-lace and board-nails, Jews-harps and spelling-books, Russia-linen and stick-liquorice, black satin and brown sugar, white muslins and blue crockery, hard soap and fish-hooks" (22). The story is carefully constructed to parallel and contrast the two women, and to present its debunking of artifice most artfully: the "Russia-linen and stick-licorice, black satin and brown sugar" are as pleasing literary tropes as the rhyming description in the previous story of hands that had been "thickened and roughened, reddened and toughened." Like the satire of Ruthy's aestheticism, the argument against Caroline's evasion of nature works by literary methods that are radically different, but no less conscious of technical skill, than their "*beau ideal*" predecessors.

Although Betsey's "Recollections" are a witty deflation of the popular Romantic notion of a ladylike woman's aspirations, they still portray marriage itself as holding out the possibilities of affection and empathy, as well as pragmatic compromise. However, the *Offering's* story "The Wedding Dress," by "Hannah," pushes far beyond this benevolent view to a much more sardonic investigation of the institution. The story is set in the contemporary factory world of Lowell and begins with two operatives engaged in one of their most pleasurable activities, "namely, a shopping expedition" (1: 33). The playful and satiric tone, which assumes a good deal of familiarity in the audience with the conventions of popular romances, appears immediately in the description and naming of the two women workers: "The taller of the two had the brightest eyes, and the reddest cheeks, and a profusion of long ringlets, mingling with the laces and roses which adorned the interior of her pink silk bonnet; yet, though possessed of far more outward beauty than her companion, she is not the heroine of my tale, and will be dismissed without even the mention of her name." The true heroine, "milder and less brilliant," is Laura, "for upon that pretty name we have decided, albeit our hero is no Petrarch" (34, 35). The Lowell of the story is an avowedly materialist city, with the shopkeepers "lounging over their counters" in the daytime, while the operatives work, waiting for the evening's business after the women are released to spend their wages. In the meantime, they read books and newspapers, "from which they gleaned intellectual wealth, during those intervals in which the acquisition of any other was denied them." Laura is shopping for silk for a bridal gown, despite the complete absence of any likely groom: "I will purchase the dress, and perhaps kind fortune will send the man" (33, 34). Kind fortune does indeed send a man, but in this witty account of marital and material compromise, the man and the woman must make adjustments not to each other's character traits but to their physical and financial shortcomings in the worldly exchange of the marketplace of marriage.

Mr. Smith, Laura's suitor, is old and thus must sacrifice a certain degree of beauty and social rank in the woman he is likely to win. Laura, the (merely) moderately pretty daughter of a poor farmer, must accept gray hairs and an occasional touch of rheumatism in her wealthy suitor in return for her modest attractions. The imminent marriage portends "sad disaster to some of Mr. Smith's relatives, who had calculated upon his passing his life in a state of single blessedness." Laura's family, by contrast, thinks "of the manifold advantages which would accrue to their daughter" by her union with a rich man (36, 37). The language and action of the story are pervaded by the economic metaphors of calculation and advantage. Mr. Smith courts Laura by sending her a letter with a ten-dollar bill in it, an action the author says surprises the heroine but gives to the contents of the letter "a definite character, and an importance which would not otherwise have attached to them" (37). When Laura goes for advice not to her minister but to her factory superintendent, he, being "a plain, matter-of-fact, common sense sort of a man," examines the ten-dollar bill carefully to see if it is counterfeit (38). The curious focus, then, at the heart of this realist story is on the reality of a piece of fiction in the form of paper money, a symbolic representation of the real property that Mr. Smith owns, a symbol that is equally represented in the form of the wages that are exchanged by the superintendent for Laura's labor, and in turn passed on to the shopkeeper for the dove-gray silk for her wedding dress. The ten-dollar bill is the effective substitute for the larger material reality behind it, just as this realist story is.[15] "Hannah" distances herself from making any judgment on the mercenary marriage by arguing that it is Laura's decision and not the author's:

> It may be objected to this tale, that we have not depicted a heroine, influenced by those noble and disinterested motives, which should sway the heart of woman in her choice of a partner for life. If so, the fault is not ours; and according to the latest accounts, Laura does not regret the decision she so hastily made.

She concludes her story with a bemused account of the incongruous hopes of other Lowell girls when they engage in the traditional ritual of placing a piece of Laura's wedding cake under their pillows: they "dreamed of rich old bachelors, and love at first sight, and all such agreeable novelties" (39). Thus the factory author's satire goes to the core of her fellow workers' capacity to conflate love and money, idealism and materialism, girlish dreams and womanly reality.

Although few of the contributors to the *Offering* reach the consummate level of literary awareness of "Hannah," many are alert to the literary formulas that were beginning to characterize their magazine. In "A Letter,"

H. H. provides a witty survey of the *Offering*'s favorite genres, in the course of describing her own frustrated efforts to write something that will be pleasing to its readers. She first considers submitting a description of her birthplace, "the pond, the brook, the forest and hill," but finds she does not have the requisite skills for what was indeed a highly favored nostalgic mode, perhaps represented in the magazine more than any other category of writing. Her second choice is the question of "LABOR," its "uses and abuses and ... its consequences, moral and physical." She finds, however, that her attempted account turns so narrowly to the personal that, "like the country member's speech in parliament, 'it savored strongly of *turnips*.'" She gives up on composing something romantic such as "*moonlight on the waters,*" and she admits she has sense enough not to try poetry. She abandons a love story when she cannot think of a suitably catastrophic conclusion, and finally decides that all her wasted efforts "will do for curl-papers, if nothing more" (5: 108). Harriet Farley provides a similarly ironic account of an attempt to transcend the mundane in her essay "A Weaver's Reverie," a description of the soul's flight from the factory floor into the empyrean. She begins by leaving her "circumscribed spot" by her looms in order to look through the window at the sky and to imagine herself wafted to clouds free from noise, machinery, and all worldly burdens. Her transportation, and the language in which it is conveyed, grow progressively more ecstatic and immaterial: "I would fain be where there is no other, save the INVISIBLE, and there, where not even one distant star should send its feeble rays to tell of a universe beyond, there would I rest upon that soft, light cloud, and with a fathomless depth below me, and a measureless waste above and around me, there would I——." Just as she seems about to wax completely insubstantial, she is recalled abruptly from the void to the banal routine of the factory floor: "'Your looms are going without fill-ing,' said a loud voice at my elbow; so I ran as fast as possible, and changed my shuttles" (1: 188, 190). The juxtaposition of genius and curl-papers, transcendence and shuttles suggests a will, and sometimes a capacity, not merely to mock the old aesthetic norms but also to find modes of writing that will encompass the clashing new worlds of these aspiring operatives.

The most frequent literary device for embodying conflicts and contradictions is irony, with its juxtapositions, reversals, and parodies of conventional forms and attitudes. Occasionally, however, an author will find a symbolic figure of such richness of allusion (as with the ten-dollar bill in "The Wedding Dress") that the composition moves beyond the exposure of fake Romanticism, hypocritical idealism, and false sentiment. Rather than merely criticizing the current conventions of reading and writing, these compositions suggest their authors' recognition that consciousness itself is changing and with it the old ways of knowing and interpreting the world.[16] In "The Village Chronicle," "Lucinda" explores the various meanings of a village newspaper for a brother and sister who respond to it from very different situations. For the younger sister, who stays in the town where she has always lived, in rural New Hampshire, the local paper is a compendium of formulaic literature, tedious reports of village life, and irrelevant legal announcements. For her brother, who receives the paper in his log hut in western Kentucky, every word resonates with vital connections to the people and places that make up the mental scenery of his former life. The sentimental poetry that makes his sister "as sick as a cup-full of warm water" evokes in the brother a sense of the ethereal poet herself; the very unoriginal fiction that the sister parodies mercilessly reminds the brother of a childhood adventure with its author (2: 354). The notice of an auction of "the late old Mr. Gardner's farm" is dismissed as uneventful by the sister but marks a turning point in the brother's life, for old Mr. Gardner was the sole obstacle to his marriage to his sweetheart. In an interesting reversal of gender stereotypes, it is the brother who reads the paper in a wholly personal way while his sister makes critical generalizations. In addition to the responses of the siblings, the narrator of "The Village Chronicle" implies still another way of reading the newspaper "text" by means of her lengthy catalogue of the numerous "puffs" in it. These range from promotions of brand-name products, "Pease's Hoarhound Candy," "Bullard's Oil-Soap," "Taylor's Spool Cotton," to extravagant claims for the advertised commodities, "Universal Panacea" and "Unrivalled Elixir" (356, 361). The chronicle that bores the sister and moves the brother thus additionally becomes a reading lesson in a commodified culture that is penetrating into the remote rural byways as well as the factory towns of New England.

Not many of the *Offering*'s authors are as adept as "Hannah" or "Lucinda" at finding an adequately allusive symbol like the ten-dollar bill or the village newspaper, or even "H. H.'s" curl-paper manuscripts. Nor are they always able to yoke the contradictory attitudes they record toward religion and materialism, gender and class, morals and manners into satisfactorily poised ambiguities and pleasing ironies. Frequently the contradictions in their accounts remain contradictions. The incipient realism of the *Lowell Offering* is hesitant and sporadic; more of the contributions are sentimental and nostalgic, morbid and allegorical, and their conventional avowals of duty and love to God and family avoid rather than confront the paradoxes of the changed world. The apprehension of the new industrial order emerges in much of the writing of the operatives as a literary engagement with the rural world they left behind.[17] Although the industrialists' conception for the early New England factory system was as a semipastoral middle ground between rural and urban life, and between family shelter and personal independence, the operatives' writings suggest that the folkways of the family farm and rural community were receding fast for them into the realm of memory and legend. Both Harriet Farley's diligence in documenting the advantages of factory labor for women and Sarah Bagley's militancy in advocating reforms in working conditions focus on the present and future industrial realms, but a large number of the women who contributed to both the *Offering* and the more politically radical *Voice of Industry* turned to their disappearing past with fascination and some regret.

A long heritage of literary and folkloric tropes is available for elegiac subject matter, and the factory women repeat choruses of "Where are they now? Where those friends with whom I enjoyed so much of happiness?" with a certain formulaic regularity (ser. 1, no. 4: 58; ser. 1, no. 3: 46). With some editorial encouragement, the contributors eventually diversified from formal apostrophes and regrets to more specific recollections and produced valuable and detailed accounts of rural customs and legends, closely akin to the kind of New England lore that pervades the tales and romances of Nathaniel Hawthorne. Reminiscences of country weddings, village parties, Pope Night mischief, and parish witchcraft are related with an enthusiastic extravagance that elicited footnotes from the editors assuring readers that the stories were not fiction but had actually occurred. Many of the incidents have the quality of oft-told family and community tales, embellished and transmitted through several generations, full of colloquialisms and hints of quaint dialect. They belong to a literary mode distinct from the many pious and elevated meditations on transience and mortality that are rarely touched by vivid local color, and they are equally distant from the ironies and paradoxes of the authors' emergent realist explorations of contemporary factory life. In her study of the literature that emerged from industrialization in Britain, Susan Zlotnick notes the absence of female nostalgia for a preindustrial past.[18] By comparison, the *Offering*'s authors produce accounts of their recent heritage that are affectionate, bemused, and often tender, although they are frequently recollections of childhood rather than explorations of adult working women's experiences in the two environments. These American writers' memories are also pervaded by patriotic affection for the days of the early republic and by a sense of national loyalty. Inevitably they mitigate both class and gender as exclusive keys to any "generalizable identity" of factory women and insist on multiple sources of their self-awareness.

Besides their memoirs and reminiscences, one of the more traditional literary modes chosen by contributors to the *Offering* was poetry, also a favored form in more militantly political periodicals. Workers composed formal odes, such as "The Tomb of Washington," and satires of their own extravagant literary aspirations, such as "Parody on Hohenlinden." They also transcribed the words and music of popular songs, imitated the dialect poems of Robert Burns, and playfully burlesqued the advertisements that pervaded their lives:

When summer showers wash earth and flowers,
What can a fair girl do,
If she's without a thick and stout
Elastic Rubber Shoe? (4: 273)

One poem, "Fancy," by "Fiducia," is an interesting amalgam of Romantic yearnings for pastoral pleasures, grim Puritan distrust of frivolity, and realist acquiescence to the time- and machine-bound world of the factory. Its opening lines suggest considerable assurance on the part of the author in yoking the imagery of the mill to the vaulting imagination of the worker poet:

O swiftly flies the shuttle now,
Swift as an arrow from the bow;
But swifter than the thread is wrought,
Is soon the flight of busy thought;
For Fancy leaves the mill behind,
And seeks some novel scenes to find. (1: 117)

The truant worker relishes visions of enchantment—feasting, dancing, manly youths and leafy bowers—but recognizes the danger of such fantasies:

Remember, in thy giddy whirl,
That I am but a factory girl;
And be content at home to dwell,
Though governed by a "factory bell." (118)

The paradox of the worker eloquently articulating the need to restrain her imagination, in a poem intended for wide public dissemination, is a pleasing one that suggests that even the poetry of humility may be a pretext for self-assertion.

Some of the more ambitious poets, like Lucy Larcom, clearly used the opportunity offered by the magazine as an occasion for literary experiments in form and voice, and not simply as a way to demonstrate properly modest attitudes. An interesting case in point is the nineteen-year-old Larcom's poem "Complaint of a Nobody," in which the first-person narrator, "Y. M.," describes herself as "an unsightly weed," "vain" and "useless," yearning for oblivion: "None look upon me with delight." Harriet Farley, shaken from her usual aesthetic sophistication by the seeming self-belittlement of the young woman, added a concerned "editor's note" to the poem, stating that the author could "not mean to intimate that she is a *nobody*" (3: 207). Many years later, Lucy Larcom noted with amusement in her memoir, *A New England Girlhood*, that she had not indeed considered herself a weed, that the unhappiness of the poem was an affectation, and that many of her early "absurdities" were written "chiefly as exercises in rhythmic expression" (213, 214, 215). A number of such ambitious contributors to the *Offering* admitted the self-conscious literariness of their efforts by recounting in the course of their submissions what they knew to be the acceptable forms and subjects for the magazine, by parodying its more hackneyed genres, and by explicitly stating their dissatisfaction with their own writing and their desire to improve it. They also revealed how eagerly they studied the forms as well as the content of their factory publication. Examples of such literary engagement are rarely a feature of more activist publications like the *Voice of Industry,* where parodies of traditional literature usually serve the cause of political satire rather than concerns about the relationship of style to substance.

Sarah Bagley's and many later scholars' dismissals of the *Offering* as a refined and high-toned betrayal of workers' interests, and even more as a denial of their working-class identity, are a portent of the criticism that would recur repeatedly over the next century as a succession of other marginalized and previously unprivileged groups entered the literary field. Just as operatives hazarded the charge of class treachery if they did not focus their writing on the oppressions of factory life, so middle-class women at the same time faced the charge that their writing was a betrayal of their femininity if they did not stay within the narrow bounds of domestic and devotional topics. Later, a central critical debate on African American writing concerned its obligation to deal with racial injustice first, and the parallel contention that other literary and aesthetic concerns must not take precedence over the primary obligation to the social needs of the group. A case for the defense of the literary integrity of the *Offering* might be more easily made if it had not had the tacit approval of factory owners, and if its literary innovations had been bolder, but such a case would again raise the problems, suggested by Dimock, of trying to construct too neat a series of metonymic correspondences for a magazine that was the product of many different authors and social forces. The tendency to oppose the ladylike and aesthetic concerns of the *Offering* to the class solidarity and political militancy of the *Voice of Industry* diminishes the complicated sense of identity and conflict that was emerging in the writing of New England factory women, even in a potentially compromised magazine like the *Lowell Offering*.[19] Immersed in a world of getting and spending, the women were still adherents of an avowedly antimaterial religion that denied simultaneous loyalty to God and Mammon; feeling their wild oats as independent working women, they still felt profound obligations and affections toward families and lives left behind; displayed to the world by one group of men as model workers and exposed by another as the debased products of the factory system, they were attempting to define their own identity. What united them was their sense that books and the written word might become for the first time a powerful means of connecting working women to each other as well as to a national, and even international, literary community.

3

Across the Gulf

The Transcendentalists, the *Dial,* and Margaret Fuller

> She was at once impressible and creative, impulsive and deliberate,
> pliant in sympathy yet firmly self-centred, confidingly responsive while
> commanding in originality. By the vivid intensity of her conceptions, she
> brought out in those around their own consciousness, and, by the glowing
> vigor of her intellect, roused into action their torpid powers.
> —WILLIAM HENRY CHANNING, 1852

> She is the child of genius, and as such must be an idealist; a veil is between
> her and the rude, practical, every-day, working world. She may write,
> and teach, and call herself a laborer, but this brings her only into distant
> relationship with us.
> —*THE UNA,* 1853

In January 1843, on the receipt of the latest issue of the *Lowell Offering,* the editors of the *Dial* announced, "We are happy to learn that our modest and far-famed contemporary has a large and increasing subscription" (3: 416). When the *Dial* wistfully congratulated the *Offering* on its widespread readership, the transcendentalist magazine had been courting both obscurity and ridicule for more than two years. Its "Prospectus," issued in May 1840, had been distinctly in the ambitious and optative mood, compared to the Lowell women's humbler aspirations. The *Dial* promised that it would be "A Magazine for Literature, Philosophy, and Religion," in which fields it would "recognise every sincere production of genius," "attempt the reconciliation of the universal instincts of humanity with the largest conclusions of reason," and "seek to discover the presence of God in nature, in history and in the soul of man." Besides these lofty goals, the journal would provide instruction and amusement and also commit itself to a fixed price, a regular publishing schedule, and even a precise page length for each issue—three dollars per annum, four issues a year, each of 136 octavo pages (Myerson 47–48). By comparison, the *Offering* had committed itself to no agenda beyond the publication of factory operatives' writing, and it proved sufficiently flexible in its publication schedule to make adaptations in form, size, and frequency as conditions required. The empyrean ideals of the *Dial* and the prominent social and intellectual status of its contributors prevented an indulgent reception of the high-minded journal from the outset, unlike the generous and sometimes condescending response given to the *Offering*.

The extravagant ethereal musings of the *Dial* were immediately parodied mercilessly by other journals and newspapers, but more serious critiques also challenged the insulated elitism of its authors, as well as the magazine's intellectual irrelevance to the contemporary world, and the artistic shortcomings of its literary efforts. Nathan Hale, Jr., in a telling metaphor, found the *Dial*'s blood "more *blue* than *red*" (Myerson 49). Thomas Carlyle accused it of turning its back on the contemporary "cotton-spinning, dollar-hunting" world of the nineteenth century and urged, "Come back into it, I tell you" (56). Edgar Allan Poe wrote scathingly of William Ellery Channing's poems "they are not precisely English, nor will we insult a great nation by calling them Kickapoo; perhaps they are Channingese" (qtd. in Mott 709). Although the *Dial* never exceeded three hundred subscribers in its four years of existence, and seemed more doomed than the *Offering* to "waste its sweetness on the desert air," it has nonetheless merited a great deal of attention from literary historians. Such interest is due not only to the subsequent eminence of many of its authors but also to the magazine's emblematic representation of one extreme of American Romanticism coming to its own eccentric terms with some of the great questions of the age. Curiously, many of these questions, although framed in the remote and abstract language of transcendentalism, were quite congruent with the concerns of the *Offering*: concerns with identity and self-culture; with personal codes of belief and social reform movements; with the value of work in an increasingly materialist world; with changing attitudes toward women and the working class; and with the functions of reading, writing, and the evolution of new literary forms. Thus, although barriers of gender, class, education, and belief separated the two symbolic realms of Concord and Lowell, there was good reason for the magazine of the former to salute that of the latter with some recognition of the mutual grounds of their endeavors.

Perhaps the most remarkable similarity between the *Dial* and the *Lowell Offering* was the coincidence, in the early 1840s, of their editorship by women. Harriet Farley and Harriot Curtis edited the *Offering* from 1842 to 1845, and Margaret Fuller edited the *Dial* during its first two years, 1840–42. Both Farley and Fuller used their editorial discretion to publish a good deal of their own writing, so that, under their guidance, the journals gave something of a double measure of attention to their favorite topics. Indeed, Fuller wrote of her editorial opportunity in her private journal: "It is now proposed that I should conduct a magazine which would afford me space and occasion for every thing I may wish to do" (qtd. in Fink 61). The *Offering*, by definition, published only women writers, and it is notable that almost all contributions to the *Dial* by women were published under Fuller's editorship. Although the magazine, under Emerson, continued to publish a good deal of her personal work after she had left it, almost no other women's work appeared in it after her departure. Fuller also assumed the editorship for another reason that might have resonated strongly with the Lowell factory women—she desperately needed a source of income to contribute to her family and help send her brothers to Harvard, and her work as a schoolteacher had proved inadequate. She was promised a salary at the *Dial* of two hundred dollars per annum, but ultimately her amateur standing was assured by the failure of the journal to pay her for her considerable labors. Although Fuller's superior education and privileged membership in the bourgeoisie separated her, in terms of class, from the factory women of Lowell, she worked as an exhausted and uncompensated editor and writer at the *Dial*, sacrificing health and comfort for its elevated goals. Then, in 1844, she accepted an offer from Horace Greeley to work for his New York *Tribune* and became a regularly employed and paid working woman. Her career movement from unpaid writing to paid work is, in some respects, the reverse of some of the Lowell operatives' trajectory, from wage labor to voluntary unpaid writing, but there is a common nexus of concerns in her world and theirs with women's work, with their reputation, with the social reforms of the age, with the life of the mind, and with the struggle to find new ways of writing about these subjects.[1]

Fuller's editorship of the *Dial*, as well as her own contributions to it, emphasized particularly the relationship between women and literary and intellectual life. She questioned the appropriateness of traditional high literary forms such as poetry to writing about women's domestic conventions and Romantic aspirations; and asserted the need for women to recover or recreate a female ancestry, mythology, and body of symbols appropriate to an evolving consciousness and commitment to self-culture. She and Sophia Ripley explored the tensions between the appeal of society and that of solitude for nurturing women's self-development, and the conflicts between marriage and self-reliance. Although Emerson continued to publish Fuller's feminist writings after he took over full editorial responsibility from her, no other contributors in the last years of the magazine's life demonstrated much interest in the concerns of gender. They did, however, pursue the topics of social reform, the nature of work, communal and private experience, and the life of the mind and of the body, from a purportedly ungendered perspective, although one that was nonetheless suffused with the language of manliness. Fuller eventually challenged the association of good writing and masculinity but, like the editors of the *Lowell Offering*, she had to struggle with pervasive assumptions (including her own) about the gender and class status of the literate individual, intent on leading an examined life.

One of the recurrent preoccupations of the women writing for the *Lowell Offering*, and particularly of its editor, Harriet Farley, was with their degraded reputation as factory workers, a reputation concisely described, as mentioned earlier, by Orestes Brownson as "almost enough to damn to infamy the most worthy and virtuous girl" (370). The effort to counter such accusations of debasement goaded the *Offering*'s contributors into demonstrations of virtue, integrity, and literary refinement that led more politically militant women to rail at their ladylike aspirations and brand them traitors to their class. To be literary risked betraying their working-class credentials. For the largely middle- and upper-class contributors to the *Dial*, literariness should have posed no comparable risks, but in fact, Nathan Hale's comment that its blood was "more *blue* than *red*" raised the possibility of an even more embarrassing literary betrayal, since Hale's jibe suggests not merely the cultural elitism of the *Dial*'s contributors but a thinly veiled charge of a less than robust masculinity. This was an insult to which both Fuller (at that time) and Emerson were likely to be peculiarly sensitive, since the vocabulary of manliness and masculinity pervaded their writing as a term of critical approval. Emerson distinguished between literature with a "*feminine* or receptive" cast and that with a "masculine or creative" one, and he displayed praise for one of Fuller's *Dial* pieces by hailing it as "manly" (qtd. in Packer 447, 449). In Fuller's writing, "womanliness" eventually emerges as a high ideal complementary to manliness, an ideal to which both a female and a male writer might aspire, but the association of the prissy and the effete with the feminine was profoundly and recalcitrantly embedded in the language of the time. If male transcendentalists feared that their writing might seem feminized and lacking red blood, how much more complicated was the dilemma for Fuller, seeking to find a woman's way of writing without sacrificing her "manly" repute.

When Fuller's *Dial* essay "The Great Lawsuit" was published later in book form, as *Woman in the Nineteenth Century*, Lydia Maria Child wrote a review that suggests her tactful awareness of Fuller's predicament. Child makes a diplomatic effort to find a vocabulary that mediates between these seemingly opposing gendered ideals of womanliness and manliness, praising Fuller's powerful intellect and vigorous style, and referring to her as both "author" and "authoress," terms that were highly contested at the time.[2] She also identifies Fuller's voice as "a contralto voice in literature: deep, rich, and strong, rather than mellifluous and clear" (qtd. in L. Reynolds 220–21). Emerson, whose "anxieties ran deep," according to Barbara Packer, about the possible unmanliness of all art, urged Fuller playfully to include more controversial material in their magazine, to rival Brownson's provocative *Boston Quarterly Review* (447). "O queen of the American Parnassus, I hope our *Dial* will get to be a little *bad*," he wrote to her, without precisely proposing any specific realm of Olympian naughtiness (qtd. in Packer 446). However, when Fuller directed the magazine seriously toward the feminism of "The Great Lawsuit," it was, ironically, the "bad" boy Brownson himself who reprimanded her, and even invoked the Holy Ghost to put the queen of Parnassus in her place, reminding her that "dominion was not given to woman, nor to man and woman conjointly, but to the man" (qtd. in L. Reynolds 215). Criticized for womanly docility and unwomanly overreaching, with neither model nor peer for an American female Romantic, Fuller made her idiosyncratic way as *Dial* editor for two years and main contributor for four, both setting the agenda and remaining at the mercy of the vagaries of its other authors.

The *Dial*, like the *Offering*, displayed a variety of literary and generic forms in its writing, although one of the operatives' favorite modes, fiction, had almost no appeal for the transcendentalists. The *Dial* avoided this less elevated mode and perhaps consequently paid less attention to the daily concerns of women's lives. In fact, the only fiction in the *Dial* was by Fuller herself, in the form of allegorical and symbolic fables. Eventually she moved toward essays, albeit essays that drew on many devices, such as anecdotes, dialogue, and imagined incidents and characters that evoked the methods of fiction. The essay format proved considerably more versatile and reflective of Fuller's favorite mode—conversation—than the lush and mannered Romanticism of her fictional sketches. Whether the other *Dial* contributors felt that fiction was an innately "unmanly" genre, or whether its realist and materialist tendencies were ill suited to their transcendentalism, the magazine gave very little attention to fiction writing, even in its literary reviews. Among hundreds of book reviews over its four-year life, the only mentions of fiction are brief comments on Hawthorne's *Twice-Told Tales* and on the *Fables* of La Fontaine (3: 130–31; 413–14). Emerson has several essays on contemporary writing but there is no novel mentioned in his "Thoughts on Modern Literature," and in "Europe and European Books," he describes himself as one of those "who do not read novels" (3: 519). For this latter essay he apparently forced himself to the task, and he is largely contemptuous of the shiploads of books from England that "give some tinge of romance to the daily life of young merchants and maidens" (518). Even to discuss novels at all is, for Emerson, a descent into "gossip" which he breaks off in "mid volley," with an unfilled promise to resume at "a more convenient season" (521). Harriet Farley's "Fiction: A Dialogue" in the *Offering* had examined many of the same objections to fiction as a "trite, insipid" substitute for gossip or a distraction for "love-sick damsels" but Farley had also provided a powerful defense of novels and had ultimately condemned the "cant abroad in society" about " 'the pernicious effects of novel-reading'" (2: 255). The transcendentalists' preferred literary form was poetry, but their most successful and innovative one in the *Dial* is the essay, which they infused with poetry, fiction, and drama—with lyricism, narrative, and dialogue—and adapted variously to their individual voices.

In the first issue of the magazine, Fuller revealed her determination to balance the rather theological cast of many of the contributions with an emphasis on literature and aesthetics. She included reviews of painting and sculpture exhibitions, an essay by Emerson on "Modern Literature," and her own "Short Essay on Critics." In this essay she asserted that the true test of the critic was "manliness": "We would converse with him, secure that he will tell us all his thought, and speak as man to man" (1: 10). Since the *Dial* publications were unsigned and ostensibly anonymous, the gender of the author would lend no incongruity to this assertion. However, before the end of its first year Fuller emerged from her "man to man" posture with two pieces of visionary fiction that began to establish a distinctly female authorial voice and set a different agenda for women's writing. During Fuller's earlier years, she had thought of George Sand's fiction as a possible model for her own writing, but she had later decided that she "would not write, like a woman, of love and hope and disappointment, but like a man, of the world of intellect and action" (qtd. in Chevigny 57). The paradox of attempting "writing like a man," when her particular subject was woman's self-development and intellectual awareness, led Fuller into a series of literary experiments with Romantic fables that drew on mythic and elemental images of femaleness. These literary tropes were almost inevitably bound to echo the gendered language and attitudes of the "woman's sphere" advocates of the 1830s and 1840s, whose arguments for the creation of a female subculture drew on essential images of womanhood for conservative rather than radical purposes. Gradually she came to reconsider the salience of this imagery for her own literary vision. Fuller's fables explore the various options for the aspiring woman thinker: of entering into deep associations with men, of communing apart with other women, and of withdrawing into solitude. Like the women of the *Offering*, she struggled greatly to choose and invent literary modes to embody her new concerns: "For all the tides of life that flow within me," she wrote, "I am dumb and ineffectual, when it comes to casting my thought into a form. No old one suits me" (qtd. in Chevigny 63). Her contributions to the *Dial* reveal some of her evolving forms, but like many newly working women whose lives and identities were in flux in the nineteenth century, she progressed through many genres as her circumstances changed.

The two fables, "Meta" and "The Magnolia of Lake Pontchartrain," that Fuller published in the third issue of the *Dial* are fictions in the sense that they have imagined characters, and are allegorical, symbolic, and preternatural in their incidents, but they have nothing in common with the domestic and realist stories and novels that other women writers were fashioning at the same time. They have more kinship with the "flower" allegories that appeared in every volume of the *Lowell Offering*, although they substitute evocative Romantic scenes and situations for the simpler didactic narrations of the factory women. "Meta," originally composed in 1833, is a ghost story about the return of Meta, the dead wife of the poet Klopstock, to her mourning husband—an event that occurs in a context dense with emotive imagery and feminine symbolism. Meta's appearance is anticipated by a sad song on the harpsichord and by the shadowed radiance of the moon, "nearly at the full." Meta, clad in "a long veil of silvery whiteness," comes to console her distraught husband, a role she shares in the afterlife with her mentor, Petrarch's Laura (1: 293, 294). Taken in isolation from Fuller's other work, Meta seems a traditional embodiment of essential female virtues, devoted as she is to nurturing, inspiring, uplifting, and sympathizing—a portrait not at all incompatible with the ideal of "true womanhood." However, taken in the context of her later *Dial* pieces, the fable may be seen as an early stage of a process Jeffrey Steele calls "Fuller's sexualizing of Transcendentalist psychology," a process whereby supposedly "neutral" (though in fact male) ideals of self-culture and spiritual awareness are applied to the condition of women (Steele, *Self,* 126).

Fuller's note at the beginning of "Meta" suggests that she was familiar with Anna Jameson's *Memoirs of the Loves of the Poets* (1829), a work by an early feminist biographer that contained an account of Klopstock and Meta. Jameson professed as her intent to show "how much of what is most fair, most excellent, most sublime among the productions of human genius, has been owing to [women's] influence" (qtd. in Booth 257). "Meta," dated shortly after the publication of Jameson's book, follows the influential biographer's approach, but in her subsequent *Dial* fables, Fuller moved beyond praise for this accessory role for woman, as influence and partner to genius, into a consideration of the solitary female soul in search of its own sublimity.[3] However, even when she considers women as independent individuals (rather than partners or lovers), Fuller's early essays display the curious paradox whereby the literary feminist selects her illustrations from the same canon of foremothers, goddesses, allegorical characters, and heroines as the most conservative essentialist of her day. A similar evocation of traditional female models (Cleopatra, Joan of Arc, Minerva, Josephine, Laura) drawn from myth, history, and literature dominates the essays and allegories of the Lowell workers in the *Offering.* In their magazine, however, such writing is mixed with both topical realist fiction, with its variety of modern female protagonists, and very numerous documentary accounts of the experiences of contemporary women, laboring in a newly industrialized world. When she moved to New York, Fuller would eventually acquire a comparable field of current references for writing about women's lives, but while she was with the *Dial,* her models for womanly self-culture were more mythic than topical.

The mode of Fuller's next quasi-fictional piece, "The Magnolia of Lake Pontchartrain," is again allegorical, although unlike the *Offering*'s novice allegorists, Fuller does not belabor the correspondences. Nevertheless, the suggestions of the flowers, queens, vestals, and princesses that pervade the "Magnolia" clearly indicate that the fable is once again about gender and spiritual aspiration. The sketch tells of a sorrowful male stranger on the banks of the lake who is drawn by a magnolia's fragrance into a conversation with the female flower. The man is sensitive to the language of flowers and listens avidly as the magnolia tells of her previous incarnation as an orange tree. In that role, she suggests, she lived too vividly and too much in the world: "I was never silent. I was never alone. I had a voice for every season, for day and night." After she undergoes a wintry death in which she loses all feeling, she is reincarnated as a "vestal princess" in the form of the magnolia, "purer, of deeper thought, and more capable of retirement into my own heart." Withdrawal from the world, self-cultivation, even a season of wintry dormancy all contribute to her present ability to "feel the Infinite possess me more and more" (302, 303, 304, 305). Jeffrey Steele, in his detailed reading of the fable, concludes that "the Orange has changed from being an other-directed 'true woman,' valued only for the 'fruit' she bore, into the independent Magnolia, dedicated solely to her own spiritual development." He suggests that the magnolia, like Fuller herself, is able to resist the voices that call her back from assuming her role as solitary spiritual adventurer: "She could relinquish the sanctioned roles of wife and mother for that of 'imperial vestal' dedicated solely to her own development."[4] Interestingly, Harriet Farley, in "A Weaver's Reverie," was simultaneously seeking such solitary transcendence. However, whereas Fuller permits a mystical reincarnation of her "other directed woman," Farley forces her cloud-borne factory idealist back into the realities of her class and gender with the intrusion of a "loud voice" that reminds her, "Your looms are going without filling" (1: 190). Even if the factory woman is able to renounce the socially sanctioned claims of gender, she cannot renounce the economic necessities of class that bind her to her looms. Eventually, Fuller, too, would acknowledge other contingencies that hindered women's intellectual and spiritual development, but during her tenure at the *Dial* she devoted her writing largely to questions of gender and to the self-reliant woman's relationships to male models and mentors.

Reviewers responded to the third issue of the *Dial,* containing the "Meta" and "Magnolia" pieces, with disgruntled comments on its dreamy mysticism, calling it "rich in the profoundly allegorical and the hopelessly obscure" (qtd. in Myerson 62). However, in the context of her later work, Fuller's sketches are clearly a step toward her goal of generating female legends and creating alternative divinities to the masculine ideologies she believed pervaded the spiritual consciousness of her New England contemporaries.[5] She followed up "Magnolia" in the fourth issue with the even more ecstatic fable "Leila," a visionary evocation of a female spirit and "Saint of Knowledge," who is conjured from the nighttime depths of a lake (465). Leila is a mysterious and powerful female divinity, wrought from contradictions and paradoxes, evoked in rhapsodic prose drawn from the symbolism of nature and the suggestions of myth, far outside time and history. The contributors to the *Lowell Offering* likewise insisted on the mysterious forces of female energy and authority in a series of essays on heroines and queens, including Zenobia, Joan of Arc, Cleopatra, and Pocahontas; and in their repeated allusions to a canon of women writers. However, despite the frequent presence of supernatural females in their imaginings, from ghosts and witches to fairies and sprites, they did not (like Fuller) take the more daring intellectual step of creating rival female divinities or elevating the goddesses of other mythologies to equal status with the divinities of their Christian religion.

Fuller's speculative boldness contrasts with the more traditional religious attitudes of the Lowell workers. For example, although they shared with her a fascination with the Shakers and with their female spiritual leader, Mother Ann Lee, they stopped far short of endorsing Lee's views on the male and female duality of God. Fuller, by comparison, was willing to combine highly unorthodox beliefs with Christianity to create what Steele calls "theological hybridity" (*Transfiguring* 103). He argues that Fuller was becoming increasingly aware of the need for women to gain control of some means of "ideological reproduction" that might counter the power of male-generated theological myths from the pulpits of New England ("Limits" 118, 130). By making Leila into what Steele calls "a composite goddess who blends facets of Diana, Isis, the Virgin Mary, and Sophia into a female messiah-figure" (*Transfiguring* 83), Fuller moved well beyond the factory operatives' orthodox frame of reference. Curiously however, Leila, as a hybrid female divinity, has one womanly attribute that might well have received the enthusiastic approval of the Lowell factory women: she is strong and vibrant rather than frail and delicate. Wild-haired, bare-foot, dynamic, Leila has none of the physical fragility that had come to be associated with the feminized spirituality and virtue of the nineteenth century. If consumptive imagery was burdensome to women like Fuller, from privileged and educated backgrounds, who wished to associate female power with robust assertiveness, it was doubly so for factory women who, despite performing arduous physical labor, were praised for being pallid, slight, and genteel in their demeanor. Thus Fuller's definitions of vigorous female divinities were, in a bodily if not yet in a spiritual sense, more appropriate to the lives working-class women were leading.

A few months later, Fuller added "Yuca Filamentosa" to the developing pattern of her *Dial* pieces, exploring, by means of exotic nature imagery, "in woman what is most womanly" (2: 287). The narrator here searches for a floral emblem to represent the goddess Diana and finds it in two *Yucca filamentosa* plants that flower together in the light of the full moon. Once again, spiritual authority emanates from female divinities and flowers with feminine associations and magical powers. Steele notes Fuller's attribution of the origins of her botanical narratives to a personal family acquaintance, Dr. William Eustis, who related the stories to her during a visit in October 1840 (*Transfiguring* 72–73). However, the botanical field of reference was already a central convention in women's writing, exploring not only the aesthetic beauty of flowers but also their mystical associations with occult languages, mythologies, and systems of reference. The *Lowell Offering*'s authors turned continually in their tales and allegories to botany and especially to the suggestive qualities of flowers, but Fuller extended the boundaries of this allusive and allegorical mode in her *Dial* pieces in conjunction with a more original feminist investigation of imperial selfhood and solitude. She used her fables in original ways to explore the sacrifices and rewards of female withdrawal from worldly affairs and from human companionship, and she used flowers like the yucca, the orange tree, and the magnolia that were outside the most familiar range of codes of correspondence. Later, as she moved into the writing of journalism and history, and into more pragmatic considerations of contemporary women's experiences, her frame of reference shifted to the topical world of politics and society, and the allegorical receded in the face of the real.

Fuller took her first major step away from the mystical mode in the January 1842 issue of the *Dial* with an essay on Bettine Brentano's letters to Goethe, followed by her own translation of extracts from a series of German letters between two women friends, from Brentano's epistolary novel *Die Günderode*. Published under the title "Bettine Brentano and her Friend Günderode," the essay's critical idiom is markedly different in its restrained and analytical tone from the rhapsodic excesses of her fictionalized sketches. Fuller continues to pursue the question of female self-development but now with a new wariness of male mentors. She contrasts Bettine's slavishly adoring relationship to Goethe to the reciprocal and complementary one revealed in the correspondence with her woman friend. The relative equality of the two female friends makes possible such benefits as "harmonious development of mind by mind, two souls prophesying to one another, two minds feeding one another, two human hearts sustaining and pardoning one another" (2: 322). Fuller does not pretend to argue that it is solely the discrepancies of gender that make the relationship of Bettine and Goethe seem "fantastic or even silly" (322). She concedes that there are large gaps between the two in age, achievement, and worldly power, but other examples in her essay of female intellectual intimacy suggest that she now sees the more equal relationship between two women as a preferable model to that of "Idol and Idolater," as she refers to the imbalance between male mentor and female admirer (314). Fuller uses her translation and commentary on the women's letters as an inventive way to pursue her own evolving ideas about alternative modes of living for the woman who wishes to lead a life of the mind, either actively immersed in the world, like Bettine, or meditatively withdrawn, like Günderode.

The literary genre of translation and Fuller's own intervention into the correspondence of two women with preoccupations highly compatible with her own is a compositional strategy that allows her to commune intimately with other women's texts and pursue a kind of discipleship with them.[6] The *Dial* published many other translations and numerous critical commentaries, but only Fuller produced a hybrid literary form that blended the two into a creative symbiosis that illustrated the model of female interaction that was her subject. Fuller argues that an intimate friendship such as exists between the two young women is "essentially poetic," a quality that she finds equally present in the sympathetic exchanges of "very common-place girls," whose correspondence is marked by "a fluent tenderness, a native elegance in the arrangement of trifling incidents, a sincere childlike sympathy in aspirations that mark the destiny of woman" (319–20). Although her actual association with such commonplace young women was still some years away, Fuller's intimation of the poetic nature of their lives and friendships had its parallel in the Lowell factories, and especially in the artistic vision of the young Lucy Larcom, at this time a nineteen-year-old beginning her literary career at the *Lowell Offering*.[7] Larcom described her factory friendships as based on the grounds of the workers' "deepest sympathies and highest aspirations, without conventionality or cliques or affectation" (*New* 225). Her response to them would eventually result in *An Idyl of Work*, her epic poem about the poetic community of young working women, itself a significant vindication of Fuller's insights and hopes.

The culmination of Fuller's writing in the *Dial* came in her long essay "The Great Lawsuit. Man *versus* Men. Woman *versus* Women" in the July 1843 issue. The title alone indicates a large shift from the flower symbolism, timeless mythology, and mysticism that pervaded the earlier semifictional sketches to a dialogue with social institutions and contemporary reality, a shift that was signaled even more clearly in the blunt and topical title of the expanded and revised book version, *Woman in the Nineteenth Century* (1845). Despite an introductory section replete with transcendental abstractions, Fuller soon moves to the contemporary condition of women in her society with a provocative allusion to the common championship by reformers of the situation of women and of "the enslaved African" (4: 9–10). She employs imaginary dialogues, invented characters, literary and historical allusions, sober analysis, and extravagant proclamations in order to argue for female self-reliance or "self-centeredness," and to propose means and assess obstacles to its attainment. Although she reiterates some of the themes of the earlier allegories, such as the need for women to detach themselves from the world and from the mentorship of men in order to "come forth again, renovated and baptized," the evolution of her thinking on questions of gender is marked by a new-found resistance to male imagery as a positive trope for describing female achievements (46). Miranda, her fictional alter ego in the essay, notes that formerly she had been flattered when a friend said that she "deserved in some star to be a man"; she had acceded to calling an admirable woman in literature "manly"; and had agreed to praising a strong woman by affirming that "she has a masculine mind" (16, 17). Now she writes of women: "Were they free, were they wise fully to develop the strength and beauty of woman, they would never wish to be men, or man-like" (23). Now she appears to be reevaluating the power of mythical and classical literary women. After reviewing the reputations of Sita, Isis, Ceres, Diana, Vesta, Cassandra, Iphigenia, Antigone, and many others, she notes the discord between the imaginative force of these women and the actual status and power of women in ancient societies. She constantly returns to this paradox. Large portions of the essay are devoted to the discrepancy between representations of the "Idea of woman" and the distorted reality of women's lives, born of the gap between the "mental faith" embodied in the images and "the practice" pursued in the world (22, 27). As an ardent lover of literature, Fuller takes pleasure in the great female creations of past cultures. Nevertheless, she boldly asserts the restrictions and incongruities imposed on the imagination of the modern woman by a failure to scrutinize the favorite myths of the past.

Fuller's movement throughout "The Great Lawsuit" is progressively toward a focus on the condition of real women in the present time, but her sense of the contemporary American woman at this stage in her life is a decidedly class-bound one that envisions women as leisured, domestic, and largely outside the pressures of the marketplace. They have time to read books and, unlike men, "are not so early forced into the bustle of life, nor so weighed down by demands for outward success"; "Their employments are more favorable to the inward life than those of the men," and they are generally exempt from "a low, materialist tendency" that is characteristic of the larger American society (39). If such women lead confined and restricted lives, it is nonetheless a privileged confinement that comports strangely with analogies to slavery, and takes no account of working women less insulated from the marketplace and its low materialist tendencies. Indeed, Sarah Bagley at Lowell had somewhat sardonically remarked in the *Offering* that a great advantage of factory life was the opportunity for silent meditation enforced on women by the deafening machinery (ser. 1, no. 2: 25). Fuller's immunity to the circumstances of the majority of women would change dramatically for her with her move to New York and her experiences as a reporter among women with no chance to seclude themselves from the bustle of life. When she did later encounter them, in forcible seclusion in Sing Sing, Fuller proved more than capable of bringing them into her circle of womanhood. She observed the incarcerated women to be "frank" and "decorous," explained to them that she was writing about Woman, and found that they replied to her "in the same spirit in which I asked." Looking back to her literary "Conversations" with the gentlewomen of New England, she commented on the prisoners, "All passed much as in one of my Boston classes." In 1846, when she visited the Mechanics' Institutes in Manchester and Liverpool, where instruction in the "higher branches" of education had been recently extended to working-class girls, she approved the development as evidence of a society where "true civilization is making its way" (qtd. in Chevigny 335, 349).

In "The Great Lawsuit," Fuller continues to propose, as she had done in her mystical sketches, some notions of womanhood that are essential in that they belong naturally to the sex, but at the same time are not necessarily present or dominant in individual women. She argues that such womanliness or "Femality" is ideally part of a complex balance of male and female qualities that exist in differing combinations in individual men and women: "Male and female represent the two sides of the great radical dualism. But, in fact, they are perpetually passing into one another. Fluid hardens to solid, solid rushes to fluid. There is no wholly masculine man, no purely feminine woman" (43). Thus what might seem a gendered stereotype of the sexes becomes a rallying call for fusion: "Let us have one creative energy, one incessant revelation. Let it take what form it will, and let us not bind it by the past to man or woman, black or white" (44).

Since Fuller's interest in "The Great Lawsuit" is not so much in what she calls the "Apolloizing of man" as in the "Minervaizing of woman" she explores how women may best develop their intellectual consciousness. Pursuing the suggestions of her "Magnolia" and "Bettine" pieces, she advises them to withdraw from the tutelage of men, "retire within themselves, and explore the groundwork of being till they find their peculiar secret." "Let her put from her the press of other minds," she proposes, "and meditate in virgin loneliness." Thus the goal of the "self-centred" woman is to be achieved by temporary withdrawal from the world of men, by education under the guidance of women teachers and mentors, by celibacy, and by retirement inward to explore "the groundwork of being" (46). Although Fuller mentions, without censure, the more activist roles played by some of her contemporaries—in seeking women's suffrage, in public speaking, in the reform of property laws, in the abolitionist movement—her emphasis, in accord with her transcendentalist contemporaries, is on the mental revolution within the private individual rather than in reforming structures and laws. Although Fuller expanded the public and practical reform implications in her revision of "The Great Lawsuit" for its publication as a book, she also enhanced what Larry Reynolds characterizes as its "residual intellectual elitism" (x). Her efforts to negotiate between an original feminist impulse and an inherited literary language of traditional womanhood, between the need for private revolution and that for public reform, between the larger condition of women and the unique situation of Margaret Fuller brought inevitable contradictions and inconsistencies of argument and style into her essay, which was greeted with praise and censure from all points on the ideological spectrum. Like most of the other *Dial* Romantics, except perhaps Bronson Alcott, the more closely their idealism encountered the realities of the time, the more likely they were to engage in a dynamic exchange with those realities. This was increasingly true for Fuller after she left the *Dial* and the Boston world, but the seeds of her future conflict and its direction were already sown in her writing for the magazine that she hoped to make her instrument.

George Eliot, who reviewed the expanded book form of Fuller's essay, *Woman in the Nineteenth Century*, immediately noted both the vagaries of the author's literary strategies and the paradoxes they revealed. Noting that Fuller's mind was "like some regions of her own American continent, where you are constantly stepping from the sunny 'clearings' into the mysterious twilight of the tangled forest," Eliot found abrupt transitions from "forcible reasoning" to "dreamy vagueness." However, Eliot was sympathetically conscious of the dilemma Fuller was facing: "On one side we hear that woman's position can never be improved until women themselves are better; and, on the other, that women can never become better until their position is improved—until the laws are made more just, and a wider field opened to feminine activity" ("Margaret" 233–34). Eliot has no difficulty envisioning a current of action and reaction that might flow back and forth between the former idealist and the latter realist positions, but Fuller's circle at home was less attuned to such worldly compromises and more willing to challenge her motives as personal rather than universal. Her friend Sophia Hawthorne wrote to her mother somewhat caustically of Fuller's "Great Lawsuit," "What do you think of the speech which Queen Margaret Fuller has made from the throne? It seems to me that if she were married truly, she would no longer be puzzled about the rights of woman" (qtd. in Chevigny 231–32). Even Fuller's friend and ongoing patron Horace Greeley found inconsistencies between her literary insistence on egalitarianism between the sexes and her personal ladylike expectation of traditional male courtesies. He noted that "while she demanded absolute equality for Woman, she exacted a deference and courtesy from men to women, *as* women, which was entirely inconsistent with that requirement" (qtd. in Chevigny 236). Such comments suggest not merely the censorious nature of Fuller's audience, especially in her own circle, but also the limitations of her personal experience and class background that inevitably hampered her efforts to reconcile, as the *Dial*'s original proclamation put it, the largest conclusions of reason with the universal instincts of humanity.

Contemporary feminists, looking back to the 1840s, have pondered the virtually irresolvable question of the extent to which Fuller was the product of her time and the extent to which she was consciously adopting some of its language and values in order to challenge others more effectively. Donna Dickenson, in considering this question of the "'hegemony' of a cultural discourse," notes the extent to which "The Great Lawsuit" reflected "the baleful influence of the cult of True Womanhood," but she suggests that this was the language Fuller *had* to speak in order to reach her audience. Of Fuller's Romantic individualism, Dickenson is equally understanding: "Clearly Fuller should not be blamed for failing to foresee a twentieth-century analysis of the actual harm that individualism does to women"; instead, "she should be praised for eventually beginning to sense the inadequacy of Transcendental self-reliance in her own way, in her own time" (112, 139). There is a general willingness to allow that Fuller's essay was indeed radical for its time and to withhold judgments based on more current feminist thinking about questions of essentialism or the appropriateness of Romantic ideals of individualism for women's movements that have later put a high premium on community and cooperation.

Fuller's class-bound notions of universalism have drawn less comment in the modern context, although one of the most interesting challenges to her bourgeois limitations emerged very soon after the publication of *Woman in the Nineteenth Century*. In a serialized novel, "Stray Leaves from a Seamstress's Journal," published in 1853 in the early feminist journal, *The Una*, the anonymous author sharply criticizes Fuller's class bias. Writing in the persona of a working-class woman who has eagerly read her book, she writes of Fuller: "She is the child of genius, and as such must be an idealist; a veil is between her and the rude, practical, every-day working world. She may write, and teach, and call herself a laborer, but this brings her only into distant relationship with us." The seamstress wishes that Fuller could "but come into our attics, our cheerless, comfortless homes, where there is nothing beautiful" so that she might realize, "how difficult, how almost impossible is self development where there is only the means of keeping soul and body together" (qtd. in L. Reynolds 231). *The Una's* critique is *not* of the aspiration to beauty, creativity, and self-culture in Fuller's work but of her failure to acknowledge the yearnings of women outside her own educated and privileged class, despite her many expressions of "universal sympathy." The writer asks, "Who will give to those who have artists' souls, (and such there are) the means to attain" (231, 232)? It is a question that tantalized and taunted working women as they confronted the strange yoking of opportunity and exploitation that accompanied the dramatic changes in their labor and their literacy and the discovery of their voices as speakers and writers. Fuller acknowledges the question in a narrow context in the *Dial* but is, as yet, unconscious of the larger group of women who were trying to negotiate an identity that assumed the better parts of womanliness and manliness and also allowed them self-development without betraying other acute needs of their fellow workers. Her revulsion, like that of many in the *Dial's* circle, from the "low materialist tendency" of American society at large kept her, at this stage of her career, somewhat remote from the dilemma of *The Una's* seamstress or the *Offering's* factory operatives. Her later experiences in New York and Europe led her into more direct engagement with lower-class women and the opportunity to test her *Dial* theories in a radically different sphere.

One of the areas in which Margaret Fuller did find herself in harmony, perhaps unknowingly, with her working-class contemporaries was in her challenge to the assumption that marriage and dependency on men was the natural and desirable condition for women. Barbara Packer notes that Fuller "is even willing to hail as a sign of greater self-reliance the growth of that class contemptuously called 'old maids.' (No greater proof of Fuller's courage could exist than her willingness to make that claim in print)" (534). Fuller does indeed celebrate the advantages of the woman, "not needing to care that she may please a husband," who may turn all her thoughts "to the centre, and by steadfast contemplation enter into the secret of truth and love, [and] use it for...all men" (4: 36). However, when Fuller published these comments in the *Dial* in 1843, the *Lowell Offering* had already tackled and thoroughly explored "that unlucky, derided, and almost despised set of females, called spinsters, single sisters, lay-nuns etc." in both satirical essays and sentimental fiction (ser. 1, no. 1: 4). "Betsey's" comic "Letter about Old Maids" in the first issue of the operatives' magazine had suggested that they were part of a providential design to make valuable contributions to every aspect of a community's life, not least of which was that "they are extremely useful in carrying the news" (5). In the next issue of the *Offering*, "Tabitha" had pursued the subject farther with a contribution on "Old Maids and Old Bachelors: Their Relative Value in Society," arguing that Old Maids exerted a better influence even though they were the offspring of an old woman whose name is "Necessity" and who dwells "in the Valley of Want" (ser. 1, no. 2: 30). In the second series of the *Offering*, begun in 1841, "F. G. A." published the story of "Susan Miller" who, on her father's death, gives up her prospects of marriage and leaves her home village for factory work in Lowell, in order to pay off family debts. Susan is rewarded not only by "the approbation of conscience" but also by "strong friendships among her factory companions" (1: 170). A "Maiden Meditation" in the 1844 *Offering* promotes "single blessedness" and ridicules the narrow mental focus of married women on their children (5: 122). Although some of the "Old Maids" who are defended in the *Offering* have come by their status through necessity rather than choice, and use it for helping others rather than for contemplation and self-development, others claim to have chosen their single condition because "the very thought of matrimony always affected me like a fit of ague" (121). The liveliness of the magazine's defense of their situation—as independent, self-sufficient, and happy in their women companions—suggests that the debate on female celibacy and autonomy was very much in the spirit of the times for working-class women when Fuller joined it in the *Dial*.

Fuller's challenge to marriage for women was actually preceded in the *Dial* by a feminist essay on the topic by Sophia Ripley, a close associate of Fuller who later became, with her husband George, one of the organizers of Brook Farm. Published in the first year of the magazine and entitled "Woman," Ripley's style in this essay is as simple as Fuller's is extravagant—exposition largely unadorned by historical and mythological allusions or dramatized scenes of conflict. Ripley suggests that the topic of "the sphere of woman" is current and controversial, and her ironic tone implies she will not be timid in tackling it: "even the clergy have frequently flattered 'the feebler sex,' by proclaiming to them from the pulpit what lovely things they may become, if they will only be good, quiet, and gentle, attend exclusively to their domestic duties, and the cultivation of religious feelings, which the other sex very kindly relinquish to them as their inheritance" (1: 362). At the core of Ripley's brief essay is an effort to align the ideals of individual self-reliance with the ideals of marriage, a goal that raises a lingering and tacit question about whether the two states are, even in their most perfect manifestations, ever quite compatible. In this tentative way, Ripley prepares for Fuller's more radical call for female celibacy. Ripley is more conventional in her assumption that marriage is the condition to which most women naturally aspire, but also more liberated from mythic notions of femaleness. Her satirical account of poetry's idealized Eves or Ophelias "wrapt in a silvery veil of mildest radiance" (362), or of woman etherealized as an angel who hovers and glides around her literary lover, is uncomfortably close to

Fuller's Romantic Leila and Meta. Ripley argues that such a "spiritualized image of that tender class of women [that the poet] loves the best" is "one whom no true woman could or would become" (362). For her, the true woman is she who is "encouraged to think and penetrate through externals to principles," who questions, anticipates, forms her own ideal, and walks alone: "She should feel that our highest hours are always our lonely ones, and that nothing is good that does not prepare us for these" (365). However, for Ripley, walking alone means, somewhat paradoxically, being married to a "chosen companion," on whom woman should not, nevertheless, depend. Instead she should "attend on him as a watchful friend" and with him fulfill "her high vocation of creator of a happy home" (365, 366). The tension between lonely hours and true companions, between tough thoughts and happy homes, between walking alone and attending on a friend reveals the fundamental oxymoron that is a transcendentalist marriage and the frustrations of defining one.

The consideration of the mutual aspirations of a transcendental partnership was a task assiduously avoided by male transcendentalists, with the exception of the celibate Thoreau. He acknowledges the tacit paradox of Ripley's essay in his *Dial* poem "Free Love," in which he recognizes an inherent contradiction between the freedoms and compromises of idealist partners. Thoreau, unlike most of the male contributors to the *Dial,* did not marry, and the logic and rhetoric of much of Sophia Ripley's essay would seem to lead to the same conclusion for woman, who, she argues, is currently "a dependent," "half a being," "an appendage," and "under possession" (364, 363). However, Ripley suggests neither withdrawal from male society nor the necessity of education and tutelage by other women. Indeed, in the present state of society, she seems to be wary of the leadership of women, whom she sees as more ready to censure the woman who aspires to self-reliance. Between them, Fuller and Ripley, despite their class-bound limitations, raised questions of profound importance about the applicability of the philosophy of Romantic individualism beyond the realm of its first privileged male adherents. However, their feminist challenge was largely ignored elsewhere in the *Dial,* despite its many other efforts to scrutinize the reform movements of the age in the light of its idealism.

A review of the male contributions to the *Dial* gives no hint that the situation of women was among the controversial reform questions of the age, or that the ideals of transcendentalism and Romantic individualism might, if applied to both sexes, cause grave turmoil in the lives of many of the *Dial's* authors. Only Thoreau risked, obliquely, pursuing the intellectual implications of partnerships between equally aspiring men and women, although Emerson would eventually come, in later years, to support women's suffrage. Ironically, the blindness of male transcendentalists to the difficulties their idealist pursuits imposed on their wives and families produced a sardonic literary response from some of the women most directly affected. Emerson's wife, Lidian, wrote a satirical "Transcendentalist Bible" in 1845 that mocked those who rejected "sympathy" in favor of "the noble, self-sustained, impeccable, infallible self" (qtd. in Cole 74). Bronson Alcott's wife, Abigail, complained in her journal of the "invasion of my rights as a woman" and less privately, his daughter, Louisa, parodied her father's Fruitlands experiment in her "Transcendental Wild Oats," noting the burden placed on her mother by her father's idealism (qtd. in Rose, *Transcendemtalism* 127). The *Dial*'s male contributors displayed a lively interest in the abstract appeals and pitfalls of social reform as well as its specific manifestations in the fields of economics, labor, education, and communal living experiments, but they were more reluctant to pursue the area of reform that might have intruded most deeply into their personal lives and domestic arrangements. Curiously, even when they looked at the great changes taking place in factories and in the condition of the laboring class, they largely ignored the presence of women. Just as Ripley and Fuller tended to see women as a middle-class category, so the men of the *Dial* tended to see the working class as male; in both cases, working women were effectively excluded from their vision and were left to adapt whatever applications of Romantic idealism they saw fit.

John Sullivan Dwight's "Ideals of Every-Day Life" is representative of many essays by male contributors to the *Dial* in seeming, from its title and organization, more comprehensive than is its actual limited content. The two-part essay's structural division into "Work" and "Home" suggests a focus on realms often considered as male and female dominions, but in fact, Dwight's ideals take no account of gendered experience at all. In "Work," he argues that drudgery is subjectively determined by the attitude of the worker rather than the nature of the work: "There are intellectual and fashionable drudges. And there are hard-working, humble laborers, more free, more dignified and manly, in all they do, or look, or think, than any who look down upon them" (1: 310). Such an argument suggests a class awareness, albeit a nostalgic one, since the only example of an actual laboring person in the essay is the farmer, whose work is uplifted by his being "conversant with nature, the glorious scenery of his labors" (311). The outdoor and ever-changing environment of the farmer makes it easier for Dwight to heal the rift between mental and manual work that so troubled his contemporaries as they looked at the mechanized world of factory labor. He recommends that "thought" (310) be brought into the worker's everyday job, a task considerably more appropriate to farm work that to that of the operative, for whom "thought" was the escape from, rather than the intellectual accessory to, tending her looms.

If Dwight's recommendations in "Work" take no account of the labor of women, it might be expected that his essay "Home" would have a contrary bias, especially as he introduces the domestic world by way of the Bible parable of Mary and Martha. However, it is immediately apparent that Dwight's concern is with the home life of the *pater familias*, who moves between fireplace and marketplace, between the intimate circle and "one's business abroad" (1: 447). The plight of the father, lacking "inspiration" because his feelings are "soured or deadened by the anxieties, the severities, the questionable morals of a selfish system of trade," is alleviated only by the presence in his home of "a faithful angel . . . whose heavenly patience, whose devoted love, whose pure forgetfulness of self" enables her husband to recover himself through her self-abnegation (456). Writing as both a Christian minister and as a transcendentalist, Dwight is the first of many *Dial* writers to endorse the role of sacrificial Christian wives enabling the self-fulfillment of transcendentalist husbands, a pattern echoed implicitly, if not explicitly, in Ripley, Emerson, and Alcott.

Theodore Parker, like Dwight an ordained minister, published in the same first year of the *Dial*'s life his "Thoughts on Labor." Although a far more radical essay than Dwight's in its class consciousness, it is again indifferent to the dramatic changes in labor wrought by women's entry into the public workforce. Parker begins not with an individual ideal of life but with a social reality—the increasing disparity in mid-nineteenth-century America between the condition of people who produced and those who consumed or, in his metonymy, between "hands" and "mouths." Parker notes at the outset that every person has been provided equally with a pair of hands and a mouth: "the inference is unavoidable, that the hands are to be used to supply the needs of the mouth"(1: 497). Thus he chooses to subordinate the preferred allegory of his contemporaries, of hands and heads, to one that is wholly material and economic. His America is a place where a large class of "hands" labors disproportionately to feed a small class of "mouths" who have learned to be contemptuous of work and have acquired the means to avoid it. He notes an insidious tendency in his own class for rank and status to be associated with idleness while hard labor becomes increasingly the burden of the poor: "this aversion to labor, this notion that it is a curse and a disgrace, this selfish desire to escape from the general and natural lot of man, is the sacramental sin of 'the better class' in our great cities" (499). His socially egalitarian solution is to divide labor and its rewards equally, which would mean that people presently privileged would "sleep less softly, dine on humbler food, dwell in mean houses" as a result of work being more justly distributed (504). For Parker, the redistribution of work and wealth would have to take place at the social rather than the personal level in order to ensure that all workers would have time for the life of the mind. Although his language is colored with Emersonian rhetoric, it is not the specialization of work so much as the excessive weight of it that threatens the large class of people for whom he is concerned: "It is only a proper amount of work that is a blessing. Too much of it wears out the body before its time; cripples the mind, debases the soul, blunts the senses, and chills the affections. It makes the man a spinning jenny, or a ploughing machine, and not 'a being of a large discourse, that looks before and after.' He ceases to be a man and becomes a thing" (501). It is the exploited body rather than the delegated intellect that reifies Parker's laborers: his solution is a restructuring of work so that all members of society will have time to spend in "intellectual, moral, aesthetic, and religious improvement" (503).

Parker's essay appeared almost simultaneously with an account of a utopian dream, entitled "A New Society," in the *Lowell Offering* in 1841. Its author, "Tabitha," envisages a perfected American society (supposedly having come into existence by 1860) where no person should work more than eight hours a day and there will be a daily obligation of three hours of manual labor (or work for the general benefit), and three hours "cultivation of the mental faculties." Tabitha's ideally balanced life of "industry, virtue and knowledge" comes very close to the values articulated by Parker. Her most significant concern in addition to those of Parker, however, is her requirement that women be given identical wages to men, and that "every father of a family who neglects to give his daughters the same advantages for an education which he gives his sons, shall be expelled from this society, and be considered a heathen" (1: 191–92). Thus "Tabitha's" utopia would make precise provision for the oversights and omissions of noble universalist designs like Parker's that assume inequalities between classes but not necessarily within them, in the different conditions of the sexes.

By contrast with "Tabitha's" playfully imagined world (which also requires that young women engage in the art of writing) Parker ends with a dystopian parable about the imaginary village of Humdrum where inequalities in the distribution of labor create a class of criminals who are "the victims not the foes of society." His position is a strikingly deterministic shift away from the self-reliant codes of other transcendentalists, who must surely have felt some reservations about his statement that "their bad character was formed FOR them, through circumstances more than it was formed BY them, through their own free-will" (512). Parker's sense that individuals are not responsible for crimes that derive from social conditions leads him to look outward, rather than inward, when he contemplates reform, unlike his fellow *Dial* contributors Emerson, Dwight, and William Ellery Channing. Channing's 1840 lecture "On the Elevation of the Laboring Classes" noted with compassion the human destruction wrought by an industrial and market economy, yet finally insisted that workers must assume responsibility for their own condition and strive to remedy it by the elevation of their souls. The *Lowell Offering*, despite its respect for Channing, Emerson, and their principles of individual responsibility, published a sardonic "Laborer's Remonstrance" in 1842 that suggests that factory workers wanted more than compassionate admonitions to virtue from those with the power to effect social change. In this piece, a symbolic common man, Jonathan, castigates "nonproducers" and warns, "if you would reconcile me to my fate, consider the cause of the poor, and point out a remedy for the evils which they suffer. Look to the laws of society—look to the laws of the Statute Book; and if they not coincide with the laws of eternal justice, revise and correct them" (3: 20). Thus, although Theodore Parker may have omitted any consideration of the particular situation of working-class women in his "Thoughts on Labor," his sense of incipient class antagonism was shared and vindicated even in so generally apolitical an outlet as the operatives' magazine.

Among transcendentalists, the tensions between their growing awareness of the currents of power embedded in an industrial and urban society and their faith in the individual's capacity for self-determination were a counterpoint to the debates among workers in the *Lowell Offering*. The operatives demonstrated in their writing a comparable consciousness of economic determinism and private conscience, material conditions and spiritual aspirations. They, too, were distressed, like Dwight and Parker, by the increased distance between their daily work and the world of nature, although their nostalgia for their rural origins was notably more aesthetic and emotional than ideological. They remembered the beauty, the family affections, and the community celebrations of their rural past, rather than the ideally balanced and integrated life of head and hand that exerted such an allure for the Romantics. Although women factory workers fondly recalled aspects of their past lives, they were not inclined to elevate agrarian work over industrial, no matter how sharply they criticized the shortcomings of the industrial world. In "The Spirit of Discontent" in the *Lowell Offering*, two factory girls decide to compare candidly "a country life with a factory life in Lowell" and, recalling the isolation and hard labor of farm life, agree that, "since we must work for a living, the mill, all things considered, is the most pleasant, and best calculated to promote our welfare" (1: 113–14). Since the *Offering* had a policy whereby *not* all things were considered as appropriate matter for their factory writings, their enthusiasm for the mill is not entirely convincing, but their memories of the hardships of farm life are persuasively conveyed. Another piece in the *Offering*, "Life Among Farmers," presents farm life as grossly materialistic, driven by the hard work of production and the consequent heavy demands of consumption. As a result, women must provide sustaining and meat-heavy meals three times a day for men, and the outcome is that "there is a continual round of eating, cooking and sleeping, with the female portion; and no time for rest, recreation, or literary pursuits" (2: 135). Thus the farmers' daughters of Lowell noted that, for their mothers, at least, a farming existence was not especially conducive to the literary life, nor one that offered the ideal balance of physical and mental pursuits.

Only the maverick Orestes Brownson, among the transcendentalists, addressed himself directly to the impact of the alternative conditions of factory labor on women and, because of the particularly provocative qualities of his essay "The Laboring Classes," it tended to elicit militant defenses by female operatives who felt that their reputations were being impugned. Otherwise, transcendentalists, while attuned to many of the issues in debates about labor and reform, showed little interest in the transformation in women's lives that was taking place around them, although it proved to be a topic of considerable interest to Romantic fiction writers. Fiction, however, was uncongenial to the high-mindedness of the *Dial*, perhaps another reason why the journal's response to labor overlooked some of the most dramatic changes caused by women's entry into the workforce, even as its contributors turned their attention repeatedly to the changing world of work and the growing separation of classes.

Among the most frequent contributors to the *Dial* on the subjects of labor, contemporary social conditions, and the possibility of reform were Ralph Waldo Emerson and Charles Lane, the founder, with Bronson Alcott, of the short-lived experiment in idealist communal living at Fruitlands. Lane supplied a series of essays evaluating various communitarian experiments, while Emerson wrote regularly from the perspective of the independent who was skeptical of all collective activities. Although they do not engage in direct debate in the *Dial*, they constitute between them a kind of dialogue on corruption and reform in public and private life and on the role of the individual in bringing change. Emerson's first *Dial* essay, "Man the Reformer," was, like William Ellery Channing's essay "On the Elevation of the Laboring Classes," presented first as a lecture to the Mechanic Apprentices' Library Association in January 1841, the year following Channing's lecture. Anne Rose has noted that the Apprentices were already, by 1841, a slightly anachronistic group, learning a craft in an age of factory labor, and thus wary of the industrial progress that threatened their skilled status (*Transcendentalism* 110). Increasingly vulnerable to a marketplace that would force many of them into semiskilled work, the Apprentices were an anomalous audience for Emerson's appeal to the wealthy, the advantaged, and the privileged to permit the power of love to induce them to share and encourage the aspirations of the laboring classes. His advocacy of love is also tinged with a warning of the alternative: "Let the amelioration in our laws of property proceed from the concession of the rich, not from the grasping of the poor" (1:537). Emerson's rhetorical use of the first-person plural in his address suggests a consistent identification of himself and his listeners with the property owners who must concede rather than with the poverty-stricken graspers:

> See this wide society of laboring men and women. We allow ourselves to be served by them, we live apart from them, and meet them without a salute on the streets. We do not greet their talents, nor rejoice in their good fortune, nor foster their hopes, nor in assembly of the people vote for what is dear to them. Thus we enact the part of the selfish noble and king from the foundation of the world. (536)

The acute class awareness of such passages, as well as Emerson's sense of conflict and tension between "us" and "them," indicates that the questions of reform he is considering are both topical and urgent. However, early references in the address to the "demon of reform" and a long list of the many targets that are "threatened by the new spirit" (524) are advance notice that Emerson is not about to endorse any practical schemes of reform, even as he assents to the moral critiques of capitalism on which they are based.

Emerson appears more aware than many of his contemporaries, in this address, of the inappropriateness of opposing agrarianism to industrialism or commerce in a world where most young men (and it appears to be only men to whom he addresses himself) do not have access to a farm. The nostalgic return to the land and its harmonious demands on mind, body, and spirit are not available to modern man: bluntly put, "he has no farm, and he cannot get one." Since such integrated farm work is not a choice, Emerson turns to the advantages of manual labor "as a part of the education of every young man," and as a way, in an elaborately commodified world, for him to attempt to get "into primary relations with the soil and nature" (1: 527). By manual labor, Emerson appears to mean not so much arduous physical work as some kind of direct involvement in the process of producing necessities, a contact with the material sphere of life as a necessary counterpoint and prelude to encountering the realm of the immaterial. Thus, he argues, "we must have a basis for our higher accomplishments, our delicate entertainments of poetry and philosophy, in the work of our hands. We must have antagonism in the tough world for all the variety of our spiritual faculties, or they will not be born. Manual labor is the study of the external world" (528). Emerson severely qualifies his enthusiasm for manual labor later in the essay, when he admits that, for the poet, or for "men of study generally," "the amount of manual labor which is necessary to the maintenance of a family, indisposes and disqualifies for intellectual exertion" (530). Thus he seems to suggest that manual labor, at least for the man of letters, is something to be approached in a dilettante fashion, engaging in just enough to familiarize and stimulate, not so much as to enervate or debase. Alternatively, the man of letters may need to accept certain kinds of privation, including perhaps celibacy (531), in order to permit the desirable balance of conditions necessary for his pursuit of higher accomplishments.

This search for just proportions between arduous labor and mental elevation, combined with a recognition of the impositions of material needs and temptations, and of family and social obligations, is equally central to many of the factory women's contributions to the *Lowell Offering*. Contemporary communitarian movements, including the Shakers, Fruitlands, and Brook Farm, similarly struggled to adjust the balance between the life of the body and that of the mind by reorganizing the relationships between the individual and the family and the individual and the community. Romantic individualists, like Margaret Fuller and Thoreau, considered how they might reconcile their needs for solitude and society and, like many factory women, pondered the advantages of celibate lives. Emerson's essay is poised, if somewhat ambivalently, at the center of the topical debate between community reformers and individual radicals, between workers seeking the life of the mind and intellectuals searching for "primary relations" with the external world. "Man the Reformer" has been described by Robert Milder as both Emerson's most "'radical'" and his most "quietistic" pronouncement, and his advocacy of love as both "prescription" and "guilt-driven evasion" (Milder 65, 64). Anne Rose sees it as evidence of certain egalitarian strains in Emerson's thought because he addresses concerns about intellectuals to an audience of working men (Rose 117). Such a generous interpretation kindly overlooks Emerson's class recriminations and his advocacy of noblesse from the rich in order to pre-empt the urgent demands of the poor. However, Emerson's choice of topic and audience points to the important confluence of the worker, the thinker, and the reformer as central figures in the writing of Romantic idealists as well as in women operatives. Even so staunch an individualist as Emerson felt the need to participate, albeit somewhat evasively and uneasily, in one of the central cultural debates of the age and to recognize at least some of the omens of industrial capitalism that threatened a democratic republic.

Emerson followed up "Man the Reformer" with several other *Dial* essays that Milder describes as part of his journey from "social revolutionary (after his fashion) to liberal accommodationist (also after his fashion)." Milder comments that "Emerson was a hesitant or tardy reformer at best" on issues of gender, race, and class and was "disabled by his own personal and vocational anxieties about manliness from doing justice to the nascent feminist movement" (51–52). It is a severe criticism of Emerson if his per-sonal reservations might so easily subsume his principles, but it may also suggest a recognition on Emerson's part of the cataclysmic changes likely to eventuate from women's entry into the world of work, from their choice of alternatives to marriage, and from their assumption that the radical ideas he articulated were indeed universal in their application. The *Dial* essays that follow "Man the Reformer" display not only a trajectory from excitement to skepticism about the social possibilities of reform but also a complete omission of how women's concerns might affect general or universal argu-ments. Surprisingly, there is no direct engagement in the magazine between Emerson and Fuller, despite his highly interested private responses to her positions on the changing status and rights of women. Those transcen-dentalists, like George Ripley and Bronson Alcott, who included women and family life in their reform schemes quickly found themselves in con-tradictory, untenable, and seemingly hypocritical predicaments that Emer-son avoided by delaying his pronouncements until the muted and limited statements in "Woman" in 1855. In that later essay, Phyllis Cole has noted, "women were always and only wives, and the marital bond of sympathy went only from wife to husband" (Cole 85). Among male Romantics, the questions of sex and gender were most provocatively pursued by fiction writers like Hawthorne and Melville and were notable by their absence from the *Dial*, perhaps further evidence that it was genre, as well as gender, that raised obstacles for idealist essayists in treating changes in the everyday lives of people in different circumstances from their own.

Emerson continued to consider topical social and reform questions in his *Dial* essays, publishing in the third volume a series entitled "Lectures on the Times" that consisted of the essays "Introduction," "The Conservative," and "The Transcendentalist." He considered the subjects further in "Fourierism and the Socialists" and in the fourth and final volume of the magazine in "The Young American." In "Introduction," he argues for the value of studying the popular and the topical as a way of coming to understand the eternal, but in the list he makes of the elements of contemporary life that will function in the present as auguries of the future, there is no longer any evidence of the harsh view of trade and commercial life that set the opening tone for "Man the Reformer." The essay emphasizes instead the dangers of too hasty action on the part of reformers. By juxtaposing the ideal of reform with its inevitably limited reality, Emerson elevates the debate to a realm where any action is inevitably flawed and partial. Only inaction can maintain the untainted possibilities of a better future with absolute integrity. He argues, "I must act with truth, though I should never come to act, as you call it, with effect. . . . Whilst therefore I desire to express the respect and joy I feel before this sublime connexion of reforms, now in their infancy around us, I urge the more earnestly the paramount duties of self-reliance"(3: 12). The rather ominous opposition of "self-reliance" to "reform" can scarcely have been a good omen to the residents of the boardinghouses in Lowell who read the *Dial*. Emerson provides the rationale that was used by many later advocates of patience, as well as proponents of laissez-faire capitalism, to respond to demands for change. He argues that he prefers those who have "some piety which looks with faith to a fair Future, unprofaned by rash and unequal attempts to realize it." By contrast, he describes the actions of reformers as limited and self-indulgent—they demonstrate a "pusillanimous preference" of "bread" to "freedom" (3: 15, 18). Such arguments against rash and imperfect schemes of reform, and in favor of future perfectionism, will be repeated throughout the industrial novels of the remainder of the nineteenth century. However, these later novelists, as well as contemporary workers, acknowledged some degree of skepticism about admonitions to look "with faith to a fair Future" (15). Even the generally conservative and constrained Harriet Farley resists, in a *Lowell Offering* essay on long-suffering, advice to the poor to live in "silent acquiescence" and to "resign to others an undue share of the joys of this life"; and she warns, with surprising acerbity, that such tracts are unlikely to be read patiently by people who "are starving for want of bread" (2: 352).

Of Emerson's two "Lectures on the Times," "The Conservative" is particularly gnomic in manner, using riddles, myths, and fables to create paradoxes of the reforming conservative and the conservative reformer. Ultimately, Emerson decides he will abandon his "alternation of partial views" in favor of the "high platform of universal and necessary history" (3: 197). Curiously, he had, in 1842, returned Frederick Henry Hedge's

Dial submission "Conservatism and Reform" because he felt that Hedge was more interested in "intellectual play" than the issues at hand. At the time of Hedge's first delivery of the piece, as a Phi Beta Kappa address in 1841, Emerson noted in his journal, "It was the profoundest of superficiality. . . . The sentence which began with an attack on the conservatives ended with a blow at the reformers: the first clause was applauded by one party & the other party had their revenge & gave their applause before the period was closed" (qtd. in Myerson 161). Emerson's sensitivity to an audience's misappropriation of clauses that suited their predispositions and to the risks of intellectual play may well have been in his mind when he tactfully rejected Hedge's *Dial* contribution with the explanation that it was "too similar" to his own forthcoming essay "The Conservative."

In "The Transcendentalist," published in the *Dial* in 1843, Emerson adopts the rhetorical ploy of articulating the case made *against* his idealist contemporaries in amusing and exaggerated terms, cataloguing their flaws and inconsistencies. He purports to criticize the transcendentalists because "they hold themselves aloof;" "they prefer to ramble in the country and perish of ennui" (3: 303); "they are the most exacting and extortionate critics"; and they expose the flaws in their fellow men so that, for them, "the richly accomplished will have some capital absurdity" and "every piece has a crack" (305). Emerson invents facetious conversations between idealists and "the world," in which the former, when challenged, cling with comic high-mindedness to their principles, nonetheless acknowledging that "We are miserable with inaction. We perish of rest and rust" (308). Emerson's ultimate rhetorical strategy is to turn the humiliation, uncertainty, and irrelevance of the transcendentalists into the price of their loftier goals, and make their persecution, ridicule, and exclusion the cost of their integrity. Thus transcendentalists may justifiably withdraw from the current struggle for justice by the slave, the factory worker, or the pauper because their own demands are more exacting, their aspirations higher, since "they eat clouds, and drink wind" (306). Although it is a witty metaphor, it seems unlikely to convince the Lowell operative who is forced back from her own empyrean flight by her employer's demand that she fill her looms, or the seamstress who notes in her journal "how almost impossible is self development where there is only the means of keeping soul and body together" (qtd. in L. Reynolds 232). "The Transcendentalist" begins by admitting that idealism may be limited in the forms it takes by the particular historical context of its practitioners, but the author displays even more distaste for the materialist reformers whose objectives are "made up into portable and convenient cakes and retailed in small quantities to suit purchasers" (3: 307). Emerson does not question the similarly expedient appropriation of the idealist impulse by opponents of reform, in the equally convenient advocacy of self-improvement and future perfectionism.

The continuing paradox of Emerson's celebration of the idealism of democracy and diversity in a society of increasingly unequal opportunity culminates in his final *Dial* essay, "The Young American," published in the magazine's last issue in April 1844. The essay extols the future development of the nation's majestic natural resources by means of science and commerce. Railroads and canals have opened the vast territory of the nation, and now engineers, architects, and agriculturalists will subdue it: "This great savage country should be furrowed by the plough, and combed by the harrow; these rough Alleganies should know their master; these foaming torrents should be bestridden with proud arches of stone; these wild prairies should be loaded with wheat; the swamps with rice; the hilltops should pasture innumerable sheep and cattle; the interminable forests should become graceful parks, for use and for delight" (4: 489). This imperial subjugation of the land is presented as a natural law that exploits the present for the improvement of the future. Nature engages in a "cruel kindness, serving the whole even to the ruin of the member," and it brooks no interference on the part of tenderhearted reformers who would try to moderate the harsh effects of this natural law on those who are wasted in its service. Emerson argues now, almost fatalistically, "It resists our meddling, eleemosynary contrivances. We devise sumptuary laws, and relief laws, but the principle of population is always reducing wages to the lowest pittance on which human life can be sustained" (4: 493). He notes with pity the plight of Irish immigrants in his neighborhood, constrained to labor fifteen or sixteen hours a day, but even in this cruelty he finds a natural mitigation—the grueling work may act as a safety valve "for peccant humors; and this grim day's work . . . though deplored by all the humanity of the neighborhood, is a better police than the sheriff and his deputies" (487).

The harsh satisfaction that absolute exhaustion will prevent the Irish from following their devilish instincts is somewhat countered by Emerson's confidence in their American opportunities: "their children are instantly received into the schools of the country; they grow up in perfect communication and equality with the native children" (4: 487). Can the Irish immigrant then become the Young American? Can he evolve into the superior New England youth, who is destined, according to this essay, to emerge as the natural aristocrat of a movement toward a superior society? ("Which should lead that movement, if not New England? Who should lead the leaders, but the Young American?") Emerson does not explore whether this triumphant New England sectionalism might include either Irish laborers or women, who are, according to this essay, "trapped in an air-tight stove of conventionalism" (501). While he rejects the corrupting influence of the marketplace on men's lives, it is at least a vital and dynamic arena compared to the "custom" that he sees dominating women's existence and excluding them from any consideration as "Young Americans." In this, his final *Dial* essay, Emerson both celebrates an expansionist nation and acknowledges the existence within it of people who seem outside his definition of young Americanism. That such marginalized people should aspire to Romantic idealism or leadership was not perhaps beyond the reach of his imagination, but it was certainly outside the articulation of it in his *Dial* essays.

Between the conclusion of Emerson's "Lectures on the Times," in January 1843, and his final essay for the *Dial* in April 1844, the magazine published a series of articles by Charles Lane that explored many of the same social concerns as Emerson's. He also reported on a number of current communitarian and associationist experiments that attempted to implement the reforms of which Emerson was so skeptical. Lane was the cofounder, with Bronson Alcott, of the Fruitlands Con-Sociate Family scheme, which began in the summer of 1843 and collapsed by December of the same year, when Bronson's wife Abigail gave notice that she intended to move herself, her children, and "all the furniture" from the settlement, saying that she "feared for her husband's sanity" (qtd. in Sears 123). Lane wrote a two-part essay, "Social Tendencies," for the *Dial,* as well as accounts of visits he made to the Shaker and Brook Farm communities; he also wrote a piece entitled "Life in the Woods" on more solitary means of existence. The interest of the Romantic individualists of the *Dial* in the efforts of more community-minded utopians to establish new ways of forming societies was further pursued by Elizabeth Peabody. She wrote a description of the Brook Farm community and provided an account of the Fourierist principles on which it was based. Emerson, as editor of the *Dial*, proclaimed his exhaustion with the topic of reform by late in 1843: it "is a word which spoken once too often sounds very hollow, & in the Dial & in the circles of the Dial we have conjugated and declined it through all numbers & modes & tenses" (qtd. in Myerson 93). Nevertheless, in this case, his pragmatic desire to publish the writings of his friends and to fill the pages of the magazine triumphed over his reservations. Thus the *Dial,* despite Emerson's desire to focus on "the state of the heavens," continued to print accounts of experiments in earthly reform (qtd. in Myerson 87).

Peabody and Lane both placed a heavy emphasis on the desire to flee from the city and embrace rural life, and to engage in work that used both body and mind. Curiously, Peabody appears less interested than Lane in Fourierist and communitarian attitudes toward what he calls women's "oppressed and degraded condition" (4: 357) and to the relationship between the institutions of associationism and those of marriage. He speculates on whether the private family is compatible with the universal family and visits the celibate community of Shakers to seek answers. Lane is very drawn to Shaker asceticism, simplicity, and renunciation—indeed his criticism of them stems from their residual worldliness, their meat-eating, coffee-drinking diet, and their dependence on trade and money for items in which they are not self-sufficient. The *Lowell Offering*'s account of the Shakers, by contrast, notes the absence of libraries, books, periodicals, lectures, and lyceums in the community. While approving the communal living arrangements, the *Offering*'s reporter ultimately has strong reservations about a way of life that "seems to be a check to the march of mind"

(1: 340). Lane, more interested in the advantages and drawbacks of communal versus solitary life, continues to debate the question in "Life in the Woods," where he concludes that "solitude is a state suitable only to the best or the worst" and thus "an association of some kind seems more suitable, as it is evidently more natural" (4: 422, 423).

The progress of Lane's and Alcott's contemporaneous experiment at Fruitlands explains his hesitation among the options of solitary living, family life, and participation in a larger community that challenged the exclusiveness of the marital unit of husband, wife, and children. The Fruitlands community was created from two nuclear families (Lane and his son, the Alcotts and their children) and a number of single adults. Although Lane expressed frequent sympathy with the hereditary wrongs of women, and avowed the importance of admitting "female influence" into public decision-making, the communal life at Fruitlands quickly came to reflect the distribution of power in the society it was intended to renounce. Lane and Alcott undertook to lecture on their communitarian theories to the public, a decision that meant they were wholly engaged in the intellectual side of their endeavor, while Abigail Alcott was left with her children to perform arduous manual labor on the farm. She was not permitted the aid of working animals, which the male leaders refused, somewhat inconsistently, to "subjugate." Anne Rose has written of Fruitlands that "community life, as it was working out, merely accentuated the contrast in antebellum society between expanding opportunities for men and the menial work expected of homebound women" (126). But Abigail Alcott and her daughters did not sacrifice in silence. Abigail engaged in copious and critical correspondence about the endeavor, and she and her two older daughters (thirteen-year-old Anna and eleven-year-old Louisa) kept diaries, which also served as repositories of their letters to one another, and of poems and songs they wrote. In fact, their remarkable literacy about their work created a sub rosa and alternative female account of the same project Lane and Alcott were advertising in the more public forum of their essays, lectures, and books.

Anna's diary records days of exhausting farm labor and study, as well as the pleasures of reading, writing, and finally being given her own room in which to carry on her activities. She writes delightedly of this solitary female privilege: "It is to be my room and I to stay by myself in it" (qtd. in Sears 102). The privacy of her room was not sufficient, however, to protect her journal from Bronson Alcott's censorship and destruction when his disappointment at the failure of Fruitlands apparently overcame his encouragement of his daughter's literacy. The final entry in Anna's diary is for September 6—thereafter it "comes to a sudden ending," according to Clara Endicott Sears, one of the early compilers of documents from the project. Sears notes that "numberless pages have been torn out carefully, and Mr. Alcott's handwriting appears in footnotes here and there, showing that it was he who destroyed the story of the later days of Fruitlands written from his youthful daughter's pen" (Sears 104). Abigail evidently had more authority than Anna to protect her diary, in which she wrote that she was "almost suffocated in this atmosphere of restriction and form" (qtd. in Rose, *Transcendentalism* 127). Louisa's diary exhibits an even more feisty and rebellious spirit, but, unlike her mother and sister, she did not limit her caustic responses to the private and vulnerable medium of a personal journal. Louisa took her opinions to the public realm of the literary marketplace, publishing a satirical allegory of Fruitlands, "Transcendental Wild Oats," as well as novels in which she explored the discrepancies between her father's Romantic idealism and her mother's practical love.

Charles Lane theorized in the *Dial* that women resisted communitarian living arrangements like Fruitlands and Brook Farm because they were unwilling to put the human family ahead of the private one. Calling it "the grand problem," Lane wrote that the maternal instinct "has declared itself so strongly in favor of the separate fire-side, that association...has yet accomplished little progress in the affections of that important section of the human race—the mothers (4: 355). Emerson, in the context of the Fruitlands experiment, wrote in his journal in November 1843: "Married women uniformly decided against the communities....The common school was well enough, but the common nursery they had grave objections to. Eggs might be hatched in ovens, but the hen on her own account greatly preferred the old way" (*Emerson in Journals* 319). Reflecting back on the schemes of association twenty years later, Emerson came to a more realistic assessment: the members of the community "were unused to labor, & were soon very impatient of it; the hard work fell on a few, & mainly on women" (*Emerson in Journals* 541). However, neither Emerson's sally about hens and eggs nor his more sober comment on the exploitation of women's labor at Fruitlands acknowledges the real source of Abigail's frustration. She was neither attached to the old ways nor afraid of hard work. She was distressed, however, to find her family without material resources or any worldly training for acquiring them, when they were left to fend for themselves by men who abjured all taint of worldliness, including even the need for food. Abigail Alcott was, according to Anne Rose, no "less vitriolic than her husband in her criticism of society," but hers was "a working-class critique" from an unskilled laborer (203). Even before the Fruitlands fiasco, she had already determined "my girls shall have trades—and the mother with the sweat of her brow shall earn an honest subsistence for herself and them" (qtd. in Rose 202). Ironically, then, one result of the most extreme experiment in idealist living by transcendentalist men was to proletarianize wives and daughters and to make them aware of the value of pragmatic female cooperatives such as Louisa describes in her novel *Work* (1873). This later realist fiction is a striking example of the voice, the perspective, and the genre least represented in the *Dial*'s response to social conditions in the middle of the nineteenth century.

In 1844, the same year that Emerson, rather gratefully, brought the *Dial* to a conclusion, Margaret Fuller left New England to begin her career as a professional writer for Horace Greeley's *New York Tribune*, for which one of her first contributions was a review of Emerson's *Essays: Second Series*. Although her review is generally positive, and frequently enthusiastic, it intimates the growing physical and intellectual separation between the two former editors. Fuller alludes often to Emerson's New England regionalism with a much more measured sense of its centrality to American life and national leadership than he himself held. "If," she writes, "New-England may be regarded as a chief mental focus to the New World," and "if we may believe, as the writer does believe, that what is to be acted out in the country at large is, most frequently, first indicated there," then Emerson's influence *there* is to be praised. However, her reiterated emphases on "there" and "that region" imply a certain marginalization or localization of Emerson himself: "His books are received there with a more ready intelligence than elsewhere, partly because his range of personal experience and illustration applies to that region, partly because he has prepared the way for his books to be read by his great powers as a speaker" (qtd. in Bean and Myerson 2–3). Later, she suggests that Emerson is preaching to the choir and that his pertinence and influence decrease outside his most familiar territory: "In New-England he thus formed for himself a class of readers, who rejoice to study in his books what they already know by heart....A similar circle of like-minded the books must and do form for themselves, though with a movement less directly powerful, as more distant from its source" (qtd. in Bean and Myerson 4–5). It is not difficult to see in these words a direct personal allusion to Fuller's intellectual relationship to her former mentor.

Fuller's position as a reporter in New York brought her into close association with those other Americans who haunt the peripheries of Emerson's essays, indeed the entire universe of the *Dial*, but are never the central subject—poverty-stricken immigrants, incarcerated prostitutes, the institutionalized insane. She quickly demonstrated an extraordinary empathic capacity, not just for observing them but also for trying to see the world through their eyes, a capacity that interacted fruitfully with her ongoing reviews for the *Tribune* of the socially conscious fiction of Eugène Sue, Sylvester Judd, Richard Hildreth, and a host of other contemporary novelists. Fuller's transcendentalism was not diluted by her growing socialism, but it was democratized by her broadened experience in the city of New York and by the opening of her mind to the more popular literary genre of the novel, as well as to the accounts by Lydia Maria Child, Eliza Farnham, and Caroline Kirkland of the lives of common people. Thus her article "The Irish Character" for the *Tribune* is based, in true journalistic style, on specific immigrants and the harrowing incidents of their lives, while her language for them is elevated and ennobling. They exhibit "delicacy of feeling," "natural eloquence," and a genius that is "exquisitely mournful, tender, and glowing too with the finest enthusiasm" (qtd. in Bean and Myerson 146–47). Fuller imagines what it must be like to be the recipient of enquiring questions, staring eyes, and mistrustful and condescending attitudes, which she attributes to an "ignorance brutal, but not hopelessly so," from which the perpetrators may be rescued by the awakening of their minds (qtd. in Bean and Myerson 130). The acute class reversals in her account of the sensitive poor, with their native genius, eloquence, and enthusiasm, and the brutally ignorant rich, who have yet to be awakened intellectually (and who are nevertheless not without hope), mark Fuller's distance, socially and imaginatively, from Emerson's "civic Boston." There, she suggests in her review of his *Essays*, he "raised himself too early to the perpendicular and did not lie along the ground long enough to hear the secret whispers of our parent life" (qtd. in Bean and Myerson 4, 5).

By 1844, the two editors of the *Dial* were charting very different personal courses in their pursuits of Romantic idealism—for Emerson a return to the "perpendicular" world of poetry, essays, and the lecture circuit, while Fuller turned to the more extreme risks of "lying along the ground." She moved toward an intellectual engagement with journalism, with the contemporary novel, and with European revolution; in her personal life she experienced an exotic love affair, motherhood, and a shocking early death. Their magazine bowed out to a more muted version of the amusement that had greeted it—a parody of transcendentalism in the *Knickerbocker,* a comment on its propensity to "vex and baffle" in the *Columbian Magazine,* and a loyal farewell in Greeley's *Tribune,* although the reviewer admitted to having lost his final copy and having to recreate the last issue from memory (Myerson 97). The magazine had not been untrue to its lofty goal of examining the ideas that impelled the leading movements of the day, especially in its focus on reform—of gender roles, work, intellectual life, community, and commerce—as the central question of the age. Yet it had also been virtually silent on slave and industrial labor, immigration and poverty, and the extraordinary changes that were being wrought by rapidly increasing technology and literacy on the bodies and minds of the population, and especially of working women. It had also chosen to ignore the realm of fiction, both in its own publications and in its choice of material for review, and by doing so had excluded the literary genre that was to prove most congenial and adaptable to these excluded subjects.

4

The Prospects for Fiction

Male Romantic Novelists and Women's Social Reality

But... recent stories have given us, who do not read novels, occasion to
think of this department of literature, supposed to be the natural fount
and expression of the age.
—R. W. EMERSON, 1843

Yes, but I have spoken to you of the truth in fiction: the display of feelings
which find no manifestation in real life; the solution of enigmas which
long have puzzled us; the confession of follies which could not be wrung
from the heart by the rack or the dungeon, the exposure of the artificial
which has deluded us in the natural world.
—HARRIET FARLEY, 1842

Margaret Fuller was the only *Dial* contributor who experienced in her
personal life the transition from literary lady to working woman;
from New England provincial to New York cosmopolite; and from American democrat to European revolutionary. Her writing and literary forms
changed with her circumstances, but after some early consideration of the
genre of the novel, she rejected it as her medium, fearing that it was too
feminine a mode for her ambitions, and unsuited to her mercurial literary talent. She avoided Romantic fiction after completing her early and
largely plotless fables, wanting instead to write "like a man, of the world
of intellect and action," and knowing herself to have an "impatience of
detail" (qtd. in Chevigny 57, 59). Several male Romantic writers, however, less impatient than Fuller with the detailed execution required of the
novelist, turned to fiction to explore precisely the nexus of topical concerns
that had absorbed the writers for the *Lowell Offering* and had been treated
more discretely and obliquely in the *Dial*. Sylvester Judd, Nathaniel Hawthorne, and Herman Melville all wrote novels and tales about the emergence
of working women from domestic anonymity to public participation,
exploring the consequences such a phenomenon might presage for future
relations between sexes and classes, and for the life of the mind and its literary expression. They questioned implicitly, and sometimes explicitly, the
adequacy and appropriateness of idealist and elitist modes of literariness in
the transition of America to an urban and industrial society, where class

divisions were sharpening and inequalities growing. Each of these three writers notably found in the changing situation of women, in workplace, marketplace, and public discourse, powerful metaphors for embodying his own social and intellectual concerns.

Hawthorne, Melville, and Judd all tested the flexibility of the conventions of mid-nineteenth-century fiction in imaginative works that dealt with varied permutations of the concerns of the *Lowell Offering* and the *Dial*: women, work, reform, social change, and the reverberations of expanded literacy and self-expression. None of these three moved so fully into documentary or realist modes as the women of the *Offering*, nor did any of them remain so hopefully or unreservedly committed to idealist forms as the *Dial*'s transcendentalists. All three demonstrated, however, the flexibility of fiction as a vehicle for articulating the intricacies and incongruities of the contemporary world in more vivid and less didactic ways than reforming essayists like Dwight, Lane, and Brownson. Melville's "Poor Man's Pudding and Rich Man's Crumbs" simultaneously explored gross class inequities and satirized sanctimonious literary men; Judd's *Margaret* exposed both the admirable diversity and the foolish limitations of rural New England life; and Hawthorne's *Blithedale Romance* brought into emotional and mental entanglement a gentlemanly writer, a self-righteous reformer, a working girl, and a feminist literary lady. Despite Fuller's impatience of the details and intellectual ingratiation necessary to writing novels, and Emerson's decidedly disingenuous assertion that he avoided reading them, fiction proved to be the most versatile literary mode for capturing the many tensions and complications of the day, as well as the form with the most democratic appeal.

Sylvester Judd, the most eccentric and transcendental of the three writers, began his career, like many of those in the *Dial* circle, as a Unitarian minister and reformer. He wrote sermons, essays, and poetry, and two remarkable Romantic novels, *Margaret: A Tale of the Real and the Ideal* (1845) and *Richard Edney and the Governor's Family* (1850). The earlier novel, *Margaret*, looks closely at the texture of late eighteenth-century rural life, and at the character and education of a young woman who helps transform the New England village of Livingston into a utopian community. The protagonist, Margaret, is a female Romantic who emerges from lower-class rural life more than a full generation before the appearance of Concord transcendentalists or aspiring literary factory workers. The novel is an eclectic compendium of arcane details that follows no known fictional model, and frequently neglects both plot and character for lengthy excursions into extravagant catalogues and inventories of spring flowers, dining room furnishings, winter birds, sweetmeats and plagues, as well as asides on throat distemper, Scotch Presbyterianism, earthquakes, and taxes. For the most part, contemporary critics of *Margaret* (with the very notable exception of Margaret Fuller) objected to a novel that mixed utopian theorizing, sermons, vulgar dialects, and low behavior with pedantic digressions into botany and ornithology. One reviewer considered it "everything a novel should not be" (Dedmond 77). However, amid the disorder and excess Judd also displays an imaginative boldness in creating the mythically ideal Margaret, a girl sprung from lowly origins and the democratic diversity of backwoods life. Judd's eclecticism does not produce an elegant and unified novel, but the immense accretion of historical and symbolic detail and incident would scarcely be acceptable in any other literary mode. If it is "everything a novel should not be," it is nonetheless difficult to imagine another literary genre so hospitable to the astonishing possibilities for human consciousness that may be embedded in the dense details of a particular time and place.

What is most striking about this novel's fictional home village of Livingston is the amazing heterogeneity of the mental life of its ostensibly homogeneous population. Erudite classicists, narrow-minded puritans, folk herbalists, freethinkers, atheists, radicals, and reactionaries are living in a community that is simultaneously repressive and conducive to every kind of dissent. At the center of the village stand the institutions of social authority: the meetinghouse, courthouse, jail, stocks, pillory, and whipping post, but also a "store, school-house, tavern...and barber's shop" (29), all competing sources of opinion and ideas. The schoolmaster's library contains the radical works of Paine and Wollstonecraft, but the villagers' mind-altering consumption of rum and hard cider is equally conducive to subversive attitudes. A hellfire-and-brimstone sermon at a camp meeting reduces some of the congregation to jerking and foaming at the mouth but leads the more skeptical to jeer and shout profanities. Judd's didactic purpose is clearly to argue for the transcendent innocence and purity in Margaret that enable her to rise above all the earthly taints of her contentious and fanatical compatriots, absorbing what is best from her multifarious education but sublimating its chaos to an innate and Christian divinity within her. However, his tolerant and affectionate chronicle of the early days of American democracy makes its disorderly vitality as appealing as the utopian order that would replace it. *Margaret* inevitably reveals not only the capacity of the novel to complicate ideas by embodying them in tangible settings and varied personalities but also its tendency to escape from its author's didactic purpose and expose more whimsical interests and less controlled speculations.

The family the child Margaret grows up in is vulgar and vital. Her first lessons in independence and fearlessness come from the boisterous atheism and disrespect for authority of her lower-class parents. She is not sheltered from the sight of violence, drunkenness, and squalor, as a more privileged girl might have been. She is allowed to wander outdoors and lavished with unqualified affection, unlike the upper class, transcendental Margaret, whose father, Timothy Fuller, admonished his three-year-old daughter "I love her if she is a good girl and learns to read" (qtd. in Blanchard 18). Judd's Margaret is free to make her own discoveries and encounter her tutors providentially, to learn the classics from her schoolmaster, superstitions from fortunetellers, and dogma from reactionary clergymen. From the man who will be her husband, she acquires a conception of Jesus as a type of New England transcendentalist, who "studied his own mysterious nature, his own manifold necessities, his own disposition; and by thus first knowing himself... knew all men" (223). Margaret's uniqueness seems to arise paradoxically from a life among common people, not in opposition to them, but drawing directly on the opportunities already present in their world. Well before the advent of lyceums, libraries, and lecture series, Judd suggests that there is a mental vigor in these ordinary folk that will seek out a rich, informal education where a formal one is lacking.

If her lowly origins are auspicious for her idealist aspirations, so, too, is Margaret's rural New England environment. Although Judd first introduces her as an infant symbol of the possibilities for spiritual fulfillment available to a child in *any* culture or nation of the world, he rapidly moves to identify the Northeast with the particular possibilities for an American idealism. Indeed, he provides a catalogue of the real lacks and the ideal compensations of New England life that notably anticipates both Emerson's celebration of the natural purity of America and Henry James's jeremiad on the same subject:

> We have no resorts for pilgrims, no shrines for the devout, no summits looking into Paradise. We have no traditions, legends, fables, and scarcely a history. Our galleries are no cenotaphic burial grounds of ages past; we have no... chapels or abbeys, no broken arches or castled crags.... All these things our fathers left behind in England, or they were brushed away by contact with the thick, spiny forests of America. Our atmosphere is transparent, unoccupied, empty from the bottom of our wells to the zenith, and throughout the entire horizontal plane. (231–32)

To Margaret's response to this catalogue—"So you think New Englanders are the best people on the Earth?"—the sage Mr. Evelyn replies, "I think they might become such; or rather I think they might lead the august procession of the race to Human Perfectibility" (232). Although Margaret Fuller criticized Emerson for the regional limitations of his New England vision, she reviewed Judd's "Yankee novel" very positively, seeing in it "a genuine disclosure of the life of mind and the history of character," and concluding, "Of books like this, as good and still better, our new literature shall be full" (qtd. in Dedmond 80).

Curiously, Fuller had little to say in her review about Judd's depiction of a specifically female idealist, although his heroine's gender is as integral to his conception of her as are her social class and environment. In the harsh and contentious world of Livingston, women learn to be tough, resilient, and hardworking, but their affinity for beauty, music, and sentiment is more readily accepted than a similar trait would be in a man. Margaret's music-loving brother Chilion is a more marginalized member of the community than the girl. Her mystical and fanciful nature, her dreams and visions, her lack of worldly ambition and indifference to material success, which would compromise a male protagonist like Chilion, operate solely to enhance Margaret's character. Judd's Romantic novel of self-culture places at its center a lower-class female, whose mind is capable of rivaling the best intellects of her society, and of pursuing its noblest ideals. He makes her ambition wholly appealing and almost convincing, at least until she becomes a rich man's wife and an unquestioning Christian. As a child of humble background and feisty upbringing, she might, a generation later, have set out for the mills at Lowell and eventually have written Romantic epics or witty defenses of "Old Maids." As it is, her bucolic world is still largely insulated from the realities of urban and industrial life, of new economic roles for women, and of the tensions of gender and class loyalties that would shortly provide a very different context for the uncommon idealism of the common girl.

Judd's second novel, *Richard Edney and the Governor's Family* (1850), considers precisely the intrusion of the culture of the urban factory world into the lives of rural New Englanders. One of the most apt terms (among the many in his Byzantine subtitle) labels the book as a "A Rus-Urban Tale."[1] Richard Hathaway describes this second novel as Judd's "implied renunciation of transcendentalism, his acceptance of limitation"; and certainly Richard is a more conventional hero than Margaret (301). He is a young man whose motto is "To Be Good, and To Do Good" and whose ambition is "to be a thorough and upright mechanic" (80). For this purpose, Richard leaves his rural home and goes to the city of Woodylin, where there are sawmills, textile mills, extremes of wealth and poverty and of temptation and deprivation. The change in setting from rural to urban does not greatly affect the wild excesses of Judd's eclectic style; however, his fascination with the texture of daily life now focuses not on birds, flowers, fish, or the multitudinous daily chores of an eighteenth-century village but on the more highly manufactured material culture of the store window displays, sawmill machinery, and boardinghouses of the industrializing city. The materiality of the urban environment is elaborately constructed and differentiated, compared to the casual and easy disorder of the countryside in the earlier novel. The people of Woodylin are stratified according to such worldly standards as the quality of the boardinghouse they inhabit, the level of the labor they perform in the mill, and the status of the church they attend. Thus, those who board where there are "Pies for breakfast" rank "higher" than those who are served simpler fare; also "there is a difference between the weave-room and the warping-room,—between a dresser and a grinder"; and even places of worship have class associations: "some of the Churches are aristocratic, while others keep to the level of common people" (94). The urban world is much farther removed from the utopian possibilities of the primitive and less hierarchical village in the earlier novel, and its capacity for reinvention more limited. Richard can, at best, only preside over secular schemes of improvement rather than earthly utopias, and his triumphs are distinctly more worldly than those of Margaret.

Although the protagonist is a male mechanic, one of the novel's most interesting characters is Plumy Alicia Eyre, a beautiful and aspiring young woman who has become a factory operative. Her allusive name suggests Judd's familiarity with the recently published and popular *Jane Eyre,* and is perhaps a sign that he was interested in producing a second novel more in tune with public tastes than the first.[2] In this minor but formidable character, Judd explores the career of an ambitious and talented working-class woman who hopes to rise from her position as a factory worker. However, Plumy Alicia is a strangely realist woman trapped in a still-Romantic genre. If she were merely a scheming seductress, out to tempt the noble Richard, she would fit the fairly simple moral scheme of the novel, but she is a woman of sufficient intelligence and integrity to recognize and desire virtue, but so thoroughly imbued with the commodified standards of her world that she is incapable of stepping outside them. The consumer luxuries of the manufacturing city have seduced Plumy, while they are merely novelties and wonders to Richard, the more recent arrival (although the allure of their novelty is powerful). When he first looks into the store windows of Woodylin, they stimulate fantasies of wonder rather than possession:

> it was a realm of enchanted vision,—a gulf opening into Paradise,—a portal of Dream-land! There were oranges and lemons in the Fruiterer's windows, that brought to Richard's memory what he had learned of Sicily, Cuba, and the evergreen Tropics. There were golden watches and bracelets, diamond rings, pearl brooches, in the Jeweller's, spread out in full view, on terraces of black velvet; and Potosi came to his mind, Golconda and the Arabian Nights. At the Confectioner's, glass globes of candies and lozenges, and all kinds of colored sugars, stood a-row, and there were sugar dogs, and sugar houses, and sugar everything,—a whole microcosm of pretty ideas in sugar. (117)

Plumy, however, is not merely stimulated by the fantasy displays of store windows but is already wholly clad in their products: "Miss Eyre had on a small white silk bonnet, with pink linings, and richly ribboned in the same color; a swan's-down victorine floated on her neck; her hands were quietly hidden in an African lynx muff" (90). She is a passionate and intelligent woman with an innate longing for elevation and nobility of character who has been educated in the city to see such virtues only within the artifices of a class and economic system that places her at the bottom. She has learned to believe, in dramatic contradiction to the democratic Margaret, in "the essential worthlessness of that large class of people among whom [she] was born" (435). Plumy cannot detach her notions of superior people from their material possessions. Even as she blames herself for despising the lower orders and betraying her own kin, she cannot escape using the language of rank and wealth as the source of her metaphors for human greatness. To Melicent, the Governor's daughter, she exclaims:

> You were born great. You cannot step out without stepping into littleness. Then how easy, how pleasant, to take a few steps in that direction,—merely passing from Wilton carpets to dusty streets,— and go home to your own greatness! But for me, born little, to step into greatness,—how hard, how hazardous! Then to go home to littleness,—to creep back, after a pleasant exaltation, into one's mean hovel,—you know not what that is! (435)

Judd's depiction of Plumy's distraught class consciousness, no matter how tawdry its embodiment in a Wilton carpet or a swan's-down victorine, gives an almost tragic quality to the mill girl's hopeless yearning.

Judd's explicit didactic purpose is to argue for the redeeming effects, on such people as Plumy, of a Christian education and of such urban reforms as will permit the city to become more like the country, its density dissipated by openness, its squalor and vice erased by the pervasive and methodical introduction of natural elements into the congested artifice of Woodylin. However, there is a huge rhetorical and conceptual chasm in Judd's second novel between his Romantic opposition of extremes of urban degradation and redeeming natural beauty and his ironic realist details of the attractions of silk bonnets and sugar-dogs, Wilton carpets and pie for breakfast. Although this gulf is never bridged or even directly acknowledged, it is at the core of the literary struggle among writers of the period to come to terms—verbally, epistemologically, and ethically—with the enormous changes that were occurring in American life. The contributors to the *Lowell Offering*, themselves the products of both a Christian education and a still countrified industrial environment, experimented with Romanticism and allegory, documentary accounts of their rural culture, and witty realist fictions, although (unlike Judd) not simultaneously. Judd attempted in his second novel to extend the Concord-like idealism of his first to the urban, industrial community of Woodylin, a town much more like Lowell than the earlier New England village of Livingston that had nurtured Margaret. However, amid the increasing class stratifications and materialism of the new setting, he created no counterpart to the classless young republican woman whose boundless idealism and mental enthusiasm had proved a fitting vehicle for his extravagant Romanticism. The warped aspirations of his factory girl Plumy seem to require the development of an urbane and skeptical realism that is scarcely compatible with Judd's eccentric genius. Margaret Fuller noted in her review of *Margaret* that it was "a genuine disclosure of the life of mind" and "a representative of transient existence which had a great deal of meaning" (qtd. in Dedmond 80). Her carefully phrased past tense suggests that the revelations of *Margaret*'s world, although a hopeful sign of future novels deeply grounded in American life, might not be prescient of the meaning of an America whose conditions were now in such dramatic flux.

In much of his fiction, Hawthorne avoided the problem Judd faced in his historical and geographical move from eighteenth-century rural to nineteenth-century urban life. In his exploration of remote historical subjects, Hawthorne did not confront directly the aesthetic and epistemological dilemma of the appropriateness of the romance mode to the dramatic changes that were occurring in contemporary society. However, in his one topical experiment in dystopian fiction, *The Blithedale Romance* (1852), he turned to the world of working women, urban life, industrial upheaval, and social reform and compensated richly for his previous neglect of current issues. He now took for his heroines a superior transcendental feminist and a working-class seamstress; for their male counterparts, an imaginative writer and a self-righteous reformer; and for their setting, the urban life of Boston and a rural utopian community based, in part, on Brook Farm. Hawthorne boldly brought many of the central intellectual, social, and literary currents of the day into striking confrontation in a novel that, unlike Judd's casual eclecticism, explores quite self-consciously its own fluctuations between the modes of realism and romance. In the preface to *Blithedale*, he describes his experiences at Brook Farm as "certainly the most romantic episode" of his life, "a daydream, and yet a fact," a statement that immediately acknowledges his consciousness of the literary quandary of genre and form on which he is embarking.[3] Thereafter in the novel, Hawthorne steadily pursues an inquiry into the ways the largest social and moral problems of the age are defined and transformed by the prejudices of characters who engage in schemes of reform. He also moves far beyond Judd in demonstrating the extent to which the literary modes of romance or realism through which the imagined world is apprehended may themselves enhance or deny the urgency for remaking existing conditions.

Many critics have noted the centrality of *Blithedale* to the growing discourse about women, labor, and literary work in imaginative writings of the mid–nineteenth century, and Hawthorne's novel has additional pertinence to the debates about the emergence of both working women and literary ladies. Both Nicholas Bromell and Amal Amireh, in their respective studies, note evidence in the novel of Hawthorne's anxiety about changes in the status and authority of women, although they locate it separately, in the two opposing female characters. Bromell proposes that women's labor as factory workers, teachers, and writers fostered a broad anxiety in male writers that is manifested in Hawthorne's work in his "repeated victimization of strong women" like *Blithedale's* formidable Zenobia who is ultimately scolded or punished by almost all the male characters in the book (109). Hawthorne's sly affirmations and denials of Zenobia's links to Margaret Fuller have ensured that Fuller can never be wholly excluded from the novel, certainly as the cultural presence that might have influenced a Zenobia or other aspiring feminists, if not as the character herself.

Hawthorne's narrator, Coverdale, introduces "Zenobia" as the pseudonym or "magazine-signature" of what the author calls in the preface "the high-spirited Woman, bruising herself against the narrow limitations of her sex" (13, 2–3). Zenobia is apparently a famous figure among obscure working women like the seamstress Priscilla who have read her "stories, (as such literature goes everywhere,) or her tracts in defence of the sex" (30–31). Both like and unlike Fuller, Zenobia in an admired celebrity at Blithedale, as Fuller was at Brook Farm, but she is a resident of the community rather than a visitor. Although many of Zenobia's qualities, such as her literariness, assertiveness, and feminism, evoke aspects of Fuller, Miles Coverdale himself takes care to avoid the identification by describing his receipt of a letter from the actual Margaret Fuller ("one of the most gifted women of the age") and simultaneously insisting on a momentary resemblance between Fuller and the fragile seamstress, Priscilla, in the penetrating gaze of the girl's eyes (47, 48). Significantly, the name Zenobia, that of an ancient queen of Palmyra, already had broad cultural resonance in the mid–nineteenth century among the working women of New England: in 1843 the *Lowell Offering* had published a biography of her in its "Portrait Gallery," a series on eminent women, lauding her "talent, genius, and energy" but most particularly the "mental superiority" of this "Oriental maid" (3: 113, 115). Thus Hawthorne's, or Coverdale's, Zenobia is an enigmatic and richly allusive figure, well befitting the symbolic magnitude of the changing consciousness of and about women at midcentury, of which Fuller was one among many manifestations.

Amal Amireh, like Nicholas Bromell, finds in *The Blithedale Romance* a reflection of Hawthorne's "worst anxieties about labor, class and gender," although she locates them in the working-class sister Priscilla rather than the literary feminist Zenobia (98). Amireh gives a persuasive account of the ways in which the other three main characters mold the young seamstress into an image that suits their own preconceptions of what such a young female must be. Coverdale, the poet, idealizes Priscilla's physical sickliness into delicate spirituality, while Hollingsworth, a sexual reactionary, finds in her demureness evidence of woman's inevitable subordination to man (104–5). Zenobia, a feminist, believes Priscilla's pallor and fragility are simply the consequence of the poor diet and working conditions of a typical urban seamstress (103). Zenobia's consciousness of the barriers of social class that separate her from the younger woman prevents her from recognizing both her literal and metaphorical sisterhood with Priscilla; indeed she collaborates in the girl's exploitation even as she bravely preaches the rights of woman. In each case, Hawthorne suggests that his three more intellectual characters are skillful at creating a verbal account of reality that rationalizes a prior, private vision. Since one of those characters is the novel's narrator, the view of reality mediated by his multiple fictions is inevitably a problematic one. Amireh argues that since the "participants in Blithedale all define the seamstress differently, and in the process define themselves and Blithedale" the consequence is that the seamstress becomes "the focus of conflicting representations and the product of conflicted discourses" (100). This astute reading of the seamstress might be applied to every major character in the novel, as well as to the contemporary debates they generate. Hawthorne is less interested in the social resolution of such disputes than in demonstrating how the discourse of an age is shaped not only by personality and prejudice but also by the language and literary forms of its intellectual interpreters.

Hawthorne's remarkable capacity to embody his double interest in the substance and the literary representation of social controversies in the emblematic characters, structure, and setting of *The Blithedale Romance* is matched by the ways he encapsulates these controversies into the smallest, seemingly incidental details of the novel. Zenobia, in responding to Coverdale's question "Do you know Hollingsworth personally?" replies, "No; only as an auditor—auditress, I mean—of some of his lectures" (21). In her slight hesitation and correction lies the whole agonized feminist debate of the day over the appropriation of feminine endings for female activities, a practice advocated by Sarah Josepha Hale in *Godey's*, that led not only to "authoress" and "editress" (adopted by the *Lowell Offering*) but also to "attorneyess," "lighthousekeeperess," and other unlikely neologisms. Similarly, when the effete Coverdale takes his urban vacation from idealist farm life, he ensconces himself in a comfortable armchair in his hotel room with a novel "purchased of a railroad bibliopolist" (136–37). For a gentleman poet, elsewhere contemptuous of the "poor little stories" that have brought Zenobia her large following, the insidious intrusion of railroad fiction into his own reading is a telling reflection of the contemporary revolution in the literary marketplace and of the impact on everyday life of mechanical and industrial change. Even so leisured and private an observer of the world as Coverdale is now traveling and living in the public sphere of trains and hotels.[4] Coverdale notes that the "torpid" quality of his railroad book serves him for a while as a barrier against the invasion of the city outside, where the "tumult of the pavements," the "foot-tramp and the clangor" of a military band, the chiming of clocks, and even the distant applause from the "exhibition of a mechanical diorama" create "an uproar so broad and deep that only an unaccustomed ear would dwell upon it" (136). The casual implication that "custom" rapidly changes consciousness is as significant as the change in Coverdale's reading: in Boston he buries himself in a soporific railroad novel to defer the shock of assimilating the modern urban world, while at Blithedale he had "read interminably in Mr. Emerson's Essays, the Dial, Carlyle's works, George Sand's romances" and the theories of Fourier and others "on the outposts of the advance-guard of human progression" (48). The material distance between Boston and Blithedale is easily traversed; less so the forms of consciousness represented by the alternatives of railroad fiction and the *Dial*.

Hawthorne's personal role as a participant in the idealist experiment at Brook Farm has naturally invited a good deal of critical interest in *The Blithedale Romance*'s account of a similar place where mind and body could be united in that balance of mental and manual labor so desired by his contemporaries.[5] Less attention has been accorded Hawthorne's meticulous and graphic description of the world from which he, as well as the dreamy idealists, was in retreat, the fictionalized version of the modern city of Boston. *Blithedale*, as reasonably as Judd's *Richard Edney*, might be subtitled "A Rus-Urban Tale," for the urban environment is the setting for the beginning, middle, and end of the novel, and the transitions between country and city, romance and reality, reformers and conservatives, idealists and materialists, are very deliberately announced in Miles Coverdale's narration as indicating shifts both in the kind of world he depicts and in his perspective on it. Coverdale likes to present himself as something of a self-indulgent dilettante who has the time, money, and inclination to dabble in different ways of living, and in their modes of representation. These ideals and forms are matters of serious conviction to their ideological adherents, but merely of bemused entertainment to the curious *litterateur*. The continuous interplay of romance and reality in Hawthorne's tales and novels prior to *Blithedale* is at the heart of the stylistic and epistemological concerns of his earlier writing, but only in *Blithedale* does this interplay become so closely connected to topical ideologies of political and social reform. In this contemporary novel, dreamy idealism is not merely the spiritualizing effect of mystic moonbeams on the perception of an innocent wayfarer but also a consciously embraced political philosophy, on whose basis a community of people have come together to establish a rustic utopia.[6] Nor is reality simply the sturdier material world revealed by the clearer light of day; now it is directly associated with the worldly skepticism of social reform that is embraced by urban merchants and conservative politicians. The novel is not, however, a simple allegory based on these oppositions but a more satirical account of the inadequacy of either a romantic or a realist lens to envision an incongruous world where nature-loving idealists compete in the marketplace and urbane realists flock to spiritualist demonstrations.

As has often been noted, the visionary rural socialists of Blithedale have fled the curse of trade and competition, only to find themselves immediately enmeshed in economic rivalry with their farming neighbors. Coverdale is struck by the irony "that one of the first questions raised, after our separation from the greedy, struggling, self-seeking world, should relate to the possibility of getting the advantage over the outside barbarians, in their own field of labor" (20). Charles Lane, himself a communitarian reformer, had noted, in the *Dial,* the same paradox in the Shakers' excessive dependence on trade. Bronson Alcott had tried to withdraw completely from such worldliness and materialism at Fruitlands, resulting in the rapid and disastrous demise of the community. In addition to their immediately compromised economic ideals, the Blithedale communitarians have also envisioned an egalitarian world that will rise above the old discriminations of gender and class, but, as Zenobia notes, it is the women who "take the domestic and indoor part of the business, as a matter of course" (16). Not only are gender roles still bound by convention but there is a considerable degree of class-based tension at Blithedale, whereby the "unpolished" members of the community do not show themselves to be as gratified by the condescension of the "people of superior culture and refinement" as the latter might wish when they embark on their "millennium of love" (23). The dreamy idealists whose aspirations are blunted by reality are not, however, the only vulnerable ideologues in the novel. It gradually appears that middle-class urbanites, those prosperous and commonsensical members of the bourgeoisie, are spending much of their supposedly valuable time at mesmeric performances and exhibitions of ventriloquism and thaumaturgy. The oppositions and equivalences that are central to allegorical representation collapse at every intersection of class, gender, ideology, and place. Even the definitive Romantic and realist realms of the country and the city are blurred in this novel. At Priscilla's final performance as the mysterious Veiled Lady in a village lyceum, Miles Coverdale notices that the men in the audience, "the schoolmaster, the lawyer, or student-at-law, the shopkeeper" all appear "rather suburban than rural," and indeed he claims to despair of finding any true "rusticity," (182) except, ironically in the heart of the city where birds thrive and trees flourish in a soil "enriched to a more than natural fertility" (137).

Coverdale engages in a good deal of aesthetic play with the notion that he may shuttle between the supposedly disparate realms of Boston and Blithedale, between cozy bachelor quarters "in one of the midmost houses of a brick-block" and the realm of the utopian day-dreamers, whose "airiest fragments, impalpable as they may be...possess a value that lurks not in the most ponderous realities of any practicable scheme" (10, 11). When he escapes back to the city for his urban vacation, he notes that his purpose is "to correct himself by a new observation from that old stand-point" (130). As a "devoted epicure of [his] own emotions," Coverdale likes to manipulate contrasting impressions for maximum dramatic effect. Looking back at Blithedale when he departs, he immediately converts the community in his mind to "part of another age, a different state of society, a segment of an existence peculiar in its aims and methods, a leaf of some mysterious volume, interpolated into the current history which Time was writing off." Looked at another way, however, he admits "it had been only a summer in the country" (135). Coverdale's self-conscious stage-managing of his own shifts in perspective suggests that the artist in him is more interested in aesthetic effects than in social causes. It is inevitable to suggest the same conclusion about Hawthorne, whose reiterated artistic concerns are so close to those of the fictional narrator whom he satirizes. Was *The Blithedale Romance* a literary effort to find the best way to represent the meaning of Brook Farm and draw morals about the state of modern society? Or did the Brook Farm venture serve as a pretext for pondering artistic questions of representation? A remarkably large proportion of the novel is given over to discussions of aesthetic and literary questions and to insinuations that the methods of apprehending the world may themselves be the fluctuating bases for different ethical responses to a changing society.

One of Hawthorne's chief implied criticisms of Coverdale, as a narrator and ideological commuter, is his tendency to make aesthetic capital of his observations and impressions, whether by apostrophizing the unnaturalness of nature in the city or meditating on saloon wall paintings of roast beef and cheese that are "so perfectly imitated, that you seemed to have the genuine article before you, and yet with an indescribable, ideal charm" (162). Coverdale is more interested in manipulating his perspective in order to conjure such paradoxes and incongruities than in committing himself to a better society, but Hawthorne permits no alternative vision of moral clarity or consistency to challenge his narrator's mental games. In the end, after oscillating between the ethereal and the substantial modes of viewing contemporary American life, Coverdale—the man of letters—abandons his efforts at writing altogether. Zenobia, the feminist ideologue, has ended her literary career even more dramatically by her suicide. Thus the two writers who go to Blithedale both fail, one ignominiously, the other dramatically, to fulfill their utopian hopes. At the end, Coverdale is living tolerably, although no longer as a writer. Whether it is as a result of his human disengagement from or his failure to find a literary mode appropriate to the modern world are questions about which he is typically indeterminate. By comparison, Zenobia, who threw herself unreservedly into both life and highly ideological literature, has seen her political and personal goals defeated and has died an early and ugly death. Although much has been made of Hawthorne's destruction of his dark literary lady antagonist in *The Blithedale Romance*, he seems to have divided the role of writer's alter ego between two very different characters, neither of whom seems able to find an acceptable mode of combining living in and writing about contemporary reality. Coverdale has reached a kind of death in life with his literary romancing and his personal suspicions of commitment, while Zenobia has not managed to survive the passionate engagements she entered into in both her life and her feminist writings.

It has proved an enduring challenge for readers of *The Blithedale Romance* to see beyond the invented failures of Hawthorne's two writer-protagonists, and especially beyond Coverdale's perversely unstable mediation as narrator, to determine whether there is a knowable vision of American society in the novel, or an endorsement of a new way to represent it. With a cast of characters consciously emblematic of the trends of the age—"the self-concentrated Philanthropist; the high-spirited Woman...; the weakly Maiden...; the Minor Poet"—and a recent utopian experiment for subject matter, Hawthorne chose to emphasize the aspects of his contemporary world that fit least easily into allegorical correspondences or convenient oppositions, like country–city, exotic–mundane, or even radical–conservative (2–3). Both John McWilliams and Nina Baym see him turning after *Blithedale* to increasingly definitive statements about the future impossibility of the romance in America, although less clearly to an endorsement of a satisfactory alternative. Although reviewers and literary journals of the day were arguing in favor of the realist genre of the novel as "the appropriate American form" to deal with current societal concerns, Hawthorne did not himself attempt that mode in the remaining years of his career.[7] In *The Blithedale Romance*, he refused to make a choice between contending, if as yet ill defined, genres for writing about contemporary American reality. Instead he concentrated on revealing the shifting sand of evidence on which such forms and genres were being erected, and as a result, he assimilated the vital questions of the time into a complex work of fiction that served his lasting interest in human psychology and perception, while providing a penetrating and sardonic account of the temper of the time and some of its liveliest debates. If his unsympathetic response to writing women, independent working women, feminism, and idealist reformers may be otherwise deduced from the totality of his literary and personal testaments, it is buried so deeply in the pervasive skepticism of the human mind in *The Blithedale Romance* that all ideology, both realist and idealist, is subsumed to the fascination of mental and imaginative processes of assimilating experience.

Hawthorne voiced ambivalence between his attraction to the "beef and ale" realism of Trollope and the kind of dematerialized romances that seemed most suited to his personal abilities; Herman Melville experienced a more tortured and many-sided conflict, not just between competing literary modes but also among social loyalties and beliefs.[8] He was tantalized by different sets of class affiliations, political sympathies, and national and cultural alignments and was burdened by the ever-present pressures of the marketplace on the nature of his literary production. There is no single equivalent in Melville's work to Hawthorne's *Blithedale Romance,* in terms of a work that provides a central matrix for so many of the social debates of the age, especially since Melville so frequently places these debates in a transatlantic and transhistorical context that projects contemporary American concerns onto other places and times. However, his 1849 novel *Redburn,* together with his short story "Bartleby the Scrivener" (1853) and his three American/British diptychs "The Two Temples" (1854), "Poor Man's Pudding and Rich Man's Crumbs" (1854), and "The Paradise of Bachelors and the Tartarus of Maids" (1855) represent a period when he was particularly keenly engaged with class consciousness and with the tensions and inequities of gender.[9] These years witnessed Melville's increasing awareness of the stratification of urban and industrial society, the changing condition of women, and his consequent concerns with the adequacy or inadequacy of prevailing modes of contemporary literature to come to terms with precipitous shifts in society. All of these works make explicit or implicit comparisons and analogies between British and American culture, and all investigate the problems of intellectual accommodation and resistance to these cultures, a process often represented at the metaphorical extremes by comfortable bachelors on one end and wretched women and delicate and enfeebled men on the other. Melville was less concerned with aspiring literary women than with a growing genteel effeminacy in American literature itself; less apprehensive of the changing nature of women's work than of the enduring nature of women. Thus he continually alludes to current events (such as the passage of legislation for immigrants, the exclusionary elitism of Grace Church, the Astor Place riots) and topical social controversies (on rural and urban life and female factory labor), while he parodies, imitates, absorbs, and resists the prevailing artistic conventions for representing them. Like Judd and Hawthorne, he wrestles with the allure of Romantic literary elevation and idealism in a world of increasing oppression, inequity, and turmoil, expanding the boundaries of fiction as he questions its suitability, indeed that of all literary efforts, for the task of reflecting reality.

Melville's early and autobiographical novel *Redburn* immediately challenges the value of literature to represent the world or guide its citizens, even as he depicts people's pervasive dependency on books selected to cater to their readers' hopes and aspirations. The Romantic adolescent Wellingborough Redburn anticipates and mediates all experience through the lens of his reading, but his account of the barely literate sailors he encounters suggests that they, too, exist in a symbiotic relationship with their more limited selection of books. Some indeed have only a single book in their possession, and it consequently exerts a disproportionate effect on them. The superstitious sailor Blunt is dominated by theories derived from his *Dream Book*; the pious cook asks for help interpreting a chapter from the Book of Chronicles in the Bible; and the suicidal sailor leaves among his effects the doubly appropriate volumes *Shipwrecks and Disasters at Sea* and *Delirium Tremens*. Lavender, the perfumed steward, has a whole supply of novels in the vein of *Three Spaniards* and *Charlotte Temple*. Only Jackson, the grim nihilist, appears to be without book-learning and contemptuous of the reading of others. Ominously, and in contrast to the sailors who read, Jackson's absent literacy does not impinge on the clarity of his perceptions. Redburn himself, otherwise ill equipped for his first voyage, has a great range of potential responses derived from his reading, although these may, ironically, function as inappropriately for him as his big-buttoned shooting jacket and his high-heeled boots. Though his father's guidebook to Liverpool demonstrates empirically that Redburn is no longer a privileged traveler in a world of revered monuments, he still strives to guarantee his pedigree by speaking the English language he has learned from his study of Addison, and to shore up his sense of enduring truths by constant reference to his Bible. From New York to Liverpool, and into the green English countryside that is guarded by man-traps and spring-guns, Redburn confronts a world of possession and dispossession, imaged in pawnshops, thieves, slavery, emigration, trespass, and beggary. He responds to it in rhetorical flourishes, quotations, allusions, analogies, literary tropes, interpretive strategies, and alternating moods of exuberance and despair. The conventions of literary genre writing—of a gentleman's first seafaring voyage—prove, however, as inadequate as his guidebook reading. They can neither comprehend the metaphysical depth nor do justice to the material evidence of the young sailor's experience, leading perhaps to Melville's own dissatisfied verdict on his novel: "beggarly."[10]

At this period in his career, Melville was apparently thinking a great deal about the appropriateness of pleasing literary tropes, about the play of witty paradox, and about the relationship of polished aesthetic detachment to subject matter that was controversial and harrowing.[11] Writing in "Hawthorne and His Mosses" in 1850, Melville not only singled out for commendation Hawthorne's "great power of blackness" but also, by contrast, disparaged Washington Irving's "studied avoidance of all topics but smooth ones." Noting that "there is no hope for us in these smooth, pleasing writers," Melville emphasizes Irving's gracefulness, his amiability, and his power to satisfy his popular readership but adds, "it is better to fail in originality, than to succeed in imitation" (129, 135). Kristie Hamilton, in her study of the "sketch" in American literature, has explored how this literary genre grew out of a British tradition of sketches and fictions, beginning with Goldsmith, that managed to be simultaneously satirically reformist, comfortably ingratiating, and fundamentally nostalgic for the personal connections and intimacies between classes in a less anonymous, preindustrial society (38). *Redburn* is a dramatic illustration that that world was no longer relevant to modern Britain or America, no matter how irrepressibly ready Redburn himself is to taste the rare roast beef or snuff the immortal loam of England in evocations of the earlier literary mode. The elements that formerly constituted such a "smooth" and "pleasing" account now no longer exist for Redburn or for a series of Melville narrators who follow him in trying to apply inherited literary paradigms and conventions to a changed reality. By the time he wrote "Hawthorne and His Mosses," Melville appears to have decided that the bonhomie and decorum of the privileged but compassionate outsider was no longer an adequate literary perspective from which to view the lower classes, no matter how appealing such a position might be. And although Melville continued, especially in his series of "diptychs," to juxtapose contrasting sets of times, places, and ethical standards, his paired sketches all avoid the satisfaction of balanced oppositions and the pleasure of synthesis. They reveal the graceful narrator to be far from a judicious or consistent mediator between his own class and an ever-expanding array of outsiders.

It was in his short stories of the 1850s rather than the novels that followed *Redburn* that Melville continued to explore most directly the impact of the Industrial Revolution on poverty and class stratification, and in which he continued his juxtaposition of transatlantic social customs and literary forms. In 1849, Melville was personally involved in a symbolic public incident that dramatically yoked together class antagonisms and cultural loyalties. His name appeared, among those of forty-seven others (including Washington Irving) on a petition supporting the performances of the British actor W. C. Macready at the Astor Place Opera House in New York, and urging him not to terminate them in the face of threatened public disruptions. These disruptions, conducted by nativist and working-class opponents of Macready who were supporters of the American actor Edwin Forrest, were the culmination of a rivalry that, according to Barbara Foley's study of the affair, "was readily incorporated into preexisting discourses of class and nation in a city already polarized by the labor struggles of the late 1840s" (99). The petitioners took it upon themselves to assure Macready "that the good sense and respect for order, prevailing in this community, will sustain you on the subsequent nights of your performances." When Macready responded positively to these assurances, his next performance, on May 10, 1849, culminated in a riot during which the National Guard fired into the crowd and twenty-two people were killed. As Dennis Berthold has summarized the event, "Workingmen's blood flowed on the streets of New York for the first time in a class struggle," and Herman Melville "was now publicly identified with New York's upper-class partisans of law, order, and Anglophilia" (429, 430).

Berthold and Foley have each reviewed the episode in detail and drawn almost diametrically opposed conclusions from it about its impact on the concerns of Melville's immediately subsequent writing, in the first half of the 1850s. For Berthold, the affair signaled a shift in Melville's class allegiance and his mode of writing, away from a populist strain in his early work to the more difficult, more elitist, and less accessible modes of his novels *Moby-Dick* (1851) and *Pierre* (1852). Berthold sees this shift anticipated by Melville's defense of the sophisticated and aristocratic style of the actor Macready and reinforced in his story "The Two Temples." For Barbara Foley, the same account of Macready's performance in "The Two Temples" is suffused not with Melville's support for Macready but with irony about his obtuse narrator's admiration of Macready's "noble" and "imposing" manner. Foley argues that Melville's "Bartleby the Scrivener" (1853) is his subtle revisiting of this painful episode of class polarization and is, in fact, a *mea culpa* for his having consorted with "the socially conservative cultural elite" in the Astor Place affair (103, 98). She writes of "Bartleby," "Melville is not simply exposing the ideological blindness and moral failure of a typical citizen of Wall Street; he is also ... working through his ambivalence about his complicity in the events that transpired at 'Massacre Place.'" She thus reads "Bartleby" as "simultaneously an expression of Melville's contempt for bourgeois moral cowardice and an admission of his own identification with this quality" (103).

While these two accounts of Melville's political and literary loyalties after the Astor Place riots may seem almost mutually exclusive, Berthold's conclusions are premised largely on the elitist difficulty of Melville's *novels* after 1850, while Foley's derive largely from the central story of a group of his more accessible short fictions. Many of the stories are set up in terms of oppositions and pairings that constitute unresolved arguments within themselves; most have first-person narrators who function as both authoritative voices and potential objects of satire; and almost all still display some of the pleasing literary tropes of Washington Irving's "smooth" manner while dealing with decidedly harsh topics. Melville certainly does not appear in them to have abandoned his sympathies for the victims of emergent capitalism, nor has he committed himself to elite and inaccessible literary styles. However, he has also not entirely shaken off the "pleasing" techniques of bourgeois belles lettres or the indulgence in extravagant Romantic apostrophes as he experiments among styles and forms for his topical subjects and simultaneously tries to write stories acceptable to a middle-class magazine readership.

Although "Bartleby the Scrivener" is not set in the immediate, mechanized factory workplace of the Industrial Revolution, its environment is nevertheless one devoted to a new and highly specialized kind of labor, remote from the world of farm, household, and workshop. In it, tasks are very narrowly defined and precisely delegated; there is a clear demarcation between management and workers; and production deadlines take precedence over all other activities. Michael Gilmore has explored the extent to which the story both evokes and resists the Dickensian model of an older and less impersonal economic order. Initially, he notes that the story recalls "the affectionate familiarity between the classes which was often presented as an ideal in British fiction of the period." Two of the central characters, Turkey and Nippers, are in fact English, and "the narrator's paternalistic attitude toward them seems more appropriate to the antiquated, vaguely feudal world of masters and servants than to the actual working conditions emerging in mid-nineteenth-century-America" (133). Gilmore contends that English novelists like Dickens, Eliot, and Disraeli believed that their kind of imaginative literature could help to make the poor visible and close the widening class gap in society but that Melville lacked such faith because he saw literature as "class-bound, written by and for the relatively privileged" (141). Such a sense of the inevitable class affiliations of "refined literature" had been at the center of the *Lowell Offering* debates between Sarah Bagley, the blunt-spoken worker, and Harriet Farley, aspiring literary lady and woman of letters. However, Bagley, Farley, and their working-class associates had carried on a long, fluent, and highly public debate in the press about how workers' voices might best serve their interests, and the factory women had made the assumption that they had the authority and the ability to communicate within a larger, literate society. Melville, by contrast, assumes an almost impassable communicative gulf between classes, a gulf that cannot be bridged either by literature or within it.

Unlike the Dickensian model, Melville's "Bartleby" is about class unfamiliarity rather than intimacy. Melville's marginalized people tend to speak in gnomic riddles and enigmatic symbolic gestures, while their middle-class observers emote and effuse their guilty consciences and argue their elaborate rationalizations. The dilemma of compassionate and privileged observers with sensitive consciences who profit from systems they know to be intolerable echoes with increasingly corrosive irony throughout nineteenth-century American literature, from Harriet Beecher Stowe's portrait of Augustine St. Clare in *Uncle Tom's Cabin* to William Dean Howells's self-lacerating Basil March in *A Hazard of New Fortunes*. However, the accompanying assumption in Melville, that the members of the working class are frail and voiceless or else part of a threatening mob, is inconsistent with the growing public and published evidence of their articulateness and literacy. Middle-class authors may have truly believed that the voices of the poor could only be translated effectively through the more refined (even if biased) perspective of the educated and conscientious observer. They may have preferred not to acknowledge the threats to their status as citizens and writers represented by the ways those voices were making themselves heard. Nevertheless, the voiceless were beginning to find words and make themselves understood, not just in the nativist heckling of a polished British tragedian but also in the written productions of factory women who were turning out not just mechanically produced blank paper but their own newspapers and literary periodicals.

Melville's story "The Two Temples," which attempts to explore the possibilities of an intellectual culture that is not class-bound, was rejected by *Putnam's* magazine because of the likelihood that it would offend the religious sensibilities of the magazine's readers and alienate the powerful and wealthy members of Grace Church, whom it satirized. Dennis Berthold notes that *Putnam's* also made a policy of avoiding any reference to the sensitive matter of the Astor Place riots, and indeed Melville's story does refer to it indirectly, alluding to a London performance by Macready (445, 446). "The Two Temples" is a two-part sketch, set—like Melville's two other diptychs of the same period—half in America and half in England. As in those, a first-person narrator visits two scenes, one on each side of the Atlantic, which are juxtaposed in a variety of ironic ways. The first visit in "The Two Temples" is to an opulent New York church, the second to a London theater. The "marble-buttressed" church is an ostentatious setting for the rich to display their goods and be entertained, while the modestly dressed narrator is disdainfully refused entrance (174). The first half of the story describes his surreptitious intrusion into the church tower, where he makes his way up a series of stairways and ladders to a small window overlooking the congregation. There he stands, his back frozen, his face scorched by the hot air rising from the church, while he observes "the theatric wonder of the populous spectacle of this sumptuous sanctuary" (178). The service, with its elaborate music, lighting, and effects, is described as "some sly enchanter's show," carefully calculated and adapted to the tastes of the audience, with a sermon on the suitable text "Ye are the salt of the earth." At the end of the performance, the narrator watches the congregation, like "gilded brooks," pouring down the "gilded aisles," but by the time he descends from his high perch, he finds that he is locked in (178, 179). He must ring the church bells to get out, and when he does, he is arrested and conducted to the Halls of Justice as a "lawless violator." The next morning, now in better clothes and thus making a "rather gentlemanly appearance," he manages to arrange a private hearing with a judge. He gets off with merely a large fine and a "stinging reprimand" for having "humbly indulged... in the luxury of public worship" (182). The episode is acutely class conscious in depicting the distortions of both religion and justice in favor of the rich, and in suggesting that democratic America is already mimicking the aristocrats and lackeys of old England.

The second part of the story retraces the same theme of a stranger at a public gathering, but this time the American narrator sits in the working-class section of a London theater and is as civilly welcomed as he had been imperiously excluded in New York. The story thus juxtaposes America and England, the church and the theater, the bourgeoisie and the working class, in each case to the detriment of the former. Although the narrator certainly has more pleasure in the shared entertainment among the friendly workers in London than in the exclusive worship in New York, Melville can scarcely be recommending British society as democratic. What is most notable in the story is the meticulous care taken to emphasize the aesthetic similarity of both performances. The theatrical experience is preferable to the church not so much for any intrinsic superiority in its elements but because it is more democratic and less hypocritical. Whether fiction, with its growing populist audience, could achieve a triumph of democracy comparable to that of the theater is a question that hangs implicitly in the background of the story.

If Melville was meditating at the time on the relative advantages of elitism or accessibility in art, the story makes a virtue of access and of the merits of a large and heartfelt response from a populist audience. The notion of participating in a public cultural experience in the company of a respectable and hospitable working-class audience may have been one of Melville's happier fantasies—certainly a desirable alternative to the violence of the New York crowd at Macready's actual performance and to the humiliation of his narrator's exclusion from the wealthy elite at the other end of New York society. In the London theater, a "ragged, but good-natured-looking boy" gives the "true blue" Yankee narrator a free mug of ale, just because he is American, and the narrator lies awake much of the following night meditating on the charity that has been extended to "a stranger in a strange land" when he could find none at home (189, 191).

Kristie Hamilton, in her study of the evolution of the sketch as a literary form, finds in Melville's stories of this period "the broadening and complication of the function and field of the literary sketch" to include social problems, although she suggests that it is only broadened sufficiently to demand of middle-class readers that they probe their private consciences about the discrepancies between their pleasures and the pains of others. Her conclusion is that "no action is requested or required." She finds that this new sketch "occupied a middle ground" between the recognition of inequity and injustice and the fatalism that accepted such conditions as natural or God-given (127–28). However, in the particular case of "The Two Temples," its rejection by *Putnam's*, and the fact that it remained unpublished in Melville's lifetime, suggests that this sketch strayed well beyond the consumer tastes of a middle-class anxious to have its conscience pricked by moral ironies without being prodded into action. It did indeed, as Hamilton argues, broaden the sketch, in this case to an unacceptably harsh satire of religious hypocrisy. Perhaps equally ominously, it presented a vision of a theatergoing and hospitable working class participating in a shared public culture, with neither envy nor ill feeling toward its social superiors. It could scarcely be read, in the aftermath of the Astor Place riots, as other than bitterly ironic.

In his next diptych, "Poor Man's Pudding and Rich Man's Crumbs," published in *Harper's* in 1854, Melville turned again to a juxtaposition of working-class poverty and wealthy indulgence, differently manifested in America and England. However, in this case the object of the satire in the American episode is not the religious hypocrisies of the rich but the fatuous complacency of their cultural spokesman, the poet Blandmour, who vindicates all the horrors of poverty in the name of natural order and laissez-faire capitalism. The English portion of the story depicts what Melville saw as an alternative and equally repugnant ideological pole—the wrath of a murderous proletariat no longer willing to be placated by the contemptuous charity of the wealthy. There is thus, in this new diptych, no national imbalance in favor of the English lower classes, or any offense to the church that might make the tales less attractive to the consumers of *Harper's* magazine. Melville's curious decision to set the piece forty years earlier, at the conclusion of the Napoleonic wars, may also have taken some of the contemporary sting from its satire, although it also leads to more intricate ironies, such as the description of a sordid area of London that strikes the narrator, in 1814, as being as "grimy as a backyard in the Five Points" (204). Thus Melville hints that the notorious New York neighborhood was already, even a generation previously, setting the metaphorical standards for urban squalor against which even London might scarcely compare.

"Poor Man's Pudding" is most evidently an attack on the prevalent literary sensibility that sentimentalizes the sufferings of the poor as part of a divine plan, and that manipulates language into cruel distortions of a supposed natural order. Thus Blandmour takes comfort that snow, in the absence of a better alternative, is "Poor Man's Manure: Distilling from kind heaven upon the soil, by a gentle penetration it nourishes every clod, ridge, and furrow" (192). A cup of cold rainwater, when substituted in a recipe, is Poor Man's Egg; it may also double duty as Poor Man's Plaster, a palliative for wounds that even the poorest of sufferers can afford. Amal Amireh proposes that Melville's story is a parody of Catharine Maria Sedgwick's 1836 novel *The Poor Rich Man and the Rich Poor Man*, which celebrates the honest and deserving poor in contrast to both the rich and the "vicious and ignorant 'very poor'" (56, 54). Amireh notes Sedgwick's endorsement of American exceptionalism, expressed in her belief that a moderate amount of hard work in America can achieve a respectable sufficiency. Melville, too, emphasizes a pattern of exceptionalism in his rural American family, the Coulters, but in his case it offers no grounds for celebration. The narrator, though resisting Blandmour's false comforts, nonetheless notes the anomalous position in which the "native American poor" find themselves. Trained to believe in "universal equality," they are humiliated by their condition and ashamed to accept relief for it. They feel shame, rather than resentment, at their poverty, and certainly the Coulters seem unlikely to emerge in any kind of rebellious fury from their unhealthy rural retirement. In London, by contrast, the situation among the poor is ripe for revolution: they see that their predicament is shared by many others; they labor under no false democratic illusion of equal opportunity; and the gulf between the classes is explicitly avowed in every aspect of their public life. In the circumstances of this story, the poor are being admitted to finish off the leavings of a Guildhall banquet for the rich, and the "lean, famished, ferocious creatures" pour like "a mob of cannibals" to fight for the aristocrats' crumbs. The narrator comments that "in this mighty London misery but maddens. In the country it softens," not an especially consoling thought for Melville's increasingly urban audience in the 1850s (204, 205).

The narrator of the story does not have a complacent literary man like Blandmour to guide him through the London portion of his poverty tour, as he did in rural America, but he has a carefully paralleled, ironic equivalent in the shape of a uniformed "civic subordinate" (203). This man displays the charities of the great city with the same relish for the providential ways of society as does the American poet. Melville thus seems to suggest that the bourgeois poet is as much a civic functionary in his support of the status quo as is the uniformed civil servant. His gentlemanly but compassionate narrator is therefore faced by something of a double dilemma about how to differentiate his democratic inheritance from the reactionary sentiments of his guides on both sides of the Atlantic and how to save his bourgeois skin when the revolution comes. In America, his private tour of the lower-class household confronts the narrator with all the conventional problems of class delicacy—misunderstandings of language, efforts not to gag on unpalatable food, attempts to show fellow-feeling without condescension, and covert efforts to absorb details without appearing to pry. He handles these embarrassments with a suave self-mockery that distinguishes him in manner, if not in substance, from Blandmour's oblivious complacency. In London, where the poor are no longer humble, and violent class war seems imminent, the narrator cannot long indulge his sardonic linguistic challenges to the values of the establishment. Now his physical safety is immediately threatened by "Lazaruses...ready to spew up in repentant scorn the contumelious crumbs of Dives," and he quickly adopts both the perspective and the behavior of the ruling class. He joins the government functionary in fighting off the beggars: "'hit that man — strike him down! hold! jam! now! Now! wrench along for your life,'" and he hears his guide address the driver of the hack in which he flees, "'Mind, Jehu...this is a *gentleman* you carry'" (208, 209). The literary middle ground of self-conscious irony seems insupportable by the end, when the narrator can merely turn helplessly to heaven and beg to be saved "equally from the 'Poor Man's Pudding' and the 'Rich Man's Crumbs'" (209). However, it is not in fact heaven that saves him but his final willingness to throw in his lot with the gentlemen.

In constructing the quasi-allegorical juxtapositions of wealth and poverty in this story, Melville for the first time introduces a veiled pattern of symbolism in which working-class women are doubly victimized—by their sexual exploitation as well as their inferior social position. Both parts of "Poor Man's Pudding and Rich Man's Crumbs" contain a good deal of bawdy innuendo about the poor farmer's wife in America being given "a Sunday ride" by the squire's man, an emperor having had "a finger in the pie" of a poor London girl, and the Prince Regent in his food choices being "uncommonly fond of the breast" (199, 206).[12] These double-entendres and allusions to the sexual use of women are never made explicit in the narrator's commentary as are his insights into the hypocrisies of democracy and charity. However, the motif of women as victims of their biology as well as their economic status is one that will become central to the last diptych, "The Paradise of Bachelors and the Tartarus of Maids" (1855), whose title gives explicit priority to the role of gender in its allegory.

This story is one in which scholars have most closely traced the echoes and satire of Washington Irving's leisurely and benevolent sketches, as well as allusions to the "hands" and "mouths" tropes of Theodore Parker's "Thoughts on Labor."[13] It is thus consciously *about* the nature of the literary discourse on gender, industrialism, wealth, and poverty as well as a contribution to it. The story moves stylistically from imitation and parody of bourgeois belles lettres to something akin to proletarian surrealism, while it addresses, thematically, the contemporary intersections of privileged and underprivileged people and the modes of expression appropriate to their lives. Melville's decision to make the representative poor in the story simultaneously female, factory workers, and producers of decorated sheets of paper that still remain essentially blank has led to some interesting critical speculation on its relationship to the *Lowell Offering*. Critics have looked at connections between the story and the magazine, which factory women produced as an amateur avocation, in contradistinction to their paid factory labor; and also at the relationship between the story and the increasing movement of women from the domestic sphere to a literary marketplace that, even as it was being feminized, was becoming progressively oriented to mass production.

Michael Newbury notes the complex and qualified nature of Melville's sympathy for the working and paper-producing women:

> On the one hand, Melville is clearly sympathetic toward the operatives, perhaps more in sympathy with these women than with the bachelors of "Paradise." On the other hand, I am suggesting that beneath this pity lies a subtext denying not only in biological but in artistic terms the idea of female originating power. The extent to which Melville imagines these operatives as exploited workers is the extent to which he explicitly and consciously sympathizes with them. The extent to which he associates them with a quasi- or even antiartistic mode of literary endeavor is the extent to which his anxieties about the commercial success of the "scribbling women" informs the particularities of this anti-industrial expression. (63–64)

The factory women who produced the *Lowell Offering* did not, of course, see themselves as "scribbling women," nor did they place any priority on commercial success, despite their pride in their creative activity, which they saw not at all as a metaphorical extension of factory labor but in conscious intellectual opposition to this mechanical activity. Melville's literary shuffling of oppositions and alignments, so that women's literary labor becomes tantamount to factory mass production, serves his literary quarrel with the marketplace better than it does any reformist concerns for improving factory conditions or liberating women from service to the machine (a situation he implies is analogous to women's own reproductive biology). Orestes Brownson had suggested that the factories contributed to women's sexual ruin; "The Tartarus of Maids" implies, by contrast, an industrial realm of enforced sexual chastity that transforms women's biological function as producers of babies into a parallel mechanical role as producers of blank sheets of paper. In Melville's story, women are less than fully human whether they are wage slaves or in thrall to their own reproductive machines. Unlike the aspiring factory women who contributed to *Mind amongst the Spindles*, they do not imagine for themselves an alternative life of the mind. Unlike the constrained Bartleby, they cannot even prefer not to be the servants of a machine that "*must* go" and of "the unbudging fatality" that drives it (252).

As in the other diptychs, there is once again a transatlantic comparison, although in this case it is doubly complicated by placing urbane bachelors in a quiet, almost bucolic setting in the heart of London, while the maids are in a noisy industrial factory in the heart of rural New England. Similarly confounding expectations, the sybaritic male dinner is both sensuous and decorous, while the female workplace is painful and grotesque. The narrator's easy assimilation into the cozy world of bachelors is tinged by his ever-present consciousness of their isolation from painful reality, but his ready sympathy for the miserable factory women is unable to bridge his feelings of estrangement from them and the grim lives they lead. In "The Paradise of Bachelors," he is poised ambivalently between self-caricature and self-indulgence in the fond memory of the bachelors' pleasures. He both satisfies and parodies the comfortable reader's expectations of literariness. Apostrophes ("Dear, delightful spot!"), poetic formulas ("the smiling month of May"), witty juxtapositions ("rise of bread and fall of babies"), even rhymes ("take your pleasure, sip your leisure") all echo the Irvingesque style (232, 228). When the privileged bachelors themselves employ literary tropes to aestheticize suffering, referring to pain and trouble as "legends" or "fables" that are not so welcome as a "spicy anecdote" for an after-dinner entertainment, Melville's satirical intentions are most apparent (237, 235). Their literary finesse collaborates perfectly with their gentlemanly status to mitigate the impact of all troubling moral questions.

By contrast, in "The Tartarus of Maids," the narrator abandons entirely such smooth verbal play for an intensely symbolic evocation of the New England paper factory. "Haggard rock," "shaggy-wooded mountains," "spike-knotted logs," and a "turbid brick-colored stream" contrast in their harsh diction with the soothing terms used to describe the Old World bucolic urban retreat in "The Paradise of Bachelors" (239). He explores all the most painful and negative permutations of his reiterated emphasis on whiteness (pallor, blankness, absence) and coldness (frigidity, virginity, rigidity). While the first half of the diptych presents careful reports of the bachelors' talk, the factory workers have no voice, either oral or written, except for the mechanically reproduced rose wreath they stamp on every sheet of paper. The mill is remote from society, freakish in its all-female work force, alien in its strange uterine machinery, and utterly resistant to all discourse between its inhabitants and the visitor from the outside world. Thus, despite the details that evoke familiar aspects of the New England factory system (neighboring boardinghouses, the rural origins of the workers, the predominance of women operatives), the paper mill is a grotesquely symbolic distortion of the real factories that existed at the time. There, women like Sarah Maria Cornell were beginning to make their voices heard in religious meetings, others like Harriet Farley and Lucy Larcom were writing and publishing their own compositions, and still others, like Sarah Bagley, were articulating the grievances of fellow workers in public forums. Simultaneously, a host of operatives were engaged in copious and lively correspondence with their friends and families. Much of their discourse was devoted to vigorous debates over their reputations *as working women* and about the best literary ways of representing themselves. Thus

Melville's symbolic decision to both silence and desex them is perhaps only conceivable as an "outside" story that embodies his most extreme sense of the otherness that existed for him in both women and poor people.

Melville's uneasiness with the "smooth" and fluent complacency of the bachelors' world leads him to create a dramatic antithesis of tortured silence and misery that can only be conveyed in the most extreme metaphors of mechanized bodies and dehumanized intellects. When Harriet Farley had worked for some time in a factory, she noticed that her feet had grown so much larger from the long hours of standing that her shoes no longer fit, and that one of her hands had become larger than the other. In her subdued and realist mode, she conceded that factory labor was, indeed, written on the body. When the women in Melville's paper mill attend their machines, the pink paper they make seems to be directly infused with blood from their cheeks, and the process of ruling the paper causes wrinkles to form on their brows. This difference between the straightforward account of industry's toll on women's bodies in Farley and the almost surreal acceleration of the same trope in Melville is not just one of degree but a qualitative step toward dehumanization that the actual women workers were far from ready to concede. Lucy Larcom's account of the concern of the *Lowell Offering*'s editors when she wrote an experimental poem of self-abnegation suggests that women factory workers were as wary of Romantically excessive obliterations of their selfhood as they were of its luxurious self-indulgence. Melville's disposition to write at the extremes, embodying in women workers the extravagant excesses of deprivation and dehumanization, was a climax of Romantic fictional engagement with their situation, but it was not a way that women writers and workers at the center of the social upheaval preferred to pursue.

Romantic novelists like Judd, Hawthorne, and Melville created dramatic literary symbols and complex allegories from the social, economic, and sexual upheavals they witnessed around them, and used these tropes to explore not merely the conditions of their world but the ways traditional techniques of literariness affected and sometimes distorted the representation of those conditions. They furthered the development of fiction as a versatile and elastic literary genre capable of incorporating complex debates about the symbiotic relationships of ideology and form, and they recognized the centrality of changing assumptions about sex and class relationships to the unsettling of their own ways of writing. If the lives and ambitions of actual working and writing women became somewhat abstracted and diminished in the process of their incorporation into this discourse, the women's own accounts, as well as the fictions of a large group of popular novelists, were more than sufficient to remind the public that there were other voices and selves vying to become part of the literary debate.

5

Fables of Lowell

The First Factory Fictions

It is singular that a place, not yet twenty-five years old, should already
have fabulous stories mingled with its history. Yet such is the case.
—HENRY A. MILES, *LOWELL, AS IT WAS, AND AS IT IS*
(1846)

It is not to be denied, however, that many, alas, too many of the
unfortunate frail ones, in all our large cities, have gone forth from those
haunts of Industry to the haunts of Infamy—turning their backs forever
upon respectability, honor, family, friends, and, worst of all, their own self-
esteem and peace of mind.
—ANONYMOUS, *ELLEN MERTON, THE BELLE OF LOWELL*
(1844)

"I am now learning to play the piano. I have various concerns that take
up my attention, such as, in the winter, attending our Institute lectures,
my singing school, sometimes a concert, and occasionally a party."
"Anything else?" he suggested.
"I sometimes—"
"Well," said Norton as she hesitated.
"Write," she said.
—"ARGUS," *NORTON: OR THE LIGHTS AND SHADES
OF A FACTORY VILLAGE* (1849)

The novels that emerged most promptly and directly from the experiences of women engaged in industrial labor in American factories
were artistically more convention-bound and less fantastic than Melville's
Tartarean fiction of pale and desexualized automatons servicing monstrous
machinery. However, they were also more ideologically open to considering a variety of attitudes toward factory work and the role it might play in
women's lives, both for good and ill. Although the plots of most of these
novels do not escape the alternative formulas of either seduction and betrayal
or virtue rewarded, the conditions and situations they depict reveal the gradual intrusion into fiction of changing ideas about the nature and needs of

working women and, most strikingly, about the role of their reading and writing in altering their own and others' perceptions of their identity.

Of twelve novels and novellas about New England factory life that appeared between 1844 and 1864, all deal with the predicament of women and girls facing the opportunities and threats of their new environment.[1] Thus they continue to explore the arguments first broached early in the century in the work of Sarah Savage and Catharine Williams, and later debated most hotly in the encounters between Orestes Brownson and the *Lowell Offering*. These arguments had offered contrary interpretations of factories: as an enlargement of the domestic sphere, where young women could aid their families and prepare themselves to be good wives and mothers, or as centers of temptation and degradation, where unprotected girls might fall irrecoverably from chastity and virtue. The new novels continue to depict the operative as both literary lady intent on reading, writing, and self-improvement; and as material girl, intent on getting, spending, and pleasure-seeking; as both virtuous and promiscuous; as both paragon and as no better than she should be. Like the earlier discourse, these novels continue to convey the double implication that women workers in American factories were exceptions to the European development of a distinct working class, and contrarily that already present within the factory population were both innately genteel and essentially vulgar types of operatives. However, despite the continuities, there are also indications that these first novels of factory life were beginning to absorb changes in attitudes about working women: among all the seduction and marriage plots, there are now also accounts of women who return to factory employment as an escape from marriage. Others choose the new mechanized labor as a more lucrative alternative to the respectable occupation of teaching school—and not just as an unselfish means of putting a brother through Harvard or paying off the mortgage on the family farm. Although happy tales of virtuous marriages to doctors and clergymen still alternate with sensational accounts of abortions, betrayals, and suicides, there is also a new willingness to consider women's sexual behavior in less absolute and condemnatory ways. There is even, finally, a tantalizing glimpse of a fictional heroine who is neither a delicate lady nor a self-indulgent hoyden but a merry and outspoken woman who leads her workmates on a picket line, in the first fictional account of a strike in American literature.[2] In formal terms, there is continuing evidence of writers' uncertainty about appropriate ways to treat their new literary and newly literate subject, the factory woman, for whom Melville's "blank paper" has now become a singularly ironic trope.

Because this first generation of what might loosely be called "Lowell novels" did not witness the emergence of any remarkable new literary talent, or evince any particularly radical political or economic theories, it is easy to overlook how dramatically the presence of the factory altered the portrayal of women as literary subjects.[3] Even when a factory setting was used merely to add novelty to a formulaic seduction plot, or to introduce some topical relevance to a Sunday school tale of the virtues of work and sacrifice, the fundamental facts of women as wage-earners, living outside the family, spending their own money, forming their own social circles, and making their own decisions (albeit burdened by many contingencies) changed symbiotically their sense of themselves and their literary representation. Later generations of more accomplished writers would refine and revise the fictions of American industrial life, developing a richer context of ideas—about social class, religion, philanthropy, capitalism, democracy, and feminism—and would engage in a more subtle aesthetic discourse beyond the didactic, the sensational, and the sentimental. Nonetheless, these earliest practitioners of factory fiction established a mythology of the factory girl and the paradoxes of her reputation that provided the sources for the development of that later and more complex tradition.

The expanding fame of the earliest American factory women was additionally enhanced later in the century by a number of autobiographical works by former Lowell workers. Lucy Larcom published a remarkable epic poem, *An Idyl of Work* (1875), that elevated the first female workers into a pantheon of democratic womanhood, unique in American literature, and both Larcom and her Lowell workmate, Harriet Robinson, went on to reminisce and reevaluate their factory experiences in memoirs written later in their lives. Even at the end of the nineteenth century, many historical novels of the early Lowell experience were still being written, and indeed the fictional allure of the subject was still notable late in the twentieth century, with the publication of novels based on Sarah Maria Cornell's Fall River experience and accounts of early New England factory women in popular adult and children's fiction.[4] Thus the terms set in these first novels of Lowell were frequently revisited and revised, and have had an enduring imaginative impact. Although clusters of similar themes and images are reiterated in them, these first novels are not monolithic in their view; nor is there a lost masterpiece among them. As Eleanor Marx Aveling later noted, when looking at the larger body of nineteenth-century American industrial novels, one looks in vain for the *Uncle Tom's Cabin* of American capitalism (77). There is no grand moral indictment of an economic and social system, and no prophetic advocacy of a new realm of women's work and possibility. These novels' innovations are not in offering degraded victims, revolutionary heroines, or noble new types of womanhood but in very slowly encroaching on the fixed typologies of female fictional characters and on conventional wisdom about the nature of women. These works are very far from the polished fictions of irony and paradox wrought (as in Howells and Wharton) with the intention of undermining fixed modes of thinking, but in their awkward, hesitant, and cruder fashion, they are the beginnings of that later development.

Two of the earliest Lowell novels, which both appeared in 1844 while the *Lowell Offering* was still being published, suggest how prevalent the stereotype of the New England factory woman had already become, and how ripe it was for both exploitation and satire. Osgood Bradbury's novel *The Mysteries of Lowell* and the anonymous *Ellen Merton, the Belle of Lowell* both label Lowell as the "Manchester of America," but a Manchester famous, unlike its debased English model, for the beauty and the intellectual aspirations of its factory operatives and for their literary publication (Bradbury 3; *Ellen* 3). Both authors engage in what are purportedly moral accounts of the hazards and temptations of factory life that run the literary gamut from semipornographic parody to playful comic irony. The author of the salacious *Ellen Merton* vows that he will not fall prey to "false delicacy" in his exposé of life in Lowell if the consequence is that such refinement should be "suffered to hoodwink Truth"; instead he will bravely reveal a world where "Vice stalks abroad untrammelled, Virtue sleeps, and Chastity lies bleeding" (4). This pious introduction is followed by a novella in the form of "confessions" by the libertine male members of the "G.F.K." club, who detail the ways they have each been seduced by eager young women. Ellen, a pure factory girl, has, however, resisted temptation so far and instead put her energies into elevating herself by her poetic contributions to the *Lowell Offering*.

While the superficial plot seems to be little more than a pretext for titillating tales of unbridled passion in crowded carriages, dimly lit church meetings, and the back rooms of stores, one curious feature of *Ellen Merton* is its extraordinary emphasis on literature itself as a subject. There are copious quotations from poetry, much mimicry of Romantic literary style, and a central thematic concern with the relationship of an individual's conduct to the kind of literary activity he or she undertakes. Henry Harford, the worldliest of the roués in the novella, justifies his rakish behavior with a self-serving pastiche of Romantic individualism:

> We have been placed here for some purpose or other, and the same Power that brought us into being, has endued us with certain capacities—feelings—inclinations; and has given us, moreover, our positions, stations and opportunities. For what? Are we to resist the dictates of those feelings—to suppress the promptings of Nature, or, if you prefer it, the will of God, as revealed within us? (6)

The lawyer Charles Howard, expelled from Dartmouth, finds vindication for his desire to pursue his inclinations justified by the "new fangled, fashionable philosophy of the day" that he encounters in Carlyle, Emerson, and Brownson (18). Although he does not so openly acknowledge it, Howard also appears to have assimilated a great deal of Poe, especially in his Ligeia-like account of his beloved Grace Melville, whose "eye, large, mild and lustrous, was blacker than the sloe; and the raven's wing could not vie with the glossiness of her long and sable curls." Grace has a glance "of more than earthly sweetness" and a brow "whiter than Parian marble," and her lover admits that "when the silvery music of her voice fell upon my ear

I could have fallen down and worshipped her" (19). In opposition to the excesses of the libertines' literary tastes, the book's upright young hero, William Walton, finds appropriate literary vindication for his own values in William Cullen Bryant's "Thanatopsis." Prior to his accidental encounter with a fragment of this solemn New England poem ("copied in his sister's hand, and placed there by his mother"), he has been "strangely enamored of a copy of Lord Byron's poems." When William comes upon the lines from "Thanatopsis," he reads them with tears of penitence for all his former errors and for the licentious path on which he was about to embark. Bryant conquers Byron and proves sufficient to turn the young hero back from his decadent companions and their "revolting confessions" to a future life of unbending integrity (26, 27, 28).

Ellen Merton, the factory girl, though of a literary turn herself, has not misspent her youth "in ephemeral poetry and novel reading." She is, however, a regular contributor to the *Lowell Offering* and thus diffuses "the fragrance of her mind" throughout society (26, 32). The "effulgence" of the *Offering* is directly opposed in this novel to a weekly scandal sheet that spreads its "ebullition of filth" in the Lowell community (29). These two papers thus become the symbolic written equivalents for the sexual alternatives of the story—modesty, restraint, and control are contrasted to the instant gratification of low appetites. The desire to read and write is portrayed as almost as instinctual as sexual desire, and, like other passions, in need of being tamed and properly cultivated. The author depicts men and women as equally strong in the ardor of their affections for both literature and the opposite sex, but men have of course had considerably more access to a wide range of experience in both realms. The novella argues for a kind of symbiosis between literary and passional attachments, in both of which men have much more latitude than women. However, women's entry into the literary realm and the workplace appears to assert a new-found initiative in human affairs, including those of the heart. Ellen Merton has come to Lowell not simply to earn money in the factories but to make a kind of proletarian debut: "it was thought expedient by her fond parents that she should see, and be seen in the world" (7). In the end, the anonymous author proves more interested in detailing seductions than in working out his intriguing theory of correspondence between literary and sexual decorum. Nevertheless, it is remarkable how much of this mildly pornographic novella of a beautiful factory girl is given over to literary allusions and imitations, and to discussions of its characters' tastes in reading and writing. It establishes the two main areas of interest that dominate most of the other Lowell novels— literariness and sexual conduct. They will recur constantly, though perhaps not always in quite such close thematic interdependency.

Osgood Bradbury's *Mysteries of Lowell* is explicitly, by its title, part of the popular literary genre of urban exposé novels, modeled after Eugène Sue's novel *The Mysteries of Paris* (1842) and *The Mysteries of London* (1844) by G. M. W. Reynolds. These begot a strain of American descendants that, according to David Reynolds, "pictured unbridled depravity among the rich and squalid wretchedness among the urban poor" (82). The *Mysteries of Lowell*, however, is less interested in exploring the social and economic gulf between classes than in investigating mysterious links that connect the owners, who run the mills, and the workers, who move from the countryside into the semiurban world of factory labor. The strange twists of the plot reveal at the end that all three of the main characters in the novel— its factory heroine, Augusta Walton, her honorable factory suitor, Edwin Gilmore, and her aristocratic, Harvard-educated admirer, Henry Seyton— are siblings. Such coincidences of hidden paternity prevent any formulaic concluding marriages among the main characters, although a more sensational climax is provided by the gory murder-suicide of the two villains. The author's real interest, however, appears to be less in the manipulative plot than in ironic literary game playing. The games involve parodies of various high styles, some sardonic mockery of Lowell "bluestockings" and their aesthetic aspirations, and a pervasive satire of the virtuous and innocent heroines of sensational seduction fiction who, as factory women, are now trapped in an absurd and patently outdated literary convention.

The narrator of *The Mysteries of Lowell* comments, early in the book, on the genius of both Henry Fielding and Eugène Sue, and these two ill-matched writers appear to be the strangely fused models for his work—an incongruous blend of irony and urban gothicism. The novel's factory protagonist, Augusta, is pursued by three suitors, and although she emerges unscathed, and also unmarried at the end, she proves in the manner of a Fielding heroine to be both fallible and calculatingly capable of self-preservation. The plot pits Augusta against a cast of characters from the conventions of melodrama: Owen Glendower, a lecherous, middle-aged factory owner; his nephew, Henry Seyton, a charming tempter; Glendower's jealous housekeeper, Adriana; and Adriana's scheming friend, Parmela, a Lowell factory worker. Amid these exaggerated types, Augusta is an oddly realist figure. Introduced as ardent, "ambitious and aspiring," she is also "naturally an honest female so far as these contending passions would permit her to be" (7–8). When the dashing and eligible Henry first takes the obligatory gentleman's tour of the factory where Augusta works, she sets out deliberately to cater to his intrusive male gaze. She takes care to make her movements about the machinery "as graceful as possible," displaying her pretty, white fingers on the end of the loom:

> She saw him look very wishfully upon her hand, and in a moment she read his thoughts; therefore she gently drummed the hard wood of which the loom was made with the ends of her fingers. She meant to let him know that her hand was alive and had sensation in it. If he had touched it as his nerves then were, no doubt he would have received a shock which would have coursed through his blood with the velocity of light. (16, 17)

Augusta also takes planned promenades past the house of the wealthy Glendower, although these do not evoke quite such dramatic reactions in the shortsighted older man as in the factory voyeur: "Mr. Glendower thought he saw a smile playing about her blood-red lips, but he was not certain as he was troubled to see at a distance without his glasses, which he did not happen to have on at that time" (12). Such willful comic subversion of melodrama by banal realism coexists throughout the novel, alongside frequent indulgence in the very histrionic formulas that are elsewhere parodied. The frequency with which such formal and stylistic inconsistencies occur in this and other Lowell novels suggests not merely the limited abilities of many of the writers but also their very real uncertainty about their elusive subject, for whom prior conventions may have seemed obsolete but new modes were still undeveloped.

When the factory heroine, Augusta, receives marriage proposals from her two rich suitors and her poverty-stricken true love, she responds neither with gratitude nor excitement but rather with a contentious desire to enter into arguments with each of them about the professions they are making. When the honorable worker, Edwin, asks tremblingly if she knows how much he loves her, Augusta replies, "Well, now Edwin, that's a good one.... How should I know how much you love me, or anyone else?...I have no means by which I can measure such a subtle etherial essence as love is" (23). To Henry's wish that he might call her his "own Augusta," she responds sharply, "if I was your property, or your own Augusta, as you say, you could sell me as they do the black females at the south" (31). To Glendower's suggestion of a trial period as his housekeeper, before she becomes his wife, she responds shrewdly that it would be "very apt to make talk among the busy-bodies" (35). Augusta's attitude to her final fate proves as complicated and realistically ambivalent as is her character. When she does not marry, but acquires instead two half-brothers and the paternal recognition of a prosperous father, Bradbury comments, "So keen were her feelings, and so strong her excitement that she didn't know whether she was happy or miserable" (40).

The muted irony of the portrait of Augusta as a young woman alone, trying to evaluate her priorities and balance desire with virtue, becomes much more robust satire in Bradbury's treatment of minor characters and in his parodic handling of the fictional conventions of the romantic mystery. When the pious and hypocritical Glendower meditates on how to set up a private, nighttime interview with Augusta, he exclaims, "I sometimes wish I was not religious" (17). When Henry embarks on his rather caddish courtship of Augusta, he is described as "full of love, as ever an egg was of meat" (18). The humor turns more sardonically to literary topics in the account of Parmela Snyder's career as a contributor to the *Lowell Offering*. Parmela, true to the Lowell mystique, is the daughter of "poor, but honest" parents in New Hampshire, who has come to the "city of shuttles and spindles," has much improved herself by education, and, by means of "great prudence, economy, and industry" has saved "a handsome sum of money," now invested at interest (14). She has already published two poems in the *Offering,* one a religious piece, the other a sentimental one undertaken in a flight of simultaneous romantic and literary optimism:

> The full moon had just arisen, and began to throw her silver light over the city; the bright stars to twinkle in the clear blue sky; the air was soft and bland and a gentle breeze played about the window as if the night air was stirred by angel's wings, and the loving Parmela drew her pencil from her heaving bosom and began to write down her peculiar sensations. (14)

The digression on Parmela has only a very minimal connection to the main plot of *The Mysteries of Lowell,* but thematically, it is central to Bradbury's pervasive comic awareness of stylistic conventions and fictional formulas. A recent addition to these formulas now apparently includes the figure of the literary factory girl, ridiculed in Parmela's midnight poeticizing, but essential to Augusta's capacity to analyze the linguistic manipulations of her suitors and invent witty verbal responses.

Bradbury continually draws attention to the formulaic elements of his own text—from his self-conscious use of quotation marks around phrases like "disinterested benevolence" and "poetry of motion" to his condescending permission to the reader to move his chapter epigraphs around to where they may "please the fancy best: for we have no predilections to be gratified" (3, 16, 7). When he opens a chapter with the statement "the full moon had just arisen," he promptly adds "(how lucky it is that the beautiful moon is always at the command of some writers!)" (21). When he digresses, he draws attention to the deviation by noting "We were saying, when we flew off from the course of our story upon the above metaphysical point" (10), and when the rather ineffectual Edwin disappears from the narrative for a considerable period, he comments "The reader may begin to enquire, where is the modest, the good and loving Edwin Gilmore all this time" (37). Bradbury also confides and analyses his own literary decisions about what to put in or exclude from his book: "We had some notion of not introducing the reader to the scene between Mr. Glendower and Miss Walton, contenting ourselves by only giving the general result of the interview" (33–34). When he employs a powerful metaphor, such as the repeated analogy between sexual desire and the charged "electric fluid" of a thunderstorm, he escalates its application of magnets, galvanic batteries, shocks, strikes, charges, conductors, and electrified currents to extravagant absurdity (5–6). There is certainly plenty of sexual titillation and didactic moralizing in Bradbury's novel, but it is impossible to believe that a major portion of the satisfaction to be derived from this little book was not from the relish of its literary playfulness in simultaneously applying and undermining contemporary conventions and stereotypes. That the representation of the female factory worker and her experiences was already, by 1844, ripe for humor, and implicitly therefore for more nuanced development, is a testament to the real historical emergence of working women whose lives challenged the simple verities of gender and class that dominated the earliest period of their literary reputation. It is also, indirectly, a hint that the political and didactic struggles for control of the operative's image by single-minded factory advocates and opponents would not dominate the fiction of the working woman to the exclusion of other more complicated stories that might be told about her.

Bradbury's novel is not, of course, typical in its literary playfulness about the genre of factory novels to which it is contributing. However, even in the most melodramatic and humorless of these Lowell novels, the authors regularly consider how the habits of mind and the literary activities of the operatives qualify or enhance their sexual vulnerability or their virtuous resistance to seduction. Surely the most extreme example of such a preoccupation is *Norton: or The Lights and Shades of a Factory Village*, published by "Argus" in 1849. The novel describes the return to Lowell, after a twelve-year absence, of Norton, a mysterious stranger who goes unrecognized by his mother and sister, and serves as the author's lens to view the customs and the culture of the "city of spindles," labeled once again "the Manchester of America" (3). Prime among his concerns is the question of seduction and its connection to literacy and to the newly awakened and ardent pursuit of self-culture by the working women of the Lowell community.

The novel performs a virtual sociological dissection of Lowell, although scarcely an impartial one, for every aspect of the factory system, from its long work hours to its careful regulation of the urban landscape, is stoutly defended. The author's sharpest attacks focus on those elements of city life where there is least oversight and control, thus, from his perspective, leading to the ruin of the female workers. Prominent among potential bad influences are libraries where women may obtain French novels; from de Kock to George Sand, these are "enough to poison the mind of any virtuous girl" (10). Male seducers quite calculatingly give eager factory readers these degrading romances, but particularly outrageous to "Argus" is their presence in the public libraries of the town. When Norton finds out this shocking piece of information, he reacts "with a look of incredulity" and exclaims, "Impossible!" (35). In opposition to French romances and to the "low flashy wit" of such plays as *A Glance at New York* by Benjamin Baker, *Norton* several times proposes what appears to be an approved canon of literature suitable for the factory girl.[5] This includes Felicia Hemans, Lydia Sigourney, Eliza Cook and Hannah More, as well as Pope, Addison, Young, Cowper, and Goldsmith. History and travel books are acceptable, as well as the botanical study of rare and beautiful flowers—always considered appropriate for young women interested in science. However, these proposals to change the offerings of public libraries insinuate an ominous agenda into the novel's endorsement of Lowell's many educational institutions, from its museum to its Institute lectures and singing school: they suggest the author's support for efforts to censor and shape workers' reading habits and thereby their minds.

The novel makes a valiant, but not entirely successful, effort to extend into the world of factory labor an older moral taxonomy of women that associates virtue with submissive and ladylike attributes and vice with female sauciness and vulgarity. In *Norton*, the factory "lady" embraces labor as noble and elevating, while the rebellious jade tries to avoid work and considers the label "mill girl" distasteful, although she detests housework even more (19). The lady reads Hemans, the jade de Kock; the lady is pale, with downcast eyes and a calm demeanor; the jade is plump and rosy, has a wild laugh, and bounds about. However, when the lady modestly defends the factory system and the jade attacks it flamboyantly, the author's elevation of pallor over rosiness, and of placidity over energy, reveals itself as a distinctly problematic trope. The rebellious young woman who criticizes factory life describes a typical day's work: "we poor girls have to leave our beds at five to run at the call of the bell, and then remain hived up in these great, noisy rooms all the day long;...From five in the morning to seven in the evening" (19). In such a context, the lady's pale face and languid movements risk losing their connotations of superiority and evoke instead Melville's grotesque apotheosis of regulated female pallor—rows of blank white girls, blankly performing blank activities.

The hard facts of factory life in Lowell, even when softened by "Argus" and presented in their most positive light, inevitably make the application of the old standards for judging women's worth seem archaic and incongruous. The celebration of physical delicacy, white skin, and a soft voice in the context of twelve-hour workdays, tending machinery amid deafening noise in an unhealthy atmosphere, is innately grotesque: it is a model of class and gender wholly inappropriate to the realities of industrial work. The ladylike Catherine Elliston's defense of her daily routine must, even in 1849, have invited a skeptical response. To Norton's suggestion that her mill employment consumes a great deal of time, leaving her little for leisure, she replies: "'Tis true we go in at five in the morning, and do not get out till seven in the evening; but from seven till ten o'clock are three hours. One hour of that time could be spent in our amusement; another hour for our private work, and then if we choose to sit up until ten, we have an hour to devote to reading" (24). Even during the hours of factory labor, Catherine asserts that employment "soothes rather than ruffles our minds," although she concedes that women less controlled than herself become "angry and excited" by petty grievances and thus suffer a great deal of "perplexity and trouble" (25). The endorsement of Catherine's even-temperedness over the scolding and fretting of her more disgruntled workmates suggests a somewhat sinister analogy between the placid lady and the acquiescent employee.

The more robust and boisterous women, manifestly more capable of enduring the long hours of labor, are excluded by their sturdiness and assertive physicality from the traditional decorousness that would make them good gender models. When Catherine is invited, on one occasion, to perform on the piano, she "blushingly" consents, sings in a "sweet, pure voice," and plays in a "retiring, unaffected manner." The moral character and the fate of the vibrant Julia, who follows her at the piano, can be forecast from the manner of her performance: "Julia's execution was striking and brilliant, and her rich full voice broke out into a gushing song of gladness" (23). Needless to say, Julia will shortly be seduced, betrayed, and dead, and "strangers will tread lightly over her ashes" (80). The paradox that the female vitality and enthusiasm necessary for the hard labor of both body and mind is dangerous to female virtue is implicit but never explicitly acknowledged in the novel, since to do so would undermine its simultaneous defense of exhausting factory work and its concern for moderation and control in all aspects of women's lives, from their emotions to their taste in library books.

Norton clings to the central theme of the older novel of seduction and betrayal, the notion that "ruin" for a woman refers exclusively to her sexual reputation, whose loss is irretrievable and whose consequence is ignominy, poverty, and death. However, even in the realm of women's sexual conduct, there are once again implicit suggestions that the reality of the factory world might be more multifaceted than such narrow moral dualism might indicate. Despite Julia's melodramatic and ominous illustration of the wages of ebullience and sin, the survey by "Argus" of the circumstances of factory life and of women's new-found earning capacity indicates that, even for fallen women, there are new opportunities in the urban industrial world for mobility, anonymity, and possibly second chances. Women may still pine away, and die from broken hearts or in unwedded childbirths, but, to judge from the evidence in *Norton* as well as from the widespread presence of abortionists in other fiction of the period, it is increasingly possible for women to deal practically with the consequences of a "fall." They are better able to conceal the evidence, find other employment, and support themselves economically in a community of not entirely unknowing or unsympathetic fellow workers. Thus, although Norton's fallen sweetheart Meg exclaims, "Man can reform—*woman, never!*" the novel suggests that a considerable number of women in Lowell are capable of resilience, if not reform, and of finding an alternative to death and suicide in the factory community, in the aftermath of their ruin (60).

"Argus" describes the dramatic decline of two ruined women, in the persons of Norton's sister Julia and his former fiancée, Agnes, who has now become the prostitute Saucy Meg. However, there is a significant disproportion between the excessive punishment and suffering meted out to these two prominent female characters and the sociological context of the novel, which insists on the pervasiveness and familiarity of vice and crime in the Lowell environment. This tension between exceptional sinners and typical conditions tempers the older theology of a fallen woman's deserved retribution with more contemporary explanatory social theories that offer understanding, if not forgiveness, of her conduct. Indeed, "Argus" places considerable weight on the need for reforms in urban life, although the changes he advocates all tend to be in the direction of greater social controls and repression. However, he has difficulty making his reformist sociological concerns fit the Procrustean bed of seduction and betrayal fiction. If he were a complete nostalgic reactionary, yearning for the traditional mores and gender roles of an older rural life and an even harsher theology, he would have a much easier task. Then his attacks on dance halls, bars, pick-pockets, cutthroats, prostitution, gaming, and legislative corruption would fit neatly into the copious school of antiurban fiction in nineteenth-century America that Adrienne Siegel has described so effectively.[6] Instead, "Argus" is an enthusiastic advocate of factories, manufacturing, and the new urban communities they help to foster. Interestingly, his hero, Norton, has made his fortune during his long absence from Lowell by working for a southern cotton merchant, so he has apparently no scruples about exploitation at either end of the cotton business. By trying to combine the promotion of modern industry with the repressive gender morality of pre-industrial ways, he exposes the inconsistencies of both ideologies and the limited malleability of traditional female literary images.

The town of Lowell itself plays a prominent role in *Norton*, with both its haunts of vice and its utopian possibilities. The latter are detailed in an idealized portrait of the city on a starlit night, when the various cultural, commercial, and residential buildings are lighted and drawn into a balanced fusion of nature and industry:

> The waning moon was shedding a soft, mellow light around them; while myriads of stars flecked and spangled the arched vault above. Below them, close at their feet, like a dim mass, lay Lowell, with its churches and its far-famed factories. Two long, continuous lines of misty light shot up over the buildings, marking out the princi-pal thoroughfares of Merrimack and Central Streets. A dull sound even now came murmuringly from them on their ears, blending with the faint roar of the waters as they rushed over Pawtucket and Hunt's Falls. Everywhere they gazed on illuminated windows of the thousand dwellings, and by those steady, unerring lights could they mark the extent and outlines of the city. Still nearer, between the two falls, sluggishly flowed the waters of the noble Merrimack. Dark shadows, from the towering mills of the Law-rence, the Merrimack, the Boott, and the Massachusetts Corpora-tions, that lined, for a long way, the southern bank, were thrown out half way across its placid surface; elsewhere it was reflected like a lake of clear glass in the falling rays of the queen of night. (26)

Order reigns in this majestic scene, where the works of man and nature, of religion and industry, coalesce harmoniously in the carefully designed city: the lines are symmetrical and architectural, the sounds are muted, and the lights unerring. The only violators of this industrial Eden are the very women who were brought to work in the factories on account of their biddability. "Argus" dismisses those reformers who say the flaws are in the factory system and in the oppression of the operatives. His improvements for factory women would include more regulation of their lives, not less; more control of their free time and leisure options; and most specifically more vetoes on the dangerous books to which they have access and which they seem so eager to read. This early campaign by "Argus" to get French romances out of public libraries is a harbinger of later and more highly organized efforts to regulate the minds of workers with appropriate reading material. It is also an early admission that working-class women's literacy was not necessarily linked to their virtue, docility, or ladylike conduct but might instead be a token of wayward desires and recalcitrant natures.

Even when the old conventions of the novel of seduction and betrayal are rigidly applied to the Lowell milieu, as in the 1850 novel *Mary Bean or the Factory Girl*, by Miss J. A. B., there is a suggestion that factory girls' intellects must be carefully guarded and controlled. The plot of *Mary Bean* does not deviate much from the factory seduction model, except in making Mary a Canadian rather than an American girl, who leaves home for the factories of Manchester, New Hampshire, rather than Lowell. Once there, the author largely neglects the factory connection, arranging for Mary's board, somewhat unusually, in a single room where she may receive daily visits from her seducer. Mary Bean, unlike many of her factory compatriots, is not a reader or a writer, but she is wholly susceptible to the seductive power of words, in the form of eloquence and "passionate speech" (16). Mary succumbs to her lover's linguistic appeal to the combination of her "*vanity and intellect*" (17)—a warning that female minds among the spindles may not be as strong and independent as their ambitious owners think. Mary's short career is a litany of betrayals: her seducer proves also to be a criminal and a murderer, and he persuades the pregnant Mary to go to an abortionist, at whose house she dies. Her body is thrown into the millstream, a solitary reminder of the factory locale that elsewhere barely colors this generic tale. Otherwise, the book focuses on the moral that women who venture away from the domestic circle are especially vulnerable to predatory men, who ensnare them with the powers of language. Miss J. A. B. does not make a specific connection between women who are duped by flattery and women who are led astray by French romances, but she manifests a comparable fear to that of "Argus" that women's minds must be as vigorously regulated as their bodies, especially in factory towns where both may be so easily seduced.

Other Lowell novels that make the specific link between the temptations of the body and the brain of the operative, and suggest that female vanity is at fault in both cases, include the anonymously published novel *The Mysteries of Nashua* (1844), and Hannah Talcott's *Madge; or Night and Morning* (1863). In *The Mysteries of Nashua*, the self-centered factory girl Elizabeth Fletcher divides her free time between a shopping spree amid tempting displays of "dazzling and gaudy finery" (21) and lecture-going. However, like French novels, the lecture, too, is a source of danger for vulnerable women, for the entrance to the hall is lined with young "rowdies" who call out coarse jests and grasp at the attendees. By contrast, the heroine, Adeline Perkins, refuses both lectures and storekeepers' goods, preferring to spend her evenings in "retrospection of the past pleasures of her childhood's home, the recollections of a father's kindness and a mother's love" (20). The heroine of *Madge*, too, demonstrates her virtue by dual resistance to material and intellectual self-indulgence, refusing to purchase the "great variety of articles temptingly displayed in the stores" (139) and wisely rejecting the young man who tries to woo her with a gift of Mrs. Radcliffe's sensational novel *The Mysteries of Udolpho*.

Whether a willingness to read Mrs. Radcliffe was a symptom of an already tainted mind or a first step toward the contamination of a pure one, these factory novels are as obsessively preoccupied with the heads and minds as with the bodies of their protagonists. The novels that present a positive picture of industrial life for women, and of virtue rewarded, are just as concerned with the proper kind of books for their factory characters to read as are the lurid exposés of urban mysteries and horrors whose operatives indulge in the sensations of de Kock. In his study *The Intellectual Life of the British Working Classes*, Jonathan Rose concludes that in Britain the culture of the working-class autodidact was, at least until the late nineteenth century, an overwhelmingly male one. However, in the United States, all the evidence of autobiographies, letters, memoirs, and the emphases of novels themselves has long denoted the keen appetite for learning, reading, writing, and participating in the life of the mind that existed among factory women. Harriet Farley noted the distinction in one of her *Lowell Offering* editorials. Acknowledging "the intellectual superiority of the males of English manufactories," she added, "In this place the females are, if not more intellectual, at all events more literary" (4: 281). Consequently, like women's appetites in general, their literary tastes were a source of both foreboding and celebration in popular fiction. Rose notes that educated people in Britain tended to find something profoundly menacing in the efforts of the working class at self-education: the nation's class hierarchy "rested on the presumption that the lower orders lacked the moral and mental equipment necessary to play a governing role in society. By discrediting that assumption, autodidacts demolished justifications of privilege."[7] Certainly the same fears moved southern slaveholders in the United States to proscribe literacy for their human chattel, but in the case of women's intellectual activity, the fears seem to have focused to an extraordinary extent on the susceptibility of women to the particular style and content of the books they read rather than merely the self-validating and empowering effects of the act of reading itself.

A. I. Cummings's 1847 novel *The Factory Girl or Gardez La Coeur* is a virtual compendium of positive instances of the harmonious coupling of mental and moral worth in female operatives. It purports to demonstrate that women's mental development is always best when it is combined with a modest sense of appropriately feminine limitations: thus women's "intellectual beauties" are best manifested in an *"acute sense of propriety,"* in a fusion of high intelligence and respectability, and in an awareness of intellectual worth coupled with humility (45). Cummings's novel thus reveals, again like *Norton*, the quandary of the woman whose mind dwells among the spindles: namely that her most striking characteristic—her eager intellect—must be constantly reined in and kept under control in order to comport with a good reputation. This self-imposed restraint might result in delaying her own education in order to support her family, or in making sure that her desire for knowledge did not outpace seemly decorum. Virtuous factory heroines are almost always poised between self-sacrifice and self-cultivation, although this rarely poses a consciously explored dilemma for them. They simply do not allow themselves to aim too high or to expect too much.

This emphasis on seemliness and moderation is equally true of their social accomplishments—they never deliberately aspire to rise significantly in social or financial status, although they almost always do, by marrying doctors and clergymen who both elevate their class standing and support their literariness. This narrative convention of the move from working-class wage-earner to professional man's wife suggests a still fluid sense of class affiliation that permits characters to be outspoken defenders of the republican values of factory labor and at the same time to "marry up" and receive the deferred economic rewards of their earlier sacrifices. The historical record of letters and memoirs from actual factory operatives shows a much more complicated mix of ambitions and outcomes than the marriage or betrayal formulas of popular fiction. Factory women often saved their wages for their own, rather than their brothers', education and envisioned other careers, or an unwed life of continuing factory work. New England could not possibly have provided enough kind doctors and upright clergymen to reward all virtuous operatives with such suitable partners. Cummings's novel still clings to the upwardly mobile marriage as payback for his deserving workers, but he also reveals incipient class tensions in the factory world that undermine the novel's complacent central narrative of virtue rewarded with a higher-class husband.

Cummings thus draws on quite antithetical ideologies of class harmony and class conflict, with no acknowledgement of their incongruity. Few authors, indeed, can have been more in thrall to formulaic literariness, or more unaware of the logical problems of drawing simultaneously on contradictory conventions, than was Cummings. For him, the sun is always Sol, the wind Boreas, Aurora daily takes her seat in "her oriental chariot," "feathered songsters" warble, and zephyrs play (17, 83). His main heroine, Calliste Barton, is a noble farm girl who goes to work in Lowell to subsidize her brother's education, meanwhile generously stifling her own wish "for more ample opportunities for mental improvement" (45). Calliste labors "with a light heart and determined purpose" and finds her work daily "less irksome" (49). She has free access to a valuable library; she attends the lyceum; she reads and writes for the *Offering*; and with her factory friend, Louisa, she lives in an elegantly furnished room, whose "every part indicated more the *sanctum* of the poet, or the *studio* of the artist, than the residence of the operative" (90). Calliste's and Louisa's careers, which culminate in their escape from scheming rakes, followed by their respective marriages to a doctor and a clergyman, might well have been the literary product of any factory propagandist eager to demonstrate how the young women who came to Lowell might make good. However, Cummings was considerably affected by an altogether different factory mythology that was equally powerful in depicting factories as distinctly antirepublican institutions that were enforcing increasing segregation on social classes, undermining democracy, and debasing the working population of New England. Thus he occasionally falls wholeheartedly into the rhetoric of the other side, of the anticapitalist denouncers of greedy monopolists and exploited workers:

> Were ye on other soil than that where *Freedom* was purchased at the point of the bayonet and the cannon's mouth, and the doctrine of *"equal rights,"* sealed with blood, ye need not blush so deeply with shame! But *here*, shame on the vile being who would fain raise an aristocracy to curse the land! The wrongs of *Factory Girls* shall not always sleep forgotten, and the instrument of high-handed monopoly go unchecked!...Ye would keep the humble and virtuous girl in a state of degradation, little above the beasts that perish, were it in your power! (135)

Perhaps a more skillful writer might have created a fruitful literary tension between these antithetical modes and ideologies, but Cummings works only in formulas that expose, apparently unintentionally, the growing rift between the factory ideal and the fear of an ominous reality.

Although there were a number of other factory fictions in which a virtuous operative found her reward in a good marriage—to a doctor in "Anna Archdale: or, The Lowell Factory Girl" (1850) and to a clergyman in Alice Neal's story "The New England Factory Girl" (1848)—they, too, display some of Cummings's ambivalence, not so much toward the factory system itself as to the whole question of incipient class stratification and class consciousness. The factory novelists almost always endorse the ideal of a classless society and hold snobs and social climbers up to ridicule. At the same time, however, their moral ranking of characters tends to replicate a class taxonomy in which the middle is the desirable level, with villainous aristocrats (frequently southerners) at one end and the vulgar, shopping mob of factory flirts at the other. Thus, in "The New England Factory Girl," young James Gordon has qualms about allowing his sister, Mary, to subsidize him with factory work at Lowell because she would be "wasting, or at least passing the bright hours of her girlhood in the midst of noise and heat, with *rude associations* for her *refined* and gentle nature" (185, emphasis added). When the laughing operatives do indeed tease Mary about her prim ways, she reveals "a tone of mind and manner...far superior to that of her companions" (197). Although the explicitly stated moral of the tale is that "*honest labor elevates, rather than degrades,*" Mary's ladylike refinement and delicacy are clearly established well before she engages in factory labor and are the result of birth rather than elevating work (219). The same point is made with even less subtlety in the case of Anna Archdale, who is forced from her splendid Boston home into the mills when her wealthy merchant father loses his fortune. Although Anna's rival in love attempts to taint her reputation with the smear that she is a flirt, this negative factory label fails to attach to someone who is clearly innately superior. Anna does not, however, marry into her original upper class but instead weds a young physician who occupies a suitable middle rank between operative and merchant.

Hannah Talcott's *Madge* offers another rather disingenuous account of the factory woman's supposed ability to transcend class stratification. The novel begins with Madge's descent to the bottom of the social hierarchy, as a "bound-girl" whose mother has died in the poorhouse. When she runs away from her abusive mistress, as a twelve-year-old, to look for work in the mill, her frail constitution causes her to be rejected by several potential employers, and her prospective landlady is initially concerned that admitting a factory girl will lower the tone of her respectable boardinghouse. Despite their reservations, Madge proves a hardworking employee and a genteel tenant, her delicate demeanor proving to be not a sign of poor health but of superior social origins, as the granddaughter of a wealthy judge. Madge pursues the factory woman's usual quest for knowledge and education, and forms a friendship with the scholarly Maurice, who proves his romantic worthiness with the gift of a writing case. Meanwhile, Madge fends off the courtship of the more vulgar James Stanley, who is so foolish as to try to woo her with (again!) *The Mysteries of Udolpho*, and to speak slightingly of *Pilgrim's Progress*. In an interesting twist on the dangers of the wrong books and literary influences, it is Maurice rather than Madge who is almost led astray by his reading on a European trip. Though warned in advance of the "infidel sentiments, which tinctured to an alarming extent, the most beautiful German literature" (235), Maurice is nonetheless diverted from his New England values when he goes abroad, and comes close to betraying Madge for an English aristocrat. In the end, Madge's virtue and intellectual diligence are rewarded with a suitable marriage to a reformed Maurice, but once again her final status seems more like a recognition of innate good breeding than of the democratic egalitarianism of the American factory world.

The struggles of early factory novelists to apply traditional class- and gender-based terms of evaluation to working women led them into many problems and incongruities. Authors seem to have had difficulty finding ways of rewarding virtue except by elevating their heroines with upwardly mobile marriages out of the working class to which they were supposedly loyal. When they applied traditional gendered terms of approval like "pale," "delicate," and "retiring," they created women who were obviously too weak for twelve hour work days. And when they advocated the values of self-restraint and intellectual limitation, they were undermining the essential quality that supposedly made these New England women admirably exceptional: namely that they had chosen to cultivate their minds in an environment that was increasingly coming to view them as "hands." Not all factory novelists, however, left their women characters happily wed or ignominiously dead, nor did they all punish their operatives' avid intellectual enthusiasm or elevate their decorum and self-censorship. Three of the Lowell novelists, all of whom appear to have had particularly close or firsthand experience of factory women's lives, chose to emphasize aspects of their female characters' lives beyond their sexual partnerships with men, whether loving husbands or seducers and betrayers. They variously created working women who were adventurers, survivors, and incipient feminists, who found their highest pleasure in their writing, or used it as a weapon in the world rather than as an intellectual ornament in the *Offering*. For these authors, the motif of the literary factory girl was more than a fictional formula. Of the three authors, one, Day Kellogg Lee, was a Universalist minister who studied many aspects of workers' lives, and the other two, Martha W. Tyler and Charlotte S. Hilbourne wrote first-person, "ostensibly autobiographical" narratives of factory women's lives that are less indebted to literary tradition than those already discussed, and more attuned to a greater variety of outcomes for working women.[8]

Day Kellogg Lee's *Merrimack; or, Life at the Loom* (1854) is perhaps the first accomplished factory novel in terms of substantial length, narrative sophistication, density of social detail, and development of character. The breadth of Lee's context is immediately established by his placement of his evocatively named heroine, Mercy Winthrop, in Salem, Massachusetts, and his initial focus on her sea-captain father and the subsequent transition in New England from a seagoing and mercantile economy to an industrial and manufacturing one. Salem, at time of the novel, is the home of a group of prosperous Quakers, a free black woman, and a man who has been driven to insanity because he has sat on a jury that imposed a death sentence—presumably all signs of the liberalizing and diversifying of a formerly intolerant and exclusionary community.

After her father's death, twelve-year-old Mercy works in a shop; then, when her mother dies, she goes into service; when she finally turns to factory work, she is seeking better wages than a servant's and a more honest alternative to the lies she is forced to tell in her sales job. While Mercy is a servant in a Quaker household, she eagerly reads what books they will permit—biographies and such novels as *The Vicar of Wakefield*. Her first purchase with her factory wages is "a little mahogany whatnot, to stand in a naked corner, and receive my books" (78). Once again, in this novel, the choice of a factory worker's reading serves as a guide to her character and likely conduct. Miss Mumby, who is "fleshy and florid," with a taste for "gay colors and glittering toys" (79), asks Mercy at their first meeting if she "had ever passed the old Bell Tavern in Danvers, or seen Eliza Wharton's grave" (80). Miss Mumby's confused fascination with the original and the fictionalized protagonist of Hannah Foster's novel *The Coquette* reveals both her emotional and her literary shallowness; by contrast, the promising young machinist, Neal Darby, quotes Washington Irving and compares Byron to Pope. Mercy finds life in a factory town an ever-expanding vista of literary and educational possibilities—she reads Sedgwick, Allston, Bryant, Hawthorne, Tennyson, and Wordsworth, and she attends lectures on astronomy. When she and her workmates publish the first issue of their periodical, "The Garden," she feels as if she has reached the epitome of female fulfillment: "We never forgot that evening. Every impulse of womanhood seemed to be aroused and inflamed in our bosoms" (204). Instead of the conventional opposition of materialism and religion as the worldly and unworldly modes of life for operatives, the life of the mind becomes the preferred alternative to the vanities of the mundane world: "Who would not abandon toys and tinsels, and retrench the expenses of the wardrobe, to buy a little more paper, and have three or four new books to read?" (205).

The great expansion of intellectual opportunity for Mercy and the other operatives comes at exactly the same point in the novel as an economic depression and major cutbacks by the corporations that reduce wages drastically and force many workers into great suffering. Mercy's response is to defend the corporations for having taught the workers independence and self-discipline so that they are now better equipped to deal with deprivation and loss. Although Mercy's literary circle encourages workers to lead examined lives, their scrutiny does not extend to the economic system that they inhabit, or to its appropriation of a religion that provides a rationale for worldly suffering. Curiously, the only one of the workers to write in defense of the rights of labor in "The Garden" is Neal Darby, who had, perhaps ominously, preferred Byron to Pope. Later Neal completes his defection when he inherits $50,000 and abandons Mercy for a nouveau riche socialite who prefers Susannah Rowson to Frederika Bremer. Mercy's effort to respond to Neal's betrayal of her comes close to a parody of nineteenth-century factory women who read too much:

> I searched my library for a book which might apply to my case, and express my mixed emotions. I read Lady Byron's reply to her lord's "Fare thee well," and found not my anodyne there. I opened "The Sorrows of Werter," and shut it before I finished the first chapter. I went to Amelia's table and took "Alonzo and Melissa," but that was intolerable and I dashed it on the floor. I took down

Irving and read with keen interest his "Pride of the Village," but found I was neither so unhappy nor so resigned as that heroine, and received little comfort from her case. (265)

Her solution is, naturally, to pen her own stanzas, "On Man's Inconstancy," and then to fall in love with another suitor, whose "nose, lips, and chin, resembled the picture of Edmund Burke's" (281).

While such an episode comes close to satire of "the operative as bluestocking," Mercy is not elsewhere a figure of fun but a resilient and critical narrator who falls in love with a man but refuses to "harbor a suspicion that he was my superior" (216), and who names her firstborn child after a handsome man she formerly loved and lost. Lee's novel repeatedly uses the literary taste of characters as a criterion for judging their true qualities. A whole chapter is devoted to a reading by the local literary circle of Emerson's "Nature." One of the most noble members of the group, Fanny Olney, translates a passage of Emerson's prose into "good blank verse of anapestic measure," while the trivial Miss Mumby, "for her life...could not get interested in the story," and pronounces Emerson's transparent eyeball "silly enough" (208, 209). Arabella Puffit asks, about the author of *Paradise Lost*, "Milton who?" and declares of Emerson's essay "I wouldn't give Charlotte Temple for a bushel-basket full of such books" (212, 214). A taste for elite or popular literature is consistently used as a way of discriminating natural aristocrats (who may be from any level of society) from the innately vulgar (also from any level of society). However, for a novel so densely packed with literary allusiveness, there is curiously little interest in the actual content of the literature, other than as the basis for assumptions and innuendoes about the types of people who might be drawn to certain styles of writing. The everyday world of the novel is filled with matters of crucial social, economic, and moral import for its characters—capital punishment is a central issue, as are racial discrimination, capitalism, prejudice against immigrants, women's rights, and the decadence of the clergy. However, there is no real effort, except in the chapter on Emerson, to move beyond cursory literary references to a deeper engagement with the ideas. Writers' names, like Bremer and Byron, or genres like poetry and fiction have already come to stand as synecdoches for admirable and disreputable sets of values and as ways of classifying the people who prefer them. Entire opposing literary canons are lined up in these early culture wars to separate the serious from the trivial, the admirable from the dangerous uses of the mind.

In the discussion of "Nature," there is considerable interest in the sentence "Infancy is the perpetual Messiah, which comes into the arms of fallen men, and pleads with them to return to paradise" and some exchange of comments like beautiful, truthful, dry, and foolish on Emerson's essay (213). Such superficial evaluation is unlikely, however, to engage the factory community very closely in any truly examined connection between their literary and their working lives. Perhaps it is significant that Lee chooses not to have his reading circle discuss "The American Scholar" rather than "Nature." Then they might have had to contend more directly with Emerson's reprimand of those who value books "not as related to nature and the human constitution, but as making a sort of Third Estate with the world and the soul" (*Selections* 67). Lee chooses in *Merrimack* to embody an enthusiastic and almost unqualified acceptance of the factory system in a text filled with a celebration of the reading of great works of literature; yet the only connection between this literature and the ideological defense of factories is that the people who prefer the superior books also happen to have the fewest criticisms of the factories. This vindication of factory labor by its association with superior culture and refinement was, of course, just the accusation Sarah Bagley made against Harriet Farley and the *Lowell Offering*. When Lee comes ten years later to record the literary lives of that first generation of working women in his novel, a taste for certain kinds of reading and writing has indeed come to seem ominously close to being a marker of refinement and acquiescence. Although Lee's workers in *Merrimack* are all aware of the many economic and social controversies of the age, the most literary characters among them are the ones most committed to a belief in laissez-faire in the operation of the factory system.

Just a year after Lee's *Merrimack* was published, Martha W. Tyler expanded the potential application of factory women's literacy by arguing passionately (albeit much less fluently) for using it to bring major changes in laws affecting their private lives within home and marriage as well as in the more public arena of their employment. Her 1855 autobiographical novel *A Book Without a Title: or Thrilling Events in the Life of Mira Dana* shows a factory woman initially using her Lowell-enhanced education to challenge the corporate exploitation of workers. However, her ultimate literary battle against oppression is with the wrongs of the institution of marriage and with unjust laws that discriminate against women. The novel is impossible to defend artistically because of its narrative inconsistency and lack of control in depicting the protagonist, its failure to subordinate the trivial to the significant, and its wild stylistic fluctuations. Nevertheless, the book sold quickly and went into a second edition within a year, suggesting that many elements in it may have struck chords with readers familiar with women like Mira, dragging out "lives of indescribable misery chained by the laws of our land to men who have ceased to be worthy of their love, and forfeited every claim to their respect by their selfish cruelty and their wilful neglect" (vii–viii).[9] The historical context in which Tyler places her account of the mistreatment of women in marriage is their comparable suffering as both factory laborers in the north and as slaves in the south. However, these two public situations are presented as ills that provoke the sympathetic support of society for their victims by contrast with women trapped unhappily in the private and socially sanctified relationship between husband and wife.

Mira Dana begins her life as a promisingly lively and assertive girl. She is a tomboy heroine, a wild romp, nicknamed "Dick," who thinks, as she makes the classic journey from the farm to the Lowell mills, "she would go out into the world, not as a passive being, but as an actor, a real worker upon life's great stage" (13). When she later leads a strike in the factory against reductions in the operatives' wages by the corporations, she proclaims confidently: "We will work together" (23). In the factory world, her feistiness and her faith in cooperation appear to bear fruit—when the corporations are forced to pay women what they have earned, it is by virtue of the election of a strike committee and the collaboration of other reform-minded people. However, when Mira attempts to challenge the legal system that victimizes her in marriage, she is almost wholly isolated from any community with mutual concerns, and the force of custom accords her much less sympathy than it does workers and slaves. Mira's recourse, after she has made fruitless efforts to try to use loopholes in the law, is to write an autobiographical novel exposing the horrors of her situation. The book brings her money, but it subjects her to charges of lowering herself "to the very depths of degradation" (293) in order to exploit her situation for profit. Her inventor and real-life counterpart Martha Tyler experienced the same charges. Tyler defended her book vigorously in the preface to its second edition, noting its liberal patronage by the public, even in the face of critical venom. Her situation was curiously similar to that of the better-known author, Fanny Fern, another victim of marital hardship whose comparable fictionalized account of her own predicament, *Ruth Hall,* was published the same year, and who wrote a similar preface defending her public novel about private wrongs. Tyler's account is a grim female *Bildungsroman* of the young factory woman who dreams of being an actor on life's stage and is thwarted at every point by her sex (from her early discovery that she can never become a doctor to her exploitation in the mills and her abuse in marriage). Nevertheless, it should not be an entirely hopeless one, as long as she has access to publication and can tell her story. However, even a highly fictionalized account of marital suffering by a wronged woman needed to be prefaced with extensive apologies and explanations in order to distance it from any suggestion that it was a personal plea for justice or an expedient attempt to make money.

An equally difficult literary dilemma for Martha Tyler is that she and her fictive counterpart, Mira, have not entirely shaken off traditional beliefs about the nature of women and marriage. When Mira, as a young and rebellious factory woman, is accused by her boss of being very impudent, she responds saucily "I thank you for your compliment" (29). However, any comparable challenge to marital tyranny is deeply compromised by Mira's ingrained sense that a woman's love and loyalty can overcome any obstacle. Thus, when her villainous husband, after years of brutality and vicious schemes, pretends to effect a reconciliation with her, the womanly Mira is overcome with affection: "she only remembered that he was the father of her children—the partner of her life—she threw her arms about his neck and kissed him fondly, exclaiming, 'How long, dear husband, have we been estranged—let us forget the wrongs of the past'" (264–65). The burden on Mira of simultaneously recognizing her husband's villainy and acting to secure the welfare of her children, while retaining her womanly tenderness and forgiveness, appears to be driving her almost to insanity. Ironically, this is one of the accusations her husband makes against her when he tries to have her incarcerated in a prison or an asylum. Mira has indeed some mental collapses; she is susceptible to vivid and prescient dreams; and she is (like Ruth Hall, the protagonist of Fanny Fern's novel) betrayed by her own brother, who allies himself with her husband. In the hands of a more skilled author, Mira might be a convincing forerunner of the protagonist of "The Yellow Wallpaper," falsely accused of mental weakness and simultaneously driven to it. However, such a transformation would require not only the finesse of Charlotte Perkins Gilman but also a considerable evolution in readers' expectations of how much is reasonable for a wife to endure.

Mira Dana finally obtains a divorce from her husband and, in the first edition of her book (1855), she obtains custody of her children. However, in 1856 Tyler published a second, expanded edition that more accurately reflected her own situation, the actual loss of access to her children. Her preface to this edition challenges laws that have made her heart "a waste of unspeakable bitterness, her life a scene of utter desolation" (viii). To judge from the comment of the *New York Times* in 1855 on Fanny Fern, the similarly wronged author of *Ruth Hall*, any changes in such laws, or the social values underlying them were not imminent: "we cannot understand how a delicate, suffering woman can hunt down even her persecutors so remorselessly. We cannot think so highly of [such] an author's womanly gentleness" (qtd. in Warren, *Fanny Fern* 124–25). Tyler, too, despite her bold creation of the first woman strike leader in American literature, seems initially to have held back from the temerity of suggesting that a wife might not forgive an erring husband, even while she challenged the laws that put her at his mercy. Her novel suggests that the new self-culture and self-reliance of young, unmarried women in the workplace did not yet presuppose an equivalent shift in the domestic sphere, or indeed broad public sympathy for such a change.

On the other hand, some Lowell novelists were beginning to suggest that factory work could provide a practical escape route from marital bondage as a lesser evil. It might offer women refuge from seduction and marriage alike, or at least provide them with a period during which they could lead an independent single life, free to make considered choices about their futures. For the first-person narrator of Charlotte S. Hilbourne's 1863 novel *Effie and I; or, Seven Years in a Cotton Mill*, the mills of Lowell provide not just an interlude in a young woman's life but a place to return for financial security and companionship after a failed marriage. Although Hilbourne engages in an excess of rhapsodic propaganda for the bucolic pleasures of a factory town, and argues that Lowell is "an asylum for the oppressed, a home for the home-less, and a broad highway leading to wealth and honor" (6), her extravagances do not wholly taint the case she makes for the value of an institution that offers women employment, lodging, and a modest degree of self-sufficiency in lives that are otherwise vulnerable to every hazard of fortune. Hilbourne also incorporates the arguments of factory opponents into her novel, though scarcely impartially, by having a Mrs. Allstone voice the extreme indictment, in her introduction, in a rhetorical style that verges on parody:

> Then go into those living tombs, those slave-palaces, and see the pale, shrinking, overtasked thousands, toiling on, year after year, for the mere pittance to prolong a miserable existence,—and for what? To fill the coffers of the wealthy capitalists, and rear marble palaces for their aristocratic sons and daughters, who would not deign to have them touch the hem of their golden drapery, lest it should be polluted by their plebeian proximity. (5–6)

The remainder of the novel then announces itself as the response of the factory worker Rosa Lynd Hartwell to Mrs. Allstone, a response that at times seems equally parodic in its excesses. However, the plot and details of the novel reveal a more tempered vision than the partisan extremes of its rhetoric suggest.

When Rosa's large and happy childhood family is rapidly decimated in the opening chapters by ill health, poverty, and the hand of God, she makes the traditional journey to Lowell, though not before first penning a few verses, entitled "Childhood Home." Her first encounter with the City of Spindles is not auspicious—a narrow bed in the boardinghouse must be shared with a "fat, blowsy maiden... troubled exceedingly with scrofula and salt rheum" (45). Among Rosa's five bedroom companions are two spinster sisters who grimly recite a litany of complaints about Lowell—of "reductions," "turnouts," "stump speeches," "clerical sympathy," and "legal interference" (45–46). Compared to the "sumptuous breakfasts" served up by the other literary defenders of Lowell, Rosa Lynd is sickened by the sour bread, rancid butter, and ersatz coffee of her boardinghouse, although she soon learns that there are better alternatives. Her first experiences of factory labor are likewise repugnant: she suffers "excruciating headaches, sickening sensations," and a terror of demonic machinery that, "like the treacherous whirlpool," seems to seek to draw her into its "fearful embrace" (48, 49). Soon however, as in many of these factory novels, the monotony of routine begins to replace the first frantic responses, she adjusts to the ways of Lowell, and she eventually begins to compose poetry as she works. When all else in Rosa's life seems ephemeral, the factory endures. Family members back at home continue to die, the old homestead itself disappears, even the old oak tree that sheltered it has gone, but the boardinghouse still stands, the factory bells still ring, and the sisterhood of operatives provides an easily replenished kinship, less prey to fate than her doomed family.

With the introduction of the title character, the youthful Effie Lee, the author investigates not just the emotional burden of isolation and abandonment for young women but also the practices and institutions of pauperdom, dependency, and charity in New England that accompany it. It is a tacit but pertinent reminder that the alternative to factory labor for girls might be a kind of indentured servitude, with even less opportunity for books, leisure, and companionship than is accorded them in the mill. Rosa promises Effie that the factory will be a superior substitute for the world of her past: "you will even learn to love the scenes and associations which at first seem so uncongenial and repulsive to a delicate and sensitive nature," and she assures her that industrial labor is a task "where any and all may acquire a competence, independent and free from the degradation which charitable obligation demands" (78). Effie's eventual marriage takes her away from Lowell and into the declining career of a neglected wife, lowlier than a servant and yet, like Mira Dana, still capable of "idolatrous and undivided affection" for her husband (179). Eventually he abandons her, steals her property, and tries to have her incarcerated in a lunatic asylum as a way of taking her child from her—a virtual recapitulation of Tyler's plot. However, in this case, the marital disaster is dramatically juxtaposed to the authentic, "familial" warmth of the factory community, as well as to the coldness of poorhouses and the hypocrisies of benevolent missionary societies that neglect the needy at home while abroad they attempt to "moralize, naturalize, and humbugize the whole human family into one loving knot of brotherhood" (187).

Although Hilbourne includes some stories of factory women who have married well, even they are described as having entered the "hymenial noose" (199). Rosa, too, commits herself to a neglectful husband who forces her into onerous home employment in the shoemaking business, which is depicted as the exploitive and degrading opposite of her factory labor. In an interesting fusion of the metonymical "hands" of labor with the hands of the artist, Hilbourne says that Rosa's "delicate fingers" were not intended for "any thing but to write poetry, paint on velvet, thread a shuttle, and tie a weaver's knot" (239–40). When her husband deserts her, Rosa's return to Lowell is her only source of consolation. There, she listens happily to the "merry music" of the factory bells vibrating in her "desolate heart"—surely one of the strangest descriptions ever of this symbol of industrialization and regimentation.[10] However, in the context of Rosa's earliest loathing of being hurried from her sleep by the summons of the bells, and her growing sense that only factories offer stability amid the vagaries and insecurities of human life, the change in her imagery speaks eloquently to the nature of her education in the hazards and dependencies of women's lives. Her idyllic childhood picture of farm life undergoes a parallel transformation, from early memories of corn-huskings, appleparings, quiltings, dances, and sleigh rides to a later remembered sense of the isolation and brutal harshness of rural life, outside the immediate circle of family prosperity. Since the large city is represented in the novel as a center of decadence and vain amusement, in Hilbourne's moral geography the factory town becomes the pastoral middle ground between the hard and uncouth life of the country and the dissipation and indolence of the city.

Hilbourne goes even further than her rhapsody on the factory bells in her final paean to factory women and to the happiness they find in their work. She celebrates the

> pure, innocent, elevated joys of an unaspiring, unassuming factory girl, who rises in the early morn, tuning her cheerful lays with the earliest matins of the lark, as she trips lightly to her task, called by the merry chiming of the factory bells, inhaling the first fragrant breath of dewy morn from shrub and flower, with the flush of health on her cheek, and the light of vigor and buoyancy of spirit in the eye, contentment and tranquility in the heart. (227)

This poetic romance of factory life must already have palled considerably by 1863, when *Effie and I* was published. However, behind the romance there is a grim recognition of the reality of many women's lives and their need for factory employment as a path out of their absolute economic dependency and the subsequent abuses that arose from it. This novel, replete with foolish rhapsodies and sentimental poetry, with manifest distortions and exaggerations, nonetheless has at its core an admission of the fundamental terror of dependent women's lives. The constantly looming threat of isolation and insecurity makes the factories seem, if not a haven, then at least a feasible alternative, no matter how cynically represented by their agents and promoters, to conditions of parasitism, indigence, and servitude.

Taken as a group, the early Lowell novels do not offer much hope for the advent of the *Uncle Tom's Cabin* of American capitalism—Stowe's novel is a much harsher indictment of capitalism than any fiction that came out of the New England factory world before the Civil War. In the later decades of the nineteenth century, beginning with Rebecca Harding Davis and Elizabeth Stuart Phelps, factory novelists would begin to focus on the inequities of the economic and industrial system as well as on the iniquities of the workers and the particular injustices in working women's lives. What the minor Lowell novelists contributed to this body of literature and to the broader development of a school of American literary realism was a first fascinated consideration of the traditional notions of womanhood—of delicacy, purity, patience, acquiescence, and decorum—encountering the doubly challenging context of the conditions of working-class labor and Romantic intellectual self-culture. The new circumstances of these two revolutionary changes demanded strong bodies, tough minds, and a degree of assertive vitality and passion that jarred incongruously with the slight, pallid, and genteel women William Scoresby described in his account of the Lowell mills, who had no element of boldness or vulgarity about them.

The first novelists made a tentative effort to approach the perceived paradoxes of feminine vulgarity and working-class boldness and even to think about working women for the first time in a context outside their emotional and financial connections to men. They engaged in some humorous literary play with the novelty of female intellectuals and in some serious concern with factory workers' reading and writing. They revealed how thoroughly assimilated the stereotype of the Lowell worker had become and how ripe it was for revision, and they helped to establish a literary provenance both for later novelists and for the notable factory poet Lucy Larcom, who engaged in much bolder permutations of both content and genre.

6

The Working Woman's Bard

Lucy Larcom and the Factory Epic

I dwell in Possibility—
A fairer House than Prose—
More numerous of Windows—
Superior—for Doors—
—EMILY DICKINSON (1862?)

If we must classify our sisters, let us broaden ourselves by making large
classifications.... Even poorer people's windows will give us a new
horizon, and often a far broader one than our own.
—LUCY LARCOM (1889)

The critics say that epics have died out
With Agamemnon and the goat-nursed gods;
I'll not believe it.
—ELIZABETH BARRETT BROWNING, *AURORA LEIGH* (1857)

The extraordinary emphasis in the early novels of Lowell on the literariness
of the factory women nevertheless rarely resulted in a full-fledged fictional portrait of the artist as a young woman.[1] Although the ardent reading
and writing of the protagonists of factory fiction might lead, if they read
the wrong books, to their seduction and, if they read the right ones, to their
salvation and success, they did not generally lead to a career in literature.
However, such a career was, in fact, the outcome for a number of these
New England women: several of the early Lowell workers who contributed to the *Offering* went on to careers in writing and to autobiographical
accounts of their literary lives. Both editors of the *Lowell Offering*, Harriot
Curtis and Harriet Farley, published books that assembled many of their
early writings from the magazine and demonstrated their interest in the
connections among women's rights, class consciousness, and the factory
system: in 1847 Curtis published *S. S. S. Philosophy* and Farley *Shells from
the Strand of the Sea of Genius*. Among the memoirs of Lowell, the most
interesting were books by two former operatives, Lucy Larcom and Harriet
Hanson Robinson, written late in their lives and taking a distinctly backward and elegiac glance. Each of them acknowledges that she is dealing

with a discrete era in the industrializing of the nation that nurtured, for a few years, the hope that America would be an exception to the patterns of Europe in fostering literary and self-reliant women workers.

Larcom's memoir *A New England Girlhood* (1889), and Robinson's *Loom and Spindle* (1898), display a nostalgic benevolence toward the factory world of their youth that undoubtedly contributed to the mythologizing of Lowell, but also reveal why so many young factory workers like themselves were stimulated to write. As Lucy Larcom noted, and as Robinson later quoted her, her "natural bent towards literature was more encouraged and developed at Lowell than it would probably have been elsewhere" (Robinson 97). Such a statement certainly suggests that the factory milieu was a more congenial literary environment than the likely alternatives, for women like Larcom and Robinson, of farm or domestic labor. Whether the liberating intellectual possibilities of wage-earning, social intercourse, and wider educational opportunities blinded the aspiring writers to their exploited and regimented industrial labor has been debated hotly, beginning with Sarah Bagley's 1845 accusation that the literary ladies of Lowell were "a mouthpiece of the corporations" (qtd. in Foner 58). More recent literary discussions have focused on the extent to which the hegemony of domesticity in the mid–nineteenth century induced women workers to emphasize their womanliness over their labor and class in their writing.[2] The power of bourgeois and domestic ideals of womanhood has been invoked by many critics of nineteenth-century women's writing to explain the eagerness of so many factory workers to create genteel paradigms for their working-class existence. Susan Zlotnick, however, in her study of British writers in the nineteenth century coming to terms with the Industrial Revolution, notes the striking absence of factory women among British working-class writers, and proposes that it was the ideology of domesticity that *prevented* British factory women from finding any voice at all. For Zlotnick, the overwhelming power of the domestic ideal excluded the possibility of speaking simultaneously as a woman and a worker (173–74). She argues that the Victorian mill girl in England was initially embraced in the literature of the Industrial Revolution as an emblem of modernity and then silenced by the competing notion of women's proper place in the home. Since the British woman worker was effectively dismembered into "woman" and "worker," she did not write at all about her double identity (222). The American woman worker, by contrast, though evidently less silenced (to judge from her relatively copious publication), has appeared to many critics to have subordinated one or other aspect of herself, that of woman or of laborer.

Both Harriet Robinson and Lucy Larcom implicitly engage with the issue of their class and gender loyalties in their memoirs, although they insist on a sense of selfhood that is largely of their own molding rather than an inevitable product of biological or social conditioning. The two women are quite candid at the beginning of their books about revealing their differing agendas: Larcom's is an inspirational and Christian text, written for an audience of girls, encouraging them to "take life as it is sent to us, to live it faithfully, looking and striving always towards better life" (*New England* 13). Robinson's goals are more worldly: women's suffrage and the improvement of conditions in the contemporary factory world. Larcom's memoir is more elegantly literary in its narrative design, while Robinson's is an assemblage of anecdotes, letters, lists, and brief biographies of many of her Lowell workmates. Larcom's is a modest account of her life that certainly avoids the "conceit and egotism" she believed were often implied by the word "autobiography" (5); Robinson's is a frankly celebratory description of the lives of the first factory workers. Granted their quite different intentions, personalities, and styles, there is a remarkable consensus in these two women's accounts of the origins and the literary cradle of working women's self-discovery.

Both Larcom and Robinson were daughters of New England women who were suddenly widowed and left to support families of young children. Both mothers tried to build a bridge between their former domestic lives and their new-found need to make money by moving to Lowell and operating boarding houses there, a move that imposed early and onerous chores on their young daughters. Robinson recalls her duty to wash the dishes for forty boarders, while standing on a stool to reach the kitchen sink (18), while Larcom remembers the tedium for her small fingers of sewing what seemed like miles of sheets (146). By 1835, when she was ten years old, Robinson had begun work in the spinning room of the mill as a doffer, removing full bobbins and replacing them with empty ones (19); Larcom entered the spinning room as an eleven-year-old, in the same year, to do the same work (153–54). Although the workday began at five in the morning and lasted until seven in the evening, Robinson comments: "I do not recall any particular hardship connected with this life, except getting up so early in the morning" and Larcom says of the work, "The novelty of it made it seem easy, and it really was not hard" (20, 153). Elsewhere, both women are more critical of child labor, especially as it impinged on education; but they also imply that the alternative work, at home or in other people's homes, would have been no less burdensome for these young girls; and they each take considerable pride in their memory of their roles as wage-earners for their families.

Robinson's more rebellious and reformist instincts show early in her career, when, as a seventeen-year-old, she was excommunicated from the Congregational Church in Lowell for refusing to subscribe to its "monstrous doctrines" of literal devils, fire, and brimstone (30, 33); she was also fired from her job for chiding an overseer for his "unusually offensive" behavior with female workers (35). Larcom, much less an activist or women's rights supporter than Robinson, nevertheless felt empowered by the opportunities factory employment offered her. She describes women's entry into the workplace as comparable to "a young man's pleasure in entering upon business for himself. Girls had never tried that experiment before, and they liked it. It brought out in them a dormant strength of character which the world did not previously see, but now fully acknowledges" (199–200). Robinson expands on this extraordinary sense of independence that came to women through their employment: "Even the *time* of these women was their own, on Sundays and in the evening after the day's work was done. *For the first time in this country woman's labor had a money value.* She had become not only an earner and a producer, but also a spender of money, a recognized factor in the political economy of her time" (42, emphasis added). She dramatizes the situation of solitary older women, formerly thought of as "relicts" or "incumbrances," who came to the mills

> depressed, modest, mincing, hardly daring to look one in the face, so shy and sylvan had been their lives. But after the first payday came, and they felt the jingle of silver in their pockets, and had begun to feel its mercurial influence, their bowed heads were lifted, their necks seemed braced with steel, they looked you in the face, sang blithely among their looms or frames, and walked with elastic step to and from their work. (42–43)

Such tributes to factory labor might indeed seem to justify the accusation that the literary women of Lowell were "mouthpieces for the corporations." However, Robinson, for all her glowing rhetoric, participated in a strike against wage cuts (as an eleven-year-old), leading the walkout of the girls in her room. She later commented: "As I looked back at the long line that followed me, I was more proud than I have ever been since at any success I may have achieved, and more proud than I shall ever be again until my own beloved State gives to its women citizens the right of suffrage" (52). Thus she (and Larcom in a more private fashion) could acknowledge the liberating power of wage-earning and the abuses of the system simultaneously—the implication is that while factories empowered women to earn and spend, they also, indirectly, enabled them to see their common interests, become organized, and speak out on their own behalf for necessary reforms.

Of all the areas where Larcom's and Robinson's accounts of the Lowell mills coincide, none is more striking than their agreement on the literary and intellectual stimulation provided by the environment and the new educational possibilities for women there. Both even use the same metaphor for the factory: Larcom notes that, for twenty years, "Lowell might have been looked upon as a rather select industrial school for young people" (222), while Robinson says that since it was so central to the education of many women, she likes to call it "their *Alma Mater*" (25). The two women describe opportunities to attend lectures, take classes, borrow books from lending libraries, and, most important, to begin to write themselves for a large and interested audience. Interestingly, both attribute their early development of a poetic sensibility to their childhood exposure to hymns, certainly a common experience for almost all of these women. Larcom writes: "Almost the first decided taste in my life was the love of hymns" (58), while Robinson says the early learning of "beautiful hymns...made a lasting impression on the serious part of my nature" (26). The two girls quickly progressed to poetry and fiction reading—Robinson read "Lalla Rookh" and found "it awoke in me, not only a love of poetry, but also a desire to try my own hand at verse-making" (27). Even more intensely for Larcom, poetry soon proved to be a vital necessity: "My 'must-have' was poetry. From the first, life meant that to me" (10). For both of them, the reciprocal pleasures of reading and writing were ends in themselves, utterly separate from the satisfactions of getting and spending their wages, although similarly a result of their enhanced sense of being active agents in their own lives.

Although Larcom and Robinson were, by virtue of their later careers, among the most professionally successful writers to emerge from the New England factories, they both present their early literary aspirations as representative of those of the many working women who longed to explore the life of the mind and the imagination. Larcom was later able to unite vocation and avocation as a poet, but, like most of her literary fellow operatives, she did not look on her writing at Lowell as a practical financial resource. In this sense, factory writers were less worldly about their literary creations than many of their contemporaries among middle-class domestic novelists, who entered the literary marketplace out of financial need. Their favorite reading materials, copiously recorded by Robinson and Larcom, suggest an interesting mixture of literary classics, eminent Romantic writers, highly esteemed novelists, and a remarkable array of lesser known women writers of both fiction and poetry whose names are only now being reintroduced to the literary canon after more than a century and a half of neglect. Robinson notes that the verse and prose in the *Lowell Offering* savored of the authors the factory women read—the poetry of Milton, Pope, Byron, and Goldsmith, but also of Sigourney, Hemans, Landon, Barbauld, and More; the prose of the *Spectator*, but also of Maria Sedgwick and Lydia Maria Child (69–70). In addition to the novels of Richardson, Fielding, and Scott, Harriet Robinson read a distinctly more female range of fiction: "Charlotte Temple," "Eliza Wharton," "Maria Monk," "The Mysteries of Udolfo," and "Mary Barton" (27, 57, 59). Larcom, too, mixed many contemporary women writers into her reading of the more renowned classics, and insofar as the same range of authors is repeated in so many of the novels of Lowell life and in the pages of the *Lowell Offering*, it appears that factory women were especially alert to the development of a female literary tradition.

The extent to which working women felt drawn or pressured by the values of a more middle-class literary tradition of domesticity is a vexed question, in part because of the complex loyalties of individual writers. Of the pair, Harriet Robinson was the more active feminist, who nonetheless chose a life of marriage and motherhood; Lucy Larcom, much more of a traditionalist about women's roles, led a single and independent life. Both believed that their wage-earning labor as young women enabled them to have more choices than their mothers had, although both also admitted that by their later years, factory work, which had liberated them, had become oppressive and restricting for more recent generations of women. Robinson concedes the unlikelihood of any significant cultural achievement emerging from operatives at the end of the nineteenth century because of changed working conditions *and* a change in the nature of the workers. Somewhat ominously, she suggests that the ancestry of the later generation of workers has not provided them with the heritage the earlier New England factory population had—the "inherited germs of intellectual life" (120). Robinson appears to recognize that she is making a judgment on the innate quality of the modern workforce, specifically recent European immigrants, and she quickly attempts to qualify her own implications by alluding to their rich cultural heritage: "But is it not also possible that the children of the land of Dante, of Thomas More, of Racine, and of Goethe may be something more than mere clods?" (120). She asserts the need for these workers to struggle not only for decent wages but also for "their intellectual freedom, as well" (121). Interestingly, Robinson's memoir was published in 1898, just as major movements of intellectual, feminist, and class activism were beginning to gain ground among immigrant women workers in the garment industry, led especially by east European Jewish women, who had come from intellectual and religious traditions as lively and rigorous as those that had nurtured the first New England workers.

About the late nineteenth-century immigrants, Robinson argues, "What these poor people need is time, and a great deal of help, before it can be decided what either they or their descendants can make of themselves" (120). Her language reveals a very different conception of "poor people" and their capacities from that of her own impoverished childhood. At the beginning of her memoir, she relates that, after her father's death, she was sent to a charity school to learn to sew. When she reported to her mother that one of her teachers had referred to her as "a poor little girl," she notes that her mother replied, "You need not go there again" (17). Robinson does not attribute the instinctive pride she remembers so long ago from her own childhood to "children of the land of Dante," but whether this is a result of her sense of a deteriorated factory population, or of the degrading effects of the modern factories, is not so obvious. She recalls, again from her youth, that the earliest generation of Irish immigrants that came to Lowell "very soon adapted themselves to their changed conditions of life, and became as 'good as anybody'" (8). There is clearly some fluidity in Robinson's sense of the worthiness of workers that is affected by their ethnic ancestry, how familiarly they are known, their working conditions, and the passage of time. Those who labor may be rapidly transformed from "mere clods" to "as good as anybody," but whether this transformation is aided more by innate or environmental conditions, and thus how much early workers were an exception or a model for later generations, is something of an enigma. Clearly, Robinson finds the application of class terminology both troubling and unavoidable. Whether "class" is seen as a social hierarchy, through which it is desirable to ascend, or as a body of populist cultural traditions in which to take pride and from which to draw an identity, there was apparently for Robinson a good deal of discomfort around the subject. She asserts that, when she looks back, she does not see "what is called 'a class' of young men and women" but instead "individuals, with personalities of their own." However, she immediately concedes, "Yet they were a class of factory operatives," followed by the exclamation "So little does one class of persons really know about the thoughts and aspirations of another!" (37). The breadth of application of the loose term "class" is compounded, in Robinson's account, by the paradox that the woman worker who chose genteel employment over factory labor was often less well paid and thus less able to acquire the education that might affect her class mobility. Thus, when Robinson, Larcom, and many of the other Lowell writers turned to the works of middle-class women writers as models of female creativity, they were not inevitably subordinating themselves to ideologies of domesticity to any greater extent than they were submitting to Romantic values in their studies of Wordsworth and Goethe—they were exploring models from other kinds of writers and testing their appeal.

They were undoubtedly influenced by all of the variety of writers they read, but their literary study does not seem to have entirely squelched their own populist and original sentiments, or inhibited a certain astute pragmatism about dabbling in many literary modes before developing a personal voice. In January 1845, the *Lowell Offering* tried out a new cover, accompanied by the motto "The worm on the earth / May look up to the star." Robinson notes that contributors' resistance to this "abject" sentiment was such that the next issue immediately replaced it with the quotation from Bunyan "And do you think the words of your book are certainly true? Yea, verily" (66). Harriet Farley's editorial of March 1845 verifies Robinson's account and insists that, in choosing the first motto, "We wished to imply no mock humility—nothing like the idea that we were worms, and other people stars, but that our situations were lowly, and our aims high" (5: 72). Lucy Larcom, in many ways a more demure and decorous writer than Robinson, nevertheless shows some irreverence for her literary and social "betters" in a letter to Robinson, responding to an account Robinson had given her of a visit to Emerson's household, in 1857: "Didn't it seem funny to go a'gossiping to the house of the Seer? I don't wonder at your expecting the parrot to talk 'transcendentally.' Did the tea and toast smack of Hymettus? and was there any apple-*sass* from those veritable sops-o'-wine?... Well, it's a fine thing to be on visiting terms at Olympus" (103). Larcom's "sass" suggests that, even if the Lowell women were far from being Olympians themselves, they had a healthy skepticism about literary idols, even those they most admired.

If the memoirs of Robinson and Larcom reveal both the extent of their literary inheritance and their balky independence, an even more interesting work in which to trace the interaction of canonical and domestic literary values with the actual imaginative writing of one of the best of the Lowell authors is Lucy Larcom's remarkable epic poem *An Idyl of Work*, published in 1875. In it she explores, retrospectively, the meaning of the factory experience for a group of young women who actively debate and investigate the strands of their identity, not only as women and workers but also as Christians, consumers, artists, nature-lovers, and daughters of the new republic. Dedicated "To Working Women...by One of Their Sisterhood," the poem was written some thirty years after she left Lowell and had become a successful and well-known poet. According to Larcom's biographer, Shirley Marchalonis, it was "the most serious and sustained piece of writing she had ever attempted" (199). Although reviewers gave the poem only qualified praise in its own time, largely because of reservations about Larcom's use of blank verse rather than the prose narrative that was felt to be more suitable for its subject, the work deserves and rewards the closest attention, not only because it is an invaluable window onto what the *Atlantic Monthly*'s reviewer called "that curious life of the first manufacturing towns of New England" ("Recent Literature" 241) but also because it dares to imagine the female factory worker as the ideal citizen of a democratic America.

Larcom had begun her literary career, according to *A New England Girlhood*, almost as soon as she acquired language as a child, reading her first novel by Sir Walter Scott when she was five years old, and composing her first verses when she was seven (105, 127–28). She notes that her fascination with the sound and rhythm of language preceded even her knowledge of the meaning of words, so that she delighted in hearing, in church, such imposing words as "dispensations," "ordinances," and "covenants" (55). She assimilated the motifs and meters of hymns virtually from her infancy, and she was encouraged in her earliest creative efforts by her large and close-knit family. Larcom dreamed as a child of a career as a poet, but when her father died and left her mother to support eight children, the factory became her career instead. Although she lost her chance to go to high school, Larcom used the resources of Lowell as best she could to continue her education and her writing. Under the tutelage of her sister Emeline, she and some friends, family members, and workmates began to produce "a little fortnightly paper, to be filled with our original contributions" (170), a project that evolved first into an "Improvement Circle" and eventually, a couple of years later, into the group that issued the *Lowell Offering* (175). Larcom's first poems were published in the *Offering,* and she spent almost ten years (1835–1845) in the factory world before embarking on a journey west with some of her family. In Illinois, Larcom completed her formal education and continued to publish poems, now in the *National Era* and eventually, after her return to the Northeast, in the *Atlantic Monthly*. She won competitions, made a modest income, and eventually achieved national renown in 1857 with her solemn poem of female virtue and endurance "Hannah Binding Shoes" (*New England* 248, 272; Marchalonis, 115–118). By the early 1870s, Larcom was a reputable professional poet and writer, best known for her work in the genres of devotional, nature, and children's poetry, in the lyric mode. It was at this point in her career that Larcom turned from her technically polished short poems, with their marked competence and versatility in meter and rhyme, to a remarkable and ambitious experiment—a book-length poem in blank verse, celebrating the lives of American women factory workers.

An Idyl of Work had virtually no precedent in either American or English poetry as an extensive excursion, narrative and philosophical, into the lives and the values of working women. There had been few enough American epics, even fewer by women, and fewer again about them. The whole question of the possibility of an American epic was a vexed and contested one in the early years of the nation: could the original heroic narrative genre ever be sufficiently transformed in order to fit it for representing an enlightened, democratic, republican, and largely Christian society? A number of modern critics and literary historians have traced the evolution of the idea of the epic through many nineteenth-century developments, arguing that authors gradually began to reconceive the epic, throwing off many of its previously most fundamental requirements. Thus they abandoned the idea that the epic must be serious in tone, that it must be written in poetic form, that it must celebrate a hero, and that it must recount warrior victories. John P. McWilliams has argued that, after Barlow's *Columbiad*, in 1807, and a number of similar epics of "gargantuan dulness and unconscious ethnocentrism" had demonstrated the discrepancies between generic conventions and American principles, the path was opened for new kinds of American epics ("Epic" 36). These might appear as novels (Cooper and Melville), prose histories (Parkman and Prescott), a hybrid of Indian mythology and Finnish meter (Longfellow) or even eccentrically personal and visionary revelation (Whitman). Roy Harvey Pearce memorably called the American epic a "strange, amorphous, anomalous, self-contradictory thing" (61), but the historians of this versatile and protean literary form have consistently agreed that its elastic limits did not appear to stretch to accommodate women, either as authors or subjects. McWilliams, who noted the capacity of the epic to transform itself, does not consider Larcom's work when he reports: "I have found no American instances of women writing epic poems, of men writing epic poems about women heroes, or of women writing novels that are meant to recall the heroic tradition we think of as epic" (*American* 10). Lynn Keller also notes the general scarcity "or invisibility—of long poems by women" before the mid-20th century. She accepts the theory that the expectations of the genre—"public, objective, universal, heroic—coincide with western norms for the masculine. Lyric norms—private, subjective, personal, emotional—overlap with the concept of the feminine." She concludes from these gendered conventions that "earlier women poets did not possess the cultural authority that would legitimate their attempts at epic" (2, 14). McWilliams finds that the literary form so many nineteenth-century women chose to make their own, the domestic novel, was not conducive to epic, since it largely emphasized "womanly fortitude and Christian piety under trial" (*American* 10). Although some English women had written poetry in the epic mode in the nineteenth century and although some earlier American women's captivity narratives certainly appear to elevate Christian piety and fortitude to heroic levels, the consensus is that amid all the efforts at an American epic in the nineteenth century, women's voices and concerns were not heard.

Larcom did, however, have a powerful model of a female epic poem, written by her much-admired English contemporary Elizabeth Barrett Browning. Her *Aurora Leigh*, published in 1857, was an imposing nine-book epic in blank verse, wholly devoted to the celebration of the career of a woman writer. Set in the contemporary world, it was suffused with Christian idealism and cautious of political radicalism but keenly aware of modern women's concerns with vocation, beyond their role as wives and mothers. Immediately after this work's publication, Larcom wrote to her friend Harriet Robinson, "A *grand* poem, isn't it? I think woman is *somebody* in these days, if all the talk and writing amount to anything," and she must surely have been pleased that Harriet Beecher Stowe already considered her "an American Mrs. Browning" (qtd. in Marchalonis 106, 143). *Aurora Leigh* provided an example, for Larcom, of a long narrative poem on a subject that might, at first glance, seem more congenial to a novel, but for which the author sought the elevation, formality, and erudition of the epic mode, even as she modified it for her topical interests.

Browning's poem explores the literary career and personal life of Aurora Leigh, an upper-class woman, the life of her suitor, Romney, who has devoted himself to social reform, and the situation of women in nineteenth-century English society. Aurora initially rejects marriage to Romney because he envisions her merely as a helpmeet in his own reforming career and regards her poetry as at best dilettantism and at worst a delusional vocation. She achieves independently a considerable reputation as a writer before finally marrying the rejected Romney. In the meantime he has been injured, and disillusioned in his career, and he is now willing to take on the role in the marriage of loving "for two," while Aurora, for her part, works also "for two" (9.911–12). The role reversal whereby the bourgeois ideology of ambition, work, and public recognition becomes the woman's domain and nurturing and perfecting the private life become the sphere of the man has been noted by a number of modern critics. Among them, Rachel Blau DuPlessis sees in the poem a conflict for Aurora, the bourgeois woman who is torn between "class values" and "gender caste," between class-based norms of ambition and success and gendered values of service and support (463). However, for Marian Erle, the working-class woman in *Aurora Leigh*, there is no comparable dilemma, since a career of public intellectual achievement does not come within the realm of consideration. Marian is the victim of rape and the mother of a resulting "illegitimate" child. She and Aurora are friends, but Marian's moral predicaments have nothing to do with the intellectual dilemmas of Aurora. For the lower-class woman, a life of devotion to her child is a sufficiently noble career.

Larcom's poem, like Browning's, deals with the relationships of women to work and to the life of the mind, but its most dramatic variation, in terms of its subject, is in its exclusive concern with workers as protagonists. Larcom's subjects are women without social eminence, without high bourgeois expectations of success as a result of their individual ambitions, without assumptions that they may have alternative private lives of fulfilling personal service. As factory operatives, they are already outside the private domain, but the public realm in which they work does not encourage much assertion of selfhood or individual recognition through the nature of their work. Yet these women, like Browning's upper class Aurora, and unlike her working-class Marian, yearn to live the life of the mind just as intensely as they appreciate the emotional and physical experiences of their existence. However, unlike Aurora, in her conflict over the pursuit of male bourgeois ideals at the expense of female, the Lowell factory women of *An Idyl of Work* conform neither to typical working-class nor typical gender standards in their pursuit of literary goals. When a selection of writings from the *Lowell Offering* was published in London in 1844, it was significantly entitled *Mind amongst the Spindles*, presumably because the metonymy of "mind" for working women was pleasingly novel, substituting for the more traditionally feminine "heart" or the conventional working-class "hand." In a context where the association of "mind" and "women workers" was sufficiently anomalous to constitute a witty title, Larcom's epic celebration of the lives of female factory workers is all the more remarkable.

The title of the twelve-part *Idyl of Work* echoes, somewhat audaciously, Tennyson's twelve-book *Idylls of the King*, much of which had been published, to widespread renown, by 1875, when Larcom's poem appeared. Dedicated with a certain grandeur of simplicity "To Working-Women" by "One of Their Sisterhood," Larcom's poem investigates, in its narrative, the values of the female community at Lowell and celebrates, in its formal structure, the mental environment in which such women's lives flourished. The *Idyl* is set early in New England's industrial era, at a moment of equipoise, when the hopes for the integrity of the new factory system were still high and its associations with the earlier rural world were still powerful. However, the poem is also pervaded by the awareness that this moment of hope has passed from the historical reality of Lowell, although not from the larger life of the republic. Larcom reiterates this point emphatically in her preface: "The conditions and character of mill-labor are no doubt much changed since the period indicated; but the spirit of our national life remains the same" (viii–ix). Such a comment suggests that for all her personal modesty, Larcom was consciously embarking on a poem about the "spirit of national life," a phrase that may well be the only essential defining quality left for an American epic.

This desire to demonstrate the operation of a national ethos or spirit, as it is manifest in a particular group of Americans in a symbolically signifi-cant time and place, is a key element in the definitions of the American epic offered by two of its most eminent scholars, Jeffrey Walker and Roy Harvey Pearce. Walker, in his book *Bardic Ethos*, traces Ezra Pound's idea that the "ethos" of the American epic is "the general sensibility, the deep-down character core that underlies and determines the specific moral choices any individual will make, and that underlies also the communal institutions a society of individuals will devise" (6). Roy Harvey Pearce argues: "In the American epic what is mythified is the total milieu and ambience, what the poet takes to be the informing spirit of his times and his world" (61). For Larcom, as for Tennyson, the ethos is that of Christianity; but her ambi-ence is the yet-unseparated realms of industrial and rural life, and what is mythified is not royal and knightly but female and democratic. Camelot is replaced by Lowell, the mystical lake by Pawtucket Falls, and Arthur, Guenevere, and Launcelot by a bevy of Zillahs, Esthers, and Aramintas who tend the machinery of industrial production.

Although it is tempting to claim Larcom's ambitious poem as a working-class manifesto, a feminist polemic, and a radical aesthetic experi-ment, it is in fact far from being any of these, while at the same time it *is* a supreme assertion of working women's authority as the bearers and trans-mitters of democratic, communal, and cultural ideals. The poem depicts a real historical world of boardinghouse life, factory machinery, strikes, courtship, betrayal, leisure, and illness, suffused by religious fervor and enriched by Romantic apprehensions of nature and art. Its novel protago-nists are a group of wage-earning young women who lead their lives very much in the public eye of visitors and supervisors yet make determined efforts to cling to private definitions of their identity and to dwell in a realm that is simultaneously material and spiritual. Despite the upheavals in their former, more traditional way of life, they do not manifest any evi-dence of a modern dissociated sensibility, and although their lives are filled with paradoxes and moral dilemmas, they are competent to resolve them together and to relish the pleasure of their intellectual exploration. The poem is politically conservative insofar as it avoids analyzing the factory women as victims of class or gender exploitation, or as disenfranchised members of the nominally democratic society the poem celebrates, but Larcom's voice is confident in asserting its subjects' equality with anyone in the nation.

The *Idyl* opens with language and images that elevate three of the young mill workers to appropriately lofty poetic status. Looking down and out from their factory window perch, Larcom compares them to

> Three damsels at a casement in old time,
> In some high castle-turret, where they wrought
> Tapestry for royal mistresses. (11)

If such ladies in the past were considered apt subjects for the painter or minstrel, then, the poet declares, "full as worthy these." Her emphasis evokes Aurora Leigh's assertion that

> "The critics say that epics have died out
> With Agamemnon and the goat-nursed gods;
> I'll not believe it." (5.139–41)

Larcom avoids any hint of the perhaps expected mock-heroic, even when she comments that "New England's beautiful blue Merrimack" is "a river less romantic than the Rhine" (12). Her blank verse is assured and without condescension as she describes the gradually diminishing activity of the mill machinery as the waters of the river rise:

> . . . for the stream
> Had risen to a flood, and made the factory-wheels
> Drag slow, and slower, till they almost stopped.
> The spindle scarcely turned, the thread ran slack,
> And lazily the shuttle crossed the web. (12)

Even the lush greenery of the geraniums the workers grow in the mill windows manages to suggest their closeness to a pastoral world without demeaning their present indoor occupation.

Amid the silenced machinery, the young women debate the meaning of the word "lady," and Esther provides her answer in the first of the poem's many sets of embedded verses, "The Loaf-Giver." Esther's verses describe the Olympian goddesses Juno, Minerva, and Venus rejecting false claims of "ladyhood" from women of fashion, high birth, and leisured lives. Instead they endorse as true lady the girl who gives food to beggars, the school-teacher who brings learning to starved souls, and the farm wife who gives bread to her family. To be a lady is to give and not take, and to mix freely with all classes of people: as Venus observes, "*I* wedded a blacksmith, / And was not ashamed" (16). The classical deities Anne Bradstreet had been reluctantly compelled to foreswear two centuries earlier, because they "did nought but play the fools and lie," now return in Larcom as a pantheon of pagan goddesses endorsing Christian and republican values (72). Larcom's adherence to a sense of enduring and essential female qualities, witnessed by her classical allusions, does not prevent her from imagining a wide range of types among her protagonists, from the queenly Esther to the fragile Eleanor and the robust and hoydenish Minta. However, all of her heroines resist public and militant activism on behalf of reform issues that touch their lives, whether for higher wages, for strikes ("The very name / Of 'strike' has so unwomanly a sound"), against child labor in factories, or slave labor to produce the cotton they spin and weave (119). Such inaction may stem either from female decorum or from an Emersonian sense that any direct engagement in reform must be prefaced by a prior internal revolution in its advocates. Womanliness and idealism are so thoroughly fused in their apprehensions that it is impossible to separate the two. Elizabeth Barrett Browning's Aurora also rejects direct involvement in reform activism, embracing no solutions to the social problems of the day except, in one critic's succinct summary, her creator's "own brand of Christian love—and poetry" (Kaplan 12). Perhaps a woman of the people, like Larcom, might have been expected to consider more direct forms of amelioration than the elite English poet. Larcom does substitute five factory women for the trio of class representatives in *Aurora Leigh* (the working-class Marian, the bourgeois Aurora, and the aristocratic Lady Waldemar) and indeed her operatives vigorously debate topical reform questions. However, Larcom assimilates their thinking about these questions into a larger spiritual context, where the paradoxes and incongruities of their daily lives are acceptable within a divine scheme not yet fully revealed to them, and thus not to be rashly challenged.

Larcom's choice of five more or less equally prominent protagonists, all workers in the same Lowell factory, is an immediate signal of the democratic nature of her epic, although it was probably also the source of critical complaints by the *Scribner's* reviewer about the lightness and vagueness of the plot ("An Idyl of Work" 136). That these women, Esther, Eleanor, Minta, Isabel, and Ruth, are not only from different geographical regions but also from a range of social backgrounds suggests that the factory world may operate as a microcosm of the republic, equalizing the social status and promoting some degree of cultural variety. Set about thirty years earlier than its 1875 publication, the *Idyl's* world predates the large-scale entry of immigrants into Lowell, so the geographic variety admittedly means only the mixing of girls from the seaports of Massachusetts, who have never seen mountains, with those from interior New Hampshire, who have never seen the ocean. Their cultural divides, from a later perspective, may seem similarly minor—Methodists, Baptists, Unitarians, and Universalists—but to women leaving their parochial homes for the first time to live in "a place filled with strangers" (Zonderman 98), such distinctions were of great significance.

Among Larcom's factory group, Eleanor is the orphaned descendant of "rich ancestors," while Minta is a farmer's daughter. Esther is "born of

Puritans by the sea / That washes Plymouth Rock" while Minta is from the mountains. Isabel, Eleanor, and Esther "were from childhood bred / On the tough meat of Calvin's doctrines," while Minta is a Methodist, and Ruth attends St. Ann's Orthodox (19, 69). As in their origins and religious loyalties, so in their eventual destinies: Larcom proposes an array of possibilities that suggest social fluidity as well as alternatives to marriage. At the end, two of the young women, Isabel and Esther, seem likely to marry, one to a carpenter, the other to a doctor; Eleanor is facing an early death, perhaps a hint that her rather aristocratic origins have not toughened her sufficiently for democratic working life. Minta is going to continue her education and prepare for a career in teaching, and Ruth is going to Europe as a governess. The women's options are extended by the inclusion in the poem of a list of outcomes of other Lowell operatives, drawn from their actual histories. Those who have married are wives of sea captains, farmers, parsons, a senator, a ruling officer in Mexico, and a millionaire. Of those who have remained single, one is a painter, one a sculptor, and one a mission teacher among the Cherokee. Such an emphasis not only preempts the "Reader, I married him" plot of *Aurora Leigh* but also provides an alternative to Elizabeth Barrett Browning's focus on a single male character for whom its three females compete.

Larcom, like Browning, explores in her poem the predicament of the fallen woman in a society where female chastity depends as much on appearance as on reality, and a good name, once lost, is almost irrecoverable. Larcom describes two instances of erring workers, although with no concessions to Orestes Brownson's argument that having worked in a factory is enough to damn the most virtuous girl to infamy. The first is an account of a woman who has drowned herself because

> In her early days
> One slip she made,—you see she is not young;
> For that she never could forgive herself,
> And she has toiled in silence ever since,
> Upright and honest, but too sad to care
> For friends or life. (58)

Eleanor's response to the suicide is to decry the lack of friends who might have helped the woman to "put her weight of sin / Behind her" and "walk on with other girls…happy and forgiven" (58). Later, when it seems as if Isabel is about to make the same slip by eloping with a lover, her group of friends rallies around to save her. The pursuit of Isabel takes Esther through the dark alleyways of Boston, where the scoffing eyes of "womanhood / Sunk to its lowest" look into the pure and pitying eyes of the factory woman. The poet, like her characters, appears to view such fallen women with compassion and the promise of redemption, but with no diminution of moral revulsion from the "stench of unclean souls" (155-6).

Nonetheless, the noble Esther grows humble at what she witnesses: "her ignorance / Of life's bad possibilities appalled her" (156). In her celebration of the new world of women's work, Larcom does not ignore the grimmer chances and accidents that run counter to her Christian and democratic optimism. The dark secrets of the city remained the favored subject for the gothic novel rather than the republican epic, but Larcom is candid enough to acknowledge that there is a large area of American life of which her admirable poet-worker, Esther, and many others like her, are completely unaware.

Larcom is, however, somewhat more tolerant of her flighty Isabel, in the fate she assigns her, than is Browning of her innocently victimized working woman Marian Erle. While Marian is permitted redemption into a world of maternal happiness only by the practice of perpetual chastity, Larcom's more culpable Isabel is redeemed into a community of fellow workers and the prospect of a happy marriage to a decent young man. Since Larcom, on principle, does not see marriage as a reward for virtue or a more desirable alternative to a single life, her decision to permit Isabel's partnership seems like an act of resistance to the social stigma against women who have compromised their good name: she allows her both earthly joy and an honorable marriage. By comparison, Browning refuses to allow her admirable Romney to waste his superior abilities by marrying Marian, in a misguided effort to compensate her for her suffering. As Cora Kaplan has argued, "through the trauma of her rape Marian becomes a virtuous untouchable...a self-determining woman...but an unmarriageable one"; Marian can only be "absolved" if she is denied "self-generated sexuality" (25). By reducing the centrality of marriage in her women's lives, Larcom can afford to reduce its significance as a reward for female virtue.

The fact that Larcom's women are all independent and self-supporting wage-earners naturally enables them to view marriage more openly as a choice rather than a necessary goal for dependent females. Larcom also suggests that it is women's access to *factory* labor, as mechanized spinners and weavers, that permits them to engage in even more important intellectual activities. The factory women in her poem perform a wholly mechanical version of women's traditional handwork, which they use to support the more desirable work of the mind. Larcom's defense of factory labor is based entirely on its peripheral benefits and on the general principle of the worthiness of labor rather than on any innate value of the particular kind of work that is being done, even though it manufactures the same product—cloth—that women's traditional work had long done. Interestingly, when Isabel, the most flirtatious of the factory women in the poem, meets a rich gentleman who might have a romantic interest in her, she tells him she is a "seamstress" rather than a factory worker. Her deception suggests that he will prefer the continuing domestic and feminine associations of home sewing to the more communal and mechanical implications of factory labor. In these two epic poems about women, work, and writing, both Lucy Larcom and Elizabeth Barrett Browning resist the notion that handwork—weaving, sewing, spinning—is a positive metaphor for the ideal work of a woman, despite its long use as a traditional metaphor for literary composition. Figures of knitting, stitching, spinning, embroidering, and weaving have conventionally served as images, in both male and female writers, for the process of composition, although the actual work from which these images derive has been an almost exclusively female occupation. Perhaps for this reason, Larcom and Browning separate the poetic activity of their protagonists, quite emphatically and explicitly, from the traditional activity of women's spinning, weaving, and sewing. Larcom makes the distinction by dividing her characters' work decisively between their cloth production as mechanical "hands" and their intellectual creativity as "minds"; Browning depicts her heroine Aurora's vigorous resistance to every feminine practice that is implied by the act of sewing.

In an interesting essay, "Nor in Fading Silks Compose," on the literary trope of sewing in Browning, Anne D. Wallace has noted that the activity of sewing is often figured in *Aurora Leigh* by terms like pricking, braiding, netting, and stringing, which suggest repetitive, painful, and largely worthless activity. Aurora, early in the poem, dismisses sewing as, in Wallace's words, "constraining, superficial, trivial, spiritually retrograde, fatal to poetic arts, and economically worthless" and as "women's work" in the most contemptible sense (233). Although Aurora's enforced sewing activities as a young lady are deemed valueless, Marian Erle's work as a paid seamstress appears to be closer to a definition of productive labor. However, Browning establishes no connection between Marian's sewing and the act of literary composition, while Aurora's resistance to this feminine skill seems to enable her to move into the male world of poetry writing as a productive and financially rewarding activity. Browning's working-class Marian is destined to the female fate of so many seamstresses in nineteenth-century literature, sexual entrapment from which she can escape only into devotional motherhood. Aurora, by comparison, moves on to a successful public career outside the constrictions of her gender. Larcom, too, like Browning, chooses an alternative to the victimized seamstress for her model of the woman writer, but her imagined poets are simultaneously engaged in the main alternative to seamstresses' labor available to working women, industrial manufacturing.

The paradigm of the seamstress and the factory worker as two distinctly different ways of representing working-class women in nineteenth-century American literature has been extensively explored by Amal Amireh. She notes that the Lowell operatives were initially used in "pro factory" arguments as models of female workers who were "orderly, controlled, and paternally supervised" daughters of the republic, who did not threaten the "patriarchal order" (3). However, they were also women in the public workplace, laboring outside the domestic realm, often at their own behest, for wages, and not at all unhappy to escape from the drudgery of traditional household and farm work. Amireh finds that by midcentury, these new women workers were incapable of being molded into an emblem of womanhood that was neither incoherent nor paradoxical, so writers turned to the seamstress and her more traditionally feminine associations. By comparison with the factory worker, the seamstress, according to Amireh, proved "a relatively coherent paradigm"—"the woman who sews" (43, 52). She could be cast as a helpless widow, uncomplaining, eager for work outside the industrial establishment, still enshrined in a domestic and preindustrial setting, or as a struggling young woman, alone and vulnerable to seduction because her earnings were so low and she had no male protectors. In either case, this more coherent seamstress is a woman at the mercy of fate who stoically accepts poverty and the obligations of childbearing: in Raymond Williams's terminology, she is a residual figure, belonging to both past and present, while the factory worker resisted and challenged the standards of the world of women's preindustrial labor (56).

Larcom, writing her *Idyl* much beyond midcentury but looking back to the earlier years of industrialism, uses both the ideal image of the orderly factory woman and the more paradoxical later one, although it is the growth of intellectual ambition and self-assertion in her protagonists, rather than social or political or sexual rebelliousness, that contributes to their paradoxical complication. Larcom's factory women are poised hopefully at a historical point that had already long passed, as she admits quite candidly in her introduction to the epic. However, they represent women discovering a new frontier of experience, both physical and mental, that for a time increased the range of their lives' possibilities. Even when their circumstances changed and narrowed later in the century, her poem suggests that the same impulses still existed in factory women, waiting for a renewed opportunity.

Larcom presents the actual factory work women do, in *An Idyl of Work*, not as a Romanticized version of women's traditional work, as Sarah Savage had done in *The Factory Girl*, but as the prosaic wage-earning activity that most human beings must engage in to provide for their material necessities. The cultivation of the mind and the writing of poetry are not presented, as in *Aurora Leigh*, as a new professional field for women, but rather as an ideal way of pursuing a higher and transcendent life that is subsidized by the practical and mundane activity of industrial employment. Such activity offers women specific opportunities for education and intellectual interaction that are not available in their work at home or on the farm, and, insofar as it enables them to pursue a creative and examined life, it is distinctly beneficial for them. Jessica Lewis's study of Larcom's memoir *A New England Girlhood* has noted her repeated tendency to associate poetry with far more than the mere act of writing or with its product: it is part of a sublime experience that requires both the presence of other people to share in the transcendence, and the availability of the homelier and more banal world of work to heighten the awareness of the contrast. Lewis concludes that "'the hand to hand struggle for existence' is 'no hindrance' to poetry—it becomes the prose, the 'on-this-earthness' in which Larcom's poetic existence can thrive" (189). Thus the tedium of daily labor served Larcom both as material subsidy and as necessary counterweight to the intellectual and spiritual realm of her poetry—attitudes she projects on to the main characters of the *Idyl* in their comments on their work and their poetry.

Early in the poem, in its first book, Larcom introduces the thematic dichotomy between the prosaic world of the factory and the poetic world it makes possible: when the overseer tells the workers the river is up and they will have a holiday,

> The three glad girls
> ...went out for a walk among green trees,
> Like souls released from earth to paradise. (24)

Later in the poem, the intimate connection between poetry and walking in nature will be affirmed, but from the start, the factory is related to the earthly, the everyday, the here and now—not by any means a prison or a punitive workhouse, but the required price for surviving in the material world. Larcom describes the Sabbath day as "One welcome pause between dull sentences / Of week-long prose," with the witty surprise conclusion that the weekdays are not imprisoning but merely prosaic sentences (60).

At the crux of Larcom's epic is the question of how to preserve the delicate balance between the bodily chore of toil and the mental freedom of the worker who performs it, a freedom that is both enabled and encroached on by the arduous nature of the work. When Ruth Woodburn is introduced, she admits that although she began her factory work imagining it would be "a romantic sport," now, "I think but as a hireling of my work," and she refers ironically to her earlier attitudes as "Eden-visions" (25, 90). Although Minta becomes possessed at one point by the urge "to strike out / For something new,—to learn what's in me" she assumes she must nonetheless continue working if she is to survive:

> Work?
> As well quit living as quit work, and yet
> Heads like to be employed, as well as hands;
> Is there no way to give each a fair chance? (138)

Although the women discuss the contemporary experiment at Brook Farm that attempted to alternate the work of head and hand, they are wary of

Fourierist phalansteries. Minta's rather ambiguous comment on Brook Farm, "I will ask no man's help or blessing" (139), may be an assertion of either individual or gender independence from the male-run communal project. Larcom's factory women in the *Idyl* still live in a time and place where the balance between head and hand has not been wholly skewed, or if it is faltering, they still believe that they may make other choices. Ruth suggests, somewhat naively, that if the mill owners become tyrants, the women may simply retreat to their preindustrial origins:

> If they grind
> And cheat as brethren should not, let us go
> Back to the music of the spinning-wheel,
> And clothe ourselves at hand-looms of our own,
> As did our grandmothers. (119)

Even if a return to such an era of handcrafts was a highly unlikely prospect, young New England women in the 1840s still believed they had a wider range of options available to them than their working sisters in England. However, Larcom's perspective from 1875 leads her both to celebrate this earlier belief and to regret its diminution.

Despite Larcom's reluctance to enter into economic or social criticism of factories, her poem gives repeated voice to the fear that the people's capacity for transcendent and metaphorically poetic activity may be undermined by excesses of drudgery in unhealthy conditions. On one occasion, when English travelers arrive for the obligatory factory tour, they cannot tolerate, even for a brief visit, the conditions in which women labor fourteen hours a day:

> The carding-room
> They gave one glance, with its great groaning wheels,
> Its earthquake rumblings, and its mingled smells
> Of oily suffocation; and passed on
> Into another room's cool spaciousness. (77–78)

Miriam Willoughby, an older woman who befriends the factory workers, hints at the dilemma of balance when she comments: "Labor is beautiful: but not too much" (135). Later she ponders whether the long hours the women work in the service of a machine may not, in the end, be a perverse economy:

> But this was waste,—this woman-faculty
> Tied to machinery, part of the machine
> That wove cloth, when it might be better clothing hearts
> And minds with queenly raiment....

Here was a problem, then,
For the political theorist: how to save
Mind from machinery's clutches. (142)

Miriam, as an outsider to the factory world, is significantly more concerned with the dehumanizing effects of machinery than are the workers
themselves. Esther, the most philosophical of the group, is less upset by the
onerousness of their work than whether "much toil on the outside show of
things / Deadened the deeper faculties" (153). Her reference to "the outside show" is an allusion to the women's work she observes on her trip to
Boston—sewing, tailoring, millinery, shop-tending—and perhaps, beyond
that to a broader sense that so much of women's work is concentrated on
the making and marketing of "goods." It is part of a larger cycle of production and consumption that emphasizes the trivial, the ephemeral, and
the material in human affairs.

Esther's even more profound scruple about the nature of the women's
work, however, concerns the paradox that the labor that liberates the factory women from dependency arises directly from the enslavement of others. If the contradictions of work are at the heart of the poem, none is
more difficult to resolve than the relationship of the female wage laborer in
the cotton mills to the human chattel in the cotton fields. David Roediger
has analyzed the extent to which both analogies and contrasts to slavery
dominated much of the discourse on white-working class labor in the first
half of the nineteenth century. He notes that wage-earning workers might
use the metaphor of slavery to emphasize, by contrast, the independent and
republican aspects of their power to sell their own labor or, by comparison, the powerlessness and dependency to which they might be reduced
(45). He observes that the contradictions inherent in comparisons between
wage labor and chattel slavery were "both insistent and embarrassed," since
chattel slavery was, for white workers, both "a touchstone against which
to weigh their fears and a yardstick to measure their reassurance" (66).
Roediger's conclusion that the "comparison cut hard, and it cut in two
ways" is particularly apt for the female textile workers at Lowell, since in
addition to the dilemma of whether to celebrate their liberation through
work or resist their exploitation as wage slaves, the particular nature of their
factory labor had an even more direct and nonmetaphorical connection to
slavery (46). The cotton they worked on came from slave plantations, and
the product they made was often returned to the south as "negro cloth" for
dressing the human chattel (Zonderman 117). Larcom's Esther, speaking to
Miriam, candidly confronts the quandary:

When I've thought,
Miss Willoughby, what soil the cotton-plant
We weave, is rooted in, what waters it,—

The blood of souls in bondage,—I have felt
That I was sinning against light, to stay
And turn the accursed fibre into cloth
For human wearing....
Am not I enslaved
In finishing what slavery has begun? (135–36)

Miriam acknowledges, somewhat evasively, that "We all share the nation's
sin," but Esther is aware that her closer implication in that sin, by choosing
factory work that produces cotton over more traditional women's occupations, is a result of her own personal desire for freedom. She admits that
had she chosen housework, as a servant, it would not have allowed her
what she treasures most, "freedom for my books / Freedom of my own
movements;" and she explains:

                                                              Every one,
    Not wife or daughter, in a land like ours,
    Who does much thinking, must prefer to be
    Mistress of her own plans; no housemaid can. (136)

Esther's honesty permits the dilemma to be faced, but not resolved. The
literary tools of paradox and oxymoron can accommodate, though not
resolve, for these worker poets, the predicament of freedom bought by
others' enslavement.

Interestingly, it is the factory superintendent who coins the phrase that
best embodies the incongruities of factory labor: "work's a blessed curse"
(80). When visitors question him about the difficulties of the lives of the
workers he oversees, he admits that he, too, lives with contradictions:

    If, being here,
    I needs must solve all problems of these lives,—
    A hopeless task,—perplexed I must withdraw
    And seek a wiser man to fill my place. (79–80)

Larcom pursues the doubleness of "a blessed curse" through several other
aspects of factory labor, including the employment of children, boardinghouse conditions, and the leisure time temptations of Lowell. The little girls
who work as bobbin-changers in the mill are introduced enjoying a rare
holiday. Normally they attend school three months of the year and work
the remainder. When the older girls ask them if they are not sometimes
very tired, they reply with New England stoicism:

    Oh yes!
    But so is everybody. We must learn,
    While we are children, how to do hard things,
    And that will toughen us, so mother says. (49)

The children not only carry the burden of their work but have already assimilated a worldly and protective attitude toward their more secluded and domesticated mother—they tell how some of the spinners in the mill

> say dreadful words; if mother knew,
> She would not let us work there. But we must,
> And so we do not tell her. (49)

Like the other factory women in the poem, these young girls themselves produce poetry, in their case an appropriately childlike song about a magical, preindustrial world where fairies spun rainbows and slid down moonbeams. Now, however, the streams the fairies haunted serve to turn the spindles in the mill; now "Toil is warp, and money weft; / Not a fairy loom is left" (54). However, in their nostalgic regret for this magical greenwood past, the children appear to recognize a redemptive Christian reality in the present. In addition to the interweaving of toil and money in the factories, they acknowledge that their work is part of a more noble fabric, in which "Life is warp, and love is weft" (55). Larcom insists always, despite her misgivings about the future direction of the factories, in finding the balancing antithesis that demonstrates the positive advantage of the "blessed curse" for such children. In this case, as in several others, she endorses and celebrates human communion and love as the consolation for mutual hardship.

Larcom's exploration of the burdens of living in crowded boardinghouses is a case in point of such comfort-taking. The opportunity for these aspiring poets to have a room of their own is virtually nonexistent, but an advantage of their proximity is that their close participation in community life inspires their writing. Ruth is the rare exception to the normal boardinghouse pattern:

> Ruth Woodburn sat alone in her own room;
> A most unusual privilege,—her own,—
> Hers only,—seven feet square! (85)

However, the narrator comments on Ruth's situation:

> Tis no good place for songs,
> Dungeoned in self. Birds in a darkened cage
> Stop singing. (86)

Esther, by contrast, who shares a room with Eleanor and Isabel,

> sought the nook
> She called her own, a space between the bed
> And window, wide enough to hold one chair,
> Where she could see the stars, unjostled, move

Across the open sky-fields. Room! more room!
Her thoughts cried out for. So to live, so cramped
As not to hear your nearest neighbor's voice
Through the surrounding jargon, was it life? (96)

However, it is significant that Esther wants not silence but sufficient quiet to hear a neighbor's voice, showing a need for human companionship that the others repeatedly affirm. Miriam, too, insists that the mind's transcendence is not achieved in exclusion from others: "Who climbs to isolation from mankind, / There thinking to find wisdom, is a fool" (123). Ruth's final embedded poem, likewise, is on the theme that "each has a share in all" (176). Larcom is not so disingenuous as to suggest that overcrowded living conditions are a requirement for poetry, but she insists that the close presence of others is a requisite for the mind to be able to perform its noblest work.

Promoters of factory work for women often cited the educational and cultural opportunities of Lowell, just as opponents noted the temptations to self-indulgence and triviality. Larcom's entire poem might be considered an extended investigation of the intellectual aspirations of women workers in a simultaneously enabling and frustrating environment. She assumes that her characters are, by virtue of their ancestry, innately attuned to the power of literacy, the love of books, the spirit of curiosity: "As well forbid us Yankee girls to breathe / As read; we cannot help it" (129). She catalogues the contents of their bookshelves, their ways of circumventing the rules against reading in the mills, even Esther's particular penchant for Wordsworth. She notes that less elevated pursuits also tempt the workers. A practitioner of the contemporary fad of phrenology visits a boardinghouse,

and a tide of mirth
Flowed in around the tables, as he read
The cranial character of each to each. (96)

He is preceded by a peddler, "whose wares / The girls sat cheapening" (96), and when the scene shifts from the Lowell boardinghouse to one in Boston, the degree of triviality in the women's exchanges is intensified to "idle prattle, all / Of fashions, scandal, good looks, stylish beaux" (153). The suggestion is certainly not that Lowell is an enduring ideal, but that work and community in the "city of spindles" at this moment in time permits women to make positive gains from the inevitable process of industrialization.

The physical location of the factory world in *An Idyl of Work* is at a metaphorical midpoint between the metropolis of Boston and the mountains of New Hampshire, adjacent to a still pastoral and accessible landscape. Here the working women readily engage in one of the traditional practices that pervades the consciousness of male contemplative poets, that of walking in nature. In her study of "the excursive possibilities of walking" in *Aurora Leigh*, Anne Wallace notes that when Aurora takes a solitary walk on the morning of her twenty-first birthday, what it "means to her, plainly enough, is agency and aspiration, specifically the power to work and succeed at poetry" (235). While such nature walking for New England factory women is a less rare adventure, and almost never a solitary one, it is similarly pervaded by a sense of possibility and celebration. In the design of *An Idyl of Work*, this sense is translated into the many formal poems embedded within the larger epic's blank verse format. Larcom uses the rich resources of the New England environment to expand the realm of her poem in time and space, and to explore connections and transitions between the natural and the supernatural, the immanent and the transcendent. The result is not so much a sense of the empowerment of the individual poet, such as comes to Aurora Leigh, but of contact with the origins of poetry itself and of its function as a link between the earthly and the divine. Early in the poem, the rising Merrimack carries along on its flood "A fence, a hen-coop, torn roots of old trees, / And once a little cottage," and in doing so leads the workers to meditate on the river's "far-off sources" (23). Eventually it becomes apparent that the stream of the poem likewise incorporates the objects and experiences of the surrounding world and leads to a similar contemplation of the power that animates them.

Within the flexible time frame of the poem, legends of New England's Puritan and warlike past mix with its rapidly industrializing present. An embedded poem about the days of Salem witchcraft, and the ostracizing of an independent woman who lives alone and speaks her mind, suggests comparisons with the modern women who are now writing and publishing their ideas. An account of the early Christian betrayal of the Indian chief Wannalancet is curiously juxtaposed to the current employment of young girls in the mills, and "the strange story of a little child / Earning its living" (50). The *Lowell Offering* had included many accounts of the mistreatment of Indians as evidence of Christian hypocrisy, so Larcom's curious alignment of Indian betrayal and child labor may well suggest a contemporary manifestation of the failure of religious principle. The poem's factory women live in a dramatically changing world that is nevertheless still permeated by a regional culture and a local history, and surrounded by a rural landscape. It is from the fusion of these seemingly disparate realms that they receive their apprehensions of that larger fusion of the material and spiritual worlds that is at the heart of *An Idyl of Work*'s poetic and Christian ethos. Larcom delights in mixing and yoking observations from different areas of human experience and relishing the sense of mystery that arises from the juxtaposition. Thus, the beautiful Isabel walks through the woods to the wild rapids of Pawtucket Falls, wearing a dress whose ruffles are stained with grease from the machinery of the factory from which she has emerged. Likewise, the wildflowers along the way evoke direct sensuous pleasure in their blazing colors, but also bring intellectual delight in their suggestions of the larger natural system, "sweet with memories of Swedish

Linnaeus" (47). The minister's Sunday sermon emphasizes the presence of the divine in common things, and Esther's poem "The City Lights" envisions the lights of urban households and those of distant stars as representing equally the "window-lights of home" (154). Larcom's characters seem equally at home in their immediate surroundings and far beyond. They have no problem fusing the various realms of their experience, past and present, rural and urban, material and spiritual, in part because their religion tells them there is no epistemological barrier between the natural and the supernatural, and in part because Larcom understands the art of poetry as the celebration of that fusion.

Within each of the twelve blank verse books of *An Idyl of Work* is a poem—a song, hymn, ballad, or sonnet—that is the spontaneous outpouring of one of the *Idyl*'s characters, sometimes directly attributed to the characters, sometimes "recalled" by them as appropriate to the occasion. Any situation may suddenly be translated into rhythmical and rhyming language, whether the humorous dilemma of whether to marry a farmer or a fop, the pain of a lost love, or the elation of going up into the mountains. Esther, Eleanor, Ruth, Miriam, Isabel, and the little factory girls (already apprentice poets) all contribute their own verses and songs. The most elevated and ambitious are two sonnets "quoted" by Miriam Willoughby, "Clouds on Whiteface" and "Chocorua," that embody, in their blend of simple sentiment and formal complexity, the union of disparities that is at the core of Larcom's poetics. "Clouds on Whiteface" is about rock and cloud, the earthly and the airy, the rooted and the floating, the mutual attraction of the real and the illusory, and the capacity for transformation. The great mountain acts as a kind of magnet to the clouds,

> Draws them unto himself; their beauty shares;
> And sometimes his own semblance seems to lose,
> His grandeur and their grace so interfuse. (111)

The sonnet "Chocorua" is likewise about a mysterious symbiosis of different essences, this time of moonlight, ocean, mist, and mountain. The factory women take delight in renaming the mountains of the Presidential Range, embarking on a "christening-tour" in which they return the range symbolically to the "red man" and recall his legendary past with invocations of Passaconoway, Paugus, Wahwa, and Wannalancet. Although neither of the mountain sonnets is Christian in any explicit, doctrinal way, none of the embedded poems is wholly secular either, since for Larcom poetry is the bridge between the secular and the sacred. For Larcom and her factory protagonists, the life of the mind, their poetic compositions, and acts of meditation and devotion are intimately bound together. Unlike the ideal domesticated women of the "true womanhood" tradition, who were "warned not to let their literary or intellectual pursuits take them away from God" (Welter 23), Larcom's factory workers clearly did not feel that they were betraying any higher female duty when they hid books beneath their looms, pasted poems and stories on the windowsills of the factory, or spent their free time in reading and writing. When Miriam discovers that the mills have had to make a rule forbidding reading at work, she exclaims, "To the praise / Of mill-girls be the need of such a rule" (128), although, admittedly, she is perhaps assuming more edifying books than the variety the workers actually read (Tolbert 2–3). The early factory novelists repeatedly extended the necessity for seemliness and decorum into women's mental lives, but the enquiring and creative mind, in Larcom's vision, is so noble that it needs no restraints.

The intimate association of reading, poetry writing, and religion in the lives of Larcom's mill women certainly might be interpreted as evidence of a successful conspiracy on the part of the factory owners to secure for themselves a diligent and compliant workforce of intelligent and ambitious young women, seeking the society of like-minded people and the opportunity to enhance their education and literacy. Larcom's characters resist this demeaning view of their entrapment in a manufacturers' scheme, seeing themselves, instead, as free agents who are undertaking arduous labor but can abandon it as soon as it no longer provides a reasonable exchange in money, time, and conditions for the work that is demanded. Larcom is aware that she is chronicling a moment in time when employers and workers found tolerable mutual satisfaction in an arrangement that would soon alter drastically. The rewards for the workers would be reduced, the demands on them would steadily increase, and the possibility of their withdrawal to an alternative life would no longer be so feasible. It is in the tenuous context of a temporary balance between workers and owners, country and city, past and present that Larcom sets her *Idyl*, not an ideal world but a real realm of possibility, where a poetic life for young women is accessible through the "blessed curse" of paid factory labor.

If the poetic life for these women workers is a union of intellectual and spiritual aspiration, empowered by the worldly realm of their work and friendship, its immediate manifestation is in writing. The act of transforming experience, emotion, and thought into words is a kind of second nature for them, an activity they turn to spontaneously, frequently in their own composition but just as readily in the remembered and quoted words of others. If they take delight in the pleasures of reading and writing, they have relatively little interest at this point in gaining material rewards for their intellectual and creative activities. Unlike many middle-class American women who were finding their vocation in writing in the mid–nineteenth century, Larcom's workers are young, unmarried, and already making enough money for their own support and sometimes that of others. Many of the middle-class women who emerged into the literary marketplace during the same period were older, were married, and felt obliged to justify their materialism and temerity, in profiting from their writing, by insisting it was an act of necessity and service to their families. These

women, whom Mary Kelley, in *Private Woman, Public Stage,* has labeled
"literary domestics," hesitated to embrace a public and professional reputation unless their unladylike behavior could be vindicated by a sense of
feminine obligations, and they repeatedly asserted reluctance to compete in
the male workplace. Kelley takes as symptomatic of these literary domestics the response of Fanny Fern's fictional Ruth Hall to her little daughter
when the child asks, "When I get to be a woman shall I write books,
mamma?" The mother's answer is "God forbid" (qtd. in Kelley 138). Such
a reply is inconceivable in the world of Larcom's factory writers, not only
because they see writing as a goodly or godly activity but also because their
industrial work has already taken them, in some measure, across the gender
barrier into moneymaking, independence, and the emergence from private
life. Larcom neither apologizes for her working-class women writers nor
makes feminist pleas for their right to express themselves. She was indeed
only a very mild feminist, never willing, despite the urging of her lifelong
friend Harriet Robinson, to join the women's rights movement or advocate for female suffrage (Marchalonis 180–81). That a markedly lukewarm
supporter of women's rights should have felt no need to comment defen-
sively on the supposed presumptuousness of women's writing suggests the
extent to which Larcom's attitudes toward writing were not those of her
literary domestic compatriots. It also indicates how far her experiences of
factory labor removed her from the gendered standard of her middle-class
contemporaries.

Whether Larcom and the factory writers were as comparably free of
social ambition as they were of gender humility is a question complicated
by the precarious stage of class relationships and class consciousness existing in the period when her epic poem was set. The New England factory
system was relatively recent and still somewhat untainted by association
with the repetitive pattern of generations of industrial workers in England, whose class status at birth seemed almost as fatally deterministic of the
quality of their lives as their gender. Visitors to New England from Britain
in the mid–nineteenth century often remarked on the "mental energy" as
well as the "literariness" of these "factory ladies," all terms that never would
have been applied, except ironically, to English working women. Although
Larcom, too, in her *Idyl,* laid claim to the word "lady," she took care to
distinguish it from more conventional notions of social rank and hierarchy.
For her, "lady" was the true description of any woman, from farm wife to
Greek goddess, who shared her talents with the world. However, it seems
reasonable to assume that when visitors and outsiders applied the term
to the women of Lowell, they were implying that their literariness, linguistic fluency, extensive reading, and thirst for education were indicators
of a middle- rather than a working-class status. By such criteria, then,
working-class literariness would be a virtual oxymoron, since the penchant
for intellectual activity was itself being defined as middle-class. Susan Zlotnick has shown that, in England in the nineteenth century, the domestic

ideal had "effectively denied a voice to working-class women" (169), by defining women's writing by a female ideal of domesticity that excluded the working-class woman. Larcom and the imagined factory writers of her poem had not, in fact, been silenced by their failure to comply with such female literary ideals of home, marriage, and motherhood. However, just as ominously, they risked being appropriated by a rising middle-class culture impatient to assume the literary and intellectual world. This culture would define the notion of a mindful existence away from factory workers and assume that those who aspired to it were, at best, in need of reclassification, at worst, traitors to their class.

Was it, then, possible to be a working-class woman writer who was not upwardly mobile in the class system, especially one who, like Larcom, felt no great antagonism toward factory owners and superintendents, was largely uninterested in agitation to improve workers' conditions, and did not look on writing as a tool of social reform? The answer must be an emphatic yes, unless the working-class writer is to be limited by a narrow conception of subject matter and attitudes and the middle-class writer then permitted to claim, by default, the rest of the literary realm. Larcom's *An Idyl of Work*, without engaging in any recognizable manifestations of class warfare, nevertheless asserts the working-class, wage-earning, enthusiastically literary factory woman as an ideal norm of American, republican life. If, from the perspective of later ideals of cultural diversity, she seems an almost comically limited norm—white, female, Christian—she was, in the mid–nineteenth century, a bold and dramatic new embodiment of the representative American. She was fit for manual and mental labor, capable not only of serving the needs of industry but of settling the frontier, educating the citizens, aspiring to the highest ideals of life, and ultimately becoming the American poet.

7

Full Development or Self-Restraint
Middle-Class Women and Working-Class Elevation

What artist sense had she—what could she know—the ignorant
huckster—of the eternal laws of beauty or grandeur?
—REBECCA HARDING DAVIS, *MARGRET HOWTH* (1862)

Christ's way is a patient way. It is a pure way, it is a way that cares more
for another world than for this one, and more to be holy than to be
happy, and more for other folks than for itself.
—ELIZABETH STUART PHELPS, *THE SILENT PARTNER* (1871)

Your redic'lus notions about independence and self-cultur won't come to
nothin' in the long run.
—LOUISA MAY ALCOTT, *WORK* (1873)

By 1875, when Larcom's *Idyl of Work* was published, the notion that
factory women might ever have embraced even modest notions of
Romantic idealism and self-culture must have seemed, at best, a wry one.
Larcom herself was well aware of the deterioration in the working conditions in New England factories and of the increasing dependency of
the workers. Although she nonetheless remained hopeful that what she
called "the spirit of our national life" would remain unchanged (viii–ix), it
was precisely this spirit that seemed to alter in the latter half of the nineteenth century, with the intensification and acceleration of industrialization. While the immigrant population was growing dramatically, the codes
of urban industrial capitalism were becoming more entrenched, so that the
experience of factory labor could no longer be viewed as a chosen stage
in a worker's life from which progress or retreat was a real possibility. Even
before the war, the Concord transcendentalists had already begun what
Anne Rose describes as "the renunciation of radical social reform and
acceptance of free market capitalism." After the war, she notes, the presence of "a sea of immigrants, machine politics, and new wealth" further
disheartened the optimism of their remaining adherents (223). The diminution of the Romantic movement did not mean a waning of interest on
the part of reformers in improving the lives of industrial workers and the
urban poor, but reform efforts focused increasingly on practical changes

in institutions and services, and relinquished the belief that a Romantic internal awakening of the individual members of society must precede and accompany beneficial changes in the larger social organism.[1] Public debates after the war began to focus increasingly on the class stratification of the population and on the terminology appropriate to the groups that were being newly defined. Martin Burke has listed some of the terms in the lexicon that dominated the U.S. Senate's 1883 investigation of "relations between labor and capital": "the 'working-class,' the 'educated classes,' 'middle class,' 'laboring classes,' the 'non-laboring classes', 'class rule,' 'class struggle,' 'oppressors and the oppressed,' 'producers,' 'non-producers,' the 'upper class,' and 'lower class,' 'capital and the ruling classes,' 'privileged classes,' and 'permanent classes'" (160). Not surprisingly, the language and syntax of class began to enter the imaginative literature of working women, alongside earlier concerns with gender, as writers scrutinized the tensions and affinities between these categories.

The amount of fiction written about women workers increased enormously in the post–Civil War years, and almost all writers, regardless of the extent of their reform agendas, proved sympathetic to laboring women in noting the ways they were victimized by both poverty and sexual prejudice. Middle-class women writers were in the vanguard of a literature that ranged from philanthropically genteel to militantly muckraking as they explored the fictive lives of poorer women, toward whom they felt both empathy and revulsion. Male authors who wrote union fiction for the Knights of Labor took up the cause of working women and created ambivalent portraits of modern comrades and more traditional heroines. In addition, a new literary genre documenting "how the other half lives" included many accounts of working women's lives by middle-class women who "descended" into their ranks, either openly, as social scientists and reporters, or covertly, disguised as members of the proletariat.[2] For all their compassion, such writings inevitably objectified the woman worker (there being no doubt about which half, either in terms of class or sex, was the "other") in a way that left little space for the kind of subjectivity and self-development Lucy Larcom and the authors of the *Lowell Offering* pursued in their literary work. There was a continuing and even heightened interest in the reading habits of working women, as well as a desire to furnish clubs for their leisure and opportunities for their further education. However, such conscious philanthropy was inevitably very different from the self-reliant aspirations of the earlier generation of factory women, who had taken from Emerson and his fellow Romantics ideals rarely seen as their entitlement. In her study of female intellectuals in Romantic America, Susan Phinney Conrad has noted the double burden of derision and suspicion that fell on intellectual women, even from the "privileged" classes: "Most people would rather *not* entertain the thought that she is a cultural type... The idea of an 'intellectual woman,' that favorite phrase of her enemies, haunted nineteenth-century American women who happened to be thinkers" (4–5). Lindsey Traub has argued that, even in the case of Emerson's relationship with Margaret Fuller, "perhaps it was literally inconceivable to him that he might have known 'Woman Thinking'" (283). How much more bizarre, then, must have been the notion of "Working Woman Thinking." Yet the dream of an integrated life that balanced body, mind, and spirit had seemed, in the 1840s, no less feasible a goal for many female Lowell operatives than for the utopian residents of Brook Farm and Fruitlands. This was the dream that seemed most in danger of disappearing from the literary record of the Gilded Age.

Idealist factory women, such as those described in Larcom's *Idyl*, had imagined in the 1830s and 1840s that not only might "mind" flourish among the spindles but also a new, female version of self-culture and self-reliance might also be compatible with a Christian tradition of selflessness and community. By the 1860s, the Romantic hope of a fulfilled life in this world as well as the next was fragmenting into literary schemes for limited improvements of work and leisure conditions in the here and now, with the promise of true rewards in the afterlife. Middle-class women writers, like Rebecca Harding Davis, Elizabeth Stuart Phelps, and Louisa May Alcott emphasized Christian otherworldliness and mutual female empathy as the means of surviving the hazards of the material world, but they presented a greatly diminished role for the exuberant faith in art, learning, reading, and writing that had inspired the workers themselves earlier in the century. They proved willing to come together with their lower-class sisters in charity and communion in this world and in dreams of transcendence in the next, but they showed less interest in the intellectual and artistic ambitions of working women, even as they simultaneously explored the barriers to their own progress in the world of arts and learning. Male novelists who espoused working women's rights to improved social and economic conditions in many Knights of Labor novels also proved enthusiastic advocates for Christian faith and piety in their female comrades, but generally manifested little interest in the idea that had so intrigued the contributors to the *Lowell Offering*—that working women might find in writing and self-culture a bridge between worldly and transcendent experience. Thus middle-class women writers reached across class barriers to share their Christian but not their artistic idealism with women workers, while male union novelists for the Knights of Labor shared reform ambitions with their female comrades but promoted womanly religious virtues. Women workers were offered religion from all quarters as a panacea for this world and hope for the next, but it was no longer associated with the Romantic aspiration to integrate intellectual ambition, artistic creativity, and the celebration of a fully realized human identity.

One of the first fictional efforts by a middle-class woman to explore the connection, or rather acknowledge the gulf, between Romantic idealism and harsh industrial reality was Rebecca Harding Davis's "Life in the Iron Mills." Although her 1861 novella is often described as an account of the intrusion of dark, satanic mills into America's pastoral landscape, the work is at least as much about what kind of art and artist may be generated from industrial squalor and exploitation as about the grim economic consequences of industrialism. When Tillie Olsen undertook the notable recovery of Davis's long-neglected work for the Feminist Press in 1972, she placed Davis in the vanguard of two literary paradigms that became dominant by the end of the century—the exposé by a middle-class writer of the lower depths, and the muckraking account of the corruptions of capitalism. Much subsequent criticism of Davis's novella has concentrated on her concern for the lives of the underclass, frequently in conjunction with her emphasis on gender. However, Sharon Harris, noting that Davis's preferred title for the story (rejected by James T. Fields at the *Atlantic Monthly*) was "The Korl Woman," has recognized the importance of the work as a statement of the author's aesthetic theories and particularly of her resistance to Emerson and his brand of Romanticism (57). Jean Pfaelzer, similarly noting Davis's lengthy literary engagement with Romanticism, suggests a continuing tension between Davis's suspicions of transcendentalism as masculine egotism and her attraction to its challenge to hierarchical ways of knowing the world and its openness to feeling and subjectivity.[3]

Davis's quarrel with American Romanticism appears to have derived, in part, from her association of its qualities with the specific manifestations of them in the character of Ralph Waldo Emerson. Davis first met Emerson in Concord in 1862, the year after the publication of "Life in the Iron Mills," and she recorded her sardonic response to the occasion many years later in her autobiography, *Bits of Gossip* (1904). However, even before this meeting, she was already engaged in a quarrel not only with transcendentalist literary values but also with what she saw as a New England delusion of representativeness. In *Bits of Gossip*, she satirizes Emerson and his disciples sharply, including in her ridicule the working women who hungered for self-affirmation, and their adulation of the Seer who blew them only "beautiful bubbles":

> New England then swarmed with weak-brained, imitative folk who had studied books with more or less zeal, and who knew nothing of actual life.... To them came this new prophet with his discovery of the God within themselves.... The new dialect of the Transcendentalist was easily learned.... Up to the old gray house among the pines in Concord they went—hordes of wild-eyed Harvard undergraduates and lean, underpaid working women, each with a disease of soul to be cured by the new Healer (qtd. in Harris 86).

Davis's primary objection to Emerson and his followers was the lack of "some backbone of fact," which stemmed from a lack of experience on the part of men who "thought they were guiding the real world" but "stood quite outside of it, and never would see it as it was." She also resisted what she saw as the egocentrism of Emerson's philosophy and its elevation of the divinely inspired artist. She disliked his elitism, which she found allied to an emotional coldness that "took from each man his drop of stored honey, and after that the man counted for no more to him than any other robbed bee" (qtd. in Harris 85). Sharon Harris has charted the evidence of antitranscendentalist ideas throughout Davis's later fiction, but it is in "Life in the Iron Mills" that she sees the philosophy and aesthetics of transcendentalism most closely connected with Davis's sense of the evils of capitalism.

Davis's story is set in the early 1830s, strictly before Emerson might be held responsible for any of its rejected attitudes. Its aggressively intrusive, first-person narrator is an apparently highly educated intellectual, of indeterminate gender, who is perhaps, to judge from the presence of a "half-moulded child's head" (65), a sculptor—like the central working-class character, Hugh Wolfe.[4] Wolfe is a puddler in the iron mills who carves figures from korl, the refuse from iron ore. The other main character is Deb, a physically deformed cotton mill worker who loves Hugh with no hope of reciprocation, although he is gentle and not inconsiderate toward her. On the night on which the main action of the story occurs, Deb has brought food to Hugh in the iron mill. Thus she is an interested witness to the event that characterizes so many accounts, both fictional and factual, of the Industrial Revolution in the United States—the tour of the workplace by privileged and curious outsiders. The literary trope of the factory tour had already proved an effective way of establishing sex- and class-based juxtapositions of visitors and workers in the literature of Lowell. Now Davis inquires, for the first time, into the ethical consequences of objectifying human lives by subsuming them into aesthetic conventions of observation. She directs her concern both to the fictional tourists in the iron mill and to her story's readers, as they, too, anticipate artistic revelations of the lower depths.[5] The tour group in her story is conducted by Clarke, the workers' overseer, and consists of four men who are designed, as is often the case in Davis's fiction, to represent distinct ideological perspectives: Kirby, the mill owner's son, is undisguised in his easy manipulation of the workers; a Yankee journalist is reviewing the "leading manufactories" for his paper; and the other two are "gentlemen" who have come merely for amusement. They are a local doctor, May, who believes he is a philanthropist, and Mitchell, who, as a complete outsider to the mill and the community, is the most disinterested observer of all (28). It is primarily in the meeting of Wolfe and Mitchell ("hand" and "head") that Davis pursues her argument about the relevance of Romantic notions of self-culture to the needs and the dreams of the working-class.

Mitchell is a highly advantaged young man who is physically, intellectually, and socially superior to the others, but ominously lacking in emotional warmth. Davis's metaphors for him are very similar to those she would later use to describe Emerson: he is "a man who sucked the essence out of a science or philosophy in an indifferent, gentlemanly way...with a temper yielding and brilliant as summer water, until his Self was touched, when it was ice, though brilliant still" (29). Mitchell's response to the heat and noise of the mill and to the brutalized workers is to evoke the familiar context of Dante's *Inferno*—exactly the kind of "idle fancy" the narrator has ridiculed at the beginning of the story in inviting the reader to enter the workers' world. Readers are thus warned from the outset of their ominous similarity to privileged sightseers. The four men visiting the iron mills have deliberately chosen to take their tour at night in order to heighten the "effects," and Mitchell uses his literary sensibilities to construct a satisfyingly picturesque scene for the others: "These heavy shadows and the amphitheatre of smothered fires are ghostly, unreal. One could fancy these red smouldering lights to be the half-shut eyes of wild beasts, and the spectral figures their victims in the den" (30–31). However, Mitchell's aesthetic relish of *his* vision is abruptly violated, not by any intrusion of the reality of workers' lives into his fancy, but by his encounter with the crude and terrifying art that is one *worker's* imaginative vision of that reality: "Mitchell started back, half-frightened, as, suddenly turning a corner, the white figure of a woman faced him in the darkness,—a woman, white, of giant proportions, crouching on the ground, her arms flung out in some wild gesture of warning" (31). It is a vision for which none of the educated and privileged visitors has any ready convention of assimilation.

The worker's statue, "a nude woman's form, muscular, grown coarse with labor, the powerful limbs instinct with some one poignant longing" (32), immediately becomes the center of a lively debate on form, meaning, and ideology among the visitors. Significantly, the artifact provokes a much more animated response from the mill tourists than the workers themselves do. Dr. May, the professional anatomist, notes appreciatively the "sweep of the muscles in the arm and hand," the "bony wrist, and the strained sinews of the instep," and summons Wolfe to question him, with a smile he reserves for "these people" (32, 33). Wolfe's explanation of his sculpture's meaning directly challenges the alien suggestions of the doctor's phrase, "these people," by stammeringly asserting the statue's yearning for exactly the same qualities that animate the lives of the privileged. She is hungry, Wolfe makes clear, not "for meat" but for "Summat to make her live, I think,—like you" (33). Mitchell then rephrases Wolfe's comment: "It asks questions of God, and says, 'I have a right to know'" (33–34), and the narrator further rephrases the demand of "the dumb face of the rough image" into "the awful question, 'What shall we do to be saved?'" (35). The movement from the worker's concern to "live," to Mitchell's to "know," to the narrator's to be "saved" reflects the shifting ground of the story between the realms of the earthly and the unearthly, and its ambitious attempt to explore the physical, intellectual, and spiritual contexts that are the necessary habitation of the creative artist.

Davis continues the debate among Kirby, May, and Mitchell, now metonymized as "money," "heart," and "head," while Wolfe, the "hand," attends raptly to their words. Kirby, or "money," callously and candidly refuses all obligations to any "stray gleams of mind and soul among these wretches" (34). The doctor, or "heart," rather less candidly mouths the truisms of opportunity in "our American system" (34). When Mitchell, or "head," is finally asked to speak on behalf of "taste, culture, refinement," he presents a more sophisticated but no less self-serving rationale for washing his hands of "this lowest deep," by arguing that change for the workers must come from within them, with no interference on his part: "I am not one of them....Reform is born of need, not pity. No vital movement of the people's has worked down, for good or evil" (38–39). Although the justifications vary, the hand-washing of the privileged is unanimous. Nevertheless, despite the impersonal and dispassionate nature of their discussion, it precipitates a crisis of consciousness for Wolfe, the worker artist who listens attentively: "His squalid daily life, the brutal coarseness eating into his brain, as the ashes into his skin: before, these things had been a dull aching into his consciousness; to-night, they were reality." The immediate outcome of the "sudden light" that "flashed" over him is his decision to receive money stolen by Deb from Mitchell, an offense that will bring him a nineteen-year jail sentence. Ironically, he takes the money because he has been convinced by the visitors that it is the necessary passport to "another world than this" where he will be "free to work, to live, to love!" (40, 39,47).

In Sharon Harris's interesting reading of this story, Hugh Wolfe is transformed from a worker who had formerly aspired to raise his coworkers to one who wants to escape from them. She interprets this change as the final extension to the working-class artist of the capitalist hegemony that has already enveloped both May's philanthropy and Mitchell's Romanticism. She argues that Wolfe "usurps not only the philosophy of the powerbrokers but their 'consciousness,' rooted in force, as well....By appropriating the language of the capitalists (ownership and possession), Hugh also begins to embrace their sense of class distinctions" (47). For Harris, Hugh's artistic vision is forever tainted by his false adulation of Mitchell, who appears to have an almost godlike effect on Hugh—"a Man all-knowing, all-seeing, crowned by Nature, reigning—the keen glance of his eye falling like a sceptre on other men" (40). Indeed Hugh Wolfe is pathetically eager to find a kinship with this elegant representative of culture and mind, but Davis's presentation of the working-class artist's capitulation to bourgeois intellectual authority is qualified by her recognition of his fundamental dilemma. Wolfe can never fully consummate his vision while sickened and trapped in the squalor of the mills, but freedom from the mills will remove him from kinship with the workers and the sources of his art. In Davis's grim view, Wolfe can never be other than lost. It is true that his temporary escape from the mill causes him to feel revulsion from the workers' world, and a seeming affinity for the social class that lives comfortably at the workers' expense. However, even among the workers where he carved his korl statues, Wolfe was neither leader nor model; always an outsider, he was known contemptuously "as one of the girl-men" (24). For all his private fantasy of raising up his fellow workers, Davis makes no suggestion that Wolfe was anything other than an isolated and alienated curiosity to his workmates, a grotesque incongruity, for whom there is no place in society's present structure.

Davis's bleak account of the working man's prospects as artist and thinker is exacerbated by her decision to feminize Hugh in his sobriquet, "Molly Wolfe," in his appearance, "a meek, woman's face," and in his distaste for the male world of cockpits, fighting, and drinking (24). Such a tactic may be read as an additional step in the estrangement of the working-class artist or a tacit recognition that any artist, regardless of class and sex, is likely to be an outcast and an antagonist of the prevailing values of society. The parallel ambiguity of Davis's narrator, a seeming artist and collector who challenges and insults the reader, and who may be male or female, suggests that Davis endorses the artist's power to disturb and perplex as much as to please. Thus, despite their bewilderment at Hugh Wolfe's korl statue, the elite outsiders are both shaken and intrigued by the sculpture. The doctor later reads the newspaper account of Wolfe's sentencing to his wife, and Mitchell even visits him in prison. These contacts are evidence not so much of any sympathy that bridges the class barrier as of the enigmatic impact of Wolfe's art. The narrator proves to have been even more captivated, preserving the statue for thirty years, albeit concealed behind a curtain. Hugh Wolfe's sculpture, if rough and ungainly, is also powerful and haunting; if it elicits obtuseness from his social superiors about what exactly it signifies, no one doubts that it *does* signify.

Similarly, although Wolfe may be the dupe of a false Romantic dream of a fuller life, Davis does not completely dismiss the power of that dream. When she first introduces Wolfe, it is as a man "silent, with foreign thoughts and longings breaking out through his quietness in innumerable curious ways" (24), someone in whose soul there is "a fierce thirst for beauty,—to know it, to create it; to *be*—something, he knows not what,—other than he is" (25). Later, after his encounter with Mitchell, Wolfe's aspirations are described again, in more fluent and Romantic terms but now tinged with irony toward those who would deny the worker-artist's aspirations:

> You laugh at the shallow temptation? You see the error underlying its argument so clearly,—that to him a true life was one of full development rather than self-restraint? that he was deaf to the higher tone in a cry of voluntary suffering for truth's sake than in the fullest flow of spontaneous harmony? I do not plead his cause. I only want to show you the mote in my brother's eye: then you can see clearly to take it out. (46)

The language of this passage, "true life," "full development," "spontaneous harmony," certainly evokes the Romantic talk of Emerson and Fuller, but it is difficult to read the passage as unsympathetic to such aspirations on the part of the degraded iron-puddler. Wolfe's dreams may be grotesque and misbegotten because they divert him from the possibility of helping his own people to rise from their misery, but if Wolfe has a mote in his eye, then the implicit beam in the imagined reader's eye seems to be the requirement of "self-restraint" rather than "full development" for workers. The narrator makes a similar rhetorical challenge to the insensitive reader about the secret love of Wolfe by Deb, the hunchbacked mill worker: "You laugh at it? Are pain and jealousy less savage realities down here in this place I am taking you to than in your own house or your own heart,—your heart, which they clutch at sometimes? The note is the same, I fancy, be the octave high or low" (23). Thus there is a double edge, or perhaps an ambiguity, to Davis's irony, in criticizing workers' unrealistic Romantic and emotional aspirations, and in attacking the privileged reader who would scoff at workers for daring to aspire to spiritual or passional fulfillment.

The narrator's constant attacks on complacent readers who judge workers' lives too severely and hastily might suggest that Davis's perspective is close to that of her artist-narrator. However, the narrator's frequent sanctimoniousness and elevated literariness have raised the possibility for several critics that the narrator, too, may be the object of Davis's multivalent satire. Amy Schrager Lang goes to the heart of the problem when she notes that "in *Life in the Iron Mills* we are in epistemological difficulty from the start" (78). Lang argues that although the narrator rejects literariness in favor of honesty from the outset, "she" is immediately beset by the problem of representing life in the iron mills because she can only enter it in a literary fancy. Distanced from industrial reality by social experience, class difference, time, and the complicity of art "in the system of capitalist exploitation," Davis has no alternative to literary methods to tell her tale (Lang 78, 82). Her narrator thus fluctuates between self-conscious berating of literariness and the necessity to acquiesce to it in varying degrees. This doubleness is most problematical in the work's religious statements, which appear both hypocritically judgmental and ardently sincere. When Hugh Wolfe enters an upper-class church, "built to meet the requirements and sympathies of a far other class" (48), the narrator directs us to see the irrelevance of the reformist Christian preacher who "painted the incarnate Life, Love, the universal Man" in what, to the ironworker, is an "unknown tongue" (49). However, the Quaker woman who rescues and restores Deb is unambiguously a positive image of Christian charity, saying little but performing acts of kindness. Inappropriate and grandiose words or necessary and simple acts—these seem to be the poles of Christian conduct. Their opposition might well lead the reader to resist, as Sharon Harris does, the highly wrought verbiage of the story's conclusion.[6] At the end, the narrator looks at Hugh's korl statue and asks, "Has the power of its desperate need commanded the darkness away? While the room is yet steeped in heavy shadow, a cool, gray light suddenly touches its head like a blessing hand, and its groping arm points through the broken cloud to the far East, where, in the flickering, nebulous crimson, God has set the promise of the Dawn"

(65). The pious language, the rhetorical question, the capitalized "Dawn" might indeed be an effort to subvert the fictional narrator, as Sharon Harris argues, noting that Davis's other story "The Promise of Dawn" is further evidence of her ironic intentions (55–56). However, Davis's next novel, *Margret Howth: A Story of Today* (1862), concludes on an identical note of otherworldly uplift and hope after an account of lives marred by industrial misery, and in this case there is even less evidence of any ironic design.

Davis's struggle to negotiate between conventional literary language (with its picturesque evocations, learned allusions, idle fancies, and ingratiating apostrophes to the reader) and a bitterly satirical rejection of that language is complicated by her own tendency to a florid style. She also has to accommodate the *Atlantic* readers' expectations of moral uplift, and the tension between her provocative material and her religious faith. However, the story suggests finally that Wolfe's art speaks at best obliquely, and from a great and mediated distance, about the even more thwarted opportunity of the nation's industrial workers. Davis offers no hope for cure in this world, beyond some charitable acts of human sympathy, and appears to insist that transcendence and "full development" must be reserved for the next. Her working-class artist speaks in enigmas and riddles, and only for himself rather than as representative of the masses. Far from the spirited women of Lowell, who celebrated the presence of "mind amongst the spindles" and who, in Lucy Larcom's *Idyl of Work*, affirmed that their intellects were free from "machinery's clutches" and their hands were not yet "hands only" (142), the middle-class author presents Hugh Wolfe as a grotesque and pathetic anomaly. His artistic legacy survives out of public sight, accessible only through the charitable agency of a bourgeois artist who mediates and interprets it.

Davis's admiring correspondent Elizabeth Stuart Phelps, in her 1871 novel *The Silent Partner*, chose to scrutinize precisely the same question: to what extent had factory workers already fallen into machinery's clutches and been excluded from what she characterized as the realm of "thinking, aspiring, creating, enjoying" people (71). Many years later, Phelps acknowledged, in a tribute to Davis she wrote after Davis's death, the impact "Life in the Iron Mills" had had on her as a young writer: "The claims of toil and suffering upon ease had assumed a new form. For me they assumed a force which perhaps it is not too much to say, has never let me go."[7] Phelps's first fiction about the working class was the short story "The Tenth of January" (1868), which described the disastrous collapse in 1860 of the Pemberton Mill in Lawrence, Massachusetts. Seven hundred and fifty workers, mostly women, were trapped in the conflagration that followed the crumbling of the building; eighty-eight of them died. Amal Amireh has identified the Pemberton catastrophe as the "specific moment that symbolically represents" a shift in the public's attitude toward factory labor, from endorsements of the "golden age" of Lowell to a revulsion toward the degradation and exploitation of workers' lives (132). Phelps's fictionalizing of the

Pemberton tragedy was the prelude to a more extensive literary engagement with working-class women in *The Silent Partner*. After her account of the sensational and exceptional disaster in the short story, she turned in the novel to the shocking details of factory women's everyday lives and to their chances for "thinking, aspiring, and creating" in such circumstances.

Like Rebecca Harding Davis, Phelps had directly observed factory workers, having grown up in Andover and taught Sunday school in the nearby factory town of Abbot Hill (Kelly 6). She engaged in energetic research for "The Tenth of January," recording in her autobiography her avid pursuit of information: "I visited the rebuilt mills and studied the machinery. I consulted engineers and officials and physicians, newspaper men, and persons who had been in the mill at the time of its fall" (*Chapters* 92). Later she documented *The Silent Partner* with footnote references to official government investigations and reports on factory conditions. Phelps, like Davis, her admired forerunner, had an ambivalent relationship with her working-class subjects, sharing gender and religious sympathies with them, but conscious of a considerable gap in social and cultural attitudes. As a woman with feminist sympathies, she had an affinity for women workers; as a Christian, she was committed to a belief in both worldly reform and otherworldly justice for them; but as a comfortable member of the middle class, she was estranged from their ways of thinking and feeling. Like Davis, too, she was interested in the life of the mind and the place of art and literature in the world of working people. The narrator of *The Silent Partner* at first tries to resist using the conventional label "hands" for such people, but she finally acquiesces in the metonymy with the revealing question "Being surely neither head nor heart, what else remains?" (71).

Phelps's story "The Tenth of January," first published, like Davis's "Life in the Iron Mills," in the *Atlantic Monthly*, immediately reveals the impact of Davis's novella, not only in the complicated relationships that are set up between the fictional narrator and the imagined audience but also in the story's interest in the inner lives of workers. Phelps's story opens, like Davis's, with an implicit attack on literary efforts to aestheticize working-class lives into smooth forms and picturesque images. What Davis's narrator performs by scolding the reader Phelps's does by ironic self-parody. She begins with the comment "The city of Lawrence is unique in its way," which is followed by an unfinished sentence, almost a page long, that reveals its author to be a refined lady, repelled by the pervasive presence of sand in the city's atmosphere, especially in her "chignon." She is clearly more interested in the literariness and parallelism of her tropes than on the human dimensions of her subject:

> For simooms that scorch you and tempests that freeze; for sand-heaps and sand-hillocks and sand-roads; for men digging sand, for women shaking off sand, for minute boys crawling in sand;...for unexpected corners where tornadoes lie in wait;...for unutterable

circus-bills and religious tea-parties; for uncleared ruins, and mills that spring up in a night;...for an air of youth and incompleteness at which you laugh, and a consciousness of growth and greatness which you respect,—it— (305)

The narrator then satirically deflates her own literary affectations by questioning what she might have been intending to say when she embarked on that particularly inflated sentence. Such elegant self-mockery of the well-meaning bourgeois artist anticipates William Dean Howells and, much later, the even more corrosive self-laceration of James Agee, as they berate themselves and, by implication, their comfortable readers for assimilating misery into art. Earlier in the century Melville had resisted Irving's attraction to "smooth" topics as the only appropriately literary ones, and had urged and exemplified a turn to more harrowing and tragic subjects. Now, in a literary marketplace increasingly saturated with accounts of injustice and suffering, Davis and Phelps attempted to resist not just smooth topics but also smooth techniques that rendered social inequity in ways that pandered too easily to a taste for well-wrought compassion for the less fortunate.

Phelps pursues a number of discomfiting literary tactics in "The Tenth of January," all of which seem directed toward emphasizing and disrupting the distances between her middle-class narrator, her similarly situated audience, and her working-class subject. One of her jarring practices is the frequent shifting of narrative voice among the first-, second-, and third-person designators "I," "you," and "one." The reader must continually decide whether he or she is willing to be incorporated into the narrator's universalization of her own refined tastes and judgments, or her sudden contrary moments of identification with workers. Thus, in addition to registering the unpleasant sensation of "sand in your eyes, your nose, your mouth" as "you" try to negotiate the windy construction sites of a mushrooming factory town (305), the reader must decide how far to agree that "one never knows exactly whether to laugh or cry" at such frustrations (308). In direct contrast to this upper class–bound "you" of the story's opening, when the mill collapses, trapping the workers inside, the genteel narrator does not just refuse to avert her eyes from the horror; she transfers the reader's consciousness abruptly into the "you" of the workers and into their immediate, present experience of disaster:

a face that you know turned up at you from some pit which twenty-four hours hewing could not open; a voice that you know crying after you from God knows where; a mass of long, fair hair visible here, a foot there, three fingers of a hand over there; the snow bright-red underfoot; charred limbs and headless trunks tossed about; strong men carrying covered things by you, at sight of which other strong men have fainted. (346–47)

Such a consciousness-expanding transformation of the narrator's "you" might seem at first like a positive omen for the prospect of cross-class empathy, but the story refuses such complacent optimism. Instead, Phelps engages in a number of narrative counter-movements that insist on the barriers to mutual class awareness, especially outside the context of a uniquely devastating catastrophe that momentarily brings people together.

The story's protagonist, Asenath Martyn, is a young factory worker, cruelly abused by her drunken mother, who has scarred her daughter's face and bent and twisted her shoulders. Her daily work is painful and repugnant, from her early morning walk, "faint and weak, over the raw, slippery streets" to her long day's obligation to "stand at the endless loom, and hear the endless wheels go buzzing round, to sicken in the oily smells and deafen at the remorseless noise" (331). However, after Asenath comes home from work and changes her clothes, the narrator comments: "She came down presently, transformed, as only factory-girls are transformed, by the simple little toilet she had been making" (310). The cheerful, almost fairy-tale transformation of the deformed and exhausted operative evokes only a sense of the privileged shallowness of the narrator and her easy generalizations about "factory girls." Even some of the narrator's most careful efforts to reach across the chasm of sensibility that separates her from working women result in reaffirming rather than eliminating the distance between classes. Her description of Asenath's grim daily routine and the factory woman's anger toward her employers is a curious amalgam of revealing details about Asenath's exploitation and the narrator's easy assimilation of those details into her (and our) more privileged experience of minor complaints:

> The very fact that her employers dealt honorably by her; that she
> was fairly paid, and promptly, for her wearing toil; that the limit
> of endurance was consulted in the temperature of the room, and
> her need of rest in an occasional holiday,—perhaps, after all, in the
> mood she was in, did not make this factory life more easy. She
> would have found it rather a relief to have somebody to complain
> of,—wherein she was like the rest of us, I fancy. (332)

In this passage, the narrative "I" absorbs the factory girl's resentment into the comfortable final "us"—of human beings who like to indulge in some petty griping. However, the reader is unlikely to feel comfortable with the notion that the narrator's desire to have "somebody to complain of" is commensurate with the grievances of a worker whose employers have been finely calculating the very "limit of endurance" in her grueling toil.

Although the cataclysmic nature of the plot of "The Tenth of January" insists on the commonalty of human emotions in the face of death and judgment, Phelps does not allow the metaphysical context of the workers' tragedy to expunge the ironic fact that the disaster is mediated by a well-intentioned narrator of distinctly limited insight. She shares a code of religious faith and a sympathy of gender with her working-class subject and occasionally she displays profound empathy for her in her harrowing experience. However, the disjunctions in condition and sensibility between privileged narrator and working-class subject cannot be entirely bridged by Christian love and sisterhood. In addition, the uniquely tragic circumstances of "The Tenth of January" prevent Phelps from exploring the other realms of what she elsewhere called "thinking, aspiring, creating" human activity, where the classes might find a different kind of common ground beyond that of their shared mortality. Perhaps in recognition of this, Phelps turned almost immediately to a longer work of fiction in which she could pursue concerns inevitably excluded by the catastrophic facts of Pemberton.

In *The Silent Partner*, published in 1871, three years after "The Tenth of January," Phelps turned more fully to the normal, rather than the aberrant, condition of women workers. In the everyday realm of factory life in this novel, Phelps has more liberty to explore the possibility of what Rebecca Harding Davis, in "Life in the Iron Mills," had called the "full development" of workers' lives, a topic naturally obviated in "The Tenth of January" by their immediate confrontation with sudden death. Phelps continues her previous method of juxtaposing the consciousness of a privileged and a poor woman by providing two closely paralleled female protagonists, Perley Kelso, daughter of a mill owner, and Sip Garth, descendant of generations of mill workers. Both women have attentive lovers, and both are motherless, and lose their fathers almost simultaneously in industrial accidents. In the course of the novel, the two women develop a close acquaintanceship, and each gives up her lover and her former occupation for a life of service to the community of workers. Perley abandons her career as a lady of leisure for a life of good works, and Sip leaves her factory job for a new calling as a street preacher. *The Silent Partner* endured a long period of critical neglect through much of the twentieth century until it was reissued in 1983. Subsequently, it became something of a canonical text for scholars exploring class and gender issues and for some who ventured into the less charted field of its religious ideology and its critique of the aesthetic indulgences of the rich and educated.[8] The novel is also notable for its attempt to examine the place of art—literature, music, and painting—as a potential territory where different ranks of people may come together and find common ground in the mutual appreciation and performance of creative works. Although such a project is clearly utopian, Phelps engages in a serious investigation of both the power of art to cross the barriers of class and of art's appropriation by the powerful.

Her charming and wealthy protagonist, Perley Kelso, is a pampered and tasteful aesthete of the first rank. She views the world outside the scented warmth of her carriage as a theatrical set provided for her pleasure, and she stage-manages her own appearances to create artistic scenarios. On her way to a performance of *Don Giovanni*, she has her first glimpse of the factory worker, Sip Garth, struggling through wind and rain, also on her

way to a theatrical performance at the Blue Plum. When Perley discovers
Sip's destination, she exclaims without irony, "but the theatre is no place
for you, my poor girl" (24). Perley firmly believes that "No theatre patron-
ized by the lower classes could be a place for a poor girl" (24)—a telling
separation of "lower class" and "poor girl," as if the attributes of each label
had no overlap. Sip admits that "'The Plum does n't make much odds to
me'" but explains that she goes there to study how she might improve on
the performances that are given: "'Give me the music, give me the lights,
and the people, and the poetry, and *I'd* do it. I'd make'em laugh, wouldn't
I? I'd make'em cry, you may make up your mind on that'" (24–25). Sip's
confident assertion of her interpretive talent and her lack only of a stage
for her abilities contrasts wryly with Perley's lavish opportunities for creating dramatic effects, although as a young lady, hers must necessarily be
private and limited in their impact. Later that evening, as Perley is leaving
Don Giovanni, Sip returns to answer her criticism of the impropriety of
the "Plum" for a poor girl, noting that Perley's entertainment differs from
her own only in what she refers to repeatedly as "the plating over" (30).
She argues that the differences between Perley's high culture and her class's
popular entertainment are superficial rather than essential, that the "plating
over" performed for the rich is merely a disguised version of the candor
offered the poor, and that upper-class refinement and style clothe the same
vulgar truths the Plum presents more blatantly. This opening debate about
aesthetics and cultural stratification mirrors and anticipates the larger one in
the novel about class differences—are they, too, a form of "plating over," so
that manners, education, and possessions disguise a fundamental common
core of humanity? Or are they so entrenched in generations of workers and
owners that they have become virtually innate and immutable?

The talented factory worker Sip, who in person seems to belie such
class essentialism, becomes nevertheless one of the main proponents of the
"inborn" class theory. She refuses to marry and breed children for the
mills, giving as her justification that an underclass heritage is inevitable:
"'It's from generation to generation.... It's in the blood'" (288). Perley, by
contrast, after her gradual awakening to the realities of her workers' lives,
devotes herself to trying to demonstrate and ensure that rich and poor,
workers and owners, are not fundamentally different from one another.
At first she looks at the crowd surging outside her carriage window as
an anthropologist might view an alien tribe: "It conceived such original
ways of holding its hands, and wearing its hats, and carrying its bundles. It
had such a taste in colors, such disregard of clean linen, and was always in
such a hurry.... Miss Kelso had never been in a hurry in her life" (17–18).
Only after she leaves her insulated world and ventures into the cottages
of the workers does Perley begin to substitute individual people for the
dehumanized "it" of the species that hurried by outside her carriage. As
she gradually discovers the degrading conditions of workers' lives, she feels
like "a stranger setting foot in a strange land"; "it even occurred to her that

she should never be very happy again, for knowing that factory-girls ate black molasses and had the cotton-cough" (98). She consequently embarks on programs of physical and mental improvement for workers, from hospital and soup-kitchen to model tenement and library, thinking thereby to bring the two estranged realms of her social environment into some more equal connection.

Perley's most novel effort to assert the commonality of her upper-class friends and working-class employees is to bring the two groups together for a party of culture and socializing at her elegant home. Her friends anticipate the occasion with amused tolerance and irony, promising that they will dress soberly and inform themselves thoroughly in advance "upon the ten-hour question" (223). Her factory guests prove to be decently clad and properly comported, seemingly justifying Perley's claim that "One does not behave till one has a chance" (226). Amy Schrager Lang reads this scene in the novel as evidence that "the working-class characters are clearly admitted into the parlor on the condition that they mimic the dress and manners of their social betters. 'Society' does not accommodate them; they conform to its requirements, thus enabling the successful encounter between rich and poor." Further, Lang notes that the workers demonstrate their common humanity by their appreciation of the "'superior art' produced by a leisured class of which they are not a part." Lang sees in this episode the hand of the middle-class narrator, mediating between the privileged upper and the needy lower, bridging the gulf between capital and labor by "universalizing middle-classness" (92–93). However, Phelps also reveals her awareness of the depth of that gulf by interrupting and disrupting her own narrative of cross-class communion and mutual enjoyment of ice cream and culture.

Neither the workers nor the gentry breach the decorum of the festivities, but it is breached nevertheless, for the reader if not for the guests, by two jarring intrusions that challenge both the egalitarianism of the occasion and the communal sharing of great works of art. Perley clearly puts a good deal of thought into the programs for her parties, and, in the one that is extensively described, she has planned a reading from Victor Hugo by Sip, to be preceded by her own piano interpretation of the Andante from Beethoven's Seventh Symphony, and followed by a performance of some Scottish songs by the worker Nynee Mell. Some of the elite guests question whether the "people" will be able to appreciate Beethoven, but in fact they listen attentively, and Perley's inclusiveness seems vindicated. However, Phelps chooses just this moment to focus on Sip Garth's damaged and deaf-mute sister, Catty, who is unable to hear the music but nevertheless senses with her hands the motions of Perley's fingers on the piano keys. Phelps notes Catty's stance, "her head forward, with her lip dropped and dull," silhouetted against the shining whiteness of Perley's dress, which provides the "background to the poor creature's puzzled figure" (229). This powerful and grotesque image at the center of the soirée serves to heighten the reader's sense, if not the guests', of the inseparable gulf between the two women, not just of class but seemingly of kind, between the flawless, angelic beauty and the "creature" who was permanently damaged in utero as a consequence of her mother's fourteen-hour workdays in the mill. The image suggests the treacherous intellectual territory between Sip's belief that workers are trapped into bearing generations of ever more tainted offspring and Perley's hope for the improving powers of culture and nurture for those who are already in the mills. The scene is part of a repeated pattern of episodes in the novel that reach across the class divide but are abruptly violated by a recognition of difference.

The second narrative interruption of the smooth progress of Perley's party occurs when Sip arrives, very late, to give her reading of Victor Hugo. She comes with a tale of horror to explain her long delay at the factory: "The thermometer has stood at 115° in our room to-day. It hasn't been below 110° not since last Saturday. It's 125° in the dressing-room. There's men in the dressing-room with the blood all gathered black about their faces, just from heat;...they're all purple.... It's most as bad as hell to be mill-folks in July!" (232). When Sip moves from her personal story to the performance of Hugo's "Address to the Rich and Poor," the rhetoric is more eloquent in Hugo's revolutionary message (which Phelps does not quote), but the message to the more privileged is the same: "Your paradise is made out of the hell of the poor."[9] Curiously, as Sip proceeds with her delivery, Perley—who presumably chose and knows her text—whispers to her frivolous friend Kenna Van Doozle, "We have nothing so popular...as that girl's readings and recitations. They ring well," to which the other replies, "An unappreciated Siddons, perhaps?" (233). Although it is Miss Van Doozle who seems to bear the heavier weight of Phelps's irony, as a fashionable aesthete responding to the messenger of misery and revolution, Perley, too, seems to endorse Sip's technical interpretive skills in isolation from the revolutionary content of the performance. The two wealthy young women are as untouched by Hugo's ominous admonition for the rich to tremble before the violent vengeance that is to come as they are by Sip's grim personal prelude. Perley's efforts to mingle with the workers on the purported common ground of art appreciation prove absurd, not because the workers cannot appreciate Beethoven, but because the upper class has incorporated and defused the scourging power of Hugo into mere appreciation of his effects in performance.

A more vexing instance of Perley's ambiguous empathy for the situation of her workers follows immediately after the Hugo episode, when Perley uses her influence over her employees to talk them out of striking against the mill. Ironically, she is present to preempt the strike because she has stopped by the mill to donate a copy of John Stuart Mill's "Liberty" to the workers' library. Any retelling of such an incident in the novel seems bound to expose Perley's naiveté, or even her hypocrisy, yet Phelps is clearly not intent on ridiculing her attractive and compassionate plutocrat. She does not comment on, nor does she appear to acknowledge, the incongruity of Perley using her charm to defuse the strike and redirect the zeal of the workers just after she has listened to Sip's account of the horror of their lives and Hugo's warning of the wrath to come. Phelps herself may well have hesitated to endorse labor strikes and violence, a position that makes her use of Hugo's indictment at Perley's party doubly ironic. Amy Schrager Lang, in her analysis of the complex currents of class and gender in *The Silent Partner,* argues that Phelps finally appears to concede that the project of bridging the gulf between labor and capital by "universalizing middle-classness and naturalizing gender" is bound to fail: "Class divisions, it would seem, are irremediable except perhaps by supernatural intervention, and class affiliation is as inescapable as class harmony is improbable" (93, 97). By the novel's conclusion, Phelps has indeed turned both of her young women protagonists away from a vision of class harmony in this world, suffused by a shared life of the mind, and focused instead on the supernatural context of their lives, suggesting that the final ends of charity and communion will be realized only beyond the grave.

Perley gradually shifts her emphasis from class-bridging cultural schemes to improving workers' education and health, and Sip abandons her earlier theatrical ambition and takes up a calling as a street preacher. Even the faith she preaches appears to be class-based: "'We must have a poor folks' religion or none at all'" (296). Somewhat surprisingly, this poor folks' religion consists of berating workers for their "wicked hearts" (297) and denying that their hellish working conditions justify their transgressions. Now she appears to believe that all efforts at worldly reform are likely to be ineffectual: "laws won't do it. Kings and congresses may put their heads together, but they'll have their trouble for nothing. Governments and churches may finger us over, but we'll only snarl the more. . . . [T]here's no way under heaven for us to get out of our twist, but Christ's way" (299). The weaving images of snarling and twisting—hazards of the everyday life of mill workers—are, surprisingly, now reformulated by Sip as signs of a metaphysical condition remediable only by a supernatural agency. Phelps thus transforms her working-class heroine from an aspiring actress, whose goal is to use the power of the theater—music, lights, poetry—to make people laugh and cry, into a scourge of the workers for their sins. Sip is finally given the opportunity and the stage to speak to an audience, but her speech demands complete abandonment of what Rebecca Harding Davis, in "Life in the Iron Mills," had called a life of "full development." For Davis's aspiring working-class artist, Hugh Wolfe, that full development must be in this world, or life is not worth living. By contrast, Sip's ambitions shift, after the death of her sister Catty, to an otherworldly context in which the young woman's passionate artistic sensitivities are sublimated to a "poor folks' religion." While Davis's working-class artist asserts a common human longing, embodied in the sculpture of his korl woman, for "summat to make her live" (33), Phelps redirects Sip from her early theatrical dream to what Hugh Wolfe in Davis's story could not undertake, a life of "self-restraint" and "voluntary suffering" instead of "the fullest flow of spontaneous harmony" (46). Sip finally chooses sublimation through religion rather than art, partly in response to her sister's tragedy and partly in response to the power of two iconic images she encounters that represent symbolically two alternative philosophies of human aspiration. The first is Carl Lemude's engraving "Dreaming Beethoven," which provokes Sip to an ecstatic identification with its illustration of the tormented artist, struggling for control: "That's the way things come to me; things I could do, things I could say, things I could get rid of if I had the chance; they come in the mills mostly; they tumble over me just so; I never have the chance. How he fights! I didn't know there was any such picture as that in the world" (130). Perley, struck by the power the engraving has on Sip, makes a gift of it to her, and the worker returns to this picture repeatedly, talking to it and even turning it to the wall when it overwhelms her. She escapes its magnetism only when she comes by accident on a very different image—a crude biblical plate of the Crucifixion. Its effect is transforming: "Somehow the driving dream and the restless dreamer hushed away before the little woodcut." The struggle for mastery is relieved for Sip by her abandonment to a greater power that silences her own urge to speak: "the Cross with the Man upon it put finger on the bitter lips of Sip's trouble" (195). Thus the Romantic agony of the young working woman is soothed away by Christian acquiescence. Sip gives no indication that she feels betrayed in her shift to a career as a preacher, and Perley's last comment on Sip suggests that she is giving the workers what they need most in a "hungry world" (301). Phelps, like Davis before her, employs the multivalent metaphor of "hunger" to suggest a longing on the part of the workers for some sustenance beyond the physical, but unlike Davis, Phelps shifts the provenance of this other spiritual food entirely to the realm of religion.

Implicit in her final focus on a poor folks' religion as the only panacea for workers' lives, and the only sublimation of their yearning, is Phelps's acknowledgment that the contemporary conditions of factory labor are hardly conducive to producing workers who could ever be more than (in Lucy Larcom's words) "hands only." The juxtaposition of Sip's harrowing account of her day at the mill and her powerful performance of Victor Hugo at Perley's tea party is a grim reminder not only of the appropriation of Hugo as drawing-room entertainment but also of the sheer unlikelihood that a hand, who had repeatedly fainted in 115-degree heat, would have much opportunity to cultivate artistic sensibilities. Sip finally has time and energy to devote to her street preaching because she is presumably being subsidized by Perley—the last stage of an experiment in which Perley has committed herself to removing Sip from the mill and finding a more congenial calling that would not be an "exorbitant waste" of her ability (197). However, when Perley presents Sip with a series of alternative jobs (at all of which she fails miserably), it is noteworthy that none of them is remotely connected to Sip's originally stated ambition to make people laugh or cry, or to convey by performance whatever is represented for her by the Beethoven engraving's "driving dream." Denied all possibility of a life of full development in this world, Sip finds redemption in preparing workers for the next. Phelps does not suggest that such a career for a potential working-class artist is an "exorbitant waste," although later, in *The Story of Avis* (1877), she treated the frustrated ambition of a middle-class artist in more tragic terms. The fulfillment of Sip's artistic dreams is abandoned with less regret than the sacrifice of the bourgeois Avis's career as a painter, in large part because the factory woman has the consolation of serving her fellow workers through her religious dedication. In contrast with the bitterness of Avis's artistic frustration, the consolations of religion minimize the tragedy of the worker's lost hope of fulfillment in this world rather than the next.

The apparent impossibility, in *The Silent Partner*, of a working woman finding an occupation that is neither body- nor soul-destroying is precisely the concern taken up by Louisa May Alcott in her 1873 novel *Work*. As the daughter of Bronson Alcott, one of the most anarchically idealistic of the Concord transcendentalists, Louisa had witnessed at first hand during her childhood an extreme experiment in pursuing the life of the mind and the spirit, oblivious to the contingencies of the material environment. Her father's utopian venture into consociate living with his young family at Fruitlands in 1843–44 had exposed his daughter to the hazards of spiritual perfection without provision for the body. She had also witnessed the consequences of a male-centered Romanticism that depended on a female support system whereby female relatives enabled the Romantic goals of men by attending to the pragmatic realities of daily life. Her mother had concluded bluntly after the collapse of the idealist scheme at Fruitlands: "My girls shall have trades," and Louisa assessed her own prospects somewhat acerbically in a letter to her father on the occasion of her twenty-fourth birthday: "I think I shall come out right, and prove that though an *Alcott* I *can* support myself."[10] In fact, Louisa was impelled to support not just herself but the rest of the family as well; thus she brought to her writing of *Work* a transcendental education, a direct experience of material need, and a personal knowledge of the opportunities available to middle- and lower-class women for earning a living without compromising their independence of spirit. Alcott's novel was published in book form the same year as her satire "Transcendental Wild Oats" (1873), a fictionalized account of the Fruitlands experiment, which had been an attempt to find a means of living that would elevate and liberate the spirit. The criticisms Alcott makes of her father's failed utopian scheme are implicitly, and sometimes explicitly, incorporated into her account of the career of Christie Devon, the young female protagonist, in *Work*. The result is Christie's eventual participation in a somewhat idealized experiment in community living, albeit one distinctly different from her father's impractical and patriarchal model.

"Transcendental Wild Oats" is a witty consideration both of gender conflicts within the Alcott family between father and mother (here named Abel and Hope Lamb) and of ideological conflicts between family loyalty and the larger consociate ideals of the other founder of Fruitlands, Charles Lane (here named Timon Lion). On the surface, "Wild Oats" is a satire of the elevation of male idealism over female realism, of impracticality over common sense, and of unworldliness over worldliness. However, Alcott hints at something closer to hypocrisy in the men's determination to admit nothing to their society that "has caused wrong or death to man or beast" (131). This means, in effect, robbing no sheep of its wool, enslaving neither cow nor ox, and refusing to exploit animals by using their manure as fertilizer. The immediate consequence is that the burden of physical labor falls not on man or beast but on one woman, Hope Lamb, and, in the most extreme necessity, on the children of the community. When a newcomer questions whether the community has any "beasts of burden," Sister Hope's reply suggests the expediency of the idealists' principles: "Only one woman!" (136). Although she is an indefatigable and long-suffering member of the community, Sister Hope is far from a silent one. Her "satirical" mouth and caustic comments on the enterprise serve as amusing textual subversions of the high-flown rhetoric of the community's patriarchs, but as a wife and the mother of four small children, she does not push her rebellion much beyond her verbal skepticism. In depicting the conflict between loyalty to family and to commune, Alcott opposes the loving Hope to the grim and dictatorial Timon Lion, who believes that the consociate family requires the renunciation of the conjugal family, as did Charles Lane, who moved, after the disintegration of Fruitlands, to a celibate community of Shakers. Alcott has her admired Hope challenge Timon on both his ideas and his unwillingness to work, but, at the same time, she notes that Hope acquiesces in what she considers variously a "lunatic asylum" and "the most ideal" of all castles in Spain (134, 136), because she "merely followed wheresoever her husband led" (135). Amid all the tributes to her mother's heroic and bemused endurance in "Transcendental Wild Oats," only in the word "merely" does Alcott suggest her reservations about the waste of a woman's initiative and ability that is entailed when she makes a marital commitment to follow her husband's vagaries. Alcott's intense admiration for her mother led her to dedicate *Work* to her—"whose life has been a long labor of love." However, in pursuing in *Work* the possibility of a more practical and successful experiment in communal cooperation than the one mocked in "Transcendental Wild Oats," she appears to take very seriously Charles Lane's warnings about the threats posed to both individual and community by the power of conjugal love. In envisioning in *Work* a single-gendered association of women, Alcott rectifies imaginatively the class division that beset Fruitlands between male thinkers and female workers. She does not, however, eliminate class distinctions, even among a league of sisters dedicated to a more elevated life for all.

In *Work*, Alcott begins where many novels end, with a marriage proposal to her protagonist, Christie Devon, and an investigation of the consequences when her heroine rejects the proposal and chooses to enter the public world of work instead. Unlike middle-class heroines of earlier novels who are isolated by orphaning, widowhood, or desertion, and thus forced to fend for themselves, twenty-one-year-old Christie is not quite middle-class and definitely not abandoned financially, having both an uncle who will grimly do his duty in supporting her and a well-to-do suitor who would lay his acres at her feet. Christie, however, wants to "take care of herself," a phrase that is repeated three times on the first page, and that means considerably more to her than merely earning a living. She hopes to find work that has an object beyond money, that will not be soul-starving, that will, in her uncle's dismissive description of her "redic'lus notions about independence and self-cultur," fulfill her "higher nater" (10, 11). That she has no pretensions to be a great artist, that she is only "moderately endowed with talents," that her inheritance is merely "a head, a heart, a pair of hands," and that she has a quite ambiguous social status (as the daughter of a refined father and a poor mother) do not prevent her from having Romantic dreams (12). She reveals these to her more sympathetic aunt as the two women sit staring into the fireplace: "'Do you see those two logs? Well that one smouldering dismally away in the corner is what my life is now; the other blazing and singing is what I want my life to be'" (8). To her aunt's reply that "both will be ashes tomorrow," Christie insists that "it *does* make a difference *how* they turn to ashes" (9), an exchange that suggests a conception of life as a more secular adventure in the here and now than is possible for the working-class population of Davis's and Phelps's fiction. *Work* is thus an account of the experiences of a woman who is disadvantaged by gender, mildly privileged by class, moderately equipped with talent, and possessed of a reasonable as well as a Romantic character.

Christie begins her career at twenty-one, eager for independence, happy to live alone, jaded with the routines of rural life and domesticity, and ready to tackle any kind of work, regardless of its social reputation. However, by the end of the novel, aged forty, she is no longer asserting "I'll paddle my own canoe" but is grateful that "a skilful hand had taken the rudder" (120, 133). She has experienced near-suicidal despair from loneliness and is living in mutual dependency with others. She has come to relish life in an old-fashioned country cottage and discovered the pleasure of "sitting in a quiet corner and making shirts" for the man she loves (223). She has also discovered a certain degree of revulsion in herself from "contact with coarser natures which makes labor seem degrading" (117). Such a trajectory seems like a betrayal of Christie's initial feminist idealism, and Susan K. Harris has noted that, indeed, the first American reviewers of *Work* focused "on its appeal to traditional definitions of women's role," while it was British reviewers who "perceived its Emersonian impulse most clearly" (177). The novel is an effort to do what had not been done in the idealist venture at Fruitlands, that is, to juxtapose Romanticism and common sense, to insist on the contingencies that qualify eternal verities, perhaps to admit the power of inconsistency in human affairs, and the right of the individual to lead many different lives, each of which seems the only right one "for now" (223). It is consequently full of contradictions, reversals, and variable ideological stances, with the notable exception, however, of a steadily and inexorably escalating emphasis on Christian duty. It is also, perhaps because of its formal and ideological fluidity, a novel that explores the role work plays in women's lives in a more expansive social and intellectual context than that of any previous novel of the century.

Christie works, in sequence, as a servant, an actress, a governess, a companion, a seamstress, a laundress, a secretary, and a flower grower. She attempts, as several critics have noted, almost every career open to a woman at midcentury, with the significant exception of factory worker. She is diligent and competent in all her jobs, eager to learn, and fascinated by the revelations of life in the increasingly materialist and showy society to which her jobs expose her. As a servant, she observes sardonically the changing canons of bourgeois taste: "Madame was intent on a water-color copy of Turner's 'Rain, Wind, and Hail'" (18). As an actress, she witnesses the absurdity of contemporary theatrical costume: "Red tunic, tiger-skin over shoulder, helmet, shield, lance, fleshings, sandals, hair down, and as much cork to your eyebrows as you like" (31). She notes "the indescribable fantasies of fashion" at a mantua-making establishment and watches the "ironing, fluting, and crimping" of a skilled laundress at work on "immaculate frills and flounces" (102, 153). Christie has a saving eye for the absurd in human affairs, a quality that keeps her detached from both the luxury and dilettantism of her wealthy employers and the trivial gossip of her lower-class workmates. Her reasons for continually changing jobs almost never involve the onerous nature of the work, or any dissatisfaction with her wages. As Barbara Bardes and Suzanne Gossett have noted, Christie's job problems arise because she is "persistently a sexual object," a circumstance that arises not from the particular conditions of the jobs but from the pervasive sexual vulnerability of women, both in the public workplace and in private household employment. Arguing that Alcott "is unable to imagine a work situation where woman's sexuality is not an issue," they note that on the single occasion when Christie's sexuality is not a central concern (in the all-female mantua-making establishment), she nonetheless forfeits her job out of loyalty to her workmate Rachel, who is fired because of her compromised sexual history (101).

Otherwise, Christie's most recurrent dissatisfaction is her inability to have a home of her own, largely because so many women's jobs (such as servant, governess, or companion) require becoming an accessory in someone else's household. Ironically, only when Christie comes closest to factory labor, as a seamstress in the garment industry (where she begins to feel like a "sewing machine"), is she able to live independently: "She liked to return at night to her own little home, solitary and simple as it was, and felt a great repugnance to accept any place where she would be mixed up with family affairs again" (103, 102). Christie resists factory work, however, because it is most clearly associated for her and other "poor gentlewomen" (117) with a distinctly defined class that her pride will not permit her to accept as her own. This is not to suggest that Christie cannot make friends with working-class women—like the black cook, Hepsey Johnson, or the clear starcher, Cynthy Wilkins—but Alcott insists on the existence of barriers of rank and refinement that are acknowledged by her female characters on both sides of the class divide. Thus Mrs. Wilkins, who is both perceptive and tactful, recognizes quickly Christie's "unfitness for her present place" as a helper in her own working-class household (162). With the help of her minister, who also sees "at a glance that her place was not here," Cynthy finds her a position doing housework for a Quaker "lady" (164). Although the work scarcely differs in kind in the two households, and although both provide an affectionate environment for Christie, there is a clear consensus that she will be more in her element amid the "delicate old glass, queer china, and tiny tea-spoons" of Mrs. Sterling than in the garish Wilkins home, with "the yellow paper with green cabbage roses on it, the gorgeous plaster statuary on the mantelpiece, and the fragrance of doughnuts which pervaded the air" (173, 133).

Alcott's mild aesthetic shudder at the Wilkinses' proletarian taste in furnishings is not merely a narrative projection of her heroine's sensibilities but part of a larger comic mode that emerges in those chapters of *Work* that are dominated by lower-class characters. While families of high social rank or of sturdy middle-class respectability are accorded the literary modes of sentiment, gothicism, and romance, the adventures of the Wilkins family are the stuff of broad comedy. Among the incidents treated with farcical humor are the conflagration of little Gusty Wilkins's pinafore, a flood that drowns the family pig and almost takes Mr. Elisha Wilkins as well, and the efforts of Cynthy to manipulate her apathetic husband into volunteering to fight in the Civil War. The generic switches from melodrama and high seriousness to farce when lower-class characters enter the narrative suggest that Alcott herself sees essential differences that justify different treatment. Thus, even as the central plot of the novel comes to depict the formation of "a loving league of sisters" of diverse backgrounds, and the heroine takes on the role of "interpreter between the two classes," Alcott's skepticism about the power of shared gender to heal class difference dominates the form and style of *Work* (343, 334).

The novel's climax is a public meeting of women of various classes who assemble to discuss their mutual aspirations. The gulf between "ladies" and "women" is evidenced in every speaker at the meeting: "each proved how great was the ferment now going on, and how difficult it was for the two classes to meet and help one another in spite of the utmost need on one side and the sincerest good-will on the other" (330). Alcott's witty analysis of the speakers suggests that the "ladies" need someone like Christie to set an example for them—one of their own who has nonetheless had experiences of the "other" class and has enough practicality and common sense to restrain them from their high-flown rhetorical excursions. However, Alcott seems to have grave reservations about the readiness of the "women" to participate in social and political action. She mocks their demand for the ballot "before one-half of them were quite clear what it meant, and the other half were as unfit for it as any ignorant Patrick bribed with a dollar and a sup of whiskey" (331). The cultural inequalities among the women are so apparent that, when Christie rises to make her first speech, she is careful to ensure that "in it there was no learning, no statistics, and no politics" (333). Unable to appeal to the working women's intellects, Christie turns instead to Christian eschatology as the lingua franca for bridging the class barrier, assuring them that their humble labor is God's work and that it will surely be "a stepping-stone to something better" and to the "nobler labor, and larger liberty God meant them to enjoy" (332–33). The loving league of sisters, "old and young, black and white, rich and poor" will be dedicated to furthering "the happy end" to which women's mutual help and education aspires. However, "something better" and "the happy end" are clearly religious objectives that justify women's empathy and collaboration toward a divine purpose, but shift the focus of their efforts away from earthly inequities and worldly aspirations. Christie herself declares, in what is surely an escalating list of benefits that "in labor, and the efforts and experiences that grew out of it, I have found independence, education, happiness, and religion" (343). At the conclusion of the novel, Christie's daughter Ruth adds her small hand to the clasped hands of the other women as "a hopeful omen, seeming to promise that the coming generation of women will not only receive but deserve their liberty, by learning that the greatest of God's gifts to us is the privilege of sharing His great work" (344). The shift from the work of women to the work of God is a seamless one within Alcott's larger Christian context, but it is simultaneously an abandonment of Christie's early Romantic metaphor of the importance of living life to the fullest, even if it inevitably turns to ashes in the end. Implicitly, bringing women of all classes together to share "His great work" is a spiritual more than a social or cultural equalizer, although the distinction is obscured by the emotional tenor and elevated terms of the debate.

Just as Alcott ultimately subordinates class inequities among women to their greater mutual privilege of sharing God's work, she similarly reconstrues Christie's original need for independence, for stimulating work, for the chance to "blaze and sing" into an increasing desire for a life of service to others and, through them, service to God. Possibly Alcott is not so much abandoning the dream of liberating earthly work for women as transposing and elevating it rhetorically to a realm that had a powerful emotional appeal at the particular historical moment of her novel, since the ecstatic religious tropes she employs are coined by analogy with the emancipation of slaves and the transcendent teleological rhetoric of the Civil War. If she is pragmatically appropriating the religious rhetoric of the Civil War for another necessary emancipation, this blurring of motive and method in the novel and willingness to shift ground may well be Alcott's corrective to her father's intractably utopian pursuit of principle. Instead of her father's planned and patriarchal community, she brings together her league of sisters on the basis of mixed motivations of affection, need, and accident. In her father's utopian society, work was the activity that connected men most closely to the gross material world, and thence abstinence from labor became a source of virtue.[11] In the daughter's fictional world, the realms of material and spiritual labor are blurred, and women's work is equally vital to their earthly survival and heavenly liberation. However, somewhere in the education of Christie Devon from youthful Romantic to mature Christian, Rebecca Harding Davis's great question of a life of "full development" for a working woman, on which Christie had embarked, is redefined in a way that makes Hugh Wolfe's workman's art and Sip Garth's theatrical ambitions seem like misguided and oblique deviations from the religious advance toward "something better." Alcott's practical corrections to her father's impracticality in the realm of work and transcendence define admirable spiritual outcomes for women's work, but eventually dismiss Davis's and Phelps's tentative interest in the mind and art of the lower class.

The religious idealism that triumphs over worldly aspirations in the fiction of middle-class writers like Davis, Phelps, and Alcott is broadly representative of a pattern in the later decades of the nineteenth century whereby an optimistic teleology transcends a limited and often pessimistic view of the present state of society. The Christian beliefs of meliorist and feminist women writers worked in curious and contradictory ways, engaging writers in visions of sisterhood and charity toward their female working-class contemporaries, but also providing a convenient, otherworldly source of consolation and hope when the conditions of this world seemed dire and immutable, except to complete social upheaval. Women's accepted role in church and family as guardians of moral concerns provided a logical position from which they might write their fictions and expand their Christian sentiments into a more public sphere and, in doing so, give voice to their sense of grievance and injustice. Barbara Welter, in *Dimity Convictions*, calls popular women writers who tackled such ethical and spiritual questions "lay theologians" (129), and Susan Griffin argues that "the novel had come to be popularly perceived as woman's proper pulpit" (157). Since there was no central established church or orthodoxy for these lay theologians to represent, they had considerable latitude in the opinions they expressed, a latitude limited more by social convention and the extent of their own rebelliousness than by any official institution. Nonetheless, there was a pervasive reluctance in these Christian writers to continue what Harriet Beecher Stowe had begun at midcentury and what Edward Bellamy and

William Dean Howells would do at its end—to challenge the foundations of capitalism or endorse radical changes in class consciousness.

Fiction of the postwar period abounds in novels that reveal the misery and inequality of the current economic system yet repeatedly depict organized industrial action by workers, even nonviolent strikes and demonstrations, as sinister conspiracies against not merely capitalism but the nation itself. Numerous scholars have attempted to explain the timidity of Christian writers in challenging the fundamental basis of capitalism in this period: as a failure of their Christian ethics, as their complicity for the sake of convenience, and as a manifestation of their developing conviction of the inevitability of a permanent underclass. Middle-class women writers engaged in remarkable efforts to investigate and expose the circumstances of their working-class comrades, and simultaneously imposed consistent limitations on their literary reform agendas and on any sense of shared cultural and intellectual kinship with their lower-class sisters.[12] They were neither ignorant about the conditions in which other women lived nor squeamish about depicting them—they observed and researched carefully and drew no veils over their shocking discoveries. *The Silent Partner* came with Phelps's own notes, referring the reader to reports of the Massachusetts Bureau of Statistics and Labor for verification of her novel's grisly details. Her novel *Hedged In* (1870) tolerates no genteel restraint in its chilling opening descriptions of urban tenement horror. Rebecca Harding Davis had railed against picturesque versions of industrial life and tried to deny her readers the consolation of comfortable aesthetic responses. Alcott, although more willing to abide by literary convention, nonetheless brought to her account of women's work the authority of personal experience. All of them demanded that the reader confront the reality of working-class women's lives, and all concluded by placing those lives in a religious teleology that diminishes the concerns of the present material world, the very concerns that dominate much of the exposition of the novels.

If the transcendent Christianity of these novelists minimized the rational economic consciousness that is so prominent in the writings of the Lowell factory women, it also provided an alternative version of sublimity to the workers' own intellectual and artistic aspirations. While elsewhere Davis, Phelps, and Alcott all advocated vigorously for greater opportunities for women artists, they rarely depicted those artists as originating among the working class. Phelps did indeed present Sip Garth as a Romantic dreamer, but one finally reconciled to abandoning her acting ambitions for a life of religious service. The conclusion of Phelps's novel *The Story of Avis* (1877), about a middle-class woman artist who is thwarted by the constrictions of society and marriage, makes an interesting contrast to Sip's resignation. Avis, at the end of her story, has failed, like Sip, to find a means of fulfilling her artistic genius. She is widowed and is reading to her little daughter (named Wait) a story about a parent's quest that is fulfilled by the child of the next generation. Phelps comments editorially that the goal of women's full achievement may take much longer: "We have been told that it takes three generations to make a gentleman: we may believe that it will take as much, or more, to make A WOMAN" (246). Nevertheless, the presence of the frustrated artist's daughter is living hope of the earthly ful-fillment of that feminized Romantic ideal of Woman as a complete, rather than complementary, human being. In *The Silent Partner,* by contrast, Sip has explicitly forsworn marriage and childbearing because she believes that future generations of factory workers will be permanently trapped in their present predicament: "They'd never get out of the mills. It's from genera-tion to generation. It could n't be helped. I know. It's in the blood" (288). In this case, Phelps does not editorialize to contradict the worker's own grim essentialism. At the end of Alcott's *Work,* the aspirations of workers and ladies are again divergent, with the workers desiring better rewards, the ladies meaningful occupations, and both assured that they will come in a future world. Once again, class differences are virtually immutable in the earthly realm of the present, and transformable only in the spiritual realm of the future. Romantic idealism certainly still exists in these novelists as a feasible aspiration for the middle-class woman, but for the lower-class female worker, only the more ascetic path of Christian service leads to the satisfaction of transcending the here and now, and of having, in Davis's words, "summat to make her live."

Interestingly, the fiction published in the late nineteenth century under the auspices of the American labor press shows a similar emphasis on Christianity as the intellectual common ground of middle- and working-class women, despite organized labor's otherwise pervasive suspicion of preachers and church institutions. Even as the newly formed Knights of Labor, which grew in the 1870s and 1880s into a huge and influential movement, demonstrated a new willingness to offer women equality in membership, much of the fiction the union published showed the most admirable women as pious, compassionate, and philanthropic rather than as social radicals or intellectual rebels. In keeping with their medieval title, the Knights depicted themselves as members of a closely knit brotherhood who crusaded for social justice rather than religion, but only the male pro-tagonists in their fiction appeared to challenge traditional Christian norms of patience and otherworldliness.[13] One of the most popular Knights of Labor novels, *Sealskin and Shoddy* (1888), by W. H. Little, seems, with its focus on a female protagonist and its portraits of working women, to have been directed very clearly to a female audience and to have been enor-mously successful—the Knights' own *Journal of United Labor* claimed it had attracted many interested members and "lined up thousands in the order" (qtd. in Schofield viii). However, working women would have found an unlikely role model in Little's heroine, the college-educated daughter of a rich industrialist, and many helpless victims among the working-class female characters. The main affinity between the suffering workers and the talented and fortunate heroine is a fund of mutual sympathy and religious devotion that allows the class barrier to be bridged by their common virtue as Christian women.

The plot of *Sealskin and Shoddy* has notable parallels to that of *The Silent Partner*, although with a very different, and more conventionally sentimental, outcome. Mamie Symington, like Perley Kelso, is a privileged and wealthy protagonist. Beautiful, intelligent, pampered, and virtuous, although without a cause to animate her at the outset, Mamie is the daughter of a factory owner whose father is suddenly absent, thus opening the way for the daughter to investigate and interfere in the management of the family business. However, in dramatic contrast to Phelps's witty satire of Perley's failure to enter the male domain of economic and executive power, Little allows Mamie to demonstrate an astonishing ability in mastering the intricacies of "the purchase of raw material, insurance on plant, and goods, taxes and the general modus operandi of the concern." In addition, the tireless Mamie is particularly careful to inquire into "the methods of employing, governing and paying the help" (17). For some time, Mamie spends her mornings learning the management side of the business and her afternoons in a double disguise that enables her to descend the social scale and see how her workers live. As Mary Stillson, she views the workers' homes as a visiting nurse, and as Betty Broadbird she gets a job in her own factory and learns the work of an operative. She becomes actively involved in the Sewing Girls Protective Association, makes reforming speeches, and ultimately proposes the adoption of profit-sharing methods in the factory. Mamie's economic progress is accompanied by a conventional romantic plot in which she is courted by two men, one a rising capitalist, the other a Harvard-educated scholar who has studied advanced social thought at Paris and Heidelberg.

By comparison with the alluringly feminine yet assertive Mamie, the victimized working women in the novel are humbly grateful for Mamie's generosity to them. Their sufferings are necessary elements in the education of the reforming lady, rather than motivations to undertake the transformation of the industrial system themselves. What the different class of women shares with Mamie is religious devotion and selflessness. Lizzie Knowlton, a tubercular orphan girl, displays "sublime resignation" to her miserable life; Jennie Jameson is "a zealous worker in the Sunday school"; and Becky Francher dies ready to enter that other world that, "God forgive me, I have sometimes doubted" (4, 98, 75). Even the privileged Mamie's more activist and reforming career is justified by Christian principles and a sacrificial impulse: "I am not selfish enough to wish to sit with folded hands in the placid lap of contentment and idleness, when my fellow-beings are suffering from a cruel system, of which my comfort and affluence is one of its fruits" (46). She prays to God for justification: "Thou knowest I sought to benefit my fellow creatures.... If it so please Thee, make me Thy servant for this work" (69). She begins her efforts to help as an act of personal charity—perhaps the only acceptable way a young lady may embark on an industrial education. Gradually, Mamie's focus moves from philanthropy to justice and equity, and the "poor" become more clearly identified as exploited workers, but the collaboration she finally engineers between capital and labor is still very much the result of her personal magnanimity and her effort to pursue Christian ideals.

Not all of the Knights' novels relegated working-class women to such a secondary role as the enormously popular *Sealskin and Shoddy,* but even those novels that had more assertive and ambitious worker heroines, like T. Fulton Gantt's *Breaking the Chains* (1887), nonetheless insisted on purity and piety as essential to their admirable female characters. Gantt's novel is an intriguing one for its lively reversal of the class stereotypes associated with culture, intelligence, and refinement, and the gender stereotypes of combativeness and emotional independence. However, even with as feisty and progressive a heroine as the worker Maud Simpson, the novel still insists on the importance of domestic and devotional virtues. Maud is second to none in the seriousness of her intellectual pursuits and cultural interests. While her lover, the young plumber Harry Wallace, likes to dream about Maud, her dreams, by contrast, "are of labor organizations and black-lists, all mixed up with a confusion of the scenes in the life of the hero of 'Les Misérables'" (Grimes 39). Although Gantt's novel is ponderous and didactic in laying out the Knights' goals and agenda, the class subversions are witty and amusing. The prosperous bourgeois who employs the working-class Maud is bewildered by her indifference to the opportunity to be elevated to a more "genteel" position, to have a "salary" instead of wages. He can scarcely imagine that "this young woman had strong intellectual cravings that could only be satisfied by the intelligent men and women of her class, while the class to which he belonged would be to her an intellectual Sahara" (80). One of Gantt's Knights articulates even more explicitly the contrast he witnesses between classes:

> the men who in a few years blossom from poverty into wealth are those who are without culture, education, or refinement, with no artistic, literary, or scientific tastes to satisfy.... On the other hand, among the impoverished millions remain those of cultivated tastes and intellectual desires—men and women whose scant wages are divided between mere existence and the gratification of the nobler aspirations of the soul. (69–70)

Gantt repeatedly suggests that a change of affiliation from working class to middle class is not a step up. When Maud's lover Harry hesitates about moving into a clerical position, she accuses him of snobbishness about his status as a plumber: "Is it not possible, Harry, that you have some false pride about your own calling? Are you not disposed to encase yourself with a sort of exclusiveness, thinking, perhaps, the calling of a plumber is just a little better than any other." (95). When Harry meets the district's congressman at a performance of *King Lear*, and is asked to introduce Maud to the honorable member, he replies, "I will, sir, if she makes no objections" (81). The member is left to the amazed contemplation that he might not be worthy of the working girl's acquaintance.

Gantt's workers are in every way more highly evolved than the hard-drinking, drug-taking, bestial rich of *Breaking the Chains*. Thus a consideration of great significance for them is how they may gratify the "nobler aspirations of the soul" without rising in social and economic degree beyond their peers, and without capitulating to the intense individualism of "every man for himself and the devil take the hindmost" that pervades the upper class (69). Gantt solves the problem by divorcing the life of the mind and the creative impulse entirely from class affiliation and, indeed, even reversing the conventional associations of culture with the upper classes. Maud's life is "consecrated" to the cause of labor, and her elevation can only come alongside that of her class compatriots in a betterment that is as much cultural and intellectual as material. It requires libraries, museums, art galleries, and concerts in tandem with improvements in the physical well-being of workers. However, even in Maud Simpson's case, this progressive young working woman who has studied Adam Smith, Malthus, Ricardo, Carlyle, Henry George, and Herbert Spencer nevertheless derives her reforming zeal from the belief that "God never intended it to be so, and our Savior taught otherwise" (37). The last glimpse of the assertive and unconventional heroine of *Breaking the Chains* shows her on her knees, in prayer, asking "the Power above for further comfort and direction" (126). By framing Maud's labor activism in the larger context of Christianity, Gantt places her in the same spiritual company as the prosperous Mamie Symington, in that sisterhood of virtuous women that exists beyond class. Davis, Phelps, and Alcott, as middle-class women writers, had all found it more acceptable to project the "nobler aspirations" of their working-class protagonists into the realm of the otherworldly, where earthly distinctions could be obliterated outside the sphere of intractable class tensions. For the male authors of the Knights of Labor, and especially for Gantt, class systems were more permeable and open to alteration, but the best women were still activated ultimately by higher religious motives, rather than by a secular and independent commitment to equality and self-culture. Ironically, the Knights' goal of bringing about a revolution in the nation's political economy and establishing the working class triumphant in the republic brought them into bitter conflict with many of the churches of their time. Robert Weir notes that "Gilded Age churches were among the external forces that conspired to crush the Knights of Labor" (101). Their reluctance, then, to depart from notions of devout womanhood in their writing suggests how entrenched was the association of gender and piety, even within a movement that embraced diversity and encouraged more egalitarian treatment of women.

Despite the Knights' openness to women's concerns, and their emphasis on a working-class culture that included housewives, teachers, artists, and thinkers, they produced no significant women novelists to espouse their high aspirations. Middle-class women wrote copiously of their laboring sisters, but the best of them acknowledged in their fiction the barriers to any fully shared consciousness with workers. In the decades after the Civil War, however, one working-class woman writer produced a novel that spoke for the ambitions and reputations of working women from their own perspective. In doing so, she attacked many of the ideals of chastity, domesticity, and piety that supposedly united good women of all classes, and at the same time, she challenged many assumptions about culture and ability that supposedly kept them apart. This novel was *The Familistère* (1874) by Marie Howland, a woman who began her working career in the late 1840s as an operative in the Lowell mills and subsequently committed herself ardently to the ideal of living a self-reliant life. Howland had moved to New York in the early 1850s, where she associated with radical thinkers such as the feminist Ada Clare and the abolitionist and anarchist Stephen Pearl Andrews. Later she moved to France and lived for a time at J. B. Godin's Familistère, a communitarian and industrial settlement in Guise. After her return to the United States, she made the acquaintance of Albert Brisbane, the main American disciple of Fourierist socialism, and moved on to live in several experimental communities, including Topolobampo in Mexico and a Henry George single-tax settlement in Fairhope, Alabama.[14] Although the utopian community in Howland's novel is established in the fictional Oakdale, Massachusetts, it appears to be closely based on Godin's French original, since these Americans give their children diluted wine at mealtimes and scatter terms like *bambin, modiste, c'est bien simple,* and *poupon* freely in their conversation. The incongruities may well be appropriate, for the novel is a strange mixture in both its plot and political ideology. It is a blend of utopian and reform schemes, sentimental romance, bitter satire on marriage, and co-operative alliances among aristocrats, intellectuals, and workers that eventually prove alluring even to recalcitrant bourgeois industrialists.

Howland's novel has an interesting intellectual provenance. In establishing a vision of a utopian community close to Boston that anticipates "the dawn of the Golden Age" when "free women are worthy of free men" (373–74), it most obviously evokes Hawthorne's *Blithedale Romance* (1852), although Howland's community is both industrially based and successful, in contrast to Hawthorne's agrarian failure. Like other late nineteenth-century novels written in the aftermath of Elizabeth Barrett Browning's *Aurora Leigh, The Familistère* deals with an ideal friendship between a privileged and educated woman and an aspiring working-class woman who has been sexually "ruined" and cast out by society. However, although Howland's privileged Clara and poor Susie begin their acquaintance in the conventional mode of gracious condescension and humble gratitude, the lower-class Susie rapidly makes pragmatic use of the education she acquires in business and science. While Clara finds fulfillment in life with her husband and baby, Susie resolutely refuses a marriage proposal from her repentant seducer, achieves success in her career as a worker, and eventually becomes the fictional narrator of the book that relates both women's lives. As first-person narrator, however, Susie quickly steps back from prominence after her initial appearance. She introduces herself by saying, "I am one of the characters, but it does not matter which one. I shall not appear again in the first person after I have described my first acquaintance with [Clara Forest]" (8). Nonetheless, this curious positioning of Susie as both behind the scenes and directing the story gives the working-class character a different kind of authority from the socially superior heroine. In contrast to the vast majority of late nineteenth-century novels, the working woman takes control not only of her own life but also of the composition of the upper-class woman's story, albeit in a discreet fashion.

Some remarkable affinities also exist between Howland's novel and Alcott's *Work*, published the previous year, that suggest not so much influence as the pervasiveness of their concerns and of the available fictional modes for exploring them. The two novels explore the need for women of all classes to have a broader sphere, both practical and psychological, for their activities, than the domestic realm of the household and the emotional realm of marriage and family. Both depict communities of women of various ages and classes working and living together—"a loving league of sisters," as Alcott puts it—and, curiously, it is in the business of growing and marketing flowers that both fictional sets of women find their professional and commercial success. The emphasis on botany seems more than coincidental, recurring also, as it does, as a constant focus in the essays in the *Lowell Offering*, as a repeated motif in Larcom's *Idyl of Work*, in the fables of Margaret Fuller, and even as the desired but unattained career in Phelps's novel *The Story of Avis*. Emerson, in "Self-Reliance," speaks of the fascination with new terminology of "a girl who has just learned botany" (163), and botany was indeed the favorite choice, by a wide margin, of nineteenth-century American women who chose to be scientists. Historians have tried to explain this fact in various ways—as a result of botany's connection with women's traditional knowledge of herbal properties, of its association with familiar images in art and literature, or, more pragmatically, of the relative ease for women of acquiring amateur knowledge before pursuing professional study.[15] In women's fiction and poetry, botany serves repeatedly as a gateway to expanded intellectual and commercial opportunities and thence as the most "female friendly" of the sciences. In *The Familistère* it is botany than enables Susie to shed her reputation as a "Magdalen" and to become instead the scientist-artist whose plants are the final transforming glory of the great glass dome that stands at the heart of the workers' social palace.

Howland's novel is much more militantly feminist than Alcott's in its attack on double sexual standards, its demands for women's suffrage and divorce rights, its assault on traditional marriage, and its barely veiled efforts to discuss menstruation and abortion. It is ultimately also more Romantic in the inclusiveness of its utopian vision, its faith in a better mutual future for men as well as women, and its willingness to allow its two main male characters, Dr. Forest and Count Paul Von Frauenstein, to play central roles in the transformation of the social order. Its privileged heroine, Clara Forest, is an amalgam of elevated, traditionally female sentiments—"love was her religion—the one necessity of her higher life"—and sardonic realism about the artificial social barriers that distort true harmony between the sexes (393). She speculates satirically at one point on what women might do to men if roles were reversed and they had the "management of affairs":

> We'd give them donkeys and a side-saddle to ride on, lest immodesty and ambition should be fostered by riding astride of fine horses. We'd have them do hard work all the time, and yet we'd kiss only the hands that were soft and white. Then we'd set up our ideal for male chastity, which should be almost unattainable, through our own system of tempting them; and then we'd laugh at the presumption of any who presumed to demand the same standard for us. If they wished to vote, we'd howl at and persecute them for getting out of their sphere, and show them they had no need of the ballot, because we, their heaven-appointed protectors, represented them at the polls. (341–42)

Howland, like Alcott, emphasizes the role of reading in the expanding sphere of women's mental life, but Howland shows her working-class women's particular embrace of books and their heroic efforts to acquire learning. Susie, despite the anguish and shame of her unwed pregnancy, takes on an arduous program of study while running a difficult household. Annie Gilder, another distressed working-class girl, tells a symbolic tale of having made a large pocket to tie on underneath her dress, so that she might conceal from her father not an illicit pregnancy but the books she is reading. Howland suggests repeatedly that all women require a larger scope for their aspirations, "a wider sphere of action," in order that they might see the world in "a broad light" (171, 67). While the working-class women in the novel take risks for such opportunities, the middle-class wife of Dr. Forest prefers "a good reputation" to intellectual curiosity, and even the highly educated college teacher, Miss Marston, declares that it is "a very equivocal compliment" for a lady to be considered liberal-minded (67, 53). Thus Howland suggests that women who value their genteel status may actually be more inhibited in acquiring intellectual daring than working women who have not had the opportunity to cultivate their feminine decorum—an interesting variation on the debates between Harriet Farley and Sarah Bagley that Howland might have heard in her earlier days at Lowell.

In one area of open-mindedness, Marie Howland goes considerably beyond her contemporaries, both middle-class women writers like Davis, Phelps, and Alcott and more politically radical male authors like Little and

Gantt. She candidly abandons all religious and otherworldly justifications for social and economic reform and bases her advocacy on reason and principle alone. Her main protagonist, Dr. Forest, is an avowed nonbeliever, and Howland rejects from the outset, through Susie's narrative voice, "the unverifiable hypotheses of theology and superstition" that are "born of the general ignorance incident to the childhood of the human race" (16). In two juxtaposed chapters, entitled "Faith and Works" and "Clara Decides between Religion and Principle," Howland makes more conventional attacks on practitioners of religion who fail to apply the ethical aspects of Christian doctrine. Nevertheless, *The Familistère*, unlike many of its contemporary social novels, is not an attack on false Christianity for the sake of recalling believers to their faith. Howland, like her doctor protagonist, finds the notion of divine Providence ludicrous and pities characters like the weak-willed woman who looks beyond the grave for rewards that "a stronger and more philosophical" nature might have found in this world (20). Clara's marriage to the count is explicitly a civil, not a church, union. Even the architecture of the social palace where the community of the future will live, work, and play excludes any plans for a place of worship, although it has detailed provisions for swimming pools, gardens, schools, a theatre, library, restaurants, and a grand assembly hall. In transporting almost unaltered the design of the actual social palace of M. Jean Baptiste Godin in Guise to the fictional New England town of Oakdale, Howland makes little effort to disguise the French origins of the communal scheme, down to the details of the brick ornamentation on the walls that proclaims "LIBERTY," "EQUALITY," "FRATERNITY" (509). However, in establishing the secular basis for the community's principles, she is also careful to build a solid foundation on the ideas of the rational New England scientist, Dr. Forest. He is a genial and tolerant Yankee who is initially regarded by his community as something of a beloved eccentric. As the novel progresses, Howland gradually moves his ideas and his influence to the center and suggests that even the most intransigent of scoffers and skeptics may be won over by his decency, his integrity, and the power of his absolute reasonableness.

The Familistère itself, however, unlike Dr. Forest, did not move from the margins to the center of social thought, nor did it serve as the harbinger of a radical secular reform school of American fiction, although it undoubtedly anticipated elements of the utopian thinking embodied later in the novels of Edward Bellamy, William Dean Howells, and Charlotte Perkins Gilman. Christian idealism and practice continued to dominate the morality of reform fiction devoted to the condition of working women until the end of the century, and Christian transcendence continued to be offered as the ultimate route to their fulfillment beyond the realm of immediate material necessity. The phenomenon of "mind amongst the spindles" began to seem, by the 1890s, an evanescent one that could only have existed in an age innocent of the inevitable course of industrial capitalism. The

ambitions of working women for a life of independent economic sufficiency, within a sociable community, with opportunities for intellectual and
creative achievement, had been stimulated (if never fulfilled) by circumstances that seemed unlikely ever to return after midcentury. The women
who had come together to produce the *Lowell Offering* and a host of other
literary and political writings in the 1840s were already educated inheri-
tors of republican and egalitarian ideals, and of moral and spiritual traditions derived from their religion. They lived in close communities, read
a largely common canon of literary works, and absorbed the Romantic,
transcendental, and reformist currents of the age. While the conditions of
their labor were very far from auspicious, they elicited from literate young
women responses in a range of forms, from letters, essays, and speeches to
poetry and fiction. Although these women were objectified by the gaze
and the commentary of outsiders, they professed their own subjectivity and
pursued their self-culture with some assurance.

After the Civil War, the earlier, cohesive factory population was fragmented; new workers faced more degrading conditions, and the free-
spirited and noble young women Harriet Robinson had recalled in her
memoir of Lowell were replaced by "poor people," perhaps, in Robinson's
gingerly chosen word, of "different" mental status (120). Robinson continued to insist that the "intellectual freedom, as well as the wage-question"
of these new workers was a central concern to be fought for, but the many
middle-class women writers who chose to represent their laboring sisters
in fiction seemed less certain (121). When they recognized a higher nature
in female workers, they depicted its religious but not its artistic or literary manifestation, thus creating a distinction between aspiring mind and
humble spirit that the workers themselves had not acknowledged. Male
writers of union fiction, despite their class-based sympathy for reforms,
continued to endorse the piety and traditional virtue of laboring women,
so that, by the end of the century, it seemed that Sarah Savage's anxiety, at
the beginning, about the disruptive danger of female self-culture and self-
reliance was seriously misplaced. However, it was just at this time that a
new group of women arrived in the United States, women who were the
heirs not of a Christian tradition but of other, quite distinct, intellectual
patterns of radicalism and reform. With their arrival, and the changes they
brought to the working-class population, and especially to the garment
industry, the Romantic possibilities of the woman worker would undergo a
new transformation, and an apotheosis of the rebel girl would emerge who
might well have justified Savage's direst fears.

8

"Beautiful Language and Difficult Ideas"

From New England Factory to New York Sweatshop

What the woman who labors wants is the right to live,
not simply exist—the right to life as the rich woman has it,
the right to life, and the sun, and music, and art.
—ROSE SCHNEIDERMAN (1912)

"I hope I won't be long in this ship," said a deep eyed Russian girl,
pushing aside her stack of little Buster Brown coats to make room on the
table for her cup. "I expect to take up literature and journalism soon."
—GERTRUDE BARNUM, "IN THE JACKET SHOP" (1910)

Where would it all end? With thousands of Emma Goldmans?
—FAY BLAKE (1972)

By the end of the nineteenth century, the United States had altered from
a rural agricultural society to a wage-based, industrial one, a milestone
that was marked in the final two decades of the century by increasing episodes of economic crisis and industrial upheaval. These were accompanied
by an outpouring of criticism from workers' organizations, women's movements, and individual reporters, writers, and artists who spoke forcefully
on behalf of working women and helped to construct the public's knowledge of their world. The 1880s and 1890s saw increasing labor organization,
union activism, and dramatic (and deadly) confrontations between workers
and employers. In 1886, seven people were killed during a protest meeting
in Haymarket Square in Chicago, and five men were later executed for their
promotion of revolutionary ideas; in 1892, sixteen men were killed during
the violent Homestead steel strike; two years later, violence flared again in
the Pullman strike. Although working women were not directly involved
in these strikes, they proved active and outspoken allies of male workers. The
same period witnessed the intensification of feminist campaigns for wom-
en's suffrage and the efforts of middle-class women to form allegiances with
working women to fight for enfranchisement.[1] The final decades of the
century also saw the emergence of a school of realist and naturalist writers
who focused their imaginative and documentary literature on the injustices

that distorted the lives of their largely lower-class subjects. Such literary concern with economic and social issues in the contemporary context of working-class and feminist militancy might well have been expected to produce a literature with particular interests in the predicament of working-class women—and to a certain extent it did. Laura Hapke, in her *Tales of the Working Girl*, chooses 1890 as a significant year to mark the beginning of an outpouring of fiction about working women's lives that educated, sympathized, entertained, and titillated with accounts of the female underclass. However, although Hapke documents the extensive variety of literary approaches to lower-class and working women, the perspective she notes is often that of the voyeur from another realm. Her chapter titles are revealing: "Masculine Tenement Fiction" explores the fascination of male authors with the sexual dilemmas of poor and exploited women; "Feminine Cross-Class Fiction" looks at the response of privileged women writers to the less fortunate members of their sex. Noticeably absent, except as filtered through the observations and imaginations of those outside her own sex and class, are the voice and consciousness of the working-class woman, speaking as female worker, and as author and agent of her own vision of the world.

Outside the realm of literature, working women's voices were increasingly heard in agitation for economic and political reforms, although there was no single movement devoted to their cause. Working-class women participated actively in labor and suffrage movements, despite the fact that their contributions were regarded as ancillary in projects that pursued exclusively class-based *or* gender-based objectives. Of their efforts in industrial organizing, Meredith Tax notes that they "had to approach the established unions as suppliants, knocking on the door and asking to be let in. Working men did not accept them as equal partners in the class struggle, because the socially caused differences in their situations made them unequal" (17). When they turned to suffrage, as one step toward rectifying that inequality, they were welcomed into an increasingly bourgeois feminist movement less concerned about economic than gender disparities. Indeed, Tax argues, "by the turn of the century suffrage had become a respectable, even boring, single-issue campaign permeated with moralism and anti–working class attitudes" (166). Without a voice of their own, working women might choose their best advocates from a socialism that was too sexist and a feminism that was too bourgeois. Toward the end of the century, a variety of movements and organizations came into existence that attempted to better integrate working women's concerns into their agendas. Tax calls them "a united front of women," which she defines as "the alliance, recurring through time in various forms, of women in the socialist movement, the labor movement, the national liberation movements, and the feminist movement" (13). This alliance existed in changing coalitions until it eventually collapsed under the stresses of World War I and fragmented into "its left and its feminist parts," with "both divided from labor" (22).

An even looser ideological nexus, which permitted the interaction of a much wider range of radicalism relevant to working women's interests, existed at the same time among sundry groups and individuals who were committed to anarchism. Anarchism provided a context for the untrammeled exploration of human potential, unlimited by social constrictions or narrowly organizational objectives. Among anarchists, working-class women's anomalous situation as members of a class and a gender whose separate goals were not entirely compatible dissolved, since anarchists' only collective group was the entire human race. Their sphere of action was, as Emma Goldman put it, "the consideration of *every phase* of life,—individual, as well as the collective; the internal, as well as the external phases" (*Anarchism* 56). Anarchism exerted a widespread fascination at the end of the nineteenth century, as a loosely defined movement that combined radical idealism with occasional rare but spectacular acts of lawbreaking and violence.[2] It provided an intellectually radical context against which more limited, pragmatic, and reformist groups might define themselves, and like the earlier transcendentalists, with whom anarchists were eager to claim kinship both direct and oblique, anarchists insisted on the authentic Americanism of imported European ideas, vigorously remade in a new environment. As women factory workers in the 1840s had been drawn to the Romantic aspirations of transcendentalism, remote as they seemed from the daily circumstances of their lives, so female immigrants who poured into the garment industry at the turn of the century found a provocative and challenging set of ideals defined by anarchism. These ideals likewise encouraged them to believe their own thoughts, walk on their own feet, and speak their own minds in "self-reliant" ways that reached beyond the immediate political objectives of both socialism and feminism.

In the case of both transcendentalism and anarchism, a controversial and atypical woman demonstrated a way to live intensely a life that combined intellectual aspiration, social activism, and emotional extravagance. As Margaret Fuller took the lead in translating Emersonian Romantic transcendentalism into terms applicable to women's lives, so did Emma Goldman take on the role of interpreter of an anarchism that looked both to American Romantic and European radical origins. As a literary editor and radical thinker, Margaret Fuller had emerged from an intellectual New England background into the Romantic movement, melding its lofty idealism with her later direct experiences among the urban poor, prostitutes, and prisoners. Eventually she committed herself to the risks of love and motherhood, and to the support of political goals that were served by revolutionary violence. Half a century later, Emma Goldman emerged from an immigrant Jewish background and associated with intellectuals, workers, convicts, bourgeois feminists, histrionic lovers, and violent insurrectionists. Goldman became, in an era of celebrity, a much more familiar icon than Fuller, not only a famous and notorious figure in the press but also the inspiration for many fictional characters in the

novels of her day. As an immigrant sweatshop worker, she was familiar from the inside with the lives of lower- and working-class women,
although, like Fuller, Goldman was no typical representative of her sex
and class. She embodied an extreme and personal manifestation of ideals
that animated a sense of possibility in more conventional people. She
stimulated a consciousness of personal freedom, and for working women
in particular, she reinvigorated and articulated a sense of personhood and
subjectivity derived from experience in the world and from the life of
the mind. Although Goldman quoted Emerson, Thoreau, and Whitman
frequently and approvingly in her writings, similarities between her anarchism and the beliefs of the leaders of the American Romantic movement
a half century earlier were as much of temperament as of theory. They all
asserted a radical individualism, a confident hope, and a brash advocacy of
their own opinions on behalf of a diverse and democratic population at
the very time that other reforming movements were becoming more organized, centralized, and politicized. Anarchists had contempt for the timid
and piecemeal legislative reforms sought by unions and suffrage associations, but for the members of those groups and their leaders, anarchists
like Goldman were a constant and useful reminder of goals beyond immediate compromises, and of individual distinctions and aspirations within
collective constituencies.

The largest group of immigrant women who flooded into the American garment industry in the late nineteenth and early twentieth centuries
were, like Goldman, largely of east European Jewish origins, spoke little
or no English, and came from cultural and religious traditions distinctly
different from those of the world into which they were moving. In these
ways, they were markedly different from that earlier generation of women
who had poured into the New England cotton mills in the early nineteenth
century with the ambition of not only earning their living but of living
their lives in a larger arena of possibility. These earlier women were native-
born farmers' daughters, at home amid the values, language, and customs
of a republic undergoing the transition to an industrial society. They came
to Lowell and other factory towns with high hopes but also with fears that
they were already being demeaned as "loose" women and belittled as a
class of operatives or "hands." They proved highly articulate in representing themselves; and they had become, in a world not yet versed in the cult
of celebrity, as famous a sight for tourists and visitors as Niagara Falls or
a southern slave plantation. They had produced and become the subjects
of an extraordinary literary outpouring, and they had engaged as well in
sharp debates about their own literariness. Was it an essential expression
of their humanity, or their acquiescence to a class-bound culture that was
eager to exploit them by co-opting their literacy to its elitist agenda? By
comparison with these daughters of the republic, however, the daughters
of the shtetl were not entirely disadvantaged in their prospects of fulfilling
comparable hopes and ambitions.

Like the Lowell women, the new arrivals were the descendants of mothers who had accepted public powerlessness in their society but had assumed a high degree of private responsibility for the support of their families: in New England they shared in farm labor and household production; in Russia they participated even more directly in money-making and business ventures. In addition, many of these Jewish immigrant women had already lived urban lives, worked in factories, and received training in industrial skills.[3] Both groups of women came from cultures that had subordinated their education to that of men but, by doing so, had served to emphasize the significance of learning—of study, literacy, reading, and their connection to the deepest currents of authority in their societies. For immigrant sisters and daughters, access to education and books came to be one of the most vital symbols of their own emerging autonomy. Like the women of Lowell, young immigrants expected to find much more in their new factory lives than the mere "means of earning a living." Susan Glenn describes the hopes they invested in their working lives in terms almost identical to those of the earlier operatives: "They...sought a social environment that would open up new possibilities for personal growth and learning" (133). Both groups of women began their careers in American industry in periods of social upheaval and participated in the ferment of ideas and the reform movements of their time. However, many east European Jewish women had already had a prior introduction to radical and revolutionary thinking through the agency of the Bund, a movement of Jewish socialists who envisioned not only a new political and economic system but also, as Susan Glenn puts it, "a blueprint for a new secular civilization" (37).

Thus, although the new immigrants lacked familiarity with the language and mores of America, they were in many ways well poised to enter the movements and organizations of the new world and to reinvigorate the Romantic sense of selfhood in working women that had long been subordinated to pragmatic group affiliations for limited reforms, or sublimated to otherworldly promises. Like the earlier generation of factory women, they were not only the objects of fascinated observation and reporting but also the authors of their own books and the editors of their own periodicals. Some pursued their ambitions in political and labor movements, others in the realm of cultural and intellectual life. And, once again, they encountered the familiar challenge to literary working-class women—how to avoid betraying their pursuit of justice in the workplace for aesthetic aspirations, and how to retain their solidarity with the goals of their class and sex while pursuing their solitary and individual creativity. The metonymic phrase that came to characterize the demands of unionized women—"bread and roses"—responds in eloquent simplicity to the first part of the dilemma, the fusion of the needs of body and soul. However, the tension between class commonalty and the aspiring individual spirit could not be so emblematically resolved, and the new immigrants found themselves repeating in other forms the debate that had raged in the 1840s between the *Lowell Offering* and the *Voice of Industry*—between bourgeois literary selfhood and female proletarian activism.

Emma Goldman proved a particularly intriguing figure in this debate. As a passionately erudite literary woman, as an ardent proponent of militant working-class activism, and perhaps most controversially, as an advocate of absolute sexual autonomy for women, she was not easily assimilated into any conventional categories. Because of her violations of law and convention, she was closely watched by both the press and the government; she was criticized and caricatured in novels; and she was repeatedly arrested and imprisoned, and eventually deported. She responded with speeches, lectures, articles, books, and her own magazine, *Mother Earth*, published regularly from 1906 until the final version of it, *Mother Earth Bulletin*, was shut down by the police in 1918. She later poured her recollections into her thousand-page autobiography, *Living My Life* (1931), with its deceptively simple title, like that of *Mother Earth*, alluding to an ideal of deliberate choice and female agency. Although it would be inaccurate to suggest that Goldman was a role model for the millions of immigrant and working women who were attempting, in more modest ways, to live their own lives in the conditions of early twentieth-century America, she was, for her antagonists, the epitome of what they feared those working women might become.[4] Goldman's anarchist philosophy was not, in the end, a theory that drew large numbers of women workers into her fold, but her example of a vivid female consciousness, unwilling to be defined by others, insisting on her own words being heard and read, resonated in the newly energized actions and confident voices of immigrant workers. In that exemplary sense, she herself represented the fusion of communal and personal ideals, of public and private life, and of political and literary impact that characterized the hopes of this new generation of factory women.

Emma Goldman was born in 1869 in a small village in Russia, but like many other immigrant Jewish women who entered the garment trade in the United States, she had already experienced urban life and factory labor before emigrating, and thus was no novice to the world of industrial work. She sailed into New York harbor as a steerage passenger in 1886 with typically (for Goldman) ecstatic hopes for the future: "the exciting anticipation of what the new land would offer stimulated my imagination and sent my blood tingling" (*Living My Life* 11). She wanted "to study, to know life, to travel," and to find love (though not marriage), but, before all else, "I would go to work" (12–13). The seventeen-year-old Goldman initially followed a pattern familiar to many immigrants—she lived with a married sister in Rochester, New York, and found factory work. She entered an early romance with another recent arrival, Jacob Kershner, and the two quickly married; when Kershner proved sexually impotent, she insisted on a separation, candidly citing her own erotic desires as the reason (*Living My Life* 20, 23). At this same period in her life, Goldman began to attend socialist meetings where she first heard accounts of the Haymarket riots and the death sentences that had been imposed on Chicago anarchists. She began to read anarchist literature, and in 1889 she left Rochester for New York City with five dollars, a sewing machine, and the address of Johann Most's anarchist paper *Freiheit* (*Living My Life* 3). Thus, by the time she was twenty, Goldman had already embraced more radical attitudes toward gender and social revolution than most of her immigrant contemporaries ever would, but these attitudes were an accelerated and exaggerated version of concerns they all shared. In the career as speaker and writer Goldman was about to begin, she would develop an intellectual and literary context for her beliefs and set an example of woman as reader, writer, and Romantic rebel. From her new home on New York's Lower East Side, where she would live for the next thirty years, Goldman began a program of educating the public through her writing, and self-education through her reading, immersing herself in both contemporary literature and the great classics of Western culture.[5]

Early in her career of anarchist activism, she decided never to go anywhere that she might be arrested without a book in her possession, in order to make the best of her imprisonment. Fifteen days in Queen's County Jail, for distributing information on contraception gave her the welcome chance to read and prepare six lectures on American literature. She read John Reed's account of postrevolutionary Russia, *Ten Days that Shook the World*, while serving jail time in Jefferson City, Missouri, transfixed by the drama of Reed's "engrossingly thrilling" story. She read Joyce's *Portrait of the Artist as a Young Man* while in the Tombs in New York waiting to be bailed out, a delay she did not mind because the book was so "absorbing" (*Living My Life* 571, 684, 612). Her literary sensibility is apparent not only in the stylistic flourishes of her autobiography but also in her penchant for modeling her behavior on fictional heroines. On one occasion she decided she would raise money for her anarchist friend Alexander Berkman ("Sasha") by emulating Dostoyevsky's Sonya in *Crime and Punishment* and becoming a prostitute:

> I visioned Sonya as she lay on her cot, face to the wall, her shoulders twitching. I could almost feel the same way. Sensitive Sonya could sell her body; why not I? My cause was greater than hers. It was Sasha—his great deed—the people. But should I be able to do it, to go with strange men—for money? The thought revolted me. I buried my face in the pillow to shut out the light. "Weakling, coward," an inner voice said. "Sasha is giving his life, and you shrink from giving your body, miserable coward!" It took me several hours to gain control of myself. When I got out of bed, my mind was made up. (91)

Fortunately Goldman also had a well-developed literary sense of irony, and thus her melodramatic effort to emulate Sonya concludes with a potential customer telling her she is "silly, inexperienced, childish," and actually paying her to abandon a profession for which she has clearly no talent (94).

Goldman's massive autobiography is suffused with a sense of her alternating impassioned engagement with life, love, ideas, and schemes and a grimly detached, even comic awareness of the preposterous consequences of her more extreme ventures in Romantic idealism. Her account of Berkman's plans to assassinate Henry Clay Frick is almost farcical, with its details of the fanatical but wholly inept amateur bomb-maker and his equally inadequate back-up methods for murder: "Sasha had taken a poisoned dagger with him. 'In case the revolver, like the bomb, fails to work,' he had said" (98). When indeed the assassination fails, the anarchists wrestle with the endless moral quandaries of true ideologues—prominent attorneys offer their services free to Berkman but must be declined because "It was inconsistent for an anarchist to employ lawyers" (100); Goldman is advised to use an assumed name to protect her from any repercussions after Berkman's arrest, but refuses on principle to deny her identity (103); the conspirators need to raise money, but it is against their beliefs "to engage in business," a dilemma they resolve curiously by deciding that running "an ice-cream parlour might prove the means to our end" (82).

An equally absurd situation arises later when Goldman uses her anarchist magazine *Mother Earth* as a platform from which to attack religion and then discovers that her current lover, Ben Reitman, is conducting a Sunday school class in the magazine's office. Goldman, sardonically aware that "To maintain consistency in a world of crass contradictions is not easy," defends her lover on the basis of his right to free speech and then discovers "the height of tragicomedy"—that Reitman is also having an affair with one of the Sunday school pupils. She comments: "It was all so absurd and grotesque" (582). Nothing is more grotesque, however, than what Goldman discovers when she is deported to Russia: the betrayal of the revolution, the resistance of her American supporters when she tries to report it, and Lenin's assertion to her that "Free speech is a *bourgeois* prejudice" (766). Even amid the crushing failure of her hopes in Russia, Goldman does not lose her literary eye for the telling detail or the foolish anomaly. When she and Berkman agree to travel around Russia in a railroad car, collecting material for a Museum of the Revolution, she is sent to the Winter Palace to assemble supplies for the journey. As a result, she notes that the deported "arch-anarchists" set out on their proletarian mission furnished with "the crested linen and china of the Romanovs" to travel through the ruins of the Russian revolution, "an Inferno awaiting the master hand of a Russian Dante" (798, 814).

Such bitter satirical awareness alternates effectively in *Living My Life* with the histrionic Goldman, who lives and writes at the emotional extremes: escaping from Russia by train in 1921, she writes "My dreams crushed, my faith broken, my heart like a stone....I clutch the bar at the frozen window-pane and grit my teeth to suppress my sobs" (927).

Goldman's anarchism emerges from her autobiography as a strange blend of intellectual fervor, emotional intensity, and corrosive irony. She reveals a selfless willingness to endure stoically and a more self-centered pleasure in moments of hedonism, and, pervasively, an absolute confidence that her own apprehensions are the keys to universal insights. It is in these seemingly incongruous elements that she is most like the American Romantics she came to admire and identify as her forebears, and most especially like Henry David Thoreau, whose life and writings exerted a profound influence on her. Alice Wexler has noted Goldman's attraction to the earlier Romantic tradition of Emerson, Thoreau, and Whitman, in whom she found "an American anti-authoritarian tradition congenial to her own anarchist vision" (103). Strangely, of them all, it was to the chaste New England naturalist that she felt the most powerful personal affinity. She traveled to Concord, met Thoreau's biographer, Frank B. Sanborn, and spent several apparently fruitless hours trying to convince him of Thoreau's anarchism. She afterward expressed her amazement that Sanborn had been a contemporary of "the most anarchistic period of American thought" yet was "scandalized" by Goldman's appropriation of Thoreau to her own intellectual tradition (585). In her address to the jury in 1917, before her final imprisonment and deportation from the United States, her last quotation was from Thoreau, challenging Emerson: "what are you doing outside, when honest people are in jail for their ideals?" (qtd. in Shulman 327). She reprinted many of the poems and essays of other American Romantics in *Mother Earth*; but her own literary method is most evocative of Thoreau. She displays the same intense subjectivity (both hyperbolically egotistical and whimsically self-deprecating), tough, logical lucidity, and continuous fruitful interaction both with the minds of others and with the immediate stimuli of the physical world.

Although there is no evidence that Goldman was familiar with the *Dial*, her own periodical, *Mother Earth*, demonstrates her faith in the same conviction as Margaret Fuller: that journals, "which monthly, weekly, daily, send their messages to every corner of this great land...form, at present, the only efficient instrument for the general education of the people."[6] While Goldman's magazine was not nearly as radical in its aesthetics as in its politics, she nonetheless used it to insist on the centrality of art and literature to social movements and their underlying ideals. Indeed, so pronounced was her interest in literature and culture that early issues of the magazine brought down on her the criticism that the magazine "was not revolutionary enough, perhaps not revolutionary at all" (Morton 47). Originally she had intended to title it *The Open Road*, after Whitman, a plan that was waylaid because, as she noted with her usual sense of the ridiculous, someone had already copyrighted the title and threatened to "set the law on us for infringement" (378). Still, she anticipated the magazine's appearance with her usual enthusiasm: "I walked on air. At last my preparatory work of years was about to take complete form! The spoken word, fleeting at best, was no longer to be my only medium of expression, the platform not the only place where I could feel at home. There would be the printed thought, more lasting in its effect, and a place of expression for the young idealists in art and letters" (377). In March 1906, the first issue of *Mother Earth* proclaimed its mission in terms as optimistic and untrammeled as those of the *Dial*, equally the medium of a woman who placed literariness at the heart of ideology. The *Dial* sought to fuse lofty intellectual ideals, free expression, and social progress, while *Mother Earth* announced that it would appeal "to those who strive for something higher, weary of the common- place; to those who feel that stagnation is a deadweight on the firm and elastic step of progress; to those who breathe freely only in limitless space" (March 1906: 4).

Goldman originally hoped that contemporary writers would contrib- ute to this Romantic ideal, but Craig Monk, in his study of the magazine, notes that "*Mother Earth* did not attract the promising new writers that Goldman envisioned," and "she would later concede that a substantive dif- ference existed between her and the modern writers" (118). Indeed, Gold- man found herself in a quandary with regard to the literary world that was not unfamiliar to the working women of Lowell, who wished to believe that there was no conflict between their ardent embrace of literature and their commitment to better lives for working women. She faced the trou- bling possibility that artistic criteria, especially in the case of the aesthetic vanguard, might be class-bound. One prominent member of that vanguard, whom Goldman was initially excited to meet, was Margaret Anderson, the editor of the innovative *Little Review*. After their meeting, however, each woman commented separately on her awareness of the problem of recon- ciling radical art and radical politics. Goldman noted that Anderson was a "*chic* society girl" who had thrown off "family bondage and bourgeois tradition" but was not "actuated by any sense of social injustice" (530, 531). Anderson related of Goldman that she objected to "the direction of mod- ern letters by complaining that 'the working-man hasn't enough leisure to be interested' in the seemingly opaque art then becoming fashionable" (qtd. in Monk 121). Goldman was uncomfortably aware that artistic and politi- cal innovation might not always be in step with one another. Although she used her magazine to educate readers, and to popularize Romantic poetry, realist fiction, and reforming drama, she did not provide a congenial outlet for the aesthetic experiments of modernism.

Goldman's reservations about the opacity of modern literature and its inaccessibility to workers are echoed in Jonathan Rose's study of the relationship of modernism to class in Britain in the same period. He con- cludes that British modernist writers "used difficulty to fence off and pro- tect literary property," a pattern that was repeated every time the working class "advanced" in its artistic interests (435). Rose's accusation of a virtual elitist conspiracy by the cultural vanguard to exclude the masses is more persuasive for certain aspects of high modernism than for other literary movements in their emergent stages. Romanticism, realism, and naturalism all had democratic aspects distinctly sympathetic to elements of political and social radicalism, while modernism had, at best, ambiguous sympathies for populist ideals. Goldman struggled uneasily in *Mother Earth* to advocate for the Romantic and realist literature she loved against criticisms from both social activists who accused her of turning away from the most vital concerns of the masses and from literary innovators who felt that she was too preoccupied with the morals of art to do justice to its aesthetic dimensions.[7] Nevertheless, despite criticism from all sides, Goldman used *Mother Earth* as a means to broaden the intellectual scope of her readers by introducing them to a wide range of European writers, from Tolstoy, Chekhov, and Gorky to Strindberg, Ibsen, and Hauptmann. As Margaret Fuller had done in the *Dial*, she insisted on the internationalism of literature, and as the editors of the *Lowell Offering* had done, she asserted her own autonomy to vindicate her literary choices.

Goldman chose in her magazine not to speak as a stranger in the land or as the marginalized voice of a particular class, sex, or ethnic group but as an assured and self-reliant individual, a woman who was at the center of what was happening in the intellectual and political life of her time. She assimilated events, ideas, and opinions into her own perspective and confidently emphasized, subordinated, and interpreted on the authority of her own independent consciousness. She displayed the confidence of Emerson in believing that what was true for her in her private heart was true for all, and the independence of Thoreau in refusing to be a member of any society she had not joined. Like Thoreau, Goldman went to jail (in her case for claiming the right to speak freely on birth control and for challenging the government's draft laws). However as a working-class immigrant and especially as a woman, Goldman's rejection of the conventions and loyalties of her newly acquired homeland proved more controversial than Thoreau's resistance to the obligations of a slave-holding republic. Most shocking were her opinions on marriage, childbearing, religion, and violence, particularly as she publicized them in her flamboyant and uninhibited style.

In her essay "Marriage and Love," published in *Mother Earth,* she noted that the two were antagonistic and that marriage "makes a parasite of a woman, an absolute dependent. It incapacitates her for life's struggle, annihilates her social consciousness, paralyzes her imagination, and then imposes its gracious protection, which is in reality a snare, a travesty on human character." Marriage, she argued, was more degrading than prostitution and more oppressive than the factory. It was a crime against motherhood, causing children to be conceived in hatred and compulsion. On religion Goldman was no less emphatic—it was "a superstition that originated in man's mental inability to solve natural phenomena," and Christianity, specifically, was "most admirably adapted to the training of slaves" and was "the complete disregard of character and self-reliance." She argued that "Blessed are the meek, for they shall inherit the earth" was "a preposterous notion!"

and that Christianity was "the conspiracy of ignorance against reason, of darkness against light, of submission and slavery against independence and freedom."[8] However, Goldman gained her earliest and most enduring notoriety from her endorsement of revolutionary violence. In *Living My Life* she provides a telling account of her own first act of political violence, which was to leap at the throat of a woman who was speaking contemptuously of the fate of the Chicago Haymarket anarchists: "'Out, out,' I cried, or I will kill you!" (10). Although she was prevented from doing any more harm than throwing a pitcher of water in the woman's face, Goldman emphasizes the emotionally *reactive* nature of her violent impulse, a theme she reiterates in her later political explanations of anarchist violence. Such acts are the responses of people whose "supersensitiveness to the wrong and injustice surrounding them... compels them to pay the toll of our social crimes" (*Anarchism and Other Essays* 86). Goldman also argues, perhaps a trifle inconsistently, that anarchists have been repeatedly blamed for acts of violence perpetrated by others, although she never denies her part in the action in which she was most directly implicated, the assassination attempt on Henry Clay Frick by Alexander Berkman. She describes the decision to strike at Frick as an *Attentat,* or act of propaganda by deed, that "would re-echo in the poorest hovel" and "strike terror in the enemy's ranks and make them realize that the proletariat of America had its avengers" (*Living My Life* 87). By the time Leon Czolgosz shot President McKinley in 1901, claiming to have been "set on fire" by Emma Goldman, many of Goldman's anarchist colleagues had come to doubt seriously the expediency of the *Attentat,* but Goldman defended Czolgosz's emotional logic passionately for many years, despite the revilement and isolation she suffered as a consequence (Wexler 104, 109–10).

Goldman's challenges to the proprieties of women's attachments, to family, church, and nonviolence as well as to loyalties of class and country, were not, in substance, unprecedented in earlier writers of the nineteenth century, but there was no previous model for her style, her decorum or lack of it, her self-assertiveness, and the wide reach of her radicalism. The gradual disappearance of working women's voices from the literary record later in the century had culminated in their appropriation by male and middle-class female writers, or in nostalgic backward glances of factory women like Harriet Robinson and Lucy Larcom. The last radical literary voice to emerge from a working-class woman had been Marie Howland's novel *The Familistère* (1874), a book that had broached many of the controversial issues Goldman would pursue, insisting on a woman's right to sexual freedom, birth control, education, and self-expression and mocking religion as superstition and dependency. Howland had taken a different line on the peaceful evolution of a communitarian society and the possibilities of collaboration between labor and capital. However, a curious aspect of Howland's forward-looking book was the disappearance, after the opening, of the first-person narrative of Susie Dykes, a working-class "fallen" woman, whose voice is overtaken by a third-person, omniscient narrator and whose central presence in the novel is replaced by that of Clara Forest, the privileged doctor's daughter. As Susie notes self-deprecatingly at the beginning, "I am one of the characters, but it does not matter which one. I shall not appear again in the first person" (8). With Emma Goldman, what returns most dramatically to women workers' writing is precisely that assertive first person, with all it implies of self-awareness and lack of reservation. Other immigrant writers, as well as a new generation of middle-class sympathizers, were simultaneously eliciting understanding and support for the aspirations of the woman worker, but it was Goldman who demonstrated how forceful a figure she might be. Her powerful sense of self made her a literary icon in her own writing and a literary character in the works of others. If she was not often a positive character, she was nevertheless a formidable one, whose silencing required ceaseless efforts.

Among the novels in which Goldman appears in fictional form are *The Warners* (1901), by Gertrude Potter Daniels, *By Bread Alone* (1901), by Isaac Kahn Friedman, *Toilers and Idlers* (1907), by John McMahon, and *Comrades,* by Thomas Dixon Jr. (1909). The authors speak from quite different points on the political spectrum, but for all of them she is what the critic and bibliographer Fay Blake calls "an obsessive symbol of evil" (61). Blake notes that the Goldman character is depicted as a tireless fomenter of trouble who nonetheless makes no headway with her devious schemes: "She plots violence out of sheer malice. She uses her sex appeal to ensnare co-conspirators. She finds the way infallibly to the heart of any dissension and fans it into an uncomfortable explosion.... And in all the novels she comes to a bad end" (62). Yet Blake also observes the curious irony that many of the novelists were sympathetic to a better future for the masses that was not entirely antithetical to Goldman's vision. It was her uninhibited manner and force that disturbed and enraged them. Thus, Blake concludes, "they kill her off, send her into wandering exile," or "consign her to a lonely outcast's life, as a warning and an object lesson" (63). Blake does not note that they sometimes adopt even more sinister ways of repressing the irrepressible Goldman—by making her into precisely the dependent woman she reviled, a submissive wife and mother, and a pitiable female who relies emotionally on her male partner. Some of the novels attribute power to her as a fanatical schemer and effective rabble-rousing speech-maker, some acknowledge her aversion to marriage, but none depicts her as a prominent advocate of sexual autonomy for women or as an influential thinker.

Of the four novels that recreate Goldman, the two that vilify her most (Daniels's *Warners* and Dixon's *Comrades*) are also those that depict industrial conflict as part of an atavistic process whereby males and females revert to the purportedly essential behavior of their gender. The Goldman figure in each is introduced as a radical associate of a violent revolutionary man, and initially as an eloquent platform speaker and sexually independent lover. In each novel, as men and women revert to their "true" natures, the "new" woman who is an active, assertive individual becomes more passive, vulnerable, and dependent. Since womanliness, for both Daniels and Dixon, is at odds with self-sufficiency and intellectual militancy, they turn the Goldman figure into a pathetic victim, driven and destroyed by her emotional ties to her lover. Friedman, too, presents his Goldman surrogate as alien and anomalous, a person who has no place in a world where men are strong and protective and women weak and vulnerable. Friedman does not punish this incongruous figure so much as make her finally irrelevant. Even McMahon, who presents a somewhat more appealing female rebel, nonetheless finds her endorsement of violence "darkly problematical," and finally leaves her alone and estranged from society (171). All of the novels associate the anarchist woman with a certain exotic foreignness in name, manners, or appearance—her ethnicity reinforces her sexual tendency to emotionalism rather than rationality. All of them juxtapose her to a more wholesome and traditional antitype—in every case a white, Anglo-Saxon, native-born man who also happens, in three of the four novels, to be the son of a wealthy businessman who is converted to a philanthropic interest in workers' welfare. Thus improvements in the workers' lot are assured by the powers that be, and the aggressive female outsider is safely humiliated or excluded.

The only one of the four novels that lacks a redemptive scion from the privileged classes is *The Warners: An American Story of Today*, by Gertrude Potter Daniels, a book whose highly derivative narrative is a reductive and peculiar mix of elements of Horatio Alger and Frank Norris. Its protagonist, Cyrus Warner, is an ambitious orphan boy who begins life selling papers and blacking boots on city streets, later works doggedly as a factory hand, and by the midpoint of the novel has acquired a pretty wife and daughter, an idyllic country cottage, and a productive oil well. However, when a business magnate tries to pressure Cyrus to sell his property, the affable protagonist suddenly finds himself in the grip of a wholly unanticipated regressive instinct "that makes beasts of men when the necessity forces" (91). Hereafter, the story of Cyrus and his wife imitates Norris's *McTeague* in the reversion of its characters to primitivism and the transformation of its setting from modern city to elemental wilderness. A parallel plot pursues the decline of a second pair of lovers: Kirby, the anarchist friend of Cyrus, and the Goldman figure, Ida Fisher, who is renowned for her speaking abilities. Ida is pretty, petite, and possessed of "an unhappy, haunted face. Her lips were constantly quivering; her eyes looked at everything beseechingly" (50). Ida's speech is "gentle," although Kirby reports that, on the stump, "she lammed the capitalists something immense. The Bloody Shirt dripped" (40). The initial inconsistencies between the private, vulnerable Ida and the feisty, public orator grow more extreme and incredible as the novel develops. Daniels seems literally incapable of fusing the incongruous notions of "female" and "anarchist" into a credible and consistent character. After Kirby and Ida's marriage, he becomes a drunken and tyrannical husband who brutally exploits his fragile wife and their sickly child by insisting that Ida and their son participate in a potentially violent street demonstration. The "wretched" woman never thinks of disobeying him, and she and the child are killed after a bomb is thrown (171). The anarchist woman is thus depicted as a helpless sexual victim, despite her fiery rhetoric and revolutionary sentiments. Ultimately, the novel retreats entirely from any political concerns raised by urban industrial labor—it moves instead into a realm of atavistic violence and human endurance where essential instincts triumph. In this world of raw power and appetite, where only accident can thwart the brutality of natural law, there is certainly no place for the anomalous figure of the eloquent female anarchist.

In the same year as the publication of *The Warners* (1901), Isaac Kahn Friedman produced *By Bread Alone*, a more sophisticated novel of political ideas, if only because of Friedman's greater familiarity with the contemporary labor movement and with actual workplace experiences. The protagonist of this novel, as well as its indisputable hero, is Blair Carrhart, the handsome and intelligent son of a wealthy wholesale grocer, who decides to reject both his father's business and a possible career as a minister in order to rectify social injustice. He takes a job as a common laborer at the North-Western Rolling-Mills, he lives among Polish immigrants in urban tenements, and he discovers the dangerous working conditions of laboring people, as well as the harshness of their private lives. He also becomes familiar with various reform movements, from peaceable unionizing socialism to militant syndicalism and violent anarchism. Friedman explores institutions like the Catholic Church and the Settlement House movement in a novel that, while not exactly a *roman à clef*, nevertheless has many characters and incidents that allude to historical originals. The Haymarket bombing of 1886, the Homestead steel strike of 1892, the attempted assassination of Henry Clay Frick, and the characters of Goldman and Berkman all have echoes in the novel, although no single episode or character is explicitly paralleled.

The Goldman figure here is more ominous and forceful than Daniels's hysterical and pathetic character, although, in the end, almost as irrelevant to the welfare of the masses. Sophia Goldstein is a polyglot Russian with "a suggestion of cruelty, of hardness, of fanaticism about her long swarthy face" (91). Elsewhere her foreignness is emphasized in her strange physical features and her "savage black eyes" (97). She lives in a Polish slum where she is visited constantly by the aristocratic anarchist, La Vette, another anomalous character whose well-dressed figure is "strikingly out of place" in the working-class neighborhood (96). Goldstein and La Vette are portrayed as alien in intellect, class, and education from the workers, who respond almost ferally to their bloodcurdling rhetoric. Friedman, like Daniels, refuses to scrutinize the anarchists' theories of violence in his novel, a significant reluctance since his most powerful scenes focus on the extraordinary and capricious violence to which workers are daily exposed in the mills. He describes gory industrial accidents in language that might easily refer to an intentional anarchist bombing:

> The men, white with fear, scattered in all directions, yelling and crying as they ran. They could have gained but a few feet when there came a terrific crash; the building shook and tottered; the converters rocked on their trunnions. Sparks shot in every direction and burst with the roar of exploding shells against the walls, lighting the room ominously, appearing and disappearing through the heavy smoke like candle flames shining afar in a blinding mist. Screams and groans and shrieks of the wounded throbbed to heaven piteously. (116)

The repetition of such industrial accidents, followed promptly by the arrival of mill photographers and doctors who "coolly" go about their duties, suggests that the owners are engaged in callous calculations of injury and profit (117). Although Friedman does not endorse retaliatory violence, he extends great sympathy to workers, whom he depicts pityingly and condescendingly as wounded animals. However, the anarchists are excluded from any meaningful part in their world, La Vette as a bourgeois, and Sophia doubly estranged as a woman and an intellectual.

Friedman explores the gulf between the bestial existence of the working class and the life of the mind on several occasions in the novel, always with a sardonic reflection on those who view laborers from any perspective other than the immediate dramatic need to improve their physical conditions. While the anarchists are reviled for their sinister efforts to exploit workers for remote ideological goals, middle-class Settlement House workers who seek to encourage literacy and culture are also cruelly satirized for their self-delusion. A typical instance occurs at the opening celebrations of a neighborhood Settlement House where the reading room is staffed by "young ladies" and an "anemic young man, all glasses, no nose and a feminine voice" whose intention is "regenerating the laboring man in a month at the outermost" (279). The hero, Carrhart, disguised as a working man, cruelly parodies this effeminate literary weakling's fantasy that he is serving humble workers, eager for enlightenment. Carrhart tells the gullible young man of his nightly efforts to read Shakespeare, "when I came home so tired that I couldn't crawl. I spelled the words out by the aid of a candle-light. I might add that I saved enough money to purchase the work by going without my supper." When the messenger of culture replies that such a noble sacrifice must have been difficult, the hero's irony escalates: "Not so very. Two meals come easy by practice. Besides, I found nurture in the poetry, drank in his words and devoured his pages" (280). Friedman ridicules Romantic sentiment about awakening workers' minds when their stomachs are empty. His pragmatic socialism rejects the cultural idealism of the middle class as foolish and the revolutionary idealism of anarchists as dangerous. Sophia Goldstein's last appearance in the book is as a kind of savage harpy, "her black eyes snapping, her long prehensile fingers clutching," (457) as she urges her young lover on toward the assassination of the mill owner. When the assassination fails and the "deluded youth" is arrested, Sophia disappears, in another fictional erasure of Goldman's power, although one that apparently needed to be repeated again and again.

John McMahon's 1907 novel *Toilers and Idlers* provides a less unsympathetic look at the Goldman character, perhaps because the fictional Sonia Sofronsky is more obviously a blend of Goldman and some of the other immigrant women who were becoming active in unionizing the New York garment industry. McMahon's Sonia is petite and curly-haired, at nineteen already president of the Ladies Shirt Waist Union, and an avid lover of reading who, when asked if she has a degree, says, "Yes, from the sewing machine" (54). The details suggest that her model is not only Goldman but also union activists like Clara Lemlich, later a leader of the Shirtwaist Uprising (in 1909–10), and Pauline Newman, who would claim that her college education was at "the Triangle Waist Company."[9] Like Friedman's novel, *Toilers and Idlers* has a wealthy protagonist, Rensen, who decides on a whim to answer a "Man Wanted" advertisement. He takes a job in the Atlantic Foundry to find out what it is like to be a worker there: later he discovers that the business is among his own properties. Rensen finds that he likes both the work and the education it brings, including his acquaintanceship with Sonia, who has a "boyish beauty" (52) and a powerful and allusive manner of speech. McMahon, like Friedman, explores the place of the life of the mind in his toilers. Although he satirizes the artistic affectations of the privileged, and Sonia argues that it would be preferable to have Settlement Houses in the neighborhoods of the rich, so that *they* might learn about the culture of the poor, the novel permits a more fertile exchange among classes and ideologies than *By Bread Alone*. Despite the repeated hints that Sonia, as a working-class woman, a thinker, and a proponent of violence, is an incongruous creature (signified often in the ambiguous male/female imagery for her), the hero, Rensen, admires the "spirit and knowledge of this young ardent girl" (102). When Rensen argues for the evolution of a new society, Sonia replies, "A child is born all at once. It does not breathe, digest food and circulate blood by steps, but all together. So must the new society come into being after violently breaking every bond with its parent" (169–70). Rensen finds this response "darkly problematical, a tragic maze," but this is a considerably more sanguine reaction than Friedman's encapsulation of his anarchist woman in witch-like metaphors (171). When Sonia's lover, Zienski, is killed during an act of sabotage at the foundry, she is forced to move on; thus, once again she is eliminated from the final scenes of cooperation between capitalists and pragmatic unionizing moderates. Her fictional fate lies finally in her irrelevance.

Thomas Dixon Jr.'s 1909 dystopian novel *Comrades* is the least historically grounded of this group of novels in dealing with Goldman's anarchism, in that Catherine, her fictional manifestation, participates in a planned socialist community that is subsidized by the wealthy father of the novel's allegorically named hero, Norman Worth. Norman's father wishes to demonstrate to his son the inevitable failure of idealist social schemes, so the utopian society is conceived as a kind of puppet state, orchestrated by one powerful man, and thus quite incompatible with Goldman's anti-authoritarian convictions. The conflict at the heart of the novel is between gradual and pragmatic social reforms and an instantly imposed socialism that ignores the obstacles in human nature. Thus the utopian socialists find, like the Puritans who attempt a model settlement in Hawthorne's *Scarlet Letter*, that one of their first institutions must be a jail, rapidly followed by other punitive measures. Dixon satirizes broadly the idealists' efforts to gratify competing individual desires within a tightly knit community. He also anticipates the tyrannical social controls Goldman herself found when she went to the Soviet Union, but the novel is most distant from reality in associating Catherine, her fictional manifestation, with a belief in repressive dictatorship and in depicting Catherine primarily as a woman scorned in love.

Catherine is the "affinity" wife of the scheming leader, Herman Wolf (who has distinct physical resemblances to Goldman's early lover Johann Most). She is also the surrogate mother of a beautiful young woman whom Wolf intends will displace her. Thus the bold, real-life avatar of independent womanhood is portrayed fictionally as both proxy wife and proxy mother. Catherine is notable initially for her showmanship, for her easy command of the platform, her fluency in foreign languages, and her history of industrial activism and imprisonment for her beliefs: she "had led two great strikes of women workers in New York and had been arrested, convicted, and sentenced twice to the penitentiary for exciting riots" (50). She is learned, austere, even fanatical, and wholly devoted to Wolf and their cause. This fictional decision to bind her utterly in ideology and emotional loyalty to Wolf (as opposed to Goldman's public horse-whipping of Most and her decision to take other lovers) makes it possible for Dixon to transform her into a conventional jealous virago.[10] The next step is to reduce her to a formulaic victim, whimpering, caressing, begging, and finally gasping, "I give up" in "a feeble, childish voice" (312). Catherine is punished for her intellectual and political overreaching by being rejected as a woman, as a lover and a mother, and by being abandoned in humiliation. To reduce the utterly nonconforming Goldman to the monstrous cliché of Catherine is a somewhat ambiguous literary victory for Dixon, since it necessitates not only the distortion of the original but also, less acceptably, the betrayal of his own imagined character, who was originally a figure of dignity and stature. However, Dixon's novel, like Daniels's, is suffused with an atavism that is attributed pervasively to foreign ideologues and native American workers alike. After he has abolished all semblance of democracy in the socialist community, Hermann Wolf affirms that "there's but one power that counts now in the world of realities in which we live—the elemental force of tooth, and nail, and claw" (312); indeed, it is eventually the army that overcomes the socialists with volleys of bullets in "a withering fire" (319).

Although Catherine, unlike Goldman, has no particular association with artistic and literary people, Dixon includes them in his dystopia, where their mental acumen quickly capitulates to brute physical discipline. The poet, Roland Adair, speaks eloquently against tyranny and prejudice until he is "flogged unmercifully"; then he quickly becomes "a mere cog in the wheel of things" (300). Dixon assumes an inevitable conflict between the pragmatic needs of society and the vain and aesthetic indulgences of people eager to escape from "real" work to the gratifications of culture. A man assigned to cleaning drains complains, "I came here to climb mountain heights and find my way among the stars. You have sent me back to the sewers" (161). When members of the community are given the option (as in Bellamy's *Looking Backward*) of choosing their occupations, of the thousand members, 175 men and 63 women wish to be editors, and the majority of women between the ages of fourteen and thirty-five wish to go on the stage.

Dixon has the same sardonic attitude toward Romantic aspirations to culture as Friedman and McMahon, but with less sympathy for social change. Catherine is presented as unique and unnatural in her foreignness, her love of books, her skepticism about marriage, and her labor militancy, despite the fact that such attributes were becoming increasingly prevalent during the first decade of the century when these novels were published. Ardis Cameron suggests that "the strident woman radical" evoked a horror born of her incongruous combination of supposedly opposed qualities of femininity and fierceness, and certainly the fictional portraits of Goldman suggest that she was almost literally inconceivable as a woman and an anarchist (69). McMahon, in his Sonia Sofronsky, comes closest to acknowledging the connection between Goldman's extravagant ideas and conduct and the attitudes of a much larger class of immigrant working women. However, even in Sonia's case, she, like Ida, Sophia, and Catherine, is punished for her unconventional ideas by being subjected to the most conventional of female fictional fates—she is left abandoned and alone. Only when the unique figure of Goldman was replaced in the public eye by more typical immigrant women who participated in 1909–10 in the Shirtwaist Strike, and who suffered the horror of the Triangle Fire in 1911, was it possible for fiction writers to depict a more sympathetic version of self-reliant working women. Even then, their literary tastes and habits continued to raise concerns about where these anomalous creatures might belong in a society ever more stratified by fine discriminations of status and cultural affinities among its members.

The flamboyant assertiveness of Emma Goldman as the apotheosis of the new immigrant working woman brought her to fictional bad ends, but these novels were not the only ones to explore the new industrial "rebel girl." A significant number of novelists described the circumstances and hopes of working-class women less infamous than Goldman, who nevertheless insisted on their subjectivity and a sense of their rights. Middle-class authors, and some from the immigrant community itself, portrayed the new women workers and produced a more dynamic version of working-class characters than had emerged from the fiction of the "lay theologians" of the late nineteenth century. These earlier authors had avoided the intractable qualities of their working-class subjects by placing their desires for change and transcendence in a context of religious otherworldliness. The novels that appeared in the early years of the twentieth century were more open to depicting working women who led strikes, picketed, doubted God, challenged marriage, went to jail, and edited and wrote provocative newspapers. Their ardent advocacy on behalf of class and gender was even beginning to be depicted as spirited and admirable, although none of the fictively approved workers had the extreme intellectual acumen or political subversiveness of a Goldman. Clara Lemlich, the enthusiastic organizer of the shirtwaist makers, appeared in a variety of fictional manifestations, and proved a more acceptable female activist. Like Goldman, she was an outspoken Jewish immigrant (though not an anarchist) but as a petite and fashion-conscious girl and, later, as a devoted wife and mother, she did not challenge conventions so blatantly.[11] Lemlich made one of her earliest fictional appearances in 1907 in McMahon's *Toilers and Idlers*, and with greater frequency after the Shirtwaist Strike in 1909–10. However, even before her first appearance, novelists were exploring the intellectual aspirations of more ordinary working women than Emma Goldman and their ambiguous relationship to their more erudite sympathizers from other classes. The desire for a life of the mind or for a vocation as an artist was still considered incongruous in the working-class woman, but it was beginning to emerge as a theme in fiction about her and a focus of controversy about her progress toward self-knowledge.

Vida Scudder, a Wellesley professor, pursued the question of a full life for working women in her 1903 novel *A Listener in Babel*. She fictionalized and expanded some of her own experiences as a Settlement House worker and female intellectual in a novel set among the immigrants of the imaginary community of Brenton, "a thinly-veiled Boston version of the famous Chicago venture" at Hull House (Hapke, *Tales* 57). The protagonist is a prosperous young painter and art historian, Hilda Lathrop, who is socially progressive in her attitudes and something of a freethinker in religion. The novel, true to its title, presents a series of arguments among advocates of contending values—of the business world, religion, unionizing, socialism, and anarchism—whereby they seek to influence workers. Hilda's particular interest is in the aesthetic and intellectual experiences of women workers. She attempts on one occasion to teach a sensitive immigrant worker, who has already memorized Wordsworth's "Lucy" poems, that she is capable of dwelling on a higher plane than her tangible surroundings by ascending into her "mind-sky," a place peopled by beautiful thoughts. The immigrant responds to what Scudder labels "transcendentalism made easy" by admitting that she wants beauty in her life as well as in her head. Scudder's novel (like those of Davis, Phelps, and Alcott decades earlier) explores the gaps in sensibility between educated young ladies and aspiring workers (229). Katie, the poetry-loving worker, relishes the mindful pleasures of language and literature, but she also envies the bourgeois marriages and comfortable households that more privileged feminists are trying to escape. That Katie might prefer to be in a pretty parlor with a baby in her arms rather than a laundry with Wordsworth in her head is hardly a rejection of Romantic idealism, and Scudder does not suggest that working women would prefer marriage to paid labor (although some did). However, she acknowledges that liberated and privileged women may be making assumptions based on what they feel is best for workers rather than trusting them to know what is true for themselves.

A similar critique of middle-class intellectuals, even those most sympathetic to the working class, occurs in Florence Converse's *Children of Light* (1913), which is dedicated to Scudder. Converse, like Scudder, satirizes her bourgeois idealists with their childlike naiveté and self-indulgence, but like Scudder, she makes these genteel reformers the focus of her novel, while the strikes, violence, hunger, and disease of immigrant workers provide only the sensational and colorful context. *The Children of Light* is a somewhat mannered novel, filled with fey letters and poems written by leftist-leaning literati, all of whom dwell in realms of possibility that only occasionally collide with material reality. Although the book is divided into two parts, "Celestial Light" and "Common Day," suggesting a turn from idealism to realism, at the end the bourgeois revolutionaries continue to pen their *aubades* and edit their papers amid labor violence, death, and imprisonment, undeterred by sacrifice and suffering.

The novel opens in a late nineteenth-century New Hope community that evokes Fruitlands and Louisa May Alcott's satire "Transcendental Wild Oats," in the utter obliviousness of its residents to the abysmal failure of their venture. The narrator is a high-principled and literary eleven-year-old girl, Clara, whose precocious innocence is an effective means of exposing the dubious value of living on cowpeas and drinking typhoid-contaminated water as a way of carrying the "leaven of cooperation into the great world of competition" (26). The notion that such elevated purposes are merely a form of decadent child's play is furthered in Clara's cousins, Cyrus and Lucian, who imagine themselves followers of St. Francis, and their mother, Pauline, who indulges in pastoral activities after the manner of Marie Antoinette. Converse implies a charming but foolish moral equivalency in the fantasies of the utopians, the children, and the pampered woman, all eagerly embracing self-denying schemes of self-fulfillment. The "Celestial Light" portion of the novel ends with the foreclosure of the mortgage at New Hope and the evolution of the children into young adults, committed to poetry and socialism. The coming of "Common Day" might be expected to moderate their enthusiasm and precocity amid the travails of organizing strikes, relief efforts, and political electioneering, but the idealists are irrepressible and oblivious amid hostility, rivalry, and violence.

Converse presents the immigrant working class as pragmatic and goal-oriented, compared to the impractical speculations of those educated more thoroughly in Marx and Ruskin. Bertha Aarons, a fictional version of Clara Lemlich, delegates women to organize the union in various sweatshops, while the poet, Lucian, searches for the perfect motto for their new periodical. When he begins to declaim his choice, "We hurry onward to extinguish hell," he is patiently interrupted by the immigrant anarchist, Lazarus Samson, trying to discuss everyday finances (155). Converse concurs with Scudder in emphasizing a pragmatic, community-oriented materialism in her workers that is quite at odds with the Romantic selfhood of their would-be mentors. She finally endorses socialism as a movement in which practical workers and dreamy intellectuals can march together, but the class differences between realist workers and visionary intellectuals means that the former make social and the latter artistic progress. Converse's workers, both men and women, do not aspire to sublimity in art or religion, even though these come ultimately to be endorsed as the noblest paths to full humanity. Thus a novel that began with a playful mockery of such idealism comes in the end to affirm it but to assume that the new immigrant proletariat must first struggle with more tangible priorities.

James Oppenheim also chose, in his novel *The Nine-Tenths* (1911), to place a well-educated, native-born, middle-class American, with powerful family connections to older American radical traditions, in the context of the new immigrant radicalism of the women who led the Shirtwaist Strike. Oppenheim's protagonist, the printer Joe Blaine, runs his business in a New York City building that houses a hat-making factory on its top floor. Blaine is the son of a mother who was nurtured in the Boston radicalism of the 1860s and belonged to an abolitionist generation that drew its idealism from Whitman, Whittier, and Longfellow. This earlier tradition permitted its women to be the inspirers and encouragers of male sacrifice and heroism in the Civil War, but not themselves to be participants in the great social cataclysm of their time. Now, in the early twentieth century, the same mother encourages her son to enter the "new war" in the tenements and sweatshops (60). However, this time she avers, "I'll go with you" and begins the process of escaping her "flat, stale, meaningless" existence by immersing herself in her son's labor education and in the immigrant life of the city (60). When a fire modeled after the one in the Triangle Shirtwaist Company destroys the hat factory and takes the lives of many of the young women workers, Joe abandons his business, moves with his mother to Greenwich Village, and begins to publish a newspaper, the *Nine-Tenths*, dedicated to the cause of workers.

Joe's mother's earlier democratic idealism is reborn among the "new women"—Irish, Italian, and Jewish immigrants—whose outspokenness and vitality are juxtaposed to her older tradition of female integrity and moral example. The new breed of women is represented by Sally Heffer, who demonstrates "the new emancipation; the exodus of woman from the home to the battle-fields of the world; the willingness to fight in the open, shoulder to shoulder with men; the advance of a sex that now demanded a broader, freer life, a new health, a home built up on comradeship and economic freedom" (168). Sally, one of several Clara Lemlich figures in the novel, is a hat factory worker who makes a passionate speech at a mass meeting of workers at Carnegie Hall and writes on "the woman question" for the *Nine-Tenths*. Other qualities of the fiery young strike leader are given to Fannie Lemick, a worker who escapes the fire, and Rhona Hemlitz, who is arrested as a picketer during the Shirtwaist Strike and serves a sentence (like Goldman) in the workhouse on Blackwell's Island. Oppenheim's interest in these intense and daring young women is conveyed through the perspective of Joe Blaine, and their impact on his political awakening is dramatic. However, although Joe is powerfully attracted to the emancipated Sally, he chooses in the end to marry a more conventional and restrained schoolteacher who is not nearly such a new woman. His mother reflects in disappointment on the rejected worker: "She was hardy and self-contained, and would never be dependent.... Sometimes Joe's mother felt that Sally was a woman of the future, and that, with such, marriage would become a finer and freer union" (289). Joe's mother, however, proves more progressive than her son in accepting changing sexual roles; despite his admiration of the "new" woman, he is more at ease and familiar with the "true" one.

Oppenheim's immigrant women are feisty and independent but still very much objectified through Joe's outside perspective. Only in Arthur Bullard's *Comrade Yetta* (1913) is there a serious imaginative effort to explore the subjective awareness of the new immigrant working woman, once again modeled on Clara Lemlich. Like *The Children of Light* and *The Nine-Tenths*, the novel has a central concern with relationships between working women and middle-class intellectuals and sympathizers; and once again a newspaper, the *Clarion*, becomes the location for exploring personal and political encounters among them. There is a distinct suggestion in Bullard's novel, consonant with that in Converse's, that privileged intellectuals are engaged with socialism and labor activism as a way of finding and fulfilling themselves as individuals, while for the newly engaged workers, the work of organizing, writing, and speaking for the labor movement is a commitment to class and gender solidarity, with less concern for the self. Although Clara in *The Children of Light* affirms from childhood a creed of cooperation, as an adult she still wonders "How would it feel...to have a heart big enough to ache over something not purely personal" (169). The well-to-do women who support the Women's Trade Union League in *Comrade Yetta* have an array of "purely personal" motives: some like the idea of being thought eccentric; one has "morbid instincts" that "were tickled by the stories of desperate misery which circulated in the League"; and all are attracted by the prospect of making the acquaintance of one of the grandest of New York's society ladies (125). These characters are not the decadent bourgeoisie that will populate the proletarian novels of the Great Depression, two decades later, but Bullard hints that it is the atypical, the eccentric, and perhaps the misfits among them who are intent on allying with the workers. By comparison Yetta, the working-class heroine, is healthy, wholesome, and normal. She leads a walkout from the sweatshop not because of her own predicament but because of her sympathy for workers who are suffering more than she is. Her impulsive action is followed by her union-directed education in economics, philosophy, and the organizing tactics that will fully develop in her a new class consciousness. However, it is significant that the seed that led to her commitment to the workers was planted long before the catalytic strike incident, during her childhood reading of *Les Misérables*. Thus her literary temperament, as well as her workplace experience, shapes her response to reality.

Bullard explores the dynamic nature of the consciousness of his working-class characters, with the young immigrant Yetta representing the best possibilities of growth from ignorant and exhausted sweatshop worker into educated and disciplined labor organizer. Yetta, unlike Clara, does indeed have a "heart big enough to ache over something not purely personal," but Bullard effectively demonstrates how such a heart may be shrunk to a preoccupation with the immediate personal contingencies of survival (like the older and weaker women in the factory) or expanded, in an atmosphere of study, companionship, and basic comfort to a life that combines private satisfactions of mind and body with service to the larger mass of humanity. Yetta's first awakening to the possibilities of escape from the grim dreariness of factory life is inspired by her cousin Rachel's flight with a young man; and for a while, Yetta aspires to follow this route. She is rescued from making a foolish decision by her impulsive purchase of a ticket for the Women's Trade Union League ball. There she finds herself "hypnotized by the pack of humanity about her. She was becoming one with that crowd of struggling toilers, one with the vast multitude of workers" (78). Under the influence of the occasion and her first taste of champagne, Yetta makes an impromptu speech that draws the attention of union organizers, who take her into their circle and set about the business of educating her for the workers' cause.

To the Women's Trade Union League, Yetta is a potential orator and organizer to be cultivated and led to serve their sincerely held ideals. However, to the nineteen-year-old orphan, these new friends are the source not only of an awakening to a cause but of a dramatic new consciousness of her own existence as an individual. The head of the League sends Yetta a letter with some randomly selected pamphlets in it; "to Yetta, the letter seemed importance itself. It was the first she had ever received" (111). She pores over the pamphlets, taking their comments personally, imagining herself the subject of their criticisms. While the labor intellectuals engage in a debate as to whether her education should fit her for organizing garment workers or form her mind, whether she should read Marx and Engels or Marcus Aurelius, economics or biology, Yetta sits thrilled and fascinated. For her it is an "immense event," while for her mentors it is merely another item on the day's agenda. Bullard stops short of suggesting that Yetta is an objectified victim of their calculating expediency, as later novelists critical of unionizing tactics would do.[12] However, he raises important questions about the individual working woman's consciousness and about the sense of personal significance that comes to her along with her group aware-ness of class and gender. Sarah Eisenstein, in her study of the emerging consciousness of working-class women at the beginning of the twentieth century, comments on the paradoxes of the situation:

> Although they recognized and appreciated the importance of unions in establishing decent wages and working conditions, women tended to stress other factors in describing what was important to them about belonging in a union.
>
> They emphasized, first of all, that participation in the union developed their intellectual abilities and broadened their percep-tion of themselves and the world. (29)

However, although Yetta finds a life of the mind among books a very appeal-ing one, in the end Bullard emphasizes her service to her fellow workers as her real act of self-discovery and her delight in her husband and children as her highest joy. Laura Hapke astutely calls this tactic the "Victorianizing" of Clara Lemlich (*Labor's Text* 153).

Yetta's marriage to the editor of the socialist *Clarion* and the birth of her two children parallels Clara Lemlich's marriage in 1913 to Joe Shav-elson (a printer) and anticipates her combination of family life and labor activism. Since the real Lemlich's life and the fictive Yetta's life were not sexually unconventional, Bullard turns to other characters to hint at a new openness to different sexual mores. Two intellectuals, Walter Longman and Beatrice Karner, engage in a happily unmarried relationship, and Mabel Train, the leader of the Women's Trade Union League, lives in an unspoken, apparently lesbian partnership with Eleanor Mead, affectionately known as "Saph," supposedly for her sapphire blue eyes but clearly suggesting Sappho (100). The working-class characters in the novel tend to be given the more conservative attitudes toward sex, and Bullard seems reluctant, despite Yetta's newly aroused consciousness, to permit her a sexual awaken-ing, except in the fulfillment of motherhood. Laura Hapke senses a general tendency, especially among male novelists, to domesticate the female striker, although this may well follow from their initial choice of Clara Lemlich as a model (*Labor's Text* 153). Ironically, despite her acceptable family image,

Lemlich's life was "wracked by conflicts" between her domestic and public lives (Orleck 219). Bullard's conclusion, by contrast, allows Yetta a perfect fusion of private love and labor activism. The young woman who dreamed of combining a life of the mind with a life of action in the world ends by arguing that "it all seems to centre around the babies. They've given Socialism a new meaning to me, have brought it all nearer, made it more intimate and personal, more closely woven into myself " (445). Such a definition of selfhood is a somewhat oblique fictional resolution for the ambitions of the Thoreauvian young worker who had "venerated books" and manifested an "all-consuming hunger" for knowledge (216). While he is initially very sympathetic to the woman worker's pursuit of a life of the mind, Bullard ultimately segregates it from a working-class life and substitutes a modernized yoking of union activism and domesticity.

Perhaps the most remarkable novel to derive from the life of Lemlich and the Shirtwaist Strike was *The Diary of a Shirtwaist Striker* (1910), by Theresa Malkiel, herself a Jewish immigrant garment worker and later a union organizer. Her book was an act of surprising literary boldness by a Russian-born woman who arrived in New York in 1891 as a seventeen-year-old. The novel is narrated in the first-person voice of a native-born American girl who has gradually been drawn into strike activity through her close observation of immigrant Jewish activists. To have written the book as a personal immigrant diary would itself have suggested the self-awareness that Lucy Larcom and Harriet Robinson recalled in the first generation of New England factory women. However, Malkiel takes a more audacious fictional step by entering the consciousness of an imaginary American girl who is turning her gaze on the immigrant outsiders; it is a complicated and ironic literary game that reveals a certain confidence that the outsider may be capable of the more complex double vision. As a member of the Socialist Party of America and the Women's Trade Union League, Malkiel had to steer a careful course between her own commitments to women's rights and the more conservative positions of her party and also between her own outlook on sexual mores, which was traditional and Victorian, and more radical feminists' campaigns for sexual liberation. However, as a fictional experimenter, she was decidedly adventurous in assuming the voice and perspective of an "authentically American" working girl.[13]

The *Diary's* narrator, the Christian, native-born Mary, is initially very conscious of the differences between herself and the Lower East Side Jewish women in the factory. She notes their long, bushy hair, emotional excesses, and extravagant rhetoric about wage slavery, which is distinctly alien both to her more decorous manners and her satisfaction in being a better-paid, free-born American. However, Mary also senses an enviable vitality in the workers when they discuss going out on strike, and her participation in their activities makes her feel "like a real grown-up person" (81). This new-found self-awareness pervades her strike diary, suggested effectively in her gushy, gossipy, celebrity-infused style: "It's strange, when you come to think of all the noise us girls have made for the last two days. Why, the Vanderbilts themselves ain't in it any more—the people are too busy with us" (83). She notes that "it really feels good to be somebody," and later, when she attends a mass meeting of strikers at the Hippodrome, this new-found selfhood even takes on transcendent qualities: "I felt as though I had been born anew and became a power" (83, 106). Her sense of belonging to a community of women workers even causes her to think for the first time about whether her real affiliation is with her church or her work community. Midway through the strike, she goes to the Church of the Ascension and hears a sermon that moves her because, she says, "It wasn't about religion at all, nor about heaven nor hell; just about the men and women we meet with every day of our lives, the injustices we are suffering under and the hope for a better future" (136). On Christmas Day, Mary makes a choice and goes to the picket line instead of the church. Originally, she had resisted picketing as a degrading activity, but when she is forced to confront newspaper advertisements for "hands wanted," she decides that it is employers who degrade working women by depriving them of their identity as a "mother's daughter, or brother's sister, or Miss So-and-So" in favor of "a good, swift pair of hands.... We don't count at all" (85–86). Mary recovers this lost identity by acting for the good of the group, since, she argues, "it teaches us self-respect" (88).

Mary's feminism begins to emerge simultaneously with her sense of class solidarity in this very didactic novel. Her father, himself a union man, tells her that striking is not "a woman's place." Ironically he helps to bring her to an understanding of her equality: "Ain't I of the same flesh and bone as a man?...I walk under the same sky and tread the same earth as men do. I, too, have senses, moods and reasons" (100). She comes to see the need for women's suffrage, although she concedes it is lower on the agenda than the strike: "us girls have something else to think of just now" (104). She even begins to rethink the advantages of marriage to her boy-friend Jim: "I was never so sure that a working girl gained so very much by getting married" (134). However, in the somewhat utopian conclusion, Jim becomes a convert to the women's cause and to Mary's feminism, and Mary then proposes marriage to him. Mary's feminism expands consider-ably during her time in prison, when she scrubs floors in the workhouse with prostitutes from whom she shrinks at first in horror. She tells one of them proudly, "I didn't want to work for starvation wages and struck; that's the crime I've committed," to which the girl replies, "An' I couldn't go on livin' on starvation wages any longer and had to sell my body instead of my hands" (183). Mary immediately regrets her hasty judgment of other wom-en's lives, although her tolerance and fellow-feeling operate only when she looks down, rather than up, the social scale. She grows increasingly resent-ful of the "mink brigade" of wealthy women associated with the Women's Trade Union League. The timorous gratitude of working women in earlier novels for the sympathy of their rich sisters is revised in this novel so that the rich Mrs. Belmont, who rents the Hippodrome for the union's mass meeting, and others of her philanthropic kind "ought to be thankful to us girls for giving them a chance to do a good deed" (104). Wealthy women get no credit and a good deal of blame for their interference in workers' lives, and there is no significant middle-class intellectual figure in the novel. Perhaps the day-by-day format of a worker's account of a highly dynamic three-month strike obviates the exploration of any larger context of ideas, or any broader education for the heroine. Her immersion in immediate actions like ordering placards, holding meetings, getting parade permits, and organizing pickets is the most vital step in altering her consciousness.

Certainly Malkiel's *Diary* is an interesting advance in literary form, as a working woman's narrative that does not obliterate the worker's consciousness in favor of assumptions about the greater objectivity or sophistication of a middle-class perspective. The novel is confident (if not always accomplished) in suggesting the voice of a young working woman whose sensibilities have been shaped by her culture and her peers. Her account of the work stoppage in her shop reveals both the youthfulness of the girls and the naiveté of their action: "Before you could say Jack Robinson we all rose, slipped on our duds and marched down the stairs, shouting, yelling and giggling about our walkout, as they called it" (82). When she is in the workhouse, Mary reports with a certain childish glee on a fight that breaks out between one of the prisoners and one of the matrons or "watchdogs": "In an instant, before the other dogs had time to get near them, she threw her opponent down on the floor and gave her a few digs with the feet. I could have laughed and cried at the sight" (188). Even her correctly socialist and feminist attitudes toward conspicuous consumption and fashionable clothes are occasionally suffused with a certain defensive longing for material indulgences: "I don't know as anybody could blame us for wanting pretty things—we're still young and would like to appear to our best advantage" (135). Such remarks seem quite consistent with Clara Lemlich's comment on the Shirtwaist Strike to reporters: "We like new hats as well as any other young women. Why shouldn't we?" (qtd. in Glenn 165). Malkiel does not give Mary a childhood acquaintance with Victor Hugo, or a longing to read poetry, or even a prison introduction to Thoreau. Her mind is not attuned in these ways to the literariness of the earliest factory women of the nineteenth century, or even that of the Jewish immigrants who led the labor activism. However, her dramatic encounter with other working women provokes her to become a literary woman, in the sense of authoring her own life and the lives of others in a piece of imaginative writing. Mary is thus a version of Malkiel herself, a working-class woman who is empowered by her ability to write. More important, however, is the fact that she is an invented character quite distinct from her author and thus testimony to Malkiel's confidence that she may speak for others outside her own group. The capacity to find a voice is a notable stage in the self-assertion of marginalized people, but the assumption of the multiple perspectives that imaginative literature requires is a triumph of an entirely different order.

Theresa Malkiel, like Emma Goldman and many of the generation of activist Jewish immigrants to which they belonged, was a public speaker before she was a writer. Both women used platform oratory to advance a vision of a differently ordered society and to promote changes in attitudes toward law, government, property, and gender. However, Goldman, Malkiel, and many of the most notable members of their generation—like Rose Schneiderman, Clara Lemlich, Fannia Cohn, and Pauline Newman—also interested themselves in very different uses of language from these public and didactic purposes, uses that affected individual consciousness more directly than communal awareness and that were literary and intellectual rather than polemical and doctrinaire.[14] Historians of these female immigrant factory workers have repeatedly noted their avid pursuit of the life of the mind and, in particular, their absorption in literature as readers, critics, editors, and authors. Like the New England farmers' daughters who had poured into the Lowell mills several generations earlier, these later working women were stimulated to a new kind of self-awareness by their industrial employment as well as provoked to rebellion against it. They came to the factories believing, according to Annelise Orleck, that education was the "key to independence from all masters" (20), but they also sought education in order to know themselves or, in the words of Anzia Yezierska, to become "a person" (qtd. in Glenn 220). Thus, when they had opportunities for learning they chose to read works of literature, to pursue courses in art appreciation in their workers' schools and study groups, and to write fiction and even literary criticism.[15] Orleck comments on their reading: "Reveling in beautiful language and debating difficult ideas made them feel that they had defeated those who would reduce them to machines" (41). Sarah Eisenstein notes the premium women put on developing their intellectual abilities and broadening their sense of themselves and their world. She reports that women who participated in unions "insisted that the most important thing about the union was that it made them think," an interesting inversion of the notion that raising the workers' consciousness would bring them to the union (30).

The reiterated emphasis on self-awareness, on the intellect as the antithesis of the machine, and on the importance of being defined fully as a person all recall the urgency of the discovery of "mind amongst the spindles" in the 1840s and the dismay of Harriet Farley when the young Lucy Larcom submitted a poem to the *Lowell Offering* entitled "Complaint of a Nobody." In a brief lapse of her literary sophistication, the distressed Farley tried to reassure the magazine's readers that the factory girl could not possibly have meant to "intimate that she is *a nobody*" (3: 207). Indeed she was right—Larcom was demonstrating one of the most powerful affirmations of her identity, the capacity not merely to think, to find a voice, and to write a poem but also to transcend herself in an imaginative identification and communion with others, even people who thought they were nobodies. Not many women, either from the mills of Lowell or the sweatshops of New York, were able to achieve the accomplished artistry of a Larcom, but in their practice of imaginative writing and reading, they could engage in the kind of intellectual exchange that verified how much more they were than "hands only." For the fictional Mercy Winthrop, her part in publishing a New England factory magazine "aroused and inflamed" in her bosom "every impulse of womanhood" (Lee, 204), and in a similarly ecstatic vein, Emma Goldman recounted that even after years of public speaking, when she first published her writing in *Mother Earth*, "I walked on air" (*Living My Life* 377).

It is from the accounts of these working women who *wrote* that we also get a sense of the much larger group of workers who *read* and of the importance of that experience for them. Harriet Robinson was one among many Lowell authors who made lists of the books and periodicals read in factory boardinghouses. The fictional accounts of Lowell in the popular novels of the day testify equally to the appetite of operatives for literature of every kind, as does the necessity for factory rules banning books in the workplace. Sixty years after reading was forbidden at Lowell, Pauline Newman read Dickens, George Eliot, Thomas Hood, and Shelley with her fellow workers at the Triangle Shirtwaist Factory; Clara Lemlich walked from the factory daily to read in the East Broadway branch of the New York Public Library; Rose Schneiderman formed a lifelong taste for literature after reading Zola in her Yiddish evening paper; and Fannia Cohn taught her workmates in sleeve-making shops to read and write. Cohn then went on to develop schools for working-class women whose chief aspiration, she believed, was "for personal development through education."[16] Emma Goldman recalled her lovers according to the books she had read with them: Racine, Corneille, and Molière with Ed Brady, Strindberg and Nietzsche with Max Baginski, and Kipling with Ben Reitman (*Living My Life* 188, 239, 425). She judged the prisons where she was incarcerated by the quality of their libraries, even becoming involved in a "silly prison flirtation" with the librarian on Blackwell's Island because the prison library "had some good literature, including the works of George Sand, George Eliot, and Ouida" (*Living My Life* 145).

Not all working-class readers, of course, were subscribing to literary magazines or tackling Nietzsche or even Zola. A chorus of contempt and anxiety about the low quality of much of working women's reading runs through the accounts of it by both insiders and outsiders. In the 1850s and 1860s, the earliest novels about factory workers created frequent plot links between a woman's taste for salacious French fiction and her own inevitable sexual downfall. Even Harriet Robinson, late in the century, noted that she would no longer advise such "indiscriminate reading" among young women as she herself had engaged in as a Lowell operative (27). Dorothy Richardson, a middle-class woman who "descended" in disguise into the world of New York's working women in 1905, devotes a chapter of her subsequent nonfiction book *The Long Day* to their tastes in reading, noting a preference for "trashy fiction" that dealt with exotic romances and unlikely adventures (81). Richardson gives an amusedly condescending account of the workers' enthusiastic retelling of the plot of their favorite novel, "Little Rosebud's Lovers," and their lukewarm response to her advocacy of *Little Women*: "that's no story—that's just everyday happenings.... They just sound like real, live people" (86). However, contrary to Richardson's overtly censorious purpose, what emerges from her chapter is evidence of a working-class appetite for reading that is as omnivorous as her own, and an attention to textual details that is no less acute.

Richardson's chapter "In Which Phoebe and Mrs. Smith Hold Forth upon Music and Literature" opens with the question "Don't you never read no story-books?" put to her by a woman who looks at her "curiously out of her shrewd, snapping dark eyes" (75). After this first challenge, the working woman displays her vivid memory of her own reading, showing "increasing animation" as she engages in discussion, critical acumen, and even a sly ability to parody Richardson's genteel pronunciation (77). Finding that she is making little headway in persuading Mrs. Smith of the superiority of her own tastes and standards, Richardson abandons her losing verbal battle with her and turns to a description of what has been going on among other workers while the literary discussion was taking place:

> The quartet at the table immediately in front of us had been making inane doggerel rhymes upon the names of their workmates, telling riddles, and exchanging nasty stories with great gusto and frequent fits of wild laughter. At another table the forthcoming ball of the "Moonlight Maids" was under hot discussion, and at a very long table in front of the elevator they were talking in subdued voices about dreams and omens, making frequent reference to a greasy volume styled "The Lucky Dream Book." (86–87)

Elsewhere another group of women prepares to sing the "maudlin stanzas" of "The Fatal Wedding," "the rather pretty melody of which was not sufficient to redeem the banality of the words" (87). Inane doggerel, nasty stories, greasy books, maudlin stanzas, wild laughter, banal words—the revulsion of the refined from the vulgar permeates the author's language even as she describes working-class women who are clearly engaged in literary, imaginative, interpretive, and aesthetic activities. They are inventing and playing with language, retelling tales, disputing meaning, and enjoying the pleasures of rhythm and rhyme. Leonora O'Reilly, one of the most articulate of the working-class women who was at that time engaged in the formation of the Women's Trade Union League, reacted angrily to Richardson's "insufferably condescending" book because it made working women seem "picturesquely immoral, interestingly vulgar, and maudlinly sentimental" (qtd. in Tax 117). However, Richardson seems well aware of the ironic discrepancies that exist in her elitist account of the common tastes and sharp minds of her working companions and of the priggishness and incongruity of her own responses to their mental pleasures. Her intellectual vanity is tempered not only by self-parody but also, as the workers make music together, by the most traditional of female levelers and bridge-builders—the "frank and unconcealed emotion" of her sympathetic tears (90).

In the incongruous mixture of her affinity and distaste for working-class women, Richardson forms one of the many links in the chain of literary ladies who turned their attention to the nation's newly industrialized factory workers during the century spanning Sarah Savage's *Factory Girl* in 1814 and Florence Converse's *Children of Light* in 1912. Catharine Williams believed, in 1833, that she heard the ghost of the murdered factory worker Sarah Maria Cornell speaking to her in a moonlit graveyard, whereupon she decided to speak for the voiceless operative. A decade later, Margaret Fuller relayed her conversations with jailed prostitutes who confided in her what she believed they could not otherwise say. Rebecca Harding Davis, Elizabeth Stuart Phelps, and Louisa May Alcott articulated their lower-class subjects' yearnings for transcendence and offered them the consolations of religion. Vida Scudder's middle-class heroine gave her fictional workers "transcendentalism made easy" and then regretted her elitist condescension. It would be false to suggest that middle-class ladies confidently assumed they understood the workers well enough to be their authentic mouthpieces, for they constantly expressed remorse for their ignorance and inadequacy. However, it is equally apparent that they did not manifest much faith in the ability of working women to speak and write for themselves, without the aid of their more educated and artistic sisters. Davis's symbolic korl woman testified mutely to the thwarted possibilities for workers of a fully developed artistic voice; and the feminist periodical *The Una* spoke eloquently on behalf of an anonymous seamstress who could not pursue self-culture until she had enough to eat. Middle-class women writers proved capable of enormous leaps of imagination and empathy in their literary response to working women; nevertheless, they believed that in the arts of rhetorical persuasion, in the superiority of their education, taste, and sophistication, and in the assurance of their values and judgments, they were the logical mediators and articulators of working women's stories.

Leonora O'Reilly's prickly reaction to the genteel Dorothy Richardson's account of working women's literary tastes is likewise part of a vital and continuing response from generations of working-class women to their middle-class chroniclers, sympathizers, and mentors, and to the troubling notion of literature's bourgeois provenance. The antagonism of the militant factory worker Sarah Bagley toward the ladylike editor of the *Lowell Offering* Harriet Farley did not stem solely from the magazine's refusal to engage in labor disputes or criticisms of the factory system. Bagley's parodies of

Farley's genteel language and elegant style imply that she suspected that such literariness was itself an attribute of class. Lucy Larcom's *Idyl of Work* and Charlotte Hilbourne's *Effie and I*, by contrast, demonstrated that reading and writing might cross class barriers and make class labels irrelevant. Indeed Larcom even suggested much later that it was time for the graduates of Lowell to stop posing as olden-time factory girls: "It is very much like politicians boasting of carrying their dinners in a tin pail in their youth" (qtd. in Robinson 105). Marie Howland's *Familistère* argued that affinities for reading and for the life of the mind are even stronger in working-class than in convention-bound middle-class women, who shrink from indecorous intellectual pursuits, while Theresa Malkiel resisted bourgeois feminists' and sympathizers' condescension and challenged their motives. Emma Goldman's writings and speeches encompass the broad and lively spectrum of working-class women's responses to the middle-class writers who were their sometime allies and advocates: she appreciated feminist solidarity, relished intellectual exchange, and suspected social co-optation.

Goldman, whose sweatshop experiences and anarchist activities place her in an ambiguous relationship to both class and classlessness, pondered repeatedly in her writing the tangled connections between literary and class affinity, artistic radicalism and political ideology, the mental life of the individual and the welfare of the oppressed. She found allies for her anarchist cause among aristocrats and enemies among Wobblies, who chastised her for "educating the bourgeoisie" (*Living My Life* 539). She felt betrayed by the New York literati who failed to support her magazine and commented bitterly, "To most of them art meant an escape from reality," while "*Mother Earth* pleaded for freedom and abundance in life as the basis of art" (395). She derided university professors as "intellectual proletarians" who were "even more dependent upon their employer than ordinary mechanics," and she attacked bohemian artists and middle-class dilettantes who were unwilling "to give up external success for the sake of the vital issues of life" (*Living My Life* 477; *Red Emma Speaks* 185). However, despite her scorn for the timidity of the bourgeoisie, Goldman also noted candidly that she scarcely knew any comrades from "the working masses." Unlike Margaret Fuller's reportedly frank discourse with women prisoners, Goldman averred that she and her fellow inmates "belonged to different worlds. It would have only made them self-conscious of their lack of development had I broached my ideas to them or discussed the books I read" (*Living My Life* 668, 671). Some of the immigrant poor gave her an enthusiastic reception and enhanced her belief in the life of the mind, but she also repudiated the masses for their acquiescence to authority and manipulation. Contemptuous of mental cowardice, Goldman spoke and wrote fearlessly for her revolutionary ideals, went repeatedly to jail for them, and was eventually deported to Russia in 1919—to witness there the aftermath of revolutionary upheaval and the establishment of the new workers' republic. Irrepressibly optimistic, she explained to Lenin her faith in the free literary circulation of ideas and the danger of persecuting people for their opinions: "His reply was that my attitude was *bourgeois* sentimentality" (*Living My Life* 766). Fortunately, one of Goldman's literary talents was a keen sense of the ironic and the absurd; otherwise, she might have seen a lifetime's dedication to radical intellectual aspiration perish in a moment.

Just as Goldman was one of the most energetic recorders of the mutual attractions, repulsions, suspicions, and ambivalences that united and separated the intellectuals of different classes, so, too, she was one of the most enthusiastic witnesses to the Romantic fervor of the newly awakened worker for the life of the mind. The practical advantages of reading, writing, and study for women in factories and sweatshops were widely apparent in terms of the likely material improvement in their lives, but to Goldman, as to so many working women, such mental efforts attained true significance in their awareness of themselves as thinking and creating people. Reading, for Goldman, was a source not of practical information but of mental exhilaration; writing was a "fascinating and absorbing" endeavor. She believed that human beings craved the affirmation of their humanity; that human development came through self-expression based on experience *and* imagination; that the human mind quested for knowledge and variety; and that, in order for human beings to acquire a philosophy of living, they needed to develop their capacity to enter mentally into the lives of other people and "make their lives and experiences our own."[17] At the core of working women's pursuit of self-culture was the belief, repeatedly avowed during their first century of factory employment, that they were more than "hands only." It is this conviction that echoes in Sarah Maria Cornell's satisfaction in thinking "seriously" about texts, and in the motives of women who came to work in Lowell "on account of the literary advantages to be found there" and "for the express purpose of getting books." It continues in the immigrant women who entered the New York garment industry wanting to have a "voice not only in the world but about how the world is," and who found self-affirmation not only in writing union fiction but in reading dime novels.[18]

Although factory women were praised for reading Wordsworth and Bryant and censured for reading "Little Rosebud's Lovers," all of their reading served, in the words of Lucy Larcom, "to save / Mind from machinery's clutches" (*Idyl* 142). And despite the qualitative range in their compositions, from foolish riddles and banal lyrics to epic poems and utopian novels, these, too, were an assertion of their authors' membership in a community beyond the material realm of their industrial employment. Sarah Savage, the first literary lady to promote the cause of working women, had early noted the dangers of "self-reliance" that might arise in working women from the coincidence of their economic independence and literary empowerment. However, the Romantic aspirations of wage-earning women were extensive enough to include Lucy Larcom's patriotic, Christian affiliations and traditional sexual values as well as Emma Goldman's espousal of anarchism, atheism, and free love. Both women cherished the autonomy and elevation that came to them through the life of the mind and the power of the word, although the possibility that any two women might pursue such divergent ideals with equal integrity was surely at the heart of Savage's misgivings. Each of them, as well as a host of more ordinary working women, refused to accept any class or gender limitations on the noble Emersonian goal of Man Thinking, regardless of whether such people as themselves had ever been envisioned in its original formulation. Their simultaneous entry into money-making and literary opportunities from the early nineteenth until the early twentieth century had a profound impact on women of all classes in creating a consciousness of both worldly and transcendent possibility as a result of their own agency.

Working-class women had reason to be soon disappointed with their material progress in the industrial world, and many of the most articulate of them turned their abilities to organizing, unionizing, and appealing on the platform and in their publications for tangible improvements in working conditions. In this endeavor, they gained the attention and support of many middle-class women who dedicated their political, philanthropic, and literary efforts to the working women's cause. Those workers who pursued more literary and intellectual interests had to face the accusation from their own class that such pursuits were a bourgeois diversion and from more privileged women a lack of empathy and the substitution of religious devotion as a preferred means to transcendence. The full dimensions of working women's efforts to pursue self-culture and the life of the mind are part of a history that must be documented from a literary record that is extensive, although also sporadic, and somewhat eccentric. That record nevertheless reveals in several generations of female "hands" the central presence of working women who refused to allow themselves to be defined and limited by the nature of the work for which they were paid, and who chose to study, read, and write not for the marketplace but because such pursuits were, in themselves, more truly rewarding.

Notes

INTRODUCTION

1. There are a number of interesting studies of the paradoxes inherent in the conflict between later working women's assertions of their subjectivity and the questionable forms their self-expression took, in consuming, imitating, abetting, parodying, and resisting middle-class values. Elizabeth Ewen, *Immigrant Women in the Land of Dollars* (1985), Kathy Peiss, *Cheap Amusements* (1986), and Nan Enstad, *Ladies of Labor, Girls of Adventure* (1999) all explore different aspects of the contradictions in their studies of turn-of-the-century working-class women in America, while Lise Shapiro Sanders takes up the same questions for London shopgirls in her *Consuming Fantasies* (2006). While scholars of the first generations of New England factory women tend to classify them as either genteel or radical, following Philip S. Foner's groundbreaking anthology *The Factory Girls* (1977), these studies of later nineteenth-century working women are more wary of oppositions that assume either co-optation or rebellion. Elizabeth Freeman, however, in "What Factory Girls Had Power to Do" (1994), notes even in the first generations of women at Lowell their complicated dialogue between submission to the new norms of capitalist enterprise and their self-transformation as working-class female authors.

2. Historians of the early New England factory system who noted the literary predilections of the operatives include Caroline F. Ware, *The Early New England Cotton Manufacture* (1931); Hannah Josephson, *The Golden Threads* (1949); more recently Thomas Dublin, *Women at Work* (1979) and *Transforming Women's Work* (1994); and David A. Zonderman, *Aspirations and Anxieties* (1992). Mark Pittenger's 1997 *American Quarterly* article "A World of Difference" is a valuable overview of the wide array of what he calls "down-and-out investigators operating between 1877 and 1929" who produced studies of working-class culture (57, n. 17). The relationship of literacy and literariness to early republican womanhood is a topic of Linda Kerber, *Women of the Republic* (1980), in the context of women's role in educating their children for citizenship. Bruce Burgett, *Sentimental Bodies* (1998), and Sarah Robbins, *Managing Literacy, Mothering America* (2004), both pursue the connection between the private world of domestic literary culture and the public realm of politics and nation building. In each case, the women are middle-class rather than working-class, inhabitants of a private domestic sphere rather than operatives in industrial employment.

3. The literary discourse includes a number of canonical authors, on whom there is a great deal of secondary scholarship to which I am indebted, and a number of now obscure and little-read authors who exist largely outside any literary critical tradition, although they have been of interest to historians. There are interesting discrepancies in emphasis between literary and historical scholarship. In literary studies, nineteenth-century women writers, largely of middle-class backgrounds, are now a large and significant area of interest. In history, there is a comparable scholarly industry on working-class factory women with considerable attention to their writing as it reflects their social rather than their literary concerns. A parallel

discrepancy exists between the modest extent of American literary scholarship on the impact of the Industrial Revolution on American writing and British scholarship on the equivalent topic. The gap between the United States and Britain is particularly curious, since scholars generally agree that there was no parallel phenomenon in Britain to the peculiar literariness of American women factory workers. Jonathan Rose, *The Intellectual Life of the British Working Classes* (2001), Susan Zlotnick, *Women, Writing, and the Industrial Revolution* (1998), and Martha Vicinus, *The Industrial Muse* (1974), all note the paucity of evidence of literary and intellectual interests among British factory women.

4. The empowering effects of reading and its subversive potential for middle-class American women are explored by Barbara Sicherman, "Sense and Sensibility," in *Reading in America* (1989), edited by Cathy N. Davidson; Patrick Brantlinger, *The Reading Lesson* (1998), looks especially at the dangers of novel reading for a nineteenth-century British audience; and Ana-Isabel Aliaga-Buchenau, *The "Dangerous" Potential of Reading* (2004), applies the question to American and French readers of the same period. Julia Swindells, *Victorian Writing and Working Women* (1985), and Kelly J. Mays, "When a 'Speck' Begins to Read," in *Reading Sites,* edited by Patrocinio P. Schweickart and Elizabeth A. Flynn (2004), expand the topic to include British working-class women. Harriet H. Robinson's memoir of her days as a Lowell operative, *Loom and Spindle* (1898), makes explicit the precise links that Sarah Savage viewed with foreboding—between women's factory labor, the transformative effects of wage-earning and literary pursuits, and a new-found feminist activism.

5. Lora Romero's *Home Fronts* (1997) is a thoughtful approach to the question of whether the literary domesticity of nineteenth-century middle-class women is hegemonic or countercultural. Cathy N. Davidson and Laurence Buell pursue and summarize the debate and its extensive scholarship in introductory essays to a special issue of *American Literature* (September 1998). The *embourgeoisement* of the working class by engagement in literary activities is discussed and qualified by Mays, "When a 'Speck' Begins to Read," with reference to British autobiographies. Michael Newbury, *Figuring Authorship in Antebellum America* (1997), Kristie Hamilton, *America's Sketchbook* (1998), and Amal Amireh, *The Factory Girl and the Seamstress* (2000) all pursue the suggestions of the dichotomy between "genteel" and "militant" women, introduced by Foner in *The Factory Girls*. Foner anthologizes some of the earliest versions of the class-based accusations, in 1845, by two of the more radical Lowell operatives (70, 66–68).

6. The *Lowell Offering* is often contrasted, following Foner's lead in *The Factory Girls*, with the more political and militant *Voice of Industry*, which was published between 1845 and 1848 in Fitchburg, Lowell, and Boston. Judith Ranta, *Women and Children of the Mills* (1999), is an invaluable annotated bibliographical guide to literary sources on the rise of the textile industry. In "Offerings and Voices: Periodicals of Women's Work" (chap. 3), she lists the many New England factory magazines and papers, with details of their literary and reformist sympathies. The scholarly debate on the origins and ideology of literary realism in the United States is extensive. Important challenges to conventional assumptions that realism was essentially a post–Civil War, post-Darwinian, and largely male-originated genre of writing (and thus as much opposed to the preceding female, sentimental, and domestic mode as to the Romantic tradition) have been made by Sharon M. Harris, *Rebecca Harding Davis and American Realism* (1991); Joyce W. Warren, ed., *The*

(Other) American Traditions (1993); Dale M. Bauer and Philip Gould, eds., *The Cambridge Companion to Nineteenth Century American Women's Writing* (2001); and Susan S. Williams, *Reclaiming Authorship* (2006). See also Jean Pfaelzer, "Introduction: Discourses of Women and Class: Subjection, Subversion, and Subjectivity," *Legacy* 16, 1999 (1–10) for a discussion of changing assumptions about realism and its relationship to working-class women. Joanne Dobson, "The American Renaissance Reenvisioned," in Warren, *The (Other) American Traditions*, makes a very persuasive case for tracing the roots of the "emerging realist aesthetic" back to the writings of women between 1820 and 1870. She finds the seeds of later realism present in these women writers' "imaginative engagement with pressing social and political issues, a representative range of racial, ethnic, and gender experience, accurate representation of ordinary life, [and]...a compelling embodiment of female subjective experience" (167). Although the female authors of this period are more usually associated with the middle-class, domestic literary tradition, I believe that the women factory writers for the *Lowell Offering* were similarly contributing to the development of realism, particularly in their acute literary consciousness of the impact of money and materialism on everyday life, and in their efforts to square such an awareness with their obligatory religious commitment to otherworldliness.

7. Not only were the contributors to the *Dial* aware of the existence and success of the *Lowell Offering* (saluting their "modest and far-famed contemporary" in their January 1843 issue) but there is ample evidence of the familiarity of the factory workers with transcendental and Romantic writing. Harriet H. Robinson, in *Loom and Spindle* (1898), refers to the likelihood that the *Dial* was one among the many periodicals subscribed to in the Lowell boarding houses and includes her correspondence with Lucy Larcom on the transcendental intellectual milieu of Emerson (56–57, 103). Freeman, "What Factory Girls Had Power to Do," notes the beginning of "what might be thought of as a working-class feminine transcendentalism" among the contributors to the *Lowell Offering* (113). The *Voice of Industry* reviewed the work of Emerson and Carlyle and reprinted Margaret Fuller's correspondence from Europe to the *New York Tribune* (21 January 1847, 1–2; 25 February 1847, 4). Lucy Larcom's sonnet to Emerson is quoted by Shirley Marchalonis, *The Worlds of Lucy Larcom* (1989), 216. Marchalonis also notes the misattribution of Larcom's anonymously published poem "The Rose" to Emerson, an error that caused it to be read with "appropriate seriousness" (139).

8. Deborah Carlin, "'What Methods Have Brought Blessing,'" in Warren, *The (Other) American Traditions*, notes the extent to which women's reform writing was philanthropic in nature and emphasized the obligations of the privileged class to the less fortunate, without challenging the underlying assumptions of the economic structure (213). Carlin notes numerous literary examples "of both a valorized American individualism and of a conservative, middle-class protectionism" that encouraged Christian charity to the working-class but retained the social status quo (214). I would add that authorship and artistic and intellectual culture were also assumed by these writers to be part of that charitable dispensation that might be donated by the upper class, but not generated from the lower. Brantlinger, *The Reading Lesson*, indicates additional complications in the response of middle-class writers to potential working-class literacy and self-expression in nineteenth-century Britain. He notes the somewhat opposed beliefs that the working class is "incapable of adequate self-expression" and, contrarily, that it is "all too clamorous, articulate, and capable of representing itself." While Harriet Martineau hoped, in early

nineteenth-century Britain, that mass literacy might lead to "the secular salvation that comes through individual culture," Brantlinger observes in later industrial writers the fear that such literacy might instead produce anarchy (94–95, 104).

9. The gendered literary battles between virile writing, "savage" realism, and effete realism and "feminized" sentimentalism in the early twentieth century are well summarized by David Shi, *Facing Facts* (1995). Lawrence Levine, *Highbrow/Lowbrow* (1988), is the definitive study of the establishment, by the beginning of the twentieth century, of a clearly hierarchical structure of intellectual and artistic culture.

CHAPTER I

1. See Jane Tompkins, *Sensational Designs* (1985), and Cathy N. Davidson, *Revolution and the Word* (1986), for accounts of women's role in the development of the American novel, as authors, readers, and subjects.

2. See Thomas Dublin, *Women at Work* (1979), Caroline Ware, *The Early New England Cotton Manufacture* (1966), and David A. Zonderman, *Aspirations and Anxieties* (1992), for valuable historical accounts of the rise of the mills in New England and of the alterations they brought in women's work and lives.

3. I am indebted to Margaret Moore, "Sarah Savage of Salem," for details on Savage's publishing career and especially for the quotation expressing her reservations about "self-reliance" in her final novel, *Trial and Self-Discipline* (258).

4. See Patricia Caldwell, introduction to *Fall River*, xvi–xvii; and David Richard Kasserman, *Fall River Outrage* (1986), 239, 245. For examples of continuing fictional treatment, see Mary Cable, *Avery's Knot* (New York: Putnam, 1981), and Raymond Paul, *The Tragedy at Tiverton* (New York: Viking, 1984).

5. See Kasserman, *Fall River Outrage*, for an account of disputes over the exclusion of the doctor's hearsay evidence at the trial (69, 141). He notes: "Outside the courtroom, however, the doctor made no secret of what had transpired" (69). Thus Williams had some license for her directly reported speech.

6. Jeanne Elders DeWaard, "'Indelicate Exposure'" (2002), scrutinizes the tensions between sentimental and legal discourses and between feminine privacy and public welfare in Williams's narrative.

7. Among the many commentators on factory women's dress and taste for small luxuries in jewelry and confectionery, and their assimilation of middle-class styles of dress, are William Scoresby, *American Factories and Their Female Operatives* (reprint, 1968), 16, 31, Henry A. Miles, *Lowell, As It Was, And As It Is* (1846), 124–25, and Zonderman, *Aspirations and Anxieties*, 93, 120. See also the advertisements and the numerous articles and stories in the *Lowell Offering* on how factory women might spend their wages.

CHAPTER 2

1. For details of factory women's magazines and *Mind amongst the Spindles*, see Judith Ranta, *Women and Children of the Mills* (43–55, 38).

2. Henry Miles, *Lowell, As It Was, And As It Is* (1846), notes the legendary status the town of Lowell had acquired within a quarter century of the first establishment of factories there and the "fabulous" nature of the stories associated with it (7). Lawrence Buell, *New England Literary Culture* (1986), 46–47 and 322–34, and Anne C. Rose, *Transcendentalism as a Social Movement* (1981), 94–99,

are among many scholars who explore the significance and the mythologizing of Concord.

3. Joel Myerson, *The New England Transcendentalists and the "Dial"* (1980) traces the history of the *Dial* under the editorship of Margaret Fuller (54–76). Benita Eisler, *The Lowell Offering* (1977), 33, Philip Foner, *The Factory Girls* (1977), 57, and Harriet Robinson, *Loom and Spindle* (reprint, 1976), 60–61, discuss Farley's career as editor of the *Lowell Offering*. Foner notes that Farley soon became the main editor, with Curtis handling subscriptions (27). While Farley seems to have been responsible for writing the editorials, Robinson also comments on Curtis's impact on the factory women through the fearless originality of her speech and writings: "Among all the writers, Miss Curtis stands out as the pioneer and reformatory spirit" (79).

4. The *Lowell Offering* appeared in two series. The first, from October 1840 until March 1841, consisted of four issues, each separately paged. These are cited in the text by series number, issue number, and page number, for example, ser. 1, no. 1: 16. The second series of the *Offering* appeared between April 1841 and December 1845, usually at monthly intervals. It was published in a five volume set, each volume sequentially paged. It is cited in the text by volume and page number, for example 3: 99. For a brief publication history of the magazine, see Judith Ranta, *Women and Children of the Mills* (47–48).

5. See Brownson, "The Laboring Classes" (1840), 460; Norman Ware, *The Industrial Worker 1840–1860* (1959), 23; and Barbara Packer, "The Transcendentalists" (1995), 434.

6. Sarah Bagley is quoted by Eisler, *The Lowell Offering* (40). Among the scholars who have commented on and joined the debate over the co-opting of the *Lowell Offering* by the factory owners are Hannah Josephson, *The Golden Threads* (1949), Caroline Ware, *The Early New England Cotton Manufacture* (1966), Norman Ware, *The Industrial Worker 1840–1860* (1959), Philip Foner, *The Factory Girls* (1977), Kristie Hamilton, *America's Sketchbook* (1998), Thomas Dublin, *Women at Work* (1979), and David A. Zonderman, *Aspirations and Anxieties* (1992).

7. William Grayson's long poem *The Hireling and the Slave* (1855) cites the many defects of wage labor and the hypocrisies of those who prefer it to slavery, which secures work, food, clothing, medicine, and shelter for all.

8. Zonderman and Eisler both reprint the iconic cover of the *Lowell Offering* as it looked in August and again in December 1845 (Zonderman, *Aspirations and Anxieties*, 92; Eisler, *The Lowell Offering*, 39). The engraving shows a young woman, with book in hand, against a background of factory, church, and schoolhouse. In the foreground is a rustic cottage with flowers, fruit, and a beehive. Zonderman discusses its conflicted symbolism, especially the ambiguous balance between rural and industrial worlds (91–95). Harriet Farley gives an account of the development of the design and of disputes over the motto in her March 1845 editorial in the *Offering* (5:71–72). Hamilton argues that the symbolism of the cover associates the Lowell worker with educated leisure, domesticity, and privacy (*America's Sketchbook*, 93). The advertisements, however, suggest yet another image of the factory worker, as a wage-earning consumer, with a disposable income, eager for the latest styles.

9. See Josephson, *The Golden Threads*, 60; Robinson, *Loom and Spindle*, 51; Dickens, *American Notes* (1996), 61–62; *Lowell Offering*, 3:95.

10. See Robinson, *Loom and Spindle*, 57; 70; *Lowell Offering*, 4:71; Larcom, *A New England Girlhood* (1889), 240.

11. See *Lowell Offering* (ser. 1.3: 34–35; 4: 260); Larcom, *A New England Girlhood* (237, 244, 176); Robinson, *Loom and Spindle* (59, 57, 27).

12. Kristie Hamilton reads this story as a kind of political allegory, resisting workers' protests against their conditions and advocating stoicism. However, she also notes that "the minute detail with which this body's agony is described...quite literally sensationalizes what the author says is 'good to learn of others' afflictions'" (*America's Sketchbook,* 111). Such fascination with disease and mortality suggests that Farley may be attempting a literary naturalism that is more interested in fictional frankness than in a rather risky political analogy between cancer and factory conditions.

13. See Barbara Welter, *Dimity Convictions* (1976), especially chaps. 2 and 5, for a discussion of such attitudes.

14. Some studies that have proved valuable in formulating these generalizations about realism include Richard Lehan, *Realism and Naturalism* (2005), John Vernon, *Money and Fiction* (1984), and Susan S. Williams, *Reclaiming Authorship* (2006).

15. John Vernon, *Money and Fiction,* has a good discussion of the parallel relationship of money and the novel to reality (18–19).

16. Elizabeth Freeman, "'What Factory Girls Had Power to Do'" (1994), provides an excellent example of the richness of allusion in her reading of the *Offering* essay "The Patchwork Quilt" (111–13).

17. Chad Montrie, "'I Think Less of the Factory'" (2004), explores the Romanticizing of nature in factory workers' writings after they had left it behind.

18. See especially Susan Zlotnick, "Nostalgia and the Ideology of Domesticity in Working-Class Literature," chap. 4 in *Women, Writing, and the Industrial Revolution* (1998).

19. Two of the most interesting recent studies of the compromised position of the *Lowell Offering* are Michael Newbury, *Figuring Authorship in Antebellum America* (1997), and Hamilton, *America's Sketchbook.* Newbury examines the ways writers conceived the act of authorship. He notes the tendency of British Romantic writers to see their literary endeavor as the opposite of industrialization—individual creativity as opposed to mass mechanized reproduction. He finds a particular version of that tendency in American male Romantic writers, such as Hawthorne and Melville, who project on to domestic and sentimental writers patterns of imagery usually associated with factory labor (29). For the female, working-class authors of the *Offering,* he argues that "literary work becomes a way of denying a working-class or proletarian identity" (29). Ultimately, Newbury coincides in his judgment with the majority of historians, asserting that the magazine's writers "seek to imagine themselves as middle-class women" (71). Hamilton views the sketches in the *Offering* as again adhering to domestic ideals and literary conventions that deemphasize labor and "focus instead on experiences that take place in the home, the boardinghouse parlor or bedroom, or the genteel past of workers' imagination" (107). Hamilton sees the more socially activist sketches of the *Voice of Industry* as "breaking new ground" and heralding the advent of realism and naturalism (93).

CHAPTER 3

1. See Barbara L. Packer, "The Transcendentalists" (1995), 444, 530–31; and Steven Fink, "Margaret Fuller" (1999), 57–63, 68.

2. In *Domesticity with a Difference* (1997), Nicole Tonkovich describes Sarah Josepha Hale's campaign in *Godey's* to insist on gendered language for women. She advocated, for example, *lighthousekeeperess, Americaness,* and *attorneyess,* among many others (66–68). Interestingly, when Harriet Farley took over the editorial chair at the *Lowell Offering*, she described her pleasure in being *editress* (3: 24).

3. Fuller's note reads, in part: "Meta, the wife of Klopstock, is probably known to many readers through her beautiful letters to Richardson, the novelist, or Mrs. Jameson's popular work, 'The Loves of the Poets,'" quoted in Alison Booth, "The Lessons of the Medusa" (2000), 293. Joel Myerson, *The New England Transcendentalists and the "Dial"* (1980) notes that Fuller took "Meta" from her 1833 notebook, which means it was written within four years of the publication of Jameson's influential book (61).

4. See Jeffrey Steele, *Transfiguring America* (2001), 75, 79. Earlier he notes that the language of flowers is a "familiar semiotic code in nineteenth-century American women's writing" (72).

5. See Jeffrey Steele, *The Representation of the Self* (1987), chap. 5, "Recovering the 'Idea of Woman.'"

6. In *Transfiguring America*, Steele notes that many critics have used the doubleness of translation as a fruitful critical paradigm for exploring Fuller's writing. Steele argues that her approach is not merely double or dual but "the staging of multiple and often contradictory voices" (108). Fuller's relationship to translation has been fully explored by Christina Zwarg, *Feminist Conversations: Fuller, Emerson, and the Play of Reading* (1995).

7. See Christina Zwarg's comments, in "The Storied Facts of Margaret Fuller" (1996) on Fuller's "mutual interests" with the women of Lowell and the "Female Department" of the *Voice of Industry* (139).

CHAPTER 4

1. The full title of Judd's novel is *Richard Edney and the Governor's Family: A Rus-Urban Tale, Simple and Popular, yet Cultured and Noble, of Morals, Sentiment, and Life, Containing, also, Hints on Being Good and Doing Good.*

2. Francis B. Dedmond, *Sylvester Judd* (1980), notes possible allusions to the work of the Brontës in Judd's novel and quotes E. P. Whipple in the October 1848 issue of the *North American Review*: "Not many months ago, the New England States were visited by a distressing mental epidemic, passing under the name of the 'Jane Eyre fever,' which defied all the usual nostrums of the established doctors of criticism." Dedmond adds, "Judd, it seems, decided to get on the bandwagon, to capitalize on Charlotte Brontë's popular success; and he made his most significant borrowing" (122).

3. Nathaniel Hawthorne, preface to *The Blithedale Romance* (reprint, 1978), 2. Hawthorne lived at Brook Farm from April until November of 1841 and published *The Blithedale Romance* in 1852. I have tried to preserve Hawthorne's use of noncapitalized "romance" and "romantic" in reference to writing that emphasizes mystery, fantasy, and unreality, and to continue to use "Romantic" to refer to the philosophy of idealism and aspiration that animates the characters of *Blithedale*. However there is inevitably some overlap and ambiguity in the case of this particular work.

4. See Ronald Zboray, *A Fictive People* (1993), chap. 5, "The Railroad, the Community, and the Book" (69–82), for the ways railroads served to distribute

books, to increase people's opportunities for reading, and to affect the kind of material that was read. Zboray also cites an interesting passage from Hawthorne's journal in which he describes the dramatic alteration in consciousness wrought by the observer's need to assimilate the multiple and fleeting impressions of other lives and places produced by train travel. Zboray comments: "That the unexpected disconnectedness of those sights bothered Hawthorne enough to make note of it demonstrates the great cultural distance separating his time from our own" (77).

5. See Nicholas Bromell, *By the Sweat of the Brow* (1993), 69–71, and Michael Newbury, *Figuring Authorship in Antebellum America* (1997), 134–43, on the relationship of Hawthorne's novel to his personal search for a resolution to what Newbury describes as "a question of how intellectual work might be established" entirely outside the economy of the new industrial society (135). Newbury argues that while Hawthorne was initially attracted to Brook Farm by its "alternative economy of labor," he failed to "understand and anticipate the extensive and even overwhelming commitment to manual labor that the Farm would require" (136, 138).

6. See Winfried Fluck, "'The American Romance' and the Changing Functions of the Imaginary" (1996), 415–57. Fluck approaches the romance "as an important literary genre whose changing functions are linked in interesting ways with questions of the status of fiction and the imaginary, the liberation of the imaginary by means of fiction and, as a result of this liberation, the changing relation between fiction and social authority" (421–22). Nina Baym, "Concepts of the Romance in Hawthorne's America" (1984), 426–443, argues that in the mid–nineteenth century "the term romance was deployed in the main, indeed massively so, simply as a synonym for the term novel," but she notes that Hawthorne was exceptional in making distinctions between the two forms that have since become central to studies of the development of American literature (430, 443).

7. John McWilliams, "The Rationale for 'The American Romance'" (1994), notes Hawthorne's preference for the "beef and ale" novels of Anthony Trollope and quotes Hawthorne on his "own individual taste...for quite another class of works than those which I myself am able to write," in *Revisionary Interventions into the Americanist Canon,* edited by Donald E. Pease (1994), 80–81. See McWilliams, 81, and Baym, "Concepts of the Romance in Hawthorne's America," 443.

8. See McWilliams, "The Rationale for 'The American Romance,'" 80–81.

9. "The Two Temples" was written, submitted to *Putnam's,* and rejected by it in 1854. Raymond Weaver, in *Billy Budd and Other Prose Pieces by Herman Melville* (1963), reprints the rejection letter; the editor wrote: "my editorial experience compels me to be very careful in offending the religious sensibilities of the public, and the moral of the 'Two Temples' would sway against us the whole power of the pulpit...and the congregation of Grace Church" (173). The story remained unpublished until 1924.

10. See Newton Arvin's account, in his critical biography *Herman Melville* (1957), of the seagoing and travelogue genre and its evolution by the nineteenth century to a style that was "whimsical, humorous, lyrical, sentimental, or poetic" (78, 80). For Melville's dismissal of his "beggarly *Redburn,*" see 109–110.

11. Kristie Hamilton, *America's Sketchbook* (1998), explores in detail the reaction to Washington Irving's urbanity in Melville and other writers and the advent of a "kind of textual subversiveness, in which literary works seek to subvert dominant models of social detachment" (89); for further commentary on Washington Irving's influence and Melville's resistance to it, see Newbury, *Figuring Authorship*

in Antebellum America, and Paul Giles, "Bewildering Intertanglement: Melville's Engagement with British Culture," in the *Cambridge Companion to Herman Melville,* edited by Robert S. Levine (1998).

12. For a discussion of the range of Melville's sexual allusions in this story, see Beryl Rowland, "Sitting Up with a Corpse" (1972), 76–79.

13. See Newbury, *Figuring Authorship in Antebellum America,* 58; Hamilton, *America's Sketchbook,* 119–28; and Bromell, *By the Sweat of the Brow,* 72–73. For a very interesting reading of this story in the context of Melville's reworking of the stock figure of the factory girl, see Tom Allen, "Melville's 'Factory Girls': Feminizing the Future" (2003), 45–71.

CHAPTER 5

1. See George Mayberry, "Industrialism and the Industrial Worker in the American Novel, 1814–1890" (1942), for one of the earliest critical investigations of the factory novel genre. While Mayberry's central emphasis is not on women's role as subjects and authors, he notes incidentally many themes that are relevant to working women—the motif of seduction, the place of the factory as a refuge for women alone, and the economic benefits of labor for factory women's families. The novels and novellas, in order of original publication, are *Ellen Merton, the Belle of Lowell,* 1844; *The Mysteries of Nashua,* 1844; Osgood Bradbury, *Mysteries of Lowell,* 1844; Alice Neal, "The New England Factory Girl," 1848; Ariel Ivers Cummings, *The Factory Girl,* 1849; "Argus," *Norton: or, The Lights and Shades of a Factory Village,* 1849; Miss J. A. B., *Mary Bean: The Factory Girl,* 1850; "Anna Archdale," c. 1850; Day Kellogg Lee, *Merrimack; or, Life at the Loom, A Tale;* 1854; Martha W. Tyler, *A Book Without a Title,* 1855, 2nd ed., 1856; Charlotte S. Hilbourne, *Effie and I,* 1863; Hannah Talcott, *Madge,* 1863.

2. Fay Blake, *The Strike in the American Novel* (1972), records the "distinction" of Tyler's novel as the first fictional account of a strike. She notes that Tyler's 1855 novel was "a whole generation behind reality," since operatives had first "turned out" as early as 1828 (12).

3. "Lowell" is used here as a metonymy for the location of these early factory novels, many of which were in fact set in Lowell and all of which were set in New England.

4. As noted earlier, two late twentieth-century novels on the Fall River affair are Mary Cable, *Avery's Knot* (1981), and Raymond Paul, *The Tragedy at Tiverton* (1984). Contemporary children's fiction about life in the Lowell mills includes Katherine Paterson, *Lyddie* (New York: Dutton, 1991), and Emily Arnold McCully, *The Bobbin Girl* (New York: Dial, 1996). Modern "Lowell" novels include Elizabeth Graver, *Unravelling* (New York: Hyperion, 1997), and Judith Rossner, *Emmeline* (New York: Simon, 1980).

5. Laura Hapke, in *Labor's Text,* notes Baker's enormously popular exploration of the lives of working-class, vernacular-speaking Bowery inhabitants, embodied in the character of B'hoy Mose, who "amalgamated the street-smarts of the have-not with the economic security of the one who can always find work" (23). Such a character is the direct antithesis of the ideal decorous worker conceived by "Argus."

6. See especially "Sweet Cheats of the Metropolis: Enticements to Corruption in the City," chap. 4 of Adrienne Siegel, *The Image of the American City in Popular Literature 1820–1870* (1981).

7. See Jonathan Rose, *The Intellectual Life of the British Working Classes* (2001), 20–21. Rose notes further: "The fact that laboring men were engaged in cultural pursuits that involved no monetary reward provoked intense suspicion" (21).

8. Judith Ranta, in her valuable annotated bibliography *Women and Children of the Mills* (1999), provides information on Lee and on the "ostensibly autobiographical" nature of Tyler's and Hilbourne's books (19, 15, 239).

9. See Judith Ranta's exploration of Tyler's "representation of working-class true womanhood" in "'A True Woman's Courage and Hopefulness'" (2004).

10. Siegel comments on the "merry music" of the factory bells: "Just how distorted such rapture was in reality is seen in the use of bells to signify the heroine's reentry into paradise. For according to contemporary accounts, the Lowell operatives viewed the periodic chiming in belfries as a grim reminder of the Corporation's efforts to turn them into cogs of the textile machines" (*The Image of the American City in Popular Literature*, 96).

CHAPTER 6

1. In her introduction to Elizabeth Barrett Browning's *Aurora Leigh and Other Poems* (1978), Cora Kaplan comments: "that most difficult venture for women, writing about woman writing, is still rarely attempted in imaginative literature" (35). Certainly writing an epic poem about working-class women's writing, as Larcom did, is extremely rare, but it is also a rather logical extension of the factory women's literary revolution in the mid–nineteenth century.

2. Kristie Hamilton, *America's Sketchbook* (1998), Michael Newbury, *Figuring Authorship in Antebellum America* (1997), Judith Ranta, "'A True Woman's Courage and Hopefulness'" (2004), and Philip Foner, *The Factory Girls* (1977), are among the critics who take up this question.

CHAPTER 7

1. See Lisa Long, "The Postbellum Reform Writings of Rebecca Harding Davis and Elizabeth Stuart Phelps," in *The Cambridge Companion to Nineteenth-Century American Women's Writing*, edited by Dale M. Bauer and Philip Gould (2001), 273, and Anne Rose, *Transcendentalism as a Social Movement, 1830–1850* (1981), chap. 6, for changing attitudes toward industrialization after and even in the decade before the war. The phrase "syntax of class" alludes to Amy Schrager Lang's book title, *The Syntax of Class: Writing Inequality in Nineteenth Century America* (2003).

2. The scholarly criticism on nineteenth-century women's writing, and especially on concerns of gender and social conscience, is broad and deep. In addition to works directly cited, other valuable studies have been done by Deborah Carlin, Barbara Quissell, Susan Hill Lindley, Joyce W. Warren and Margaret Dickie, Susan Coultrap-McQuin, Sharon M. Harris, Susan K. Harris, Aleta Cane and Susan Alves, Shirley H. Samuels, Sheila H. Hughes, Naomi Sofer, Deborah Barker, Jonathan Arac, and Caroline Levander. Mark Pittenger, "A World of Difference" (1997), is a comprehensive survey of the phenomenon of "slum tourism."

3. See Sharon M. Harris, *Rebecca Harding Davis and American Realism* (1991), 27–28, and Jean Pfaelzer, *Parlor Radical* (1996), 25.

4. There is a broad critical assumption that the fictional narrator of "Life in the Iron Mills" is female, although there is no specific gender identification

anywhere in the story. This assumption has affected feminist readings of the story and has also tended to cause a perhaps disproportionate emphasis to be placed on the character of Deb at the expense of the artist figure, Hugh Wolfe.

5. Melville had expressed his misgivings about a smooth, pleasing style and easily digested subject matter, but Davis berates the audience as well as the author who panders to it. Later nineteenth-century writers on poverty and class express increasing misgivings with artistic conventions and forms that aestheticize suffering. Phelps and Alcott engage in satire of their narrators and of their audiences' expectations, uncomfortably mixed with their own acquiescence in traditional approaches. William Dean Howells carries bourgeois self-criticism to a witty climax in *A Hazard of New Fortunes* (1890) and "Tribulations of a Cheerful Giver" (1896), in which even self-deprecation becomes a convention to be relished and ridiculed.

6. See Michele L. Mock, "'An Ardor That Was Human, and a Power That Was Art,'" in *"The Only Efficient Instrument,"* edited by Aleta Feinsod Cane and Susan Alves (2001), 126, on Davis's "good Samaritan" brand of Christianity and her dislike of self-righteous preachiness. See also Sharon Harris on Davis's lifelong insistence on the value of "personal activism" and her advice to her son to "'stop praying and go out and try to put your Christianity into real action'" *Rebecca Harding Davis and American Realism,* 54–55.

7. Sharon Harris quotes Phelps (*Rebecca Harding Davis and American Realism,* 308). See also Michele Mock on Phelps's "personal indebtedness" to Davis for her "textual activism" ("'An Ardor That Was Human, and a Power That Was Art,'" 127).

8. Surprisingly few critics have made religion central to their studies of Phelps. Notable exceptions are Deborah Carlin, "'What Methods Have Brought Blessing,'" in *The (Other) American Traditions* (1989), edited by Joyce W. Warren, and Susan Hill Lindley, "Gender and the Social Gospel Novel." Jenny Franchot, "Invisible Domain: Religion and American Literary Studies" (1995), raises the question of the invisibility of religion and even of "the interior life" as a subject of literary study (835). In dealing with literary texts, especially before 1900, she notes that "we are apparently content to leave religion to historians and anthropologists" and to permit the "negation of mystery and of conscience as categories of experience that disrupt deterministic, particularizing accounts of human identity" (838, 836). Susan K. Harris, *Nineteenth-Century American Women's Novels* (1990), has provided an interesting treatment of the question of "aestheticism," noting that "aesthetic perceptions are limited to people who have no other way of knowing the world" and thus, ironically, aestheticism "signals poverty of imagination" (189).

9. Phelps presumably relied on her audience's familiarity with the Victor Hugo address. Perley announces her evening as "a Victor Hugo evening" (*The Silent Partner* and "The Tenth of January" [reprint, 1983], 228), and the novel quotes Sip speaking just the opening words: "'My Lords! I impart to you a novelty'" (233). Thereafter the reader is left to juxtapose Hugo's unquoted words with Sip's grisly account of the mill scene she has just left behind.

10. Rose quotes Abigail Alcott: "My girls shall have trades—and the mother with the sweat of her brow shall earn an honest subsistence for herself and them" (*Transcendentalism as a Social Movement,* 202). Alcott's birthday letter is cited by Toby Widdicombe in "A 'Declaration of Independence'" (1992), 228, n. 20.

11. Rose notes that the particular philosophy of abstinence embraced by Bronson Alcott and Charles Lane at Fruitlands "tended to devalue work, even

as a spiritual discipline" and, ironically, as in industrial societies, to "look to leisure for the satisfaction denied in work" (*Transcendentalism as a Social Movement,* 124, 125).

12. See Fay Blake, *The Strike in the American Novel* (1972), 21–24; Carlin, "'What Methods Have Brought Blessing,'" 212–21; and Pittenger, "A World of Difference," 53–55.

13. See Ann Schofield, "Introduction to Labor Press Fiction, 1870–1920," in *Sealskin and Shoddy* (1988), edited by Schofield; Robert E. Weir, *Beyond Labor's Veil: The Culture of the Knights of Labor* (1996), chap. 5, "Victoria's Sons and Daughters? The Knights of Labor in Fiction"; and Mary C. Grimes, introduction to *The Knights in Fiction: Two Labor Novels of the 1880s* (1986), edited by Grimes (1–26).

14. See Robert Fogarty, "The Familistère: Radical Reform through Cooperative Enterprise," introductory essay to Marie Howland, *The Familistère* (reprint, 1975), unpaged. The first edition of the novel was published in 1874 under the title *Papa's Own Girl.*

15. See Mary Creese, *Ladies in the Laboratory* (1998); Sally Kohlsted, ed., *History of Women in the Sciences* (1999); and Nina Baym, *American Women of Letters and the Nineteenth-Century Sciences: Styles of Affiliation* (2002) for comments on the remarkable prominence of botany as a choice of women scientists in the nineteenth century.

CHAPTER 8

1. See Sean Wilentz, "The Rise of the American Working Class, 1776–1877" (1989), and Michael Reich, "Capitalist Development, Class Relations and Labor History," in *Perspectives on American Labor History: The Problem of Synthesis* (1989), edited by J. Carroll Moody and Alice Kessler-Harris. There are lively debates over periodization and turning points in the different but overlapping fields of labor history, women's history, and literary history. See Ardis Cameron, *Radicals of the Worst Sort* (1993), on those who spoke for laboring women, construed their world, and shaped "the command of meaning" for them (185). Fay Blake, *The Strike in the American Novel* (1972), Meredith Tax, *The Rising of the Women* (1980), and Alice Wexler, *Emma Goldman* (1984), discuss the strikes and violence of the late nineteenth century; Tax, especially, investigates the degree of women's support for them. She also explores thoroughly the tensions and allegiances between working- and middle-class women on the question of suffrage.

2. Despite their sensational reputation, late nineteenth- and early twentieth-century anarchists, according to Arthur Redding, *Raids on Human Consciousness* (1998), "laid out a program of democracy which had little to do with the fears expressed by the popular media," although they did occasionally "put the same fears into practice as a sort of aggressive public relations tactic, a practice that habitually backfired" (74–75).

3. See Annelise Orleck, *Common Sense and a Little Fire* (1995), 18–19; Susan A. Glenn, *Daughters of the Shtetl* (1990), 8–30; and Emma Goldman, *Living My Life* (1934), 15, 20–21.

4. See Cameron on how female militants and radical women from the lower orders threatened the Victorian world by breaking down boundaries and dissolving distinctions and were consequently depicted as grotesque anomalies and figures of deviancy (*Radicals of the Worst Sort,* 69, 68).

5. See Wexler, *Emma Goldman,* 16–27, and Marian J. Morton, *Emma Goldman and the American Left* (1992), 19–20.

6. Epigraph to Aleta Cane and Susan Alves, *"The Only Efficient Instrument"* (2001).

7. See Wexler, *Emma Goldman,* 124; Richard Drinnon, introduction to *Mother Earth* (1968); and Craig Monk, "Emma Goldman, *Mother Earth*, and the Little Magazine Impulse in Modern America" (2001).

8. See Alix Kates Shulman, ed., *Red Emma Speaks* (1972), 164–65, 42, 187, 188, 191, 194.

9. Quoted by Françoise Basch in introductory essays to Theresa S. Malkiel, *The Diary of a Shirtwaist Striker* (reprint, 1990), 26. Orleck notes that Lemlich and Newman had both been engaged in "shop-to-shop organizing" since 1906 (*Common Sense and a Little Fire,* 58).

10. Goldman's very different account of her repudiation of Most and her histrionic physical attack on him is in *Living My Life* (105). Unlike Catherine's single-minded devotion to Wolf in Dixon's novel, Goldman branded Most "a traitor and a coward" in the *Anarchist*; then, when he refused to reply, she attacked him with a horsewhip at a public lecture: "Repeatedly I lashed him across the face and neck, then broke the whip over my knee and threw the pieces at him."

11. See Orleck on Lemlich's hats, veils, lipstick, and "obsession with nice clothing" (*Common Sense and a Little Fire,* 233, 247). Orleck notes the importance of her marriage to Joe Shavelson and her motherhood in bringing her "the comforts of social acceptance," but she also comments on the ambivalence and tension that existed in her private life (119). The acceptability of the woman union worker, devoted to her family and community, rather than the self-assertive and independent anarchist as a fictional figure, has an interesting possible precedent in Amal Amireh's argument, in *The Factory Girl and the Seamstress* (2000), that the factory worker was abandoned in favor of the seamstress in nineteenth-century fiction because "antebellum Americans needed an emblem that would both express and alleviate their anxieties about industrialization and its effects on their class and gender identities." They found this emblem in the more domesticated seamstress rather than the "paradoxical" factory worker (37). That a woman with politics as radical as Lemlich's could repeatedly be treated as an admirable fictional character may be seen as a considerable advance over the previous century's depiction of the rebellious working-class woman. That she had to place family and community ahead of herself suggests that self-sacrifice was still a gendered virtue.

12. See, for example, John Steinbeck's account of manipulative union organizers and innocent proletarians in his 1936 novel *In Dubious Battle.*

13. See Basch, introductory essay to *The Dairy of a Shirtwaist Striker,* 53–61.

14. Orleck, *Common Sense and a Little Fire,* juxtaposes the careers of Cohn, Schneiderman, Newman, and Lemlich. Other valuable histories and analyses of the ideas of immigrant working women are in Tax, *The Rising of the Women*, Cameron, *Radicals of the Worst Sort,* Glenn, *Daughters of the Shtetl,* Sarah Eisenstein, *Give Us Bread but Give Us Roses* (1983), and Joan M. Jensen and Sue Davidson, eds., *A Needle, a Bobbin, a Strike* (1984).

15. Among her many other activities, Goldman authored a book of literary criticism, *The Social Significance of the Modern Drama* (1914). She argued that "merely propagandistic literature" was not adequate to an understanding of social problems" and continued: "Rather must we become conversant with the larger

phases of human expression manifest in art, literature, and, above all, the modern drama" (*Anarchism* [1910], 247).

16. See Orleck, *Common* Sense *and a Little Fire,* 38, 39, 40, 169.

17. See Shulman, *Red* Emma *Speaks,* 51, 239, 379, 121, 108–9, 388.

18. See Robinson, *Loom and Spindle,* 26, 40, 70, and Cameron, *Radicals of the Worst Sort,* 13.

Works Cited

Alcott, Louisa May. "Transcendental Wild Oats." In *Critical Essays on American Transcendentalism*, edited by Philip F. Gura and Joel Myerson. Boston: Hall, 1982, 128–41.

———. *Work: A Story of Experience*. New York: Penguin, 1994.

Aliaga-Buchenau, Ana-Isabel. *The "Dangerous" Potential of Reading: Readers and the Negotiation of Power in Nineteenth-Century Narratives*. New York: Routledge, 2004.

Allen, Tom. "Melville's 'Factory Girls': Feminizing the Future." *Studies in American Fiction* 31 (2003): 45–71.

Alves, Susan. "Lowell's Female Factory Workers, Poetic Voice, and the Periodical." In Cane and Alves, *"The Only Efficient Instrument,"* 149–64.

Amireh, Amal. *The Factory Girl and the Seamstress: Imagining Gender and Class in Nineteenth-Century American Fiction*. New York: Garland, 2000.

"Anna Archdale: or, The Lowell Factory Girl." Boston: Gleason, c. 1850.

Arac, Jonathan. "Narrative Forms." In Bercovitch, *Cambridge History of American Literature,* vol 2:607–777.

"Argus." *Norton: or, The Lights and Shades of a Factory Village*. Lowell: Vox Populi Office, 1849.

Arvin, Newton. *Herman Melville*. New York: Viking, 1961.

Aveling, Edward, and Eleanor Marx. *The Working-Class Movement in America*. New York: Arno, 1969.

Bardes, Barbara A., and Suzanne Gossett, eds. *Declarations of Independence: Women and Political Power in Nineteenth-Century American Fiction*. New Brunswick, N.J.: Rutgers University Press, 1990.

Barker, Deborah. *Aesthetics and Gender in American Literature: Portraits of the Woman Artist*. Lewisburg, Pa.: Bucknell University Press, 2000.

Bauer, Dale M., and Philip Gould, eds. *The Cambridge Companion to Nineteenth-Century American Women's Writing*. New York: Cambridge University Press, 2001.

Baym, Nina. *American Women of Letters and the Nineteenth-Century Sciences: Styles of Affiliation*. New Brunswick, N.J.: Rutgers University Press, 2002.

———. "Concepts of the Romance in Hawthorne's America." *Nineteenth-Century Fiction* 38 (1984): 426–43.

Bean, Judith Mattson, and Joel Myerson, eds. *Margaret Fuller, Critic: Writings from the New-York Tribune, 1844–1846*. New York: Columbia University Press, 2000.

Bercovitch, Sacvan, ed. *Cambridge History of American Literature, vol. 2, 1820–1865*. Cambridge: Cambridge University Press, 1994.

Berthold, Dennis. "Class Acts: The Astor Place Riots and Melville's 'The Two Temples.'" *American Literature* 71 (1999): 429–61.

Blake, Fay M. *The Strike in the American Novel*. Metuchen, N.J.: Scarecrow Press, 1972.

Blanchard, Paula. *Margaret Fuller: From Transcendentalism to Revolution*. New York: Delacorte Press, 1978.

Booth, Alison. "The Lessons of the Medusa: Anna Jameson and Collective Biographies of Women." *Victorian Studies* 42 (2000): 257–88.

Bradbury, Osgood. *Mysteries of Lowell*. Boston: Williams, 1844.

Bradstreet, Anne. "The Prologue." In *American Literature: The Makers and the Making*, edited by Cleanth Brooks, R. W. B. Lewis, and Robert Penn Warren. New York: St. Martin's Press, 1973, 1:71–72.

Brantlinger, Patrick. *The Reading Lesson: The Threat of Mass Literacy in Nineteenth-Century British Fiction*. Bloomington: Indiana University Press, 1998.

Bromell, Nicholas K. *By the Sweat of the Brow: Literature and Labor in Antebellum America*. Chicago: University of Chicago Press, 1993.

Browning, Elizabeth Barrett. *Aurora Leigh*. Edited by Margaret Reynolds. New York: Norton, 1996.

Brownson, Orestes. "The Laboring Classes." *Boston Quarterly Review* 3 (July 1840): 358–95; (October 1840): 420–512.

Buell, Lawrence. "Circling the Spheres: A Dialogue." *American Literature* 70 (1998): 465–490.

———. *New England Literary Culture: From Revolution through Renaissance*. Cambridge: Cambridge University Press, 1986.

Bullard, Arthur (Albert Edwards). *Comrade Yetta*. 1913. Upper Saddle River, N.J.: Gregg, 1968.

Burgett, Bruce. *Sentimental Bodies: Sex, Gender, and Citizenship in the Early Republic*. Princeton, N.J.: Princeton University Press, 1998.

Burke, Martin J. *The Conundrum of Class: Public Discourse on the Social Order in America*. Chicago: University of Chicago Press, 1995.

Caldwell, Patricia. Introduction to Catharine Williams, *Fall River: An Authentic Narrative*. New York: Oxford University Press, 1993, xi–xxii.

Cameron, Ardis. *Radicals of the Worst Sort: Laboring Women in Lawrence, Massachusetts, 1860–1912*. Urbana: University of Illinois Press, 1993.

Cane, Aleta Feinsod, and Susan Alves, eds. *"The Only Efficient Instrument": American Women Writers and the Periodical, 1837–1916*. Iowa City: University of Iowa Press, 2001.

Carlin, Deborah. "'What Methods Have Brought Blessing': Discourses of Reform in Philanthropic Literature." In Warren, *The (Other) American Traditions*, 203–25.

Carlyle, Thomas. ["Transcendentalism."] In *Critical Essays on American Transcendentalism*, edited by Philip Gura and Joel Myerson. Boston: Hall, 1982, 55–56.

Chevigny, Bell Gale, comp. *The Woman and the Myth: Margaret Fuller's Life and Writings*. Old Westbury, N.Y.: Feminist Press, 1976.

Cole, Phyllis. "Pain and Protest in the Emerson Family." In *The Emerson Dilemma*, edited by Gregory Garvey. Athens: University of Georgia Press, 2001, 67–92.

Conrad, Susan Phinney. *Perish the Thought: Intellectual Women in Romantic America, 1830–1860*. New York: Oxford University Press, 1976.

Converse, Florence. *The Children of Light*. Boston: Houghton, 1912.

Coultrap-McQuin, Susan. *Doing Literary Business: American Women Writers in the Nineteenth Century*. Chapel Hill: University of North Carolina Press, 1990.

Creese, Mary. *Ladies in the Laboratory?: American and British Women in Science, 1800–1900*. Lanham, Md.: Scarecrow Press, 1998.

Cummings, Ariel I. *The Factory Girl; or Gardez la Coeur*. Lowell: Short, 1847.

Daniels, Gertrude Potter. *The Warners: An American Story of Today*. Chicago: Jamieson, 1901.

Davidson, Cathy N., ed. *No More Separate Spheres!* Special issue, *American Literature* 70 (1998): 441–702.

———. "Preface." *American Literature* 70 (1998): 443–63

———, ed. *Reading in America: Literature and Social History.* Baltimore: Johns Hopkins University Press, 1989.

———. *Revolution and the Word: The Rise of the Novel in America.* New York: Oxford University Press, 1986.

Davis, Rebecca Harding. *Bits of Gossip.* Cambridge, Mass.: Riverside, 1904.

———. *Life in the Iron Mills.* Old Westbury, N.Y.: Feminist Press, 1972.

———. *Margret Howth: A Story of Today.* New York: Feminist Press, 1990.

Dedmond, Francis B. *Sylvester Judd.* Boston: Twayne, 1980.

DeWaard, Jeanne Elders. "'Indelicate Exposure': Sentiment and Law in *Fall River: An Authentic Narrative.*" *American Literature* 74 (2002): 373–401.

Dial: A Magazine for Literature, Philosophy, and Religion. Boston, 1840–44. 4 vols. New York: Russell, 1961.

Dickens, Charles. *American Notes.* Modern Library: New York, 1996.

Dickenson, Donna. *Margaret Fuller: Writing a Woman's Life.* New York: St. Martin's Press, 1993.

Dimock, Wai Chee. "Class, Gender, and a History of Metonymy." In *Rethinking Class: Literary Studies and Social Formations,* edited by Dimock and Michael T. Gilmore. New York: Columbia University Press, 1994, 57–104.

Dixon, Thomas, Jr. *Comrades: A Story of Social Adventure in California.* New York: Doubleday, 1909.

Dobson, Joanne. "The American Renaissance Reenvisioned." In Warren, *The (Other) American Traditions,* 164–82.

Drinnon, Richard. Introduction to *Mother Earth.* Reprint. New York: Greenwood Press, 1968.

Dublin, Thomas, ed. *Farm to Factory: Women's Letters, 1830–1860.* New York: Columbia University Press, 1981.

———. "The Mill Letters of Emeline Larcom, 1840–1842." Edited with an Introduction. *Essex Institute Historical Collections* 127 (1991): 211–239.

———. *Women at Work: The Transformation of Work and Community in Lowell, Massachusetts, 1826–1860.* New York: Columbia University Press, 1979.

Du Plessis, Rachel Blau. "To 'Bear My Mother's Name': *Künstlerromane* by Women Writers." In Elizabeth Barrett Browning, *Aurora Leigh,* edited by Margaret Reynolds. New York: Norton, 1996, 463–66.

Eakin, Paul John. *The New England Girl: Cultural Ideals in Hawthorne, Stowe, Howells, and James.* Athens: University of Georgia Press, 1976.

Eisler, Benita, ed. *The Lowell Offering: Writings by New England Mill Women (1840–1845).* Philadelphia: Lippincott, 1977.

Eisenstein, Sarah. *Give Us Bread but Give Us Roses: Working Women's Consciousness in the United States, 1890 to the First World War.* London: Routledge, 1983.

Eliot, George. "Margaret Fuller and Mary Wollstonecraft." In *Woman in the Nineteenth Century,* edited by Larry J. Reynolds. New York: Norton, 1998, 232–34.

Ellen Merton, the Belle of Lowell. Boston: Brainard, 1844.

Emerson, Ralph Waldo. *Emerson in His Journals.* Selected and edited by Joel Porte. Cambridge, Mass: Harvard University Press, 1982.

———. *Selections from Ralph Waldo Emerson.* Edited by Stephen E. Whicher. Boston: Riverside, 1957.

Enstad, Nan. *Ladies of Labor, Girls of Adventure: Working Women, Popular Culture, and Labor Politics at the Turn of the Twentieth Century*. New York: Columbia University Press, 1999.

Ewen, Elizabeth. *Immigrant Women in the Land of Dollars: Life and Culture on the Lower East Side, 1890–1925*. New York: Monthly Review Press, 1985.

Fine, David M. *The City, the Immigrant, and American Fiction, 1880–1920*. Metuchen, N.J.: Scarecrow Press, 1977.

Fink, Steven. "Margaret Fuller: The Evolution of a Woman of Letters." In *Reciprocal Influences: Literary Production, Distribution, and Consumption in America,* edited by Steven Fink and Susan S. Williams. Columbus: Ohio State University Press, 1999, 55–74.

Fink, Steven, and Susan S. Williams, eds. *Reciprocal Influences: Literary Production, Distribution, and Consumption in America*. Columbus: Ohio State University Press, 1999.

Fluck, Winfried. "'The American Romance' and the Changing Functions of the Imaginary." *New Literary History* 27 (1996): 415–57.

Foley, Barbara. "From Wall Street to Astor Place: Historicizing Melville's 'Bartleby.'" *American Literature* 72 (2000): 87–116.

Foner, Philip S., ed. *The Factory Girls: A Collection of Writings on Life and Struggles in the New England Factories of the 1840s*. Urbana: University of Illinois Press, 1977.

Franchot, Jenny. "Invisible Domain: Religion and American Literary Studies." *American Literature* 67 (1995): 833–42.

Freeman, Elizabeth. "'What Factory Girls Had Power to Do': The Techno-Logic of Working-Class Feminine Publicity in *The Lowell Offering*." *Arizona Quarterly* 50 (1994): 109–28.

Friedman, Isaac Kahn. *By Bread Alone*. New York: McClure, 1901.

Gantt, T. Fulton. *Breaking the Chains*. In *The Knights in Fiction: Two Labor Novels of the 1880s,* edited by Mary C. Grimes. Urbana: University of Illinois Press, 1986, 29–133.

Garvey, T. Gregory, ed. *The Emerson Dilemma: Essays on Emerson and Social Reform*. Athens: University of Georgia Press, 2001.

Giles, Paul. "'Bewildering Intertanglement': Melville's Engagement with British Culture." In *The Cambridge Companion to Herman Melville,* edited by Robert S. Levine. Cambridge: Cambridge University Press, 1998, 224–49.

Gilmore, Michael T. *American Romanticism and the Marketplace*. Chicago: University of Chicago Press, 1985.

Glenn, Susan A. *Daughters of the Shtetl: Life and Labor in the Immigrant Generation*. Ithaca, N.Y.: Cornell University Press, 1990.

Goldman, Emma. *Anarchism and Other Essays*. New York: Mother Earth Publishing Association, 1910.

———. *Living My Life*. New York: Knopf, 1934.

Goldman, Emma, and Max Baginski eds. "Mother Earth." Editorial, *Mother Earth* (March 1906): 1–4.

Grayson, John William. *The Hireling and the Slave*. 2nd ed. Charleston, S.C.: Russell, 1855.

Griffin, Susan. "Women, Anti-Catholicism, and Narrative in Nineteenth-Century America." In Bauer and Gould, *The Cambridge Companion to Nineteenth-Century American Women's Writing,* 157–75.

Grimes, Mary C., ed. *The Knights in Fiction: Two Labor Novels of the 1880s*. Urbana: University of Illinois Press, 1986.

Gura, Philip F., and Joel Myerson, eds. *Critical Essays on American Transcendentalism*. Boston: Hall, 1982.

Hamilton, Kristie. *America's Sketchbook: The Cultural Life of a Nineteenth-Century Literary Genre*. Athens: Ohio University Press, 1998.

Hapke, Laura. *Labor's Text: The Worker in American Fiction*. New Brunswick, N.J.: Rutgers University Press, 2001.

———. *Tales of the Working Girl: Wage-Earning Women in American Literature, 1890–1925*. New York: Twayne, 1992.

Harris, Sharon M. *Rebecca Harding Davis and American Realism*. Philadelphia: University of Pennsylvania Press, 1991.

———, ed. *Redefining the Political Novel: American Women Writers, 1797–1901*. Knoxville: University of Tennessee Press, 1995.

Harris, Susan K. *Nineteenth-Century American Women's Novels: Interpretative Strategies*. Cambridge: Cambridge University Press, 1990.

Hathaway, Richard D. *Sylvester Judd's New England*. University Park: Pennsylvania State University Press, 1981.

Hawthorne, Nathaniel. *The Blithedale Romance*. Edited by Seymour Gross and Rosalie Murphy. New York: Norton, 1978.

Hilbourne, Charlotte S. *Effie and I; or, Seven Years in a Cotton Mill*. Cambridge, Mass.: Allen, 1863.

Howard, Leon. *Herman Melville: A Biography*. Berkeley: University of California Press, 1967.

Howland, Marie. *The Familistère*. 3rd ed. With an introduction Robert S. Fogarty. Reprint, Philadelphia: Porcupine Press, 1975. First ed. published 1874 as *Papa's Own Girl*.

Hughes, Sheila Hassell. "Between Bodies of Knowledge There Is a Great Gulf Fixed: A Liberationist Reading of Class and Gender in *Life in the Iron Mills*." *American Quarterly* 49 (1997): 113–37.

"An Idyl of Work." Unsigned review of *An Idyl of Work* by Lucy Larcom. *Scribner's Monthly*, November 1875, 135–36.

J. A. B., Miss. *Mary Bean: The Factory Girl*. Boston: Hotchkiss, 1850.

Jensen, Joan M., and Sue Davidson, eds. *A Needle, a Bobbin, a Strike: Women Needleworkers in America*. Philadelphia: Temple University Press, 1984.

Josephson, Hannah. *The Golden Threads: New England's Mill Girls and Magnates*. New York: Russell, 1949.

Judd, Sylvester. *Margaret: A Tale of the Real and the Ideal, Blight and Bloom*. 2nd revised ed. 1851. Reprint, Upper Saddle River, N.J.: Gregg, 1968. First edition published 1845.

———. *Richard Edney and the Governor's Family*. Boston: Phillips, 1850.

Kaplan, Cora. Introduction to Elizabeth Barrett Browning, *Aurora Leigh and Other Poems*. London: Women's Press, 1978, 5–36.

Kasserman, David Richard. *Fall River Outrage: Life, Murder, and Justice in Early Industrial New England*. Philadelphia: University of Pennsylvania Press, 1986.

Keller, Lynn. *Forms of Expansion: Recent Long Poems by Women*. Chicago: University of Chicago Press, 1997.

Kelley, Mary. *Private Woman, Public Stage: Domesticity in Nineteenth-Century America*. New York: Oxford University Press, 1984.

Kelly, Lori Duin. *The Life and Works of Elizabeth Stuart Phelps, Victorian Feminist Writer.* Troy, N.Y.: Whitson, 1983.

Kerber, Linda K. *Women of the Republic: Intellect and Ideology in Revolutionary America.* Chapel Hill: University of North Carolina Press, 1980.

Kessler, Carol Farley. *Elizabeth Stuart Phelps.* Boston: Twayne, 1982.

Kohlstedt, Sally, ed. *History of Women in the Sciences: Readings from "Isis."* Chicago: University of Chicago Press, 1999.

Lang, Amy Schrager. *The Syntax of Class: Writing Inequality in Nineteenth-Century America.* Princeton, N.J.: Princeton University Press, 2003.

Larcom, Lucy. *An Idyl of Work.* 1875. Reprint, Westport, Conn.: Greenwood, 1970.

———. *A New England Girlhood: Outlined from Memory.* Cambridge, Mass.: Riverside, 1889.

Lazerow, Jama. *Religion and the Working Class in Antebellum America.* Washington, D.C.: Smithsonian Institution Press, 1995.

Lee, Day Kellogg. *Merrimack; or, Life at the Loom, A Tale.* New York: Redfield, 1854.

Lehan, Richard. *Realism and Naturalism: The Novel in an Age of Transition.* Madison: University of Wisconsin Press, 2005.

Levander, Caroline Field. *Voices of the Nation: Women and Public Speech in Nineteenth-Century American Literature and Culture.* New York: Cambridge University Press, 1998.

Levine, Lawrence W. *Highbrow/Lowbrow: The Emergence of Cultural Hierarchy in America.* Cambridge, Mass.: Harvard University Press, 1988.

Lewis, Jessica. "'Poetry Experienced': Lucy Larcom's Poetic Dwelling in *A New England Girlhood.*" *Legacy* 18 (2001): 182–92.

Lindley, Susan Hill. "Gender and the Social Gospel Novel." In *Gender and the Social Gospel,* edited by Wendy J. D. Edwards and Carolyn Gifford. Urbana: University of Illinois Press, 185–201.

Long, Lisa A. "The Postbellum Reform Writings of Rebecca Harding Davis and Elizabeth Stuart Phelps." In Bauer and Gould, *The Cambridge Companion to Nineteenth-Century American Women's Writing,* 262–83.

Lovell, Thomas B. "Separate Spheres and Extensive Circles: Sarah Savage's *The Factory Girl* and the Celebration of Industry in Early Nineteenth-Century America." *Early American Literature* 31 (1996): 1–24.

Lowell Offering, 1840–1845. Ser. 1, 4 single issues. Lowell, Mass. October1840–March 1841. Ser. 2, 5 bound vols., 1841–45. Westport, Conn.: Greenwood Reprint, 1970.

Malkiel, Theresa S. *The Diary of a Shirtwaist Striker.* 1910. Reprint with an introductory essay by Françoise Basch. Ithaca, N.Y.: ILR Press, 1990.

Marchalonis, Shirley. *The Worlds of Lucy Larcom, 1824–1893.* Athens: University of Georgia Press, 1989.

Mayberry, George. "Industrialism and the Industrial Worker in the American Novel, 1814–1890." Ph.D. diss., Harvard University, 1942.

Mays, Kelly J. "When a 'Speck' Begins to Read: Literacy and the Politics of Self-Improvement in Nineteenth-Century British Working-Class Autobiography." In *Reading Sites: Social Difference and Reader Response,* edited by Patrocinio P. Schweickart and Elizabeth A. Flynn. New York: Modern Language Association, 2004, 108–34.

McMahon, John R. *Toilers and Idlers.* New York: Wilshire, 1907.

McWilliams, John. "The Rationale for 'The American Romance.'" In *Revisionary Interventions into the Americanist Canon,* edited by Donald E. Pease. Durham, N.C.: Duke University Press, 1994, 71–82.

McWilliams, John P., Jr. *The American Epic: Transforming a Genre, 1770–1860.* Cambridge: Cambridge University Press, 1989.

———. "The Epic in the Nineteenth Century." In *The Columbia History of American Poetry,* edited by Jay Parini. New York: Columbia University Press, 1993, 33–63.

Melville, Herman. "Bartleby the Scrivener." In *The Shorter Novels of Herman Melville.* New York: Liveright, 1956, 107–56.

———. *Billy Budd and Other Prose Pieces.* Edited by Raymond W. Weaver. New York: Russell, 1963.

———. *Redburn: His First Voyage.* Edited by Harrison Hayford, Herschel Parker, and G. Thomas Tanselle. Evanston, Ill.: Northwestern University Press, 1969.

Milder, Robert. "The Radical Emerson?" In *Cambridge Companion to Ralph Waldo Emerson,* edited by Joel Porte and Saundra Morris. Cambridge: Cambridge University Press, 1999, 49–75.

Miles, Henry A. *Lowell, As It Was, And As It Is.* 2nd ed. Lowell: Dayton, 1846.

Mind amongst the Spindles: A Selection from the Lowell Offering. Edited by Charles Knight. London: Knight, 1844.

Mock, Michele M. "'An Ardor That Was Human, and a Power That Was Art': Rebecca Harding Davis and the Art of the Periodical." In Cane and Alves, *"The Only Efficient Instrument,"* 126–46.

Monk, Craig. "Emma Goldman, *Mother Earth,* and the Little Magazine Impulse in Modern America." In Cane and Alves, *"The Only Efficient Instrument,"* 113–25.

Montrie, Chad. "'I Think Less of the Factory Than of My Native Dell': Labor, Nature, and the Lowell 'Mill Girls,'" *Environmental History* 9 (2004): 275–95.

Moody, J. Carroll, and Alice Kessler-Harris, eds. *Perspectives on American Labor History: The Problems of Synthesis.* DeKalb: Northern Illinois University Press, 1989.

Moore, Margaret B. "Sarah Savage of Salem: A Forgotten Writer." *Essex Institute Historical Collections* 127 (1991): 240–59.

Morton, Marian J. *Emma Goldman and the American Left: "Nowhere at Home."* New York: Twayne, 1992.

Mott, Frank Luther. *A History of American Magazines 1741–1850.* Cambridge, Mass: Harvard University Press, 1970.

Mrozowski, Stephen A., Grace H. Ziesing, and Mary C. Beaudry. *Living on the Boott: Historical Archeology at the Boott Mills Boardinghouses, Lowell, Massachusetts.* Amherst: University of Massachusetts Press, 1996.

Myerson, Joel. *The New England Transcendentalists and the "Dial": A History of the Magazine and Its Contributors.* Rutherford, N.J.: Fairleigh Dickinson University Press, 1980.

The Mysteries of Nashua: or Revenge Punished and Constancy Rewarded. Nashua, N.H.: Gill, 1844.

Neal, Alice B. "The New England Factory Girl: A Sketch of Everyday Life." *The Gossips of Rivertown; with Sketches in Prose and Verse.* Philadelphia: Hazard and Mitchell, 1850. 177–219.

Newbury, Michael. *Figuring Authorship in Antebellum America*. Stanford, Calif.: Stanford University Press, 1997.

Oates, Joyce Carol. "The Mystery of Jon Benét Ramsey." *New York Review of Books*, June 24, 1999. 31–37.

Olsen, Tillie. Biographical interpretation. In Rebecca Harding Davis, *Life in the Iron Mills*. Reprint, Old Westbury, N.Y.: Feminist Press, 1972. 69–174.

Oppenheim, James. *The Nine-Tenths*. 1911. Reprint, Upper Saddle River, N.J.: Gregg, 1968.

Orleck, Annelise. *Common Sense and a Little Fire: Women and Working-Class Politics in the United States, 1900–1965*. Chapel Hill: University of North Carolina Press, 1995.

Packer, Barbara L. "The Transcendentalists." In Bercovitch, *Cambridge History of American Literature,* 2:329–604.

Pearce, Roy Harvey. *The Continuity of American Poetry*. Princeton, N.J.: Princeton University Press, 1961.

Peiss, Kathy. *Cheap Amusements: Working Women and Leisure in Turn-of-the-Century New York*. Philadelphia: Temple University Press, 1986.

Pfaelzer, Jean. "Introduction: Discourses of Women and Class: Subjection, Subversion, and Subjectivity," *Legacy* 16, 1999 (1–10).

———. *Parlor Radical: Rebecca Harding Davis and the Origins of American Social Realism*. Pittsburgh: University of Pittsburgh Press, 1996.

Phelps, Elizabeth Stuart. *Chapters from a Life*. Boston: Houghton, 1896.

———. *Hedged In*. Boston: Fields, 1870.

———. *The Silent Partner* and "The Tenth of January." Old Westbury, N.Y.: Feminist Press, 1983.

———. *The Story of Avis*. 1877. With an introduction by Carol Farley Kessler. New Brunswick, N. J.: Rutgers University Press, 1985.

Pittenger, Mark. "A World of Difference: Constructing the 'Underclass' in Progressive America." *American Quarterly* 49 (1997): 26–65.

Prude, Jonathan. "The Social System of Early New England Textile Mills: A Case Study, 1812–40." In *The New England Working Class and the New Labor History*, edited by Herbert G. Gutman and Donald H. Bell. Urbana: University of Illinois Press, 1987, 90–127.

Quissell, Barbara C. "The New World That Eve Made: Feminist Utopias Written by Nineteenth-Century Women." In *America as Utopia,* edited by Kenneth M. Roemer. New York: Burt Franklin, 1981, 148–74.

Ranta, Judith A. "'A True Woman's Courage and Hopefulness': Martha W. Tyler's *A Book without a Title: Or, Thrilling Events in the Life of Mira Dana* (1855–56)." *Legacy* 21 (2004): 17–33.

———. *Women and Children of the Mills: An Annotated Guide to Nineteenth-Century American Textile Factory Literature*. Westport, Conn.: Greenwood Press, 1999.

"Recent Literature." Unsigned review of *An Idyl of Work* by Lucy Larcom. *Atlantic-Monthly,* August 1875, 241–42.

Redding, Arthur F. *Raids on Human Consciousness: Writing, Anarchism, and Violence*. Columbia: University of South Carolina Press, 1998.

Reich, Michael. "Capitalist Development, Class Relations, and Labor History." In Moody and Kessler-Harris, *Perspectives on American Labor History,* 30–54.

Reynolds, David S. *Beneath the American Renaissance: The Subversive Imagination in the Age of Emerson and Melville*. New York: Knopf, 1988.

Reynolds, Larry J., ed. *Woman in the Nineteenth Century*. New York: Norton, 1998.

Richardson, Dorothy. *The Long Day*. In *Women at Work*. Edited by William L. O'Neill. Chicago: Quadrangle, 1972.

Robbins, Sarah. *Managing Literacy, Mothering America: Women's Narratives on Reading and Writing in the Nineteenth Century*. Pittsburgh: University of Pittsburgh Press, 2004.

Robinson, Harriet H. *Loom and Spindle or Life among the Early Mill Girls*. 1898. Reprint with an introduction by Jane Wilkins Pultz. Kailua, Hawaii: Press Pacifica, 1976.

Roediger, David R. *The Wages of Whiteness: Race and the Making of the American Working Class*. Rev. ed. London: Verso, 1999.

Romero, Lora. *Home Fronts: Domesticity and Its Critics in the Antebellum United States*. Durham, N.C.: Duke University Press, 1997.

Rose, Anne C. *Transcendentalism as a Social Movement, 1830–1850*. New Haven, Conn.: Yale University Press, 1981.

Rose, Jonathan. *The Intellectual Life of the British Working Classes*. New Haven, Conn.: Yale University Press, 2001.

Rowland, Beryl. "Sitting Up with a Corpse: Malthus According to Melville in 'Poor Man's Pudding and Rich Man's Crumbs.'" *Journal of American Studies* 6 (1972): 69–83.

Samuels, Shirley, ed. *The Culture of Sentiment: Race, Gender, and Sentimentality in Nineteenth-Century America*. New York: Oxford University Press, 1992.

Sanders, Lise Shapiro. *Consuming Fantasies: Labor, Leisure, and the London Shopgirl, 1880–1920*. Columbus: Ohio State University Press, 2006.

Savage, Sarah. *The Factory Girl*. Boston: Munroe, 1814.

Schofield, Ann. "Introduction to Labor Press Fiction, 1870–1920." In *Sealskin and Shoddy: Working Women in American Labor Press Fiction, 1870–1920*, edited by Ann Schofield. New York: Greenwood Press, 1988, vii–xvi.

Scoresby, William. *American Factories and Their Female Operatives*. 1845. New York: Franklin, 1968.

Scudder, Vida D. *A Listener in Babel*. Boston: Houghton Mifflin, 1903.

Sears, Clara Endicott, ed. *Bronson Alcott's Fruitlands*. Boston: Houghton, 1915.

Shi, David E. *Facing Facts: Realism in American Thought and Culture, 1850–1920*. New York: Oxford University Press, 1995.

Shulman, Alix Kates, ed. *Red Emma Speaks: Selected Writings and Speeches by Emma Goldman*. New York: Random House, 1972.

Sicherman, Barbara. "Sense and Sensibility: A Case Study of Women's Reading in Late-Victorian America." In *Reading in America: Literature and Social History*, edited by Cathy N. Davidson. Baltimore: Johns Hopkins University Press, 1989. 201–25.

Siegel, Adrienne. *The Image of the American City in Popular Literature, 1820–1870*. Port Washington, N.Y.: Kennikat, 1981.

Sofer, Naomi Z. "'Carrying a Yankee Girl to Glory': Redefining Female Authorship in the Postbellum United States." *American Literature* 75 (2003): 31–60.

Steele, Jeffrey. "The Limits of Political Sympathy: Emerson, Margaret Fuller, and Woman's Rights." In *The Emerson Dilemma*, edited by Gregory Garvey. Athens: University of Georgia Press, 2001, 115–35.

———. *The Representation of the Self in the American Renaissance*. Chapel Hill: University of North Carolina Press, 1987.

———. *Transfiguring America: Myth, Ideology, and Mourning in Margaret Fuller's Writing.* Columbia: University of Missouri Press, 2001.

Stoehr, Taylor. *Nay-Saying in Concord: Emerson, Alcott, and Thoreau.* Hamden, Conn.: Archon, 1979.

"Stray Leaves from a Seamstress's Journal—No. 5." In *Woman in the Nineteenth Century,* edited by Larry J. Reynolds. New York: Norton, 1998, 231–32.

Swindells, Julia. *Victorian Writing and Working Women: The Other Side of Silence.* Cambridge: Polity Press, 1985.

Talcott, Hannah Elizabeth. *Madge; or, Night and Morning.* New York: Appleton, 1863.

Tax, Meredith. *The Rising of the Women: Feminist Solidarity and Class Conflict, 1880–1917.* New York: Monthly Review Press, 1980.

Thomas, John L. "Romantic Reform in America, 1815–1865." In *Ante-bellum Reform,* compiled by David Brion Davis. New York: Harper, 1967, 153–76.

Tolbert, Susan L. "Reading Habits of the Nineteenth-Century New England Mill Girls." www.philandsusantolbert.com/research/millgirl.html.

Tompkins, Jane P. *Sensational Designs: The Cultural Work of American Fiction, 1790–1860.* New York: Oxford University Press, 1985.

Tonkovich, Nicole. *Domesticity with a Difference: The Nonfiction of Catherine Beecher, Sarah J. Hale, Fanny Fern, and Margaret Fuller.* Jackson: University Press of Mississippi 1997.

Traub, Lindsey. "Woman Thinking: Margaret Fuller, Ralph Waldo Emerson, and the American Scholar." In *Soft Canons: American Women Writers and Masculine Tradition,* edited by Karen L. Kilcup. Iowa City: University of Iowa Press, 1999, 281–305.

Tyler, Martha W. *A Book without a Title: or Thrilling Events in the Life of Mira Dana.* 2nd ed., with additions. Boston: Printed for the author, 1856.

Vernon, John. *Money and Fiction: Literary Realism in the Nineteenth and Early Twentieth Centuries.* Ithaca, N.Y.: Cornell University Press, 1984.

Vicinus, Martha. *The Industrial Muse: A Study of Nineteenth-Century British Working-Class Literature.* New York: Barnes and Noble, 1974.

Voice of Industry. Fitchburg, Lowell, Boston. 1845–48.

Walker, Jeffrey. *Bardic Ethos and the American Epic Poem: Whitman, Pound, Crane, Williams, Olson.* Baton Rouge: Louisiana State University Press, 1989.

Wallace, Anne D. "'Nor in Fading Silks Compose': Sewing, Walking, and Poetic Labor in *Aurora Leigh.*" *English Literary History* 64 (1997): 223–56.

Ware, Caroline F. *The Early New England Cotton Manufacture: A Study in Industrial Beginnings.* New York: Russell, 1966.

Ware, Norman. *The Industrial Worker 1840–1860: The Reaction of American Industrial Society to the Advance of the Industrial Revolution.* Gloucester, Mass: Smith, 1959.

Warren, James Perrin. *Culture of Eloquence: Oratory and Reform in Antebellum America.* University Park: Pennsylvania State University Press, 1999.

Warren, Joyce W. *Fanny Fern: An Independent Woman.* New Brunswick, N. J.: Rutgers University Press, 1992.

———, ed. *The (Other) American Traditions: Nineteenth-Century Women Writers.* New Brunswick, N. J.: Rutgers University Press, 1993.

Warren, Joyce W., and Margaret Dickie, eds. *Challenging Boundaries: Gender and Periodization.* Athens: University of Georgia Press, 2000.

Weir, Robert E. *Beyond Labor's Veil: The Culture of the Knights of Labor.* University Park: Pennsylvania State University Press, 1996.

Welter, Barbara. *Dimity Convictions: The American Woman in the Nineteenth Century.* Athens: University of Ohio Press, 1976.

Wexler, Alice. *Emma Goldman: An Intimate Life.* New York: Pantheon Books, 1984.

Widdicombe, Toby. "A 'Declaration of Independence': Alcott's *Work* as Transcendental Manifesto." *Emerson Society Quarterly* 38 (1992): 207–29.

Wilentz, Sean. "The Rise of the American Working Class, 1776–1877: A Survey." In *Perspectives on American Labor History: The Problems of Synthesis,* edited by J. Carroll Moody and Alice Kessler-Harris. DeKalb: Northern Illinois University Press, 1989, 83–151.

Williams, Catharine. *Fall River: An Authentic Narrative.* 1833. Reprint edited by Patricia Caldwell. New York: Oxford University Press, 1993.

Williams, Susan S. *Reclaiming Authorship: Literary Women in America, 1850–1900.* Philadelphia: University of Pennsylvania Press, 2006.

———. "Writing with an Ethical Purpose: The Case of Elizabeth Stuart Phelps." In *Reciprocal Influences: Literary Production, Distribution, and Consumption in America,* edited by Steven Fink and Susan S. Williams. Columbus: Ohio State University Press, 1999, 151–72.

Zboray, Ronald J. *A Fictive People: Antebellum Economic Development and the American Reading Public.* New York: Oxford University Press, 1993.

Zlotnick, Susan. *Women, Writing, and the Industrial Revolution.* Baltimore: Johns Hopkins University Press, 1998.

Zonderman, David A. *Aspirations and Anxieties: New England Workers and the Mechanized Factory System, 1815–1850.* New York: Oxford University Press, 1992.

Zwarg, Christina. *Feminist Conversations: Fuller, Emerson, and the Play of Reading.* Ithaca, N.Y.: Cornell University Press, 1995.

———. "The Storied Facts of Margaret Fuller." *New England Quarterly* 69 (1996): 128–42.

Index